MW01206177

THE NATIONAL UN_

2015 Health Savings Accounts Facts

Whitney Richard Johnson, Esq.

Health Savings Accounts could quadruple their growth over the next six years.

The book you hold in your hands will enable you to make the most of all the opportunities — and avoid the pitfalls — in this flourishing market. *2015 Health Savings Accounts Facts* is the clear, concise, but comprehensive, Q&A resource that is the product of the authors' extensive experience in this rapidly growing field. And it is the one resource that all insurance agents, employee benefits & HR professionals, TPAs, accountants, attorneys, health professionals, and bank executives need to confidently answer HSA questions with authority and certainty.

The product of years of real-world advising, Health Savings Accounts Facts:

- Simplifies your work

- Explains HSA rules

- Clarifies HSA issues

- Enables you to answer authoritatively and guarantees you answer correctly

Saving you hours of time wading through unwieldy amounts of research from innumerable, disparate sources, *2015 Health Savings Accounts Facts* covers:

- HSA eligibility

- Contribution limitations

- HSA deductions

- Tax reporting

- Employer contributions

- Comparability testing

- Testing periods

And this groundbreaking resource includes regulatory materials, HSA worksheets, HSA forms, and numerous other charts, graphs, and checklists that clearly illustrate key topics.

Related Titles Also Available:

- *Healthcare Reform Facts*

- *Social Security & Medicare Facts*

- *The Advisor's Guide to Long-Term Care*

- *Tax Facts on Insurance & Employee Benefits*

- *Tax Facts on Individuals & Small Business*

- *Field Guide to Estate Planning, Business Planning & Employee Benefits*

For customer service questions or to place orders for any of our products, please call 1-800-543-0874.

2015
HEALTH SAVINGS
ACCOUNTS FACTS

- Eligibility • Establishment and Enrollment
- Contributions, Transfers, and Rollovers
- Testing Periods and Compliance • Distributions
- Taxation • Issues for Employers • Comparability
- Issues for Custodians • Impact of Affordable Care Act

Whitney Richard Johnson, Esq.

ISBN 978-1-941627-08-2

This publication is designed to provide accurate and authoritative information in regard to the subject matter covered. It is sold with the understanding that the publisher is not engaged in rendering legal, accounting or other professional service. If legal advice or other expert assistance is required, the services of a competent professional person should be sought. — From a Declaration of Principles jointly adapted by a Committee of The American Bar Association and a Committee of Publishers and Associations.

Circular 230 Notice – The content in this publication is not intended or written to be used, and it cannot be used, for the purposes of avoiding U.S. tax penalties.

ABOUT SUMMIT PROFESSIONAL NETWORKS

Summit Professional Networks supports the growth and vitality of the insurance, financial services and legal communities by providing professionals with the knowledge and education they need to succeed at every stage of their careers. We provide face-to-face and digital events, websites, mobile sites and apps, online information services, and magazines giving professionals multi-platform access to our critical resources, including Professional Development; Education & Certification; Prospecting & Data Tools; Industry News & Analysis; Reference Tools and Services; and Community Networking Opportunities.

Using all of our resources across each community we serve, we deliver measurable ROI for our sponsors through a range of turnkey services, including Research, Content Development, Integrated Media, Creative & Design, and Lead Generation.

For more information, go to http://www.SummitProfessionalNetworks.com.

About The National Underwriter Company

The National Underwriter Company is a Summit Professional Network.

For over 110 years, The National Underwriter Company has been the first in line with the targeted tax, insurance, and financial planning information you need to make critical business decisions. Boasting nearly a century of expert experience, our reputable Editors are dedicated to putting accurate and relevant information right at your fingertips. With *Tax Facts*, *Tools & Techniques, National Underwriter Advanced Markets, Field Guide, FC&S®, FC&S Legal* and other resources available in print, eBook, CD, and online, you can be assured that as the industry evolves National Underwriter will be at the forefront with the thorough and easy-to-use resources you rely on for success.

The National Underwriter Company
Update Service Notification

This National Underwriter Company publication is regularly updated to include coverage of developments and changes that affect the content. If you did not purchase this publication directly from The National Underwriter Company and you want to receive these important updates sent on a 30-day review basis and billed separately, please contact us at (800) 543-0874. Or you can mail your request with your name, company, address, and the title of the book to:

The National Underwriter Company
4157 Olympic Boulevard
Suite 225
Erlanger, KY 41018

If you purchased this publication from The National Underwriter Company directly, you have already been registered for the update service.

National Underwriter Company Contact Information

To order any National Underwriter Company title, please

- call 1-800-543-0874, 8-6 ET Monday – Thursday and 8 to 5 ET Friday

- online bookstore at www.nationalunderwriter.com, or

- mail to The National Underwriter Company, Orders Department, 4157 Olympic Blvd., Ste. 225, Erlanger, KY 41018

PREFACE

Health Savings Accounts (HSA) were established in 2003 under the Medicare Prescription Drug, Improvement and Modernization Act. HSAs are tax-advantaged, medical savings plans that work in tandem with High Deductible Health Care Plans (HDHPs). Over the past decade, HSAs have experienced explosive annual growth rates of 25 to 30 percent and are expected to have assets approaching twenty-four billion dollars with over thirteen million Americans having accounts by the end of 2014.

The 2015 edition of *Health Savings Accounts Facts* is a comprehensive compilation of the decade of questions that Mr. Johnson has answered and is designed to serve as a reference book for professionals that answer HSA-related questions. The book thoroughly reviews all the key government guidance on HSAs and provides industry best practices in areas that the government fails to address. The depth and breadth of the author's twenty years of legal experience in tax-deferred plans, his experience in answering thousands of HSA questions, attending hundreds of HSA meetings, as well as leading dozens of HSA presentations is captured and cogently presented in this publication.

2015 Health Savings Accounts Facts is written for professionals that need to know about Health Savings Accounts and their role in financial and health-care planning. This comprehensive reference will prove invaluable to a host of professionals including those working in financial institutions, HSA custodians and trustees, insurance specialists and agents, benefit consultants and other third-party administrators, human resource professionals, attorneys, accountants as well as others interested in this rapidly growing area.

2015 Health Savings Account Facts will help simplify your life by allowing you to find the answers that you need – and confidently answer questions with both authority and certainty. In order to easily enable you to find needed answers, this book is organized into an "Question and Answer" format. The questions and answers are divided into specific topics designed to enable you to easily enable you to answer questions as they arise. In addition, responses to questions are written in "plain English, rather than "legalese" supplemented by actual situations, bringing the answers to life. Many of the answers include, where relevant, a citation to statutes, regulations or other government materials such as Notices, Rulings, Publications and other support of the answer. Questions and Answers are indexed and cross-referenced to help ensure a comprehensive discernment of information needed. Ease-of-use and understanding is further enhanced by forms, worksheets and illustrative charts.

This publication is designed to provide accurate and authoritative information in regard to the subject matter covered. However, neither the publisher nor the author are engaging in rendering legal, accounting, or other professional services. If legal advice or other professional assistance is required for a specific situation, the services of a competent professional should be sought.

ABOUT THE AUTHOR

Whitney Richard Johnson, Esq. is a founder and principal of HSA Authority, LLC and HSA Resources, LLC - businesses that provide HSAs to employers and individuals as well as HSA solutions for financial institutions. Mr. Johnson has an undergraduate degree in Finance from the University of Wisconsin at Madison and a law degree from the University of Minnesota. He is an Associate Professor at St. Cloud State University where he teaches business law.

Mr. Johnson's legal and compliance background in HSAs extends through the entire history of HSAs as well as their predecessor, Medical Savings Accounts. He also worked more than a decade extensively with Individual Retirement Accounts (IRAs) which provide the legal framework for the HSA law and rules. Mr. Johnson has written and presented extensively on HSAs which has extended the opportunity to both hear and answer thousands of HSA questions from HSA professionals, owners and companies. Prior to the passage of the HSA legislation, Mr. Johnson worked as an attorney in private practice and as in-house counsel focusing on tax-deferred plans working with financial institutions. He also served as an appointed member to IRPAC, a Washington DC IRS Advisory Board. In addition, Mr. Johnson serves as an expert witness on the duties and responsibilities of a custodian and trustee.

ABOUT THE LEAD CONTRIBUTING EDITOR

Roy Ramthun, Founder, HSA Consulting Services is a nationally-recognized expert on Health Savings Accounts and consumer directed health care issues. He led the U.S. Treasury Department's implementation of HSAs after they were enacted into law in 2003. President George W. Bush then tapped Mr. Ramthun to be his health care policy advisor at the White House, where he developed the President's proposals to expand HSAs while overseeing the implementation of the Medicare prescription drug benefit (Part D). He has also served on the staff of the U.S. Senate Committee on Finance and the U.S. Health Care Financing Administration (now known as the Centers for Medicare & Medicaid Services). Mr. Ramthun holds a Master of Science degree in Public Health from the University of North Carolina, and a Bachelor of Science degree from the University of Michigan.

ABOUT THE PUBLISHER

Kelly B. Maheu, J.D., is Managing Director of the Professional Publishing Division of The National Underwriter Company, a Division of Summit Professional Networks. Kelly has been with The National Underwriter Company since 2006, serving in editorial, content acquisition, and product development roles prior to being named Managing Director.

Prior to joining The National Underwriter Company, Kelly worked in the legal and insurance fields for LexisNexis®, Progressive Insurance, and a Cincinnati insurance defense litigation firm.

Kelly has edited and contributed to numerous books and publications including the *Personal Auto Insurance Policy Coverage Guide*, *Cyberliability and Insurance*, *The National Underwriter Sales Essentials Series*, and *The Tools and Techniques of Risk Management for Financial Planners*.

Kelly earned her law degree from The University of Cincinnati College of Law and holds a BA from Miami University, Ohio, with a double major in English/Journalism and Psychology.

ABOUT THE EDITOR

Michael D. Thomas, J.D., is an editor with the Professional Publishing Division of the National Underwriter Company, Summit Professional Networks. He is responsible for the editorial process for the *2015 Health Savings Accounts Facts*. He is also responsible for the editing and development of health care publications for Summit Professional Networks.

Prior to joining Summit Professional Networks, Mike spent over twenty-five years with LexisNexis, where he was responsible for the editorial content and new product development of new online and traditional legal products, including *Health Law*, *Insurance Law*, *Social Security Law*, *Labor & Employment Law*, *Family Law*, as well as other legal research tools. In addition, he worked as a Field Agent for Knights of Columbus Insurance specializing in life, health, disability income, long-term care insurance as well as annuity sales.

Mike has a Bachelor of Arts from Tufts University and a Juris Doctorate from the University of Dayton.

ABOUT THE MANAGING EDITOR

Christine G. Barlow, CPCU, is Managing Editor of *FC&S,* a division of Summit Professional Networks. Christine has fifteen years' experience in the insurance industry, beginning as a claims adjuster then working as an underwriter and underwriting supervisor handling personal lines. Before joining *FC&S*, Christine worked as an Underwriting Supervisor for Maryland Auto Insurance Fund, and as Senior Underwriter/Underwriter for companies Montgomery Mutual, Old American, Charter Group, and Nationwide.

ABOUT EDITORIAL SERVICES

Connie L. Jump, Supervisor, Editorial Services

TABLE OF CONTENTS

APPENDICES

For substantive updates to this product please visit: pro.nuco.com/booksupplements/hsas

LIST OF QUESTIONS
PART I: INTRODUCTION

1. What is an HSA?

2. Are there taxable benefits of an HSA?

3. Are there additional benefits of an HSA?

4. Are there disadvantages of an HSA?

5. How does an HSA work?

6. Who is an "HSA Owner"?

7. Why did Congress create HSAs?

8. Are HSAs "consumer-driven" health plans?

9. Are HSAs the same nationwide or do state laws apply?

10. What law created HSAs?

11. What government agencies regulate HSAs?

12. Is an "HSA Insurance Plan" the same as an HSA?

13. Are HSA owners required to get their health insurance and HSA from the same provider?

14. Is an HSA the same as a Medical IRA?

PART II: HEALTH CARE REFORM'S IMPACT ON HEALTH SAVINGS ACCOUNTS

15. What is the Affordable Care Act?

16. How did the 2010 passage of the Affordable Care Act impact HSAs?

17. Does the Affordable Care Act build on the success of HSAs?

18. Did the Affordable Care Act change contribution limits?

19. Did the Affordable Care Act change the rule allowing for the purchase of over-the-counter drugs with HSAs?

20. Did the penalty increase for non-qualified use of an HSA?

21. Will the law change HSAs in the future?

PART III: ELIGIBILITY

Overview

High Deductible Health Plan (HDHP)
Overview of HDHPs

43. Should HSA owners show their medical insurance cards for medical services when they are still below the deductible and paying with the HSA?

44. Is a health plan that primarily covers accident, disability, dental, vision or long-term care an HDHP?

Deduction Limits

45. What are the HDHP deductible limits?

46. Do the HSA deductible limits change every year?

47. How does the deductible limit apply to a health plan year that is longer than twelve months?

48. Can cost-sharing subsidies provided under the Affordable Care Act make a person ineligible for an HSA if the deductible is reduced below the HDHP limits?

Maximum Out-of-Pocket Expenses

49. What is a maximum out-of-pocket limit?

50. Does an HDHP have to have a maximum out-of-pocket limit?

51. Can a plan without a maximum out-of-pocket expense qualify as an HDHP?

52. If a medical expense is not covered by the HDHP, does it still count toward the maximum out-of-pocket expense?

53. Do extra fees charged for failing to first get approval for a specific treatment count towards the maximum out-of-pocket expenses?

54. Can an HDHP limit benefits to "Usual, Customary, and Reasonable" (UCR) amounts in determining maximum out-of-pocket expenses?

55. If an HSA owner receives treatment outside of a physician network, does the full cost count toward the maximum out-of-pocket expense?

Lifetime Limit

56. Can an HDHP impose a maximum lifetime limit?

Deductible Credit for Mid-Year Insurance Changes

57. Can an HDHP count expenses toward the deductible that were incurred under a traditional plan when an employer changes insurance mid-year?

58. Can an HSA owner switch from self-only HDHP to family HDHP coverage mid-year and remain eligible for an HSA even if all the medical expenses count toward the deductible?

59. Can an HSA owner switch from family HDHP coverage to self-only HDHP coverage mid-year and remain eligible for an HSA even if all the medical expenses count toward the deductible?

97. Can an employee elect three plans: a post-deductible health FSA, a limited-purpose health FSA, and an HSA?

Retirement HRA

98. What is a "Retirement HRA"?

99. Are Retirement HRAs allowed in combination with HSAs?

Suspended HRA

100. What is a "suspended HRA"?

101. Are "suspended HRAs" allowed in combination with HSAs?

Non-Medical Cafeteria Plan Benefits

102. Does participation in pre-tax dependent care benefits impact HSA eligibility?

103. Does participation in pre-tax parking benefits impact HSA eligibility?

Department of Veterans Affairs (VA) and Indian Health Services (IHS) Coverage

104, Does Department of Veterans Affairs (VA) health coverage disqualify someone for an HSA?

105. Can a veteran seek preventive care, dental and vision through the VA and remain eligible for an HSA?

106. Does coverage under the TRICARE disqualify someone for an HSA?

107. Does medical coverage through Indian Health Services (IHS) disqualify individuals for an HSA?

Concierge Medicine

108. Can an individual participate in a physician retainer program (concierge medicine) and retain HSA eligibility?

Miscellaneous

109. Does COBRA continuation coverage impact HSA eligibility?

110. Can an HDHP insured individual enroll in a catastrophic insurance plan (non-HDHP), in addition to the HDHP, and still be eligible for an HSA?

111. Does coverage under a mini-med plan disqualify a person for an HSA?

112. Can an employer reimburse employees for medical expenses below the group's HDHP limits?

113. Does a company free on-site health clinic disqualify employees for HSAs?

114. Does an Employee Assistance Program (EAP) disqualify employees for HSAs?

174. Does an employer contribution to an HSA set the establishment date?

175. What is the establishment date when an employer requires employees to complete all the HSA agreements two weeks before becoming HSA-eligible?

Not the First HSA

176. What is the establishment date for someone that used to have an HSA and is now opening a new one?

177. Do HSA transfers impact the establishment date?

178. Do HSA rollovers impact the establishment date?

179. Does rolling funds from an Archer MSA to an HSA maintain the Archer MSA establishment date?

Tracking

180. Who is responsible for tracking the Establishment Date?

181. Does the HSA custodian know the establishment date of its HSAs?

Authorized Signer

Overview

182. What is an authorized signer?

183. What powers does an authorized signer have?

184. Does an authorized signer have the same rights on the HSA as the HSA owner?

185. Is having "power of attorney" the same as being an authorized signer?

186. Is having an authorized signer the same as having a joint HSA?

187. If an authorized signer is over age fifty-five; but the HSA owner is not, can the authorized signer's age be used to make a catch-up contribution?

188. Is an authorized signer also the beneficiary?

Who Can Serve

189. Can an HSA owner's spouse serve as an authorized signer?

190. Can an HSA owner name a child as an authorized signer?

191. Do HSA laws require a minimum age to serve as an authorized signer?

192. Can an HSA owner name a nanny or grandparent as an authorized signer?

"Sum-of-the-months" Rule

Full Contribution Rule

Family versus Single Coverage

Mid-Year Change In HDHP Coverage Type

Catch-Up Contributions

Tax Treatment

330. What is the tax impact of moving money from an IRA to an HSA?

331. What is the tax consequence of moving money from a Roth IRA to an HSA?

332. What is "basis" and how does it relate to IRA funding of HSAs?

333. Does an IRA to HSA funding distribution work for an IRA owner that is taking substantially equal period distributions from the IRA?

Testing Period

334. Does a "testing period" apply to money moved from an IRA to an HSA?

Types of IRAs Allowed

335. What types of IRAs are permitted for funding an HSA?

336. Can money be moved from a 403(b) into an HSA?

337. Can an individual fund an HSA with an inherited IRA?

338. Can an individual move money from an inherited SEP into an HSA?

339. Can an individual fund an HSA with a 401(k)?

340. Can individuals fund an HSA with a spouse's IRA?

Once-in-a-Lifetime

341. What is the "once-in-a-lifetime" rule?

342. Why is only one IRA to HSA funding allowed in a lifetime?

343. Who is responsible for tracking the once-in-a-lifetime requirement?

344. What are the consequences for completing a second IRA to HSA funding transaction?

345. Can an individual combine two or more smaller IRAs to reach the HSA limit?

346. Is there an exception for a second IRA to HSA funding when switching from self-only HDHP to family? What happens if the switch is from family HDHP to self-only HDHP?

Tax Reporting

347. How are IRA to HSA qualified funding distributions reported to the IRS?

348. How do taxpayers report the IRA funding on their individual income tax returns?

349. How does the HSA custodian report contributions coming from IRAs?

350. Is the IRA custodian required to withhold for income taxes for an HSA qualified funding distribution?

FSA and HRA Rollovers to an HSA

PART VII: TESTING PERIODS

Overview

Failed Testing Period

Calculating the Amount to Base Penalties

Penalties

368. What is the penalty for failure to meet the testing period?

369. Did the penalty for failure to meet the testing period increase to 20 percent?

370. Are disability and death exceptions to the testing period penalty?

371. Is obtaining age sixty-five an exception to the testing period penalty?

372. Does a failed testing period result in additional state taxes?

373. How do HSA owners actually pay the taxes and penalties for a failed testing period?

Failed Testing Period and Excess Contributions Compared

374. Is failing the testing period the same as making an excess contribution?

375. How is an HSA owner taxed when the HSA owner fails a testing period and then tries to correct it by removing it as an excess?

Reporting

376. How do custodians report failed testing periods?

377. Does the custodian have any responsibility regarding the testing period?

IRA to HSA Testing Period

Overview

378. Is there a separate testing period for IRA to HSA money movements?

379. What is the testing period for IRA to HSA funding?

380. What is the testing period if an IRA to HSA funding transaction starts in one month and finishes in the next month?

Failed Testing Period

381. What happens when an HSA owner fails the IRA to HSA testing period?

382. Do HSA owners have to amend their tax return for a failed testing period?

383. What happens when HSA owner completes two IRA to HSA qualified funding distributions and then fails the testing period?

Interaction of IRA Funding and Full Contribution Rule

384. Can the two different testing periods ever interact with each other?

385. What happens when an HSA owner funds the HSA both directly and with an IRA and then fails the testing period for the regular contribution?

386. Is it possible to pass the regular HSA contribution testing period and fail the IRA to HSA funding testing period?

Excess Contribution from IRA to HSA Funding

387. What happens if an HSA owner exceeds the HSA limits when funding with an IRA?

388. If an HSA owner's contribution exceeds the HSA limits does that result in a failed testing period?

PART VIII: DISTRIBUTIONS

Overview

389. What are the basic distribution rules for HSAs?

390. What are the different types of HSA distributions and how are they treated for tax purposes?

Qualified Medical Expenses

Overview

391. What are qualified medical expenses?

392. Is there a difference between "qualified" medical expenses and "eligible" medical expenses?

393. Is there a list of all qualified medical expenses?

394. Do HSAs follow the same rules as FSAs and HRAs as to what is a qualified medical expense?

Prescription Drugs/Medications

395. What is a prescription drug?

396. Is medical marijuana qualified with a prescription?

397. Are prescription drugs from Canada qualified?

Over the Counter Drugs

398. Are over-the-counter drugs qualified?

399. Are over-the-counter drugs purchased prior to 2011 still eligible?

Age Sixty-five Distributions

Insurance

COBRA Premiums

Medicare Premiums

Long-Term Care Premiums

Health Premiums and Unemployment Compensation

440. Can an employed HSA owner use an HSA to pay for an unemployed dependent's health insurance premiums?

Other Insurance Issues

441. Should HSA owners show their health insurance cards for medical services even if they are paying the full expense themselves with their HSA?

442. How does an insurance company track the deductible when expenses are paid with an HSA?

443. Does an HSA owner benefit from insurance company negotiated discounts on medical services?

Death Distributions
Overview

444. What happens to an HSA when the HSA owner dies?

445. Can HSA beneficiaries continue to use the HSA as an HSA?

446. Is it better to name a spouse than a non-spouse as beneficiary for an HSA?

447. Can the beneficiary of an HSA use the HSA to pay for the deceased HSA owner's remaining medical expenses?

448. What procedures should a beneficiary follow to request the HSA funds after the death of the HSA owner?

449. What if the HSA appreciated in value from the date of the death until the distribution?

Spouse Beneficiaries

450. Can a spouse beneficiary transfer the HSA assets to a different HSA?

Non-Spouse Beneficiaries

451. Can a non-spouse beneficiary keep the money in the HSA for five years after death?

452. What happens when the HSA owner fails to name a beneficiary?

453. What happens if the HSA owner names her estate as the beneficiary?

454. How do non-spouse beneficiaries pay the taxes on an inherited HSA?

455. When does the non-spouse beneficiary have to claim the HSA?

456. What if a non-spouse beneficiary does not close the HSA in the year of the death?

Timing of Distributions

457. Can HSA owners withdraw HSA assets at any time?

458. Does the HSA owner control the timing and amount on HSA distributions?

Spouses

478. Who is considered a spouse?

479. Can HSA owners use HSA funds to pay for a spouse's medical expenses if the spouse is not eligible for an HSA?

480. Does the income tax filing status of a couple impact HSA usage?

Dependents

481. Who is a dependent?

Children

482. Who qualifies as a child dependent?

483. Can HSA owners use their HSA to pay the medical expenses of adult children (up to age twenty-six) added to their insurance pursuant to the Affordable Care Act rules?

484. Why can an employee use an FSA or HRA for children up to age twenty-six but not an HSA?

485. Can HSA owners use HSA funds for a child not covered by the HSA owner's health insurance?

486. Can HSA owners use an HSA to pay the medical expenses of a child that is claimed as a dependent by a former spouse?

Qualifying Relative

487. Who is a qualifying relative?

Domestic Partners and Same-Sex Marriages

488. Did the Supreme Court's 2013 ruling that the Defense of Marriage Act is unconstitutional impact HSAs?

489. Are same-sex couples always considered spouses?

490. Is a domestic partnership or civil union the same as marriage?

491. What is the rule for a legal same-sex marriage where the couple now lives in a state that does now allow same-sex marriages?

492. What is the effective date for the changes for same-sex spouses?

493. Can an HSA owner use an HSA to pay the medical expenses for a same-sex spouse?

494. Can HSA owners use HSA funds to pay medical expenses of domestic partners?

Earnings

512. What is the tax treatment on interest, dividends, and other earnings in an HSA?

Attachment of HSAs

513. Can the IRS levy an HSA?

514. Is an HSA exempt from bankruptcy?

515. Can an HSA be garnished?

516. Can an HSA be escheated to the state?

Withholding for Taxes

517. Is an HSA distribution subject to income tax withholding?

518. Can an HSA custodian withhold for income taxes?

Tax Forms Required

519. What IRS forms are necessary for HSA owners to prepare and file income tax returns?

520. What tax forms are required if an HSA owner only used the HSA for qualified medical expenses and did not make any HSA contributions?

521. Are any tax forms required if an HSA owner has an HSA but does not make a contribution or take a distribution during the tax year?

522. Can an HSA owner file using the IRS Form 1040EZ?

Tax Reporting
IRS Form 8889

523. What is IRS Form 8889 and how is it used?

524. Is the IRS Form 8889 filed for prohibited transactions?

525. Is the IRS Form 8889 filed to report failed testing periods?

526. Are beneficiaries of HSAs required to file the IRS Form 8889?

IRS Form W-2

527. Are HSA contributions reported on the IRS Form W-2?

IRS Form 5498-SA

528. What is an IRS Form 5498-SA - Contribution Report?

529. What information gets sent to the IRS on the IRS Form 5498?

590. Can an employer make HSA contributions into the HSA of an employee's spouse?

591. When do employers have to decide how much they are going to contribute to employees' HSAs?

592. Can employers change HSA contribution amounts mid-year?

593. Do employer contributions to an employee's HSA count as earned income for the purposes of the Earned Income Credit (EIC)?

Deductibility

594. Are employer HSA contributions deductible health care expenses?

595. How do employers claim a deduction for employee HSA contributions?

Reporting

596. Are employer contributions, payroll deferral, and employee direct contributions treated the same for the purposes of IRS reporting?

597. What happens if an employer fails to report HSA contributions on the IRS Form W-2s?

Prior Year

598. Can employers make prior year HSA contributions?

599. How are employer prior year contributions reported by the employer and employee?

Payroll Deferral

Overview

600. What is payroll deferral into an HSA?

601. Does an employer that offers HDHP health insurance have to offer payroll deferral into an HSA?

602. If an employer offers an HDHP but does not help with HSA contributions, can the employee open an HSA on her own?

603. Can an employer allow HSA payroll deferral for an employee not covered by the company health plan?

604. How long can an employer hold employee payroll deferral funds prior to depositing the funds into an HSA?

Post-Tax

605. Why would an employer offer a post-tax HSA deferral option?

606. Can an employer allow for HSA contributions through payroll deferral without a Section 125 plan?

Section 125 Plan

607. What is a Section 125 plan?

608. What is involved in administering a Section 125 plan?

609. What are the benefits of using a Section 125 plan combined with an HSA?

610. Is a "Premium-Only Plan (POP) Section 125" set up to work with HSAs?

611. Are Section 125 plans subject to non-discrimination rules?

612. Is there an exception to the Section 125 plan non-discrimination rules for small employers?

613. Can an employer make a matching contribution to employees' HSAs through the Section 125 plan?

Employee Contributions

614. Are employee payroll deferrals into an HSA subject to FICA/FUTA taxes?

615. Can an employee change his or her HSA deferral election mid-year?

616. May an employer accelerate an employee's payroll deferrals to cover a large expense that occurs early in the year?

617. Can an employer provide a negative election for HSAs (automatic contribution if the employee fails to complete the election form)?

618. How long can employers hold HSA payroll deferral amounts before contributing to the HSAs?

Business Owners

619. What unique HSA rules apply to partnership members, Limited Liability Corporation (LLC) shareholders, S-Corp shareholders and sole proprietors?

620. How are business HSA contributions to non-owner employees treated?

621. Are family members of a business owner also considered owners?

622. Are HSA contributions to owners subject to the comparability rules?

Sole Proprietors

623. Is a sole proprietor allowed to deduct HSA contributions made to herself through the business?

624. Can a sole proprietor open an HSA in the business's name?

Partners

625. Are partners and members of LLCs allowed to deduct HSA contributions made to themselves through the business?

626. Is there an exception for guaranteed payments to partners?

S-Corporations

627. Are owners of S-Corporations subject to special rules for business HSA contributions?

628. Are HSA contributions to the owner of an S-Corp subject to payroll taxes or self-employment taxes?

C-Corporations

629. How are employees that are also owners of a C-corporation treated concerning HSA contributions?

Recoupment

630. What does "recoup" mean?

631. Can an employer ever recoup an HSA contribution made on behalf of an employee?

632. How can an employer take an employee's HSA money back if the money is nonforfeitable?

633. Can the employee agree to a recoupment that would otherwise not be allowed?

Exceeds Annual Limit

634. If an employer contributes amounts to an employee's HSA that exceed the maximum annual contribution, can the employer recoup the excess amounts?

635. Is the HSA limit for employer recoupments the HSA legal maximum limit or the individual's maximum limit?

636. If an employer contributes to the HSA of an employee who ceases to be a qualified individual during a year, can the employer recoup amounts that the employer contributed after the employee ceased to be an eligible individual?

637. What if an employee quits mid-year and the employer forgets to stop the HSA payments?

638. What happens when an employer contribution and an employee payroll deferral combined cause an excess contribution?

Never HSA Eligible

639. If an employer contributes to an employee who was never eligible for an HSA, can the employer recoup the HSA contributions?

Impact on Comparability

640. Can an employer recoup a mistaken employee contribution if that contribution results in non-comparable contributions?

641. Are employers subject to a 35 percent penalty for violation of the comparability rules if the employer mistakenly over contributes to an employee's HSA and cannot recoup?

Other Correction Methods

642. Can an employer seek a repayment of the mistaken HSA contribution directly from the employee rather than recouping through the HSA custodian?

643. What if the HSA custodian made the mistake rather than the employer?

Reporting

644. How is a recouped HSA contribution reported to the IRS by the custodian and employer?

HSAs, FSAs and HRAs Compared

645. What are the differences between HSAs, FSAs and HRAs?

646. Do FSAs allow for rollovers?

647. Which is the best, HSA, FSA or HRA?

648. Can an employer offer both an FSA and HSA?

649. Can an employer offer both an HRA and an HSA?

650. Can an employer offer an HRA, FSA and HSA?

651. What FSA rules do not apply to HSAs?

652. Are HSAs, FSAs and HRAs taxed in the same fashion?

653. Do FSAs avoid some of the "group health plan" rules as "excepted benefits"?

654. Are HSAs subject to the "group health plan" rules under the Affordable Care Act?

655. How is an HSA similar to a 401(k) or an IRA?

PART XI: COMPARABILITY

Overview

656. What are the HSA comparability rules?

657. When do the comparability rules apply?

658. Does employer encouragement of employees to fund HSAs on their own result in the comparability rules applying?

659. What types of HSA contributions are not subject to the comparability rules?

660. Can an employer make comparable contributions to employees if the employer does not offer health insurance?

661. Can an employer allow after-tax payroll deferral into an HSA and avoid the comparability rules?

662. Can an employer make a one-time contribution to employees' HSAs without committing to future HSA contributions?

Categories

663. What are the acceptable categories for comparability testing?

Single versus Family

664. Can an employer treat employees covered under a family HDHP differently than those covered under a single HDHP?

665. What are the family categories of coverage?

666. Can an employer treat an employee and spouse covered under a family plan differently than an employee and a child covered under a family plan?

667. How do the comparability rules apply if an employee switches mid-year from single to family coverage using the pay-as-you-go method?

668. Can an employer give a larger contribution to an employee with a larger family?

Employer Provided HDHP versus Other HDHP

669. Can an employer limit HSA contributions to employees who have health insurance coverage provided by the employer?

670. Can an employer elect to make HSA contributions to employees who do not receive their health insurance through the business?

671. How does an employer know whether an employee is eligible for an HSA when the employee is not covered by the employer's HDHP?

672. If a husband and wife both work for the same business do the comparability rules require that the business give them each an HSA contribution?

Current versus Former Employees

673. Do employers have to make HSA contributions for former employees?

674. Are employers required to make HSA contributions for former employees receiving COBRA continuation coverage?

675. What happens when an employer makes HSA contributions for former employees but cannot find a former employee?

676. Can an employer make HSA contributions only to former employees that continue to receive their HDHP coverage through the employer?

695. Can an employer give a bonus amount into the HSAs of employees that participate in a health assessment exam process?

696. Can an employer give a bonus amount to an employee that participates in a health assessment process into a Section 125 plan that the employee then elects to put in an HSA?

Employee Fails to Open an HSA
Overview

697. What if an employee fails to open an HSA?

698. How are the comparability rules satisfied if a qualified employee fails to open an HSA?

Model Notice

699. What is the IRS model language for notice to employees regarding employer HSA contributions and the consequences of failing to open an HSA?

700. Can an employer modify the model notice?

701. Can the notice be sent to employee electronically?

702. When does the notice need to be sent to employees?

703. What if an employer hires a new employee after it sent the model notice?

704. Does the model notice go to all employees or only those that did not open an HSA?

705. Do employers have to give the notice for payroll deferral or employer matching contributions made through a Cafeteria plan?

706. Is the notice required if all eligible employees establish HSAs?

Making Missed Contributions

707. How long do employers have to hold the money for employees that fail to open HSAs?

708. Are employers required to account separately for missed contributions?

709. After notified that an employee did open an HSA, how long does the employer have to make any missed HSA contributions?

710. Do employers have to pay interest on HSA money held for employees that fail to open an HSA?

711. Does an employer have to set aside HSA contributions for ineligible employees?

712. What if the failure to open the HSA is caused by a refusal of the HSA custodian to accept the employee's HSA Application?

729. Do employers have to make comparable HSA contributions to independent contractors?

730. Can an employer stop contributing to an HSA of an employee that exceeds the HSA limit and still meet the comparability rules?

Timing of Contributions

731. How often do employers have to calculate whether employer contributions are comparable?

732. Is the comparability test run on a fiscal or calendar year?

733. What are the timing methods for employer comparable HSA contributions?

734. Which payment method works best, pre-funding, pay-as-you-go, or look back?

Pre-Funding

735. Does an employer have to use the same funding method for all employees?

736. May an employer fully fund the employee's HSA at the beginning of the year?

737. What's wrong with the pre-funding option for employer HSA contributions?

738. Does an employer violate the comparability rules if it pre-funds and then an employee quits?

739. If an employer makes the full year's HSA contribution on January 1, is it done for the year?

740. If an employer pre-funds for its existing employees, can it choose to fund new employees' HSAs either on a pay-as-you-go method or a look back method?

741. Can an employer contribute the maximum HSA contribution to an employee that starts mid-year?

742. Can an employer accelerate employer HSA contributions into earlier months to help an employee with large medical bills?

Pay-as-you-go Method

743. How does the pay-as-you-go method work?

744. Can employers adjust the timing of HSA contributions to match payroll when salaried employees are paid monthly and hourly employees are paid bi-weekly?

745. What if an employer uses a different pay period for exempt versus non-exempt employee?

746. How does it work if an employee switches mid-year from single to family coverage using the pay-as-you-go method?

747. Does pay-as-you-go work if HSA contributions are made quarterly?

I

Look-back Method

748. What is the look-back method for making comparable contributions?

749. How does it work if an employee switches mid-year from single to family coverage using the look-back method?

750. Can employers change the amount of an HSA contribution mid-year?

751. Must an employer use the same method for all comparable employees?

PART XII: CUSTODIAL ISSUES

Overview

752. What is an HSA custodian or trustee?

753. Who is qualified to serve as an HSA custodian or trustee?

754. Are banks and credit unions automatically approved to be HSA custodians?

755. Are all insurance companies qualified to serve as HSA custodians?

Fiduciary

756. Is an HSA custodian a fiduciary?

757. What is the difference between a custodian and a trustee?

Contribution Responsibilities

758. Is an HSA custodian required to determine if an individual is eligible for an HSA?

759. What is the maximum HSA contribution an HSA custodian can accept?

760. Is the custodian responsible for determining whether a particular HSA owner exceeded his or her HSA limit?

761. Is the custodian required to determine an HSA owner's limit based on whether the person has family or self-only HDHP coverage?

762. Is the HSA custodian responsible to track the age of the HSA owner?

763. Do custodians have to accept the return of mistaken distributions?

764. If the custodian does accept the return of a mistaken distribution may it rely on the HSA owner's representation that it was a mistake?

Employer Contributions

765. Are HSA custodians required to differentiate between employer and employee contributions?

766. Are custodians responsible for recording whether employer contributions are pre-tax or post-tax?

Distribution Responsibilities

767. Can a custodian restrict distributions to only qualified medical expenses?

768. Does a custodian have to ensure that HSA owners' distributions were for qualified medical expenses?

769. Are custodian's required to "spot-check" documentation to prove distributions were for qualified medical expenses?

770. Can an HSA custodian use a health only debit card that prevents use for non-medical items?

771. Will the law change requiring HSA custodians to substantiate that distributions were used for qualified medical expenses?

772. How long does a Custodian have to retain contribution and distribution forms?

Establishment

773. Can an HSA custodian require that an employer open all its employees' HSAs with the custodian?

774. Can HSA custodians set up an individual's HSA before the individual is eligible?

775. Is the custodian responsible to disclose new HSA law changes?

Investment Offerings

776. What types of investments can a custodian offer?

777. Can an HSA custodian provide a cash incentive to open an HSA?

778. Can stored value cards be used for HSAs?

779. Does a custodian have to offer more than one investment choice?

780. May an HSA custodian serve as the HSA custodian for its own employees?

781. Can an HSA custodian offer an employer a discount on other services it offers if the employer agrees to open its employees' HSA with the custodian?

Fees

782. What types of fees are typically charged on an HSA?

783. Can fees be directly withdrawn from the HSA account?

784. If HSAs fees are paid from the HSA, does that increase the annual contribution limit by the amount of the fee?

PART I: INTRODUCTION

1. What is an HSA?

A Health Savings Account (HSA) is a tax-favored account used to pay for qualified medical expenses. HSA contributions are tax-deductible, or potentially pre-tax if made by an employer. It is always used in conjunction with a qualified High-Deductible Health Plan (HDHP)

The HSA is a custodial or trust account and individuals must open an HSA with an IRS approved custodian or trustee.

A less technical definition is that an HSA is a checking, savings or other type of investment account used for medical expenses with a lot of additional legal rules and tax benefits. Most HSAs today are based on checking accounts and the money is deposited at a bank, credit union or other HSA approved custodian. HSAs can be invested in stocks, bonds, mutual funds and a wide variety of other investment choices. HSA owners often use their HSA much as they would a checking account: writing checks, using a debit card or even withdrawing money from an Automated Teller Machine to pay for qualified medical expenses.

IRC Sec. 223(d)(a), See also IRS Publication 969, IRS Notice 2004-2.

2. Are there taxable benefits of an HSA?

Yes. There are a number of taxable benefits for HSA owners.

- **Tax-Free Distributions.** HSA owners can use an HSA tax-free to pay for qualified medical expenses for themselves, their spouse/partner, and their dependents

- **Tax Deductible Individual Contributions.** HSA owners can deduct HSA contributions on their federal and, in most cases, their state income tax returns. HSA owners do not need to itemize to get the tax deduction (it's an "above-the-line" deduction) and there are no income limits. There are HSA limits as to how much a person can contribute, but the limits are high compared to Flexible Spending Accounts (a common alternative to an HSA).

- **Pre-Tax Employer Contributions.** Contributions made pre-tax by an employer (employer contributions or employee payroll deferral) are not included as taxable income on the HSA owner's IRS Form W-2. HSA owners avoid federal income taxes, Social Security taxes, Medicare taxes (together with Social Security referred to as FICA), federal unemployment taxes (FUTA), Railroad Retirement Tax Act, and in most cases state income and state unemployment taxes (SUTA). Because employer contributions are never included in income, HSA owners cannot deduct them on their income tax return.

- **Earnings Grow Tax-Free.** Any interest or other earnings grow tax-free in the HSA.

See IRS Form W-2.

3. Are there additional benefits of an HSA?

Yes. There are a number of other benefits for HSA owners including:

- **Balance Rolls Over.** HSA balances roll over from year to year if HSA owners do not spend the money. No "use it or lose it" as is sometimes true for other medical spending account plans.

- **HSA Remains after Separation from Service.** An HSA remains with the HSA owner after separation from service even if the employer provided the HSA funding.

- **Transferability.** HSA owners can move their HSA to a new HSA custodian at any time.

- **Ownership.** HSA owners own the money in their HSA and can use it as they see fit. This relates to other benefits already mentioned, but also provides HSA owners the ability to name beneficiaries on the account, select investments, and decide when to take a distribution (even if the distribution is for a non-medical reason).

- **Control Spending.** An HSA gives HSA owners some additional control over their medical spending. The HSA owner can decide where to spend the money and can negotiate with providers when appropriate. This gives HSA owner some freedom to choose medical providers outside of an insurance company's network or to try alternative approaches (within the definition of "qualified medical expense").

- **Lower Insurance Premiums.** HDHPs are generally less expensive than traditional insurance.

4. Are there disadvantages of an HSA?

Yes. For an individual unable to afford traditional insurance, the High Deductible Health Plan (HDHP) and HSA combination may provide an affordable approach to insurance not possible otherwise. Many people that can afford traditional insurance also choose HDHPs and HSAs because the combination reflects a cost savings and provides more pure insurance rather than pre-paid medical. This background is important because many of the disadvantages of HSAs are only in comparison to traditional health insurance, low or no deductible health insurance. The following are potential disadvantages of a combination HDHP and HSA.

- **More Responsibility for Health Care Spending.** HSAs require individuals to take charge of their own health care spending. This will generally require more time devoted to learning about health care costs and alternatives than a person with traditional insurance coverage undertakes where much of the expense is simply paid.

- **Tax Reporting.** HSA owners are required to account for both HSA contributions and distributions each year on their income tax return. Plus, the HSA owner needs to save medical receipts.

- **HSA Rules.** HSAs, similar to all tax-driven types of accounts, can get complex. The HSA owner is responsible to learn the HSA rules and follow them or face tax consequences.

- **HSA Maintenance.** The HSA owner is responsible to maintain the HSA: pay medical bills, monitor the balance, choose beneficiaries, and otherwise maintain the HSA.

- **Higher Deductible.** An HSA owner faces a higher health insurance deductible than a person with traditional insurance and may need to pay that larger deductible amount. This can be an increased cost burden (although lower deductibles generally mean higher premiums, which is also a burden).

- **Expenses before Savings.** An HSA owner may face a large medical expense prior to having time to build a sufficient balance in the HSA.

5. How does an HSA work?

HSAs are designed to pay for day-to-day medical expenses on a tax-favored basis. HSA owners are given the control to decide what to buy, where to buy it, and how much to pay. HSAs also demand more personal responsibility in that HSA owners need to make these decisions, understand the HSA rules, and maintain receipts and other records to prove to the IRS that they acted within the rules.

In order to open an HSA, individuals must have health insurance. HSA laws require that individuals have a High Deductible Health Plan and meet other eligibility requirements. With a high deductible plan, individuals are responsible for the day-to-day expenses rather than the insurance company. To compensate for this responsibility (and to level the tax playing field), the law allows HDHP owners to open an HSA to pay for these day-to-day expenses tax-free.

The general idea is Americans can pay for routine and relatively low cost medical expenses using their HSAs. Insurance will cover serious illnesses and catastrophes. A common comparison is with automobile insurance. A car owner generally buys insurance for major accidents or loss. The day-to-day care of the car, including oil changes and minor accident repair are the responsibility of the car owner. A car owner can control the premium cost somewhat by accepting more risk through a higher deductible. The chart below illustrates this concept for HSAs.

Unused HSA Savings Covers	• Future medical expenses • Medicare of Insurance payments after age 65 • General retirement
Your Insurance Covers (Your High Deductible Health Plan)	• Major medical expenses • Preventive care • Post deductible expenses
HSA Covers	• Doctor visits • Prescriptions • Day-to-day routine medical expenses

6. Who is an "HSA Owner"?

HSAs are individual accounts and must be established in the name and social security number of an individual. The person opening the HSA is called the "HSA owner." Various other terms are also used to name the HSA owner, including the following: "account beneficiary," "account owner," "account holder," "taxpayer," and in certain contexts, "employee."

7. Why did Congress create HSAs?

Congress wanted to provide Americans with more control over their health care spending and insert the power of consumerism into health care. The belief is that consumers, spending their own money, may be able to help reduce the rate of increase in health care costs.

The goal of returning consumerism to health care spending required the creation of the HSAs as a tax-driven account. Our tax code allows employers to provide employees with health care on a tax-favored basis. Individuals that buy health insurance on their own do not get to deduct their health care premiums. This tax-driven approach to health care spending strongly encourages employers to offer health insurance coverage and for that coverage to be as comprehensive as possible so as much medical care as possible can be provided on a tax-favored basis.

The health care system that has developed due to employer provided insurance has resulted in rapidly increasing costs and a situation where the person seeking the medical service is often not directly paying the cost. Often the patient does not even know the cost of the medical service.

HSAs are not insurance and do not directly address all the tax issues. HSAs do provide individuals with direct control over some of their health care dollars and give individuals an incentive to seek cost effective health care solutions. HSAs were and are seen as part of the solution to bring consumerism back into the healthcare market.

8. Are HSAs "consumer-driven" health plans?

Yes. HSAs are part of the consumer-driven healthcare market. "Consumer-driven healthcare" refers to a broad concept of giving individuals the power to make healthcare purchasing decisions (rather than insurance companies, employers or the government). This power includes the ability to save the money if the purchase is not made or to keep the savings if a less expensive alternative is found.

Consumerism has worked in America to reduce prices, increase quality and expand choice in a wide variety of consumer products. Whether consumerism works for healthcare is controversial. HSAs have now served as a ten year test for consumerism and the results as measured by popularity of the product are a success. HSAs have grown steadily and rapidly. HSAs have also reduced the rate of increase in health care costs overall but that conclusion will require more data and more analysis before it can be made without inviting a debate.

9. Are HSAs the same nationwide or do state laws apply?

HSAs were created by the United States Congress and are available to taxpayers in all fifty states. Based in federal law, the HSA laws and rules are the same across the country for most issues. State laws apply in a number of key areas such as: whether state income tax applies, when an HSA is deemed "established," the types of health insurance available, and a number of other areas. Federal authorities, especially the Internal Revenue Service (IRS), have provided much of the regulation and guidance on the federal HSA law.

10. What law created HSAs?

HSAs were part of the Medicare Prescription Drug, Improvement and Modernization Act of 2003 (also known as the Medicare Modernization Act or "MMA"). The Act was signed into law by President George W. Bush on December 8, 2003. This law is best known for its prescription drug program called Medicare Part D.

11. What government agencies regulate HSAs?

Since HSAs are primarily tax-driven accounts, the Internal Revenue Service (IRS) provides the most guidance on the regulation of HSAs. Secondly, HSAs have a health care aspect, so Health and Human Services (HHS) provides some guidance. Thirdly, the Department of Labor (DOL) has limited involvement since HSAs are often offered through an employer plan. In addition, states may also provide some regulation as well.

Investments held in an HSA may engage an entire different set of federal and state regulators: Federal Deposit Insurance Corporation (FDIC), Securities and Exchange Commission (SEC), Office of the Comptroller of the Currency (OCC) and more.

12. Is an "HSA Insurance Plan" the same as an HSA?

No. There has been some confusion in the industry between High Deductible Health Insurance Plans (HDHPs) and HSAs. HDHPs are health insurance plans that pay for your health insurance after you reach your deductible. HSAs are an account used to pay for your day-to-day medical expenses and are not insurance (at least not in the traditional sense of paying a premium to insure against a risk). Some insurance companies advertise their HDHPs as "HSA Plans." What they mean by this is that purchasing health insurance with them will allow you to open an HSA.

13. Are HSA owners required to get their health insurance and HSA from the same provider?

No. Health insurance and HSAs are two distinct products. HSA owners can select health insurance from one provider and open an HSA account with another. In many cases, the insurance provider will offer an HSA as well as health insurance, but obtaining both from the same provider is an option, not a requirement.

14. Is an HSA the same as a Medical IRA?

No, however — HSAs were created using the legal framework from Individual Retirement Accounts (IRAs) and accordingly share many of the same attributes of an IRA. Earlier versions of the law even called the accounts Medical IRAs. IRAs and HSAs are both custodial accounts, share similar reporting requirements (IRS Forms 1099 and 5498), allow for similar investment choices, and share the same idea of giving individuals control over their savings. The two accounts differ in tax treatment of contributions and distributions, purpose of the accounts, requirements to open an account, and numerous other technical details.

PART II: HEALTH CARE REFORM'S IMPACT ON HEALTH SAVINGS ACCOUNTS

15. What is the Affordable Care Act?

The full name of the Affordable Care Act is the "The Patient Protection and Affordable Care Act." This law is also referred to as "ObamaCare," both by critics of the law and periodically by President Obama. This health care law will profoundly change our health care system by insuring thirty million previously uninsured Americans, by requiring individuals and some businesses to buy health insurance, and by providing subsidies to lower income Americans and small businesses. The law also significantly revises Medicaid and Medicare and puts the federal government, rather than the states, in charge of health insurance.

See The Patient Protection and Affordable Care Act, Pub. L. No. 111-148, 124 Stat. 119 (2010)

16. How did the 2010 passage of the Affordable Care Act impact HSAs?

The law contains only two direct changes to HSAs: (1) eliminating the ability to use the HSA for over-the-counter drugs without penalty and (2) increasing the withdrawal penalty from 10 percent to 20 percent for non-qualified distributions. The Affordable Care Act only includes the acronym "HSA" six times in the entire law. The law is not about HSAs and Congress did not significantly consider HSAs in drafting it. The indirect changes could impact HSAs, even potentially ending the growth of HSA plans. The actual impact depends on regulatory interpretation of the health care reform law as well as market response to those interpretations. Although regulators have had more than four years to work on regulations much remains to be done and we will not know the full impact of the law on HSAs until a few years from now.

17. Does the Affordable Care Act build on the success of HSAs?

From a broad perspective, the Affordable Care Act takes a different approach to health insurance than the consumer-directed health care movement that includes HSAs. The Affordable Care Act mandates insurance coverage and then provides very specific levels of detail on what health coverage must include with an emphasis on making sure essential care and preventive services are covered.

The philosophy behind the consumer-directed movement with HDHPs is that the individuals should take charge of health care dollars and pay for most routine, low-cost care, day-to-day medical procedures. Insurance should be reserved for large or even catastrophic medical payments. These two different approaches to health insurance and health care result in a number of potential conflicts for regulators in meshing the ACA with the law for HDHPs and HSAs.

18. Did the Affordable Care Act change contribution limits?

No. The law did not change HSA contribution limits.

19. Did the Affordable Care Act change the rule allowing for the purchase of over-the-counter drugs with HSAs?

Yes. Over-the-counter drugs have not been qualified medical expenses since 2011. However, if an HSA owner gets a doctor's prescription for over-the-counter drugs she can still use her HSA to pay for the items tax-free and penalty-free. The rule against buying over-the-counter drugs with an HSA does not apply to non-drug over-the-counter items such as bandages or contact lenses cleaner.

See Part Eight: Distributions — Qualified Medical Expenses — Over-the-Counter Drugs.

20. Did the penalty increase for non-qualified use of an HSA?

Yes, the ten percent penalty for using an HSA for non-qualified medical expenses increased to 20 percent in 2011.

21. Will the law change HSAs in the future?

Other than items discussed this Chapter, the ACA does not directly change HSAs. Indirectly, however, the ACA may change HDHPs in a manner that would eliminate HSA eligibility. The chart below provides areas to watch as the Affordable Care Act is fully implemented (the terms in the table are defined in this chapter).

AFFORDABLE CARE ACT'S IMPACT ON HSAS

New Law (year effective) Direct Impact to HSAs	Impact to HSAs
No Over-The-Counter (OTC) Drugs (2011)	HSA owners are no longer allowed to use their HSA tax and penalty free for OTC medicines. Non-drug OTC are still allowed. HSA owners can get a prescription for an OTC drug making the OTC drug eligible.
Increased Penalty for Non-Eligible Withdrawals to 20% (2011)	The penalty tax for early withdrawals for non-eligible medical expenses increased to 20% from 10%.
Indirect Impact to HSAs	
Preventive Care Services (2010)	Definition of "preventive care" for new law must match definition for High Deductible Health Plans (HDHPs). These definitions have worked together thus far.
Medical Loss Ratio (MLR) (2011)	Some HDHPs have had lower MLRs and could be at risk of being canceled by insurance companies. This has not been a serious problem thus far but remains an issue.
Essential Benefits (2014)	HDHPs must offer "essential benefits." This will likely expand the medical services offered by some HDHPs and increase premiums.

Insurance Exchanges and Actuarial Value (2014)	HDHPs must meet actuarial value requirements for inclusion on exchanges. Early calculations show that HDHPs will meet the actuarial requirements, but it is an area to watch.
Maximum Out-of-Pocket Expenses (2014)	The law requires all insurance plans to meet HDHP maximum out-of-pocket expenses. This change could increase the number of people eligible for HSAs.
Cadillac Tax (2018)	Impacts HSAs uniquely because HSA contributions (employer and payroll deferral) count toward the Cadillac tax cap. After the cap is reached a 40% tax applies.

22. Why is the definition of "preventive care" important to HSAs?

The Affordable Health Care Act requires that a qualified health plan offer preventive care services without cost-sharing. The obvious goal of the ACA is to encourage Americans to seek preventive care and potentially avoid more expensive care in the future. The definition of "preventive care" is crucial to both the Affordable Care Act and the law that created HSAs, the Medicare Prescription Drug Improvement, and Modernization Act. The key for HSAs is that the definitions match. If preventive care under the Affordable Care Act expands to include items that are not allowed under the HDHP rules, then HDHPs will no longer be considered qualified health plans. If that happens, individuals and companies will have to change health plans in order to avoid the tax for not maintaining health insurance.

The HDHP law provides that "[a] plan shall not fail to be treated as a high deductible health plan by reason of failing to have a deductible for preventative care…except as otherwise provided for by the Secretary." This definition allows for periodic health evaluations, routine pre-natal and well-child care, immunizations, tobacco cessation programs, obesity programs, and screening services, but does not include services to treat an illness. This definition is substantially simpler than the Affordable Care Act's definition.

Fortunately, both laws put preventive care in a special category with the Affordable Care Act requiring preventive care services at zero cost-sharing and the HDHP law allowing for preventive care services without cost-sharing. Also both laws place the details of the definition within the regulatory scope of the Secretary of Health and Human Services. So far, Health and Human Services has maintained the definition of "preventive care" such that it works both for the Affordable Care Act and HSA/HDHP laws.

The IRS-provided important guidance on the definition of preventive care under HSA law in the fall of 2013. The HSA law's definition of preventive care "…also includes services required to be provided as preventive health services by a group health plan or a health insurance issuer offering group or individual health insurance under…" the Affordable Care Act (as implemented under Section 2713 of the Public Health Services Act), and regulations and other administrative guidance.

This interpretation allows for HDHPs to offer the preventive care required under the Affordable Care Act (Section 2713 of the Public Health Services Act) without a deductible and remain

HDHPs. This interpretation, that if the Affordable Care Act requires preventive care without a deductible that requirement should not preclude HSA eligibility, is very welcome guidance to the HSA industry. The ruling also clarifies that the HSA law's previous definition of preventive care also remains in place and any item that was previously considered preventive care under HSA law remains so.

IRS Notice 2013-57.

23. What do Medical Loss Ratios have to do with HSAs?

Medical Loss Ratios (MLRs) do not directly impact HSAs, but MLRs do apply to HDHPs that are necessary to be eligible for an HSA. There is some risk that HDHPs might become less attractive to insurance companies or even unprofitable if the plans fail the MLR rules. If that happens, insurance companies may stop offering HDHPs.

The Affordable Care Act requires that health plans maintain a MLR of 85 percent for large group plans and 80 percent for small group plans. A MLR is calculated by determining the amount of insurance premiums that are used toward qualifying medical expenses. For example, if an insurance plan spends eighty cents out of a dollar of insurance premium on medical expenses, the plan has a MLR of 80 percent.

Failure to maintain the MLR of 80 percent or 85 percent results in a mandatory refund to the premium payers of the amount exceeding the permitted MLR. An insurance company with a MLR of 80 percent in the large group market (100 employees or more) must rebate 5 percent of the premiums back to enrolled participants because the plan failed to meet the required 85 percent MLR. This rule is designed to prevent insurance companies from making excessive profits.

The MLR rules are significant for the health insurance industry generally but may be especially harsh for HDHPs and HSAs. HDHP plans require that individuals pay most of the cost up to a high deductible amount thus reducing cost-sharing and the MLR. Serious medical issues drive much of health care spending, but at the margin individual cost-sharing and high deductibles will impact the MLR negatively for HDHPs. Traditional health insurance has an element of pre-paid health services built in that increases the MLR. Other parts of the MLR calculation also result in HDHPs having higher MLRs. The first two years of MLR testing under the Affordable Care Act, 2011 and 2012, did result in rebates but not in amounts resulting in any dramatic impact on the HDHP marketplace.

24. Does the Affordable Care Act's maximum deductible limit for the small group market impact HSAs?

The Affordable Care Act included the provisions described below. However, in 2014 Congress passed legislation signed by the President eliminating these provisions retroactively to the passage of the Affordable Care Act (The Protecting Access to Medicare Act of 2014, P.L. 113-93).

The rule would have required small groups that currently offer higher deductible HDHPs to lower their deductibles. The Affordable Care Act imposed a maximum deductible for the small group markets of $2,000 for individuals and $4,000 for families. These deductibles are within the current limits for HDHPs of $1,250 minimum deductible for single coverage and $2,500 (2014) for family.

Even before the law change, Health and Human Services issued regulations allowing for some flexibility for increased deductibles in the small plan market. The regulations allowed a health plan's annual deductible to exceed the annual deductible limit ($2,000/$4,000) if that plan could not reasonably reach the actuarial value of a given level of coverage without exceeding the annual deductible limit. This flexibility is no longer necessary given the repeal of the law.

45 CFR § 156.130(b)(3).

25. How do the new levels of bronze, silver, gold and platinum impact HSAs?

The Affordable Care Act creates new American Health Benefit Exchanges and it's important for HSAs to include HDHPs in these exchanges. To be included on an exchange, the health insurance must meet one of five levels: bronze, silver, gold, platinum or catastrophic.

The bronze level, the easiest to meet other than catastrophic, must provide at an actuarial value of at least 60 percent. The actuarial value is another tool to ensure that the health plan meets certain minimum requirement established by the Affordable Care Act. What the bronze level requires is that the plan must pay at least 60 percent of the expenses of an identical plan with zero cost-sharing (i.e., no deductibles, no co-pays, basically no cost to the insured other than the premium). This rule is first implemented in 2014 so at the time of this writing there was not enough data to fully understand the rules impact on HSAs. The potential impact is if HDHPs cannot meet the requirements for even the bronze level of service then HDHPS would not be offered (and then accordingly, no one buying a bronze through platinum plan on an exchange would be eligible for an HSA). That scenario did not happen for the first year of the exchanges as HDHPs were widely available.

One significant question is the extent to which HSA contributions count in the actuarial value calculation. Early rules provide that employer-made HSA contributions will be included if the employer contribution is known in advance (additional calculations may also be required). This will help HDHPs achieve a higher actuarial value and potentially a higher level metal.

The law also creates a special category for catastrophic care that provides the most lenient rules for allowance on the exchange. The catastrophic category applies to individual plans (with some cases for family coverage) and only for individuals under the age of 30 or meeting other limited exceptions for hardship (those who cannot find coverage for less than 8 percent of their income). Although the catastrophic care coverage will have high deductibles, the plans will not qualify as HDHPs necessary for HSA eligibility. Catastrophic plans under the Affordable Care Act require three office visits prior to the deductible being met and this requirement disqualifies the plans as HDHPs.

The IRS and the Department of Health and Human Services released a minimum value calculator (based on an Excel worksheet) that is designed to assist employers in determining whether an employer-sponsored health plan meets the minimum values required under the Affordable Care Act.

26. Do the new maximum out-of-pocket limits for health plans impact HSAs?

Yes, new health plans will have to comply with the HDHP maximum out-of-pocket costs potentially increasing the number of Americans eligible for HSAs. Starting in 2014, the ACA requires Qualified Health insurance plans to have maximum out-of-pocket expenses that match the current inflation adjusted HDHP maximum out-of-pocket expenses ($6,350 for single coverage and $12,700 for families in 2014). This change should increase the number of plans meeting the HDHP requirements and therefore increase the number of people eligible for an HSA.

For years after 2014, however, the Affordable Care Act uses a different inflation adjustment index than is used to adjust the HDHP limits. HSA rules use the Consumer Price Index (CPI) to adjust the maximum out-of-pocket limits for HDHPs. The Affordable Care Act uses an index tied to increases in the average per capita premium for health insurance coverage. Accordingly, the maximum-out-of-pocket numbers will diverge for years after 2014. At the time of this writing the 2015 HDHP limits were available but not the 2015 Affordable Care Act limits.

The difference in inflation adjustment methods is important for HSA eligibility because in order for individuals to be eligible for an HSA they must be covered by an HDHP. If the inflation adjustment for the Affordable Care Act increases at a significantly faster pace than the CPI, insurance companies may decide to increase their maximum-out-of-pocket limits to a point that exceeds the allowed limit for the maximum out-of-pocket for HDHP purposes. If this happens, individuals covered under those plans will not be eligible for HSAs.

If the inflation adjustment under the Affordable Care Act is close to the adjustment for HDHPs, insurance providers will have an incentive to stay below the HDHP limits so they can advertise the health insurance as HSA-eligible. The Affordable Care Act inflation adjustment is likely to result in a greater inflation adjustment than the CPI. If this is the case, at some point in the future, insurance companies will begin offering high deductible insurance with the higher out-of-pocket maximums allowed under the Affordable Care Act inflation adjustment in order to lower premium expense. History supports this assertion as prior to the Affordable Care Act, insurance companies offered catastrophic plans that failed to meet the definition of an HDHP because the plans allowed for total out-of-pocket costs that exceeded the limit for HDHPs. Although individuals selecting these plans faced large deductibles, they were not eligible for an HSA.

27. Does the Cadillac Tax have any effect on HSAs?

Starting in 2018, the Affordable Care Act law places a tax on high cost health plans (referred to as the "Cadillac Tax" starting in 2018. The Cadillac tax will be imposed on plans that cost more than $10,200 for individuals and more than $27,500 for families. At first glance, this appears to cause no issues for HDHPs and HSAs as HSA plans are generally less expensive plans. However, both employer and employee payroll deferral HSA contributions count towards the Cadillac tax cap.

The Cadillac tax does not apply until 2018, but using 2014 HSA contribution limits illustrates how this tax could impact HSAs. An employee that makes a $3,350 HSA contribution through payroll deferral (single HSA limit for 2015 that will increase by 2018) would only have $6,850 left for insurance premiums without facing the Cadillac tax. Although $6,850 for a single HDHP policy is high, most Americans are not likely to think that a cost at this level could trigger the Cadillac tax.

The inflation adjustment for the Cadillac tax makes this issue more important. The Cadillac tax limits are adjusted using the Consumer Price Index plus one percent for 2019 and after that the straight CPI. Medical inflation has outpaced the CPI in every year since 1973, when oil prices disrupted the CPI, to 2012. The rate of medical inflation has been declining since 2012 which could reduce the impact of the Cadillac tax.

The use of the CPI for the Cadillac tax will likely lead to the tax applying to more plans than expected. The Joint Economic Committees Minority Staff Report Study predicts that in just eight years after the Cadillac provisions take effect, the average priced insurance policy will be subject to the Cadillac tax. If that projection is true this provision will draw comparisons to the Alternative Minimum Tax. The inflation issue combined with the fact that employer HSA contributions, including payroll deferral, count toward the total cap, make this an issue to watch for those involved with HSAs.

For an employer group, the penalty is applied at an individual level. This means that an employer group cannot rely on averages to avoid the tax.

28. How do the Affordable Care Act's premium subsidies impact HSAs?

The Affordable Care Act provides premium subsidies to low and moderate income families (income between 100 percent and 400 percent of the Federal Poverty Level (FPL)) without access to affordable employer-sponsored insurance. The premium subsidy works as a tax credit and is available starting in 2014.

The health insurance premium subsidies should result in more Americans becoming eligible for HSAs. The premium subsidies are designed to increase health coverage overall by enticing previously uninsured Americans to buy insurance. Assuming this is successful, there is reason to believe that HDHPs may be a popular choice for Americans eligible for premium subsidies (HDHP coverage is the key to HSA eligibility).

The amount of the premium subsidy is tied to the cost of a Silver level plan on the health care exchanges. The amount of the subsidy does not increase if a person elects a Gold or Platinum plan. Given that Silver and Bronze plans are less expensive anyway, Americans receiving subsidies will be drawn to Silver and Bronze level plans. At the Silver and Bronze level, HDHPs are prominent. A logical conclusion is that HDHPs will become a popular choice for Americans receiving premium subsidies.

29. How do the Affordable Care Act's cost-sharing subsidies impact HSAs?

In addition to premium subsidies, the Affordable Care Act also provides cost-sharing subsidies to lower to moderate income Americans (incomes between 100 percent and 250 percent of the FPL). The cost-sharing subsidies are designed to increase the actuarial value of the plan by reducing an individual's share of medical expenses paid. The law allows insurance companies some flexibility in how to reduce the individual's costs. The cost savings are generally achieved through reductions in the deductible amount, the co-insurance amount, and ultimately, the maximum out-of-pocket limit. The government pays the insurance company directly for the cost-sharing measures. The cost-sharing subsidies are only available for Silver level plans on the health exchanges.

Cost-sharing subsidies, however, can change a plan from an HDHP to a non-HDHP. Whether or not the plan remains an HDHP will require a review of the HDHP requirements after the benefits of the cost-sharing measures are applied. A reduced deductible below the HDHP minimum allowed would be a case of a cost-sharing measure eliminating HSA eligibility. The insurance provider should be able to determine whether an HDHP remains an HDHP for an individual with cost-sharing subsidies.

30. What would happen to HSAs if the law prevented future HSA contributions?

If the Affordable Care Act did impact either an HSA owner's health plan or health plans in general in a manner that individuals lose HSA eligibility, existing HSA owners could continue to use any amounts in their HSAs for qualified medical expenses even if no longer eligible to contribute more. This is important to know in case changes do make HDHPs less available. The HSA remains one of the best tax favored options available. A good strategy is for people to accumulate assets now in the HSA to prepare for future changes might occur.

31. Should HSA owners change anything based on the Affordable Care Act?

The ACA is a foundational change to our health care and insurance system and mostly likely will impact everyone. For now the combination of an HDHP and HSA remain very competitive and a good choice for many businesses and consumers.

PART III: ELIGIBILITY

Overview

32. Are there eligibility requirements to open an HSA?

Yes. To be eligible for an HSA, individuals must meet the following requirements:

- be covered by a High Deductible Health Plan (HDHP)
- not be covered by another health plan that is not an HDHP
- not be eligible to be claimed as a dependent on another person's tax return
- not be entitled to Medicare benefits (enrolled in Medicare)

The detail surrounding each of these requirements can be complex. Accordingly each requirement is covered in a separate section in this part.

See the Eligibility and Contribution Worksheet, IRS Notice 2004-2, See Q 2.

33. Are there any income limits affecting HSA eligibility?

No, income level does not impact HSA eligibility. Unlike some IRAs, high income earners as well as individuals with no income are both potentially eligible.

34. Is "earned income" required to be eligible for an HSA?

No. HSA owners do not need to have "earned income" in order to be eligible for an HSA. If an individual is otherwise eligible for an HSA, she can contribute to an HSA even if she has no earned income. The money for the HSA contribution can come from savings, a gift or otherwise. Comparisons between IRAs and HSAs often raise this question because Individual Retirement Accounts (IRAs) do require earned income.

35. Can individuals without health insurance open HSAs?

No. Individuals must be covered under an HDHP to be eligible to open an HSA.

> *Example.* Ella is not covered by health insurance but would like to pay for her qualified medical expenses tax-free through an HSA. She does not have an HSA and would like to open and contribute to one. She cannot as she is not eligible for an HSA because she is not covered by an HDHP.

36. Are HSA-eligible individuals required to open HSAs?

No, but they stand to lose some tax benefits if they are eligible for an HSA and do not open one. Nationwide statistics reveal that many (up to one-half of eligible people) Americans that are eligible for an HSA do not open one. A likely reason many eligible individuals fail to open an HSA is that they cannot afford to do so.

HSA owners that do not have sufficient funds to fully fund an HSA should consider opening an HSA with just a minimum amount to set the "establishment date." Individuals cannot use an HSA for any expenses incurred prior to their "establishment date."

Example 1. Stephanie's employer provides her with an HDHP with a $2,500 deductible. The employer further offers Stephanie the ability to deduct money from her pay pre-tax to go into an HSA through its Cafeteria plan. Stephanie does not open an HSA. Subsequently, Stephanie gets hit by a bus and incurs a $10,000 hospital bill (she owes her $2,500 deductible and the insurance will pick up $7,500). She cannot use her HSA to pay for her $2,500 expense because she did not open her HSA <u>prior</u> to incurring the expense.

Example 2. Assume instead that Stephanie elected to do a one-time payroll deferral of $100 into an HSA. This required her to commit some money and do a bit of work to open the HSA, but in exchange she set her establishment date. Now if she gets hit by the bus after she opened her HSA, she can use her HSA to pay her $2,500 deductible.

The fact that she can use her HSA does not change the fact that she only has $100 in her HSA, but at least she can contribute more money to her HSA on a tax-favored basis to pay the $2,500 deductible. She could get a loan to pay the medical bill and then pay herself back from the HSA over time. She may even be able to approach the medical provider with an offer of increasing her deferral to the HSA and writing them a monthly check until the bill is paid. By running the expense through the HSA, she will save taxes and lower her overall cost.

High Deductible Health Plan (HDHP)
Overview of HDHPs
37. What is a High Deductible Health Plan (HDHP)?

"HDHP" is a legally defined term for a health insurance policy with a higher deductible than traditional insurance. These types of health insurance plans used to be called "catastrophic" plans, but the HSA law created the new name, HDHP, because HDHPs have to meet very specific requirements. In fact, many of the catastrophic plans that existed prior to HSAs did not qualify as HDHPs.

The key requirement that HDHPs must meet are the federal limits for the annual deductible and maximum out-of-pocket expenses. For individual coverage the HDHP must have an annual deductible of at least $1,300 for 2015 ($1,250 for 2014) and require that annual out-of-pocket expenses paid (includes co-payments and deductibles but not insurance premiums) not exceed $6,450 for 2015 ($6,350 for 2014). For family coverage the limits are an annual deductible of not less than $2,600 for 2015 ($2,500 for 2014) and require that out-of-pocket expenses not exceed $12,900 for 2015 ($12,700 for 2014).

HDHPs cannot provide coverage below the deductible thresholds for service other than "preventive" care. Preventive care is an important exception especially because the Affordable Care Act now requires that health plans offer preventive care coverage before the deductible is met.

IRS Notice 2004-2, See Q 3.

38. Why is having an HDHP a requirement for having an HSA?

Opponents of the HSA legislation were concerned that HSAs would become just another tax break for the wealthy. To partially counter that concern, the HSA laws require that in order to be eligible for an HSA you must be covered by an HDHP and no other health plan. This is to avoid the situation where a taxpayer could get a large deduction for an HSA contribution and then not really need the HSA to pay for day-to-day medical expenses because the person either had traditional, low-deductible insurance, or was double covered and had both traditional and HDHP coverage. People with HDHP coverage and no other health plan coverage (other than permitted coverage or coverage by another HDHP) need the benefits of an HSA because they face a high deductible. The idea behind HSAs is that HSA owners would pay day-to-day medical expenses with the HSA. Their HDHP insurance is only accessed for catastrophic events or very large medical expenses.

Congress also designed HSAs to encourage consumerism. Many individuals spend less than their deductible year-to-year. By requiring a high deductible plan, HSA owners are being encouraged to be good consumers of their health care dollars. Any money not spent in an HSA rolls over to future years and individuals directly benefit from lower cost health care services. The larger the deductible, the more HSA owners confront their medical expenses as they would other expenses. HSA owners should be more likely to become informed of what medical options exist and to make overall wise choices with their health care dollars. Congress passed the HSA law in the belief that this would lower the overall rate of health care cost increases.

39. Are there any advantages to an HDHP over a traditional health insurance plan?

Yes. Listed below are the key advantages:

- **Required for HSA Eligibility.** One significant advantage of HDHP coverage is that it is required for HSA eligibility. The benefits of HSAs are substantial and worth some effort to obtain.

- **Less Expensive.** Another advantage is that HDHP coverage is generally less expensive than traditional health insurance, often significantly so. The analogy with car insurance is apt. You pay less for car insurance if you choose a higher deductible plan. However with a higher deductible on your car insurance you likely will have to pay the full costs of a minor fender bender accident. This gives you an incentive to both avoid the accident and to find a reasonable price solution to fix your car should an accident occur. If you get in a serious accident, your insurance will cover you. HDHPs work the same way by encouraging consumers to use health services responsibly and seeking value-based care when needed. HDHPs are allowed to offer preventive care services for no cost to you, such as an annual physical, so HDHPs do provide some services prior to reaching the deduction limit (this provision reduces some criticism of HSAs that people will not seek medical care if they have to pay for it).

- **Tax Deductibility for Individuals.** The selection of an HDHP and HSA is often the most logical choice for individuals that buy their own insurance. Besides the lower cost, there are also tax benefits. Individuals cannot deduct the cost of their health insurance premiums; including HDHPs, but contributions to an HSA are tax deductible. This allows individuals to get a portion of their health care costs covered tax-free, the portion contributed to the HSA.

- **Access to Tax Benefits for Out-of-Pocket Medical Expenses.** An HDHP allows an individual to open and use an HSA to pay for out-of-pocket medical expenses. This is a significant benefit for individuals that do not have access to employer provided Flexible Spending Accounts or Health Care Reimbursement Accounts.

- **Employer Provided Insurance - Cost Savings.** When an employer provides the insurance, most Americans would likely prefer low deductible traditional insurance with no or low co-pays. Over the last decade or more however, employers have increased the deductibles on traditional insurance often to the point where there may not be much of a gap between traditional health insurance deductibles and HDHP plans. Also, many employers require the employee to pay a portion of the premium and switching to an HDHP may reduce the employee cost. When an employer switches to an HDHP from traditional insurance, a number of factors will determine whether the switch is a net positive or negative for employees. Likely it will be a positive for those that use less health services (and can build a balance in their HSA or otherwise value the flexibility of an HSA) and a negative for heavy users of health care that are satisfied with their existing choices and cost.

40. What is the process for determining if a health insurance plan is an HDHP?

The easiest and best method to determine if a particular health insurance plans meets the requirements to be an HDHP is to ask the insurance provider if it is an HDHP or an HSA-qualified plan. Insurance companies have an incentive to know whether their plans qualify as HDHP plans and often advertise the plans as "HSA Plans." If an employer self-insures, then the individual employee needs to ask the employer's human resources' staff. Businesses self-funding will need to read the details on HDHPs to make sure a self-funded plan meets the HDHP requirements.

The legal definition of HDHP gets complex and depends upon insurance policy provisions that may be difficult to find in a lengthy insurance policy. The deductible limits and maximum out-of-pocket limits are the first items to check, but there are other rules that could also disqualify the plan (for example, prior to HSAs existing many catastrophic plans with deductibles high enough to meet the HDHP requirements failed to be HDHPs because they provided first-dollar coverage for services that are not allowed in HDHPs).

41. Is proof of HDHP coverage required?

No. Most HSA custodians will not ask for proof as it is not a required part of an HSA custodian's job to verify eligibility. Some HSA custodians may want to see proof of HSA eligibility to avoid the potential liability and work of correcting mistakes with HSAs.

Employers offering health insurance will work with the insurance company and will know whether the health plan is an HDHP or not. Some employers will make HSA contributions on behalf of employees that are HSA-eligible but do not obtain their insurance through the employer. In this case, the employer may ask for proof of HDHP coverage (a copy of the policy) or more likely simply ask the employee to sign a form attesting to the fact that the employee is eligible.

HSA owners will need to provide proof of HDHP coverage in case of a state or federal tax audit. HSA owners should be prepared to provide that proof by keeping adequate insurance records (although documentation could likely be obtained after the fact from the insurance company).

42. Can a health insurance plan provide for negotiated discounts at medical providers and still meet the legal definition of an HDHP?

Yes, a health plan that otherwise meets the definition of an HDHP may provide negotiated discounts to plan participants regardless of whether the participant has reached the deductible yet or not.

> *Example.* Penelope has a HDHP issued by Best Insurance Company. Best Insurance Company negotiated with City Medical Clinic to obtain a 25 percent discount on medical services for its health insurance policy holders. Penelope is still below her HDHP deductible when she visits City Medical Clinic for a medical issue. City Medical Clinic bills Penelope $75 for the visit. The $75 charge represents a 25 percent discount from City Medical Clinic's posted fees for the service and Penelope got the special rate because she showed her Best Insurance Company health card. Her plan still qualifies as an HDHP even though it allows Penelope to benefit from the negotiated discounts prior to reaching her deductible.

43. Should HSA owners show their medical insurance cards for medical services when they are still below the deductible and paying with the HSA?

Yes. As a general practice HSA owners should provide show insurance card every time they receive medical services, even if the insurance company will not be paying for the service. HSA owners should do this because most insurance companies negotiate discounts for medical services and policy holders are entitled to those discounted rates as a member of that insurance company even if paying for the expense using an HSA (generally because the HSA owner is still below the deductible or maybe it's a non-covered area of service).

Also, by showing the insurance card, the service provider may be providing that information to the insurance company so that the insurance company is tracking expenses towards the deductible. An HSA owner can and should do this on his own by saving receipts but it is advantageous to have it done by the insurance company as well.

Of course, it's not mandatory to show the card. HSA owners are essentially paying cash when using an HSA to cover medical expenses and they may be able to negotiate an even better discount for the service than the insurance company. However, this is the exception and most of us are better off presenting the card whenever we seek medical treatment, even if not sure that the provider wants to see the card. Let the medical provider explain that it does not accept or use an insurance card rather than assume that's the case.

44. Is a health plan that primarily covers accident, disability, dental, vision or long-term care an HDHP?

No. This type of accident and other health care insurance is not HDHP insurance.

> *Example.* A plan provides coverage substantially all of which is for a specific disease or illness. This plan is not an HDHP.

IRS Publication 969.

Deduction Limits

45. What are the HDHP deductible limits?

A critical component of the definition of an HDHP is the deductible. A self-only HDHP must have a deductible of at least $1,300 (2015) and the family deductible must be at least $2,600 (2015). HDHPs must also have a maximum out-of-pocket limit. See the chart below for previous years' limits.

HDHP DEDUCTION LIMITS

TYPE	2004	2005	2006	2007	2008	2009	2010	2011	2012	2013	2014	2015
HDHP - Min Single	$1,000	$1,000	$1,050	$1,100	$1,100	$1,150	$1,200	$1,200	$1,200	$1,250	$1,250	$1,300
HDHP - Min Family	$2,000	$2,000	$2,100	$2,200	$2,200	$2,300	$2,400	$2,40	$2,400	$2,500	$2,500	$2,600
HDHP - Max Single	$5,000	$5,100	$5,250	$5,500	$5,600	$5,800	$5,950	$5,950	$6,050	$6,250	$6,250	$6,450
HDHP - Max Family	$10,000	$10,200	$10,500	$11,000	$11,200	$11,600	$11,900	$11,900	$12,100	$12,500	$12,700	$12,900

46. Do the HSA deductible limits change every year?

Yes, the minimum deductible limits adjust each year for inflation.

47. How does the deductible limit apply to a health plan year that is longer than twelve months?

If a plan year is longer than twelve months the deductible limit must be increased to meet the HDHP rules. The adjustment will be done as follows:

- **Step 1 – Multiply the Deductible Limit by Number of Months.** First, multiply the minimum annual deductible limit ($1,250 for self-only or $2,500 for family for 2014) by the number of months allowed to satisfy the deductible.

- **Step 2 – Divide the Result by Twelve.** Next, divide the result from the first step by twelve. This amount is the adjusted deductible for the longer period that is used to test compliance with the deductible limits.

- **Step 3 – Compare.** Finally, compare the amount in the second step with the plan's deductible. If the plan's deductible equals or exceeds the amount in Step 2, the plan satisfies the minimum deductible requirement.

Example. A health plan takes into account medical expenses incurred in the last three months of 2013 to satisfy its deductible for 2014. The plan's deductible for self-only coverage is $2,000 and covers fifteen months (the last three months of 2013 and the twelve months of 2014). To determine if the plan's deductible satisfies the minimum deductible limit for HDHPs, the following calculations are required.

- **Step 1 – Multiply the Deductible Limit by Number of Months.** Multiply the 2014 minimum annual deductible for self-only HDHPs, $1,250, by fifteen (the number of months allowed to satisfy the deductible. The result is $18,750 ($1,250 × 15).

- **Step 2 – Divide the Result by Twelve.** Divide the result from step 1, $18,750, by 12 to obtain $1,562.50.

- **Step 3 – Compare.** Compare the result in Step 2, $1,562.50, to the plan's deductible, $2,000. The plan's deductible of $2,000 for self-only coverage exceeds $1,562.50 so the plan qualifies as an HDHP.

IRS Notice 2004-50, See Q 25.

48. Can cost-sharing subsidies provided under the Affordable Care Act make a person ineligible for an HSA if the deductible is reduced below the HDHP limits?

Yes. The Affordable Care Act provides cost subsidies to low and moderate income Americans (income limits up to 250 percent of the federal poverty level). The cost-sharing subsides are designed to reduce the individual's out-of-pocket health care costs-including deductibles, copayments and the annual maximum out-of-pocket expenses. If the cost-sharing subsidies reduce the deductible below the HSA deductible limits ($1,300 for self-only and $2,600 for family for 2015), then the plan is no longer an HDHP. The cost subsidies are only available for Silver level plans purchased on a government run health exchange.

Note: The Affordable Care Act provides premium subsidies as well as cost-sharing subsidies. A premium subsidy does not impact HSA eligibility because the health plan remains the same. The taxpayer simply receives help in paying the cost of the premium. The cost-sharing subsidies are different in that the cost-sharing subsidies change basic features of the insurance, such as the deductible.

Example. Paul's income qualifies him for a cost-sharing subsidy under the Affordable Care Act. Paul selects a family plan offered on a government run health care exchange at the Silver level. The plan is listed on the exchange as an HDHP with a deductible of $3,000 and a maximum out-of-pocket expense of $12,900 (levels that meet the HDHP rules for 2015). However, because of the cost-sharing subsidies, Paul's deductible drops to $800 and his maximum out-of-pocket expense is also reduced. Paul is not eligible for an HSA because his plan is not an HDHP (even though it was called an HDHP prior to the application of the cost-sharing subsidies).

Maximum Out-of-Pocket Expenses

49. What is a maximum out-of-pocket limit?

Health insurance plans often include a maximum out-of-pocket limit that is the highest or total amount the health insurance plan requires an individual to pay toward the cost of covered health care. Out-of-pocket expenses include health-related expenses but not the cost of the insurance premium. These expenses include co-pays, co-insurance, prescription drugs, amounts below the deductible, and more. After an individual reaches the maximum out-of-pocket limit in expenses, the health insurance company pays all additional health care expenses. There are some exceptions to this rule and some expenses do not count towards the maximum out-of-pocket limit. Expenses that will not count include: expenses incurred out of the provider network, non-health insurance covered health expenses (dental and vision) and other expenses as well.

50. Does an HDHP have to have a maximum out-of-pocket limit?

Yes. By definition, HDHPs must have a maximum out-of-pocket expense limit of $6,450 for self-only plans (2015) and $12,900 for family plans (2015). Congress likely imposed these limits to ensure that HDHPs offered quality insurance for consumers and did not reduce coverage surreptitiously by increasing the out-of-pocket maximum (a term most consumers are less likely to on than cost and deductible).

The law setting this limit actually made HDHPs more expensive than some other types of insurance with lower deductibles because the other plans capped the maximum out-of-pocket at a higher number. The Affordable Care Act now requires all qualified insurance to use the same maximum out-of-pocket limits as HDHPs, at least for 2014. After 2014, the inflation adjustment for the maximum out-of-pocket limit is different for HDHPs versus qualified health plan requirements under the Affordable Care Act.

See Health Reform's Impact on HSAs.

51. Can a plan without a maximum out-of-pocket expense qualify as an HDHP?

No. The rules require that HDHPs meet the maximum out-of-pocket requirements. A plan may meet the requirements without specifically stating a maximum out-of-pocket expense.

Example 1. A plan provides self-only coverage with a $2,000 deductible. For expenses above the deductible, the plan pays 100 percent of the medical expenses. This meets the HDHP rules even though no specific mention is made on the out-of-pocket maximum because the plan pays all expenses after the $2,000 deductible is met.

Example 2. A plan provides self-only coverage with a $2,000 deductible. For expenses above the deductible, the plan pays 80 percent of the medical expenses and the individual pays 20 percent until the expenses reach $3,000. The plan then pays 100 percent of covered expenses. This meets the HDHP rules even though no specific mention is made on the out-of-pocket maximum because the individual faces a $2,000 deductible, plus another $3,000 in co-insurance for a $5,000 maximum out-of-pocket.

Example 3. A plan provides self-only coverage with a $2,000 deductible. For expenses above the deductible, the plan pays 80 percent of the medical expenses and the individual pays 20 percent. This plan does not qualify as an HDHP because it does not contain a maximum out-of-pocket limit and the expenses could exceed the legal limits.

IRS Notice 2004-50, See Q 18.

52. If a medical expense is not covered by the HDHP, does it still count toward the maximum out-of-pocket expense?

No. Non-covered expenses generally do not count toward the maximum out-of-pocket expense cap. Only covered benefits are required to count toward reaching that maximum out-of-pocket; however, any restriction on benefits must be reasonable.

Example. Farrid is insured under an HDHP. Experimental treatments, chiropractic care, dental care and vision care are not covered by his HDHP. Farrid incurs expenses in each of these categories but the expenses do not count towards his maximum out-of-pocket because the services were not "covered expenses."

IRS Notice 2004-50, See Q 16.

53. Do extra fees charged for failing to first get approval for a specific treatment count towards the maximum out-of-pocket expenses?

No. The penalty is not counted as an out-of-pocket expense, and therefore does not count toward the maximum out-of-pocket limit. An HDHP does not need to count a penalty for a failure to seek pre-certification towards the maximum out-of-pocket limit.

IRS Notice 2004-50, See Q 19.

54. Can an HDHP limit benefits to "Usual, Customary, and Reasonable" (UCR) amounts in determining maximum out-of-pocket expenses?

Yes. Amounts paid by individuals that are above UCR are not included in determining maximum out-of-pocket expenses.

IRS Notice 2004-50, See Q 17.

55. If an HSA owner receives treatment outside of a physician network, does the full cost count toward the maximum out-of-pocket expense?

No. An HDHP is not required to credit the full cost of the service towards the maximum out-of-pocket when an HSA owners seeks treatment outside of the insurance provider's network. A "network" plan is one that provides more favorable benefits and services (lower cost) for services provided within the insurance company's network of providers.

> *Example.* Yi has a network plan HDHP and sought treatment outside of the plan's network. The medical service cost more than it would have if Yi had used an in-network provider. The HDHP plan does not need to credit Yi with the full cost of the out-of-network medical expenses towards his maximum out-of-pocket expenses.

IRS Notice 2004-2, See Q 5.

Lifetime Limit
56. Can an HDHP impose a maximum lifetime limit?

No. The Affordable Care Act imposes rules on lifetime and yearly dollar limits that a health plan must meet in order to be a "qualified health plan." Individuals and employers will have to comply with the Affordable Care Act definitions to avoid penalties.

This question can create confusion because HSA law and IRS regulations allow an HDHP to impose a reasonable lifetime limit on benefits. Although the Affordable Care Act does not directly change the HSA rules, it essentially overrules the practice of an HDHP imposing a lifetime limit. There are limited exceptions for grandfathered plans. In the case of a grandfathered plan, the lifetime limit is not treated as a violation of the maximum out-of-pocket limit required for HSAs. A lifetime limit designed to circumvent the maximum annual out-of-pocket limits is not a reasonable lifetime limit.

> *Example.* Joe is covered by a grandfathered health plan that does not have to comply with the maximum lifetime limit under the Affordable Care Act, at least for 2015. Joe's insurance provides him self-only HDHP coverage with a deductible of $2,000 and a maximum out-of-pocket of $5,000. Joe's insurance further

provides that it has a lifetime limit of one million dollars. This lifetime limit is reasonable and does not disqualify the plan from being an HDHP.

IRS Notice 2004-50, See Q 15.

Deductible Credit for Mid-Year Insurance Changes

57. Can an HDHP count expenses toward the deductible that were incurred under a traditional plan when an employer changes insurance mid-year?

Yes. If the period during which medical expenses are incurred for the purpose of satisfying the deductible is twelve months or less and the plan otherwise satisfies the requirements of an HDHP. The new plan's taking into account medical expenses incurred during the prior plan's short year (whether or not the prior plan was an HDHP) and not reimbursed, does not violate the HDHP requirements. Insurance plans are not required to count expenses incurred under the prior plan toward the deductible on the HDHP.

> *Example.* Clear Windows, Inc. offers a calendar year health plan and switched from a non-HDHP to an HDHP on July 1. The new plan counts medical expenses incurred under the prior plan during the first six months of the year in determining if the new plan's annual deductible is met. The new plan is an HDHP.

IRS Notice 2004-50, See Q 23.

58. Can an HSA owner switch from self-only HDHP to family HDHP coverage mid-year and remain eligible for an HSA even if all the medical expenses count toward the deductible?

Yes. If an HSA owner switches from a self-only HDHP to a family HDHP, the HSA owner does not lose HSA eligibility if the insurance company allows the HSA owner to count medical expenses incurred while on the self-only policy toward the family deductible.

IRS Notice 2004-50, See Q 24.

59. Can an HSA owner switch from family HDHP coverage to self-only HDHP coverage mid-year and remain eligible for an HSA even if all the medical expenses count toward the deductible?

Yes, provided the self-only HDHP uses a reasonable method to allocate the covered expenses during the family coverage period to the self-only covered period. For example, subject to state law requirements, a plan may allocate to the self-only deductible only the expenses incurred by the individual with self-only coverage after the change.

IRS Notice 2008-59, See Q 13.

Embedded Deductibles

60. Do embedded deductibles impact eligibility for HSAs?

Yes. Some family plans have deductibles for both the family as a whole and also for each individual family member. Under these plans, when one family member's medical expenses exceed the individual deductible, the insurance will cover additional qualified medical expenses. If either the deductible for the family as a whole or the deductible for an individual member is below the minimum annual deductible for family coverage, the plan does not qualify as an HDHP.

> *Example.* Assume family insurance coverage for 2014 and that the annual deductible for the family plan is $3,500. This amount meets the minimum deductible limits for family HDHPs for 2014. This plan also has individual deductibles of $1,500 for each family member. Although the $1,500 meets the HDHP minimum deductible limit for a self-only plan for 2014, it does not meet the family minimum limit ($2,500). The plan does not qualify as an HDHP because the deductible for an individual family member is below the minimum annual deductible ($2,500) for family coverage.

IRS Publication 969, p. 4, IRS Notice 2008-59, See Q 5.

61. If an embedded deductible could result in exceeding the maximum out-of-pocket limits, does that disqualify it as an HDHP?

Yes. In order to be a family HDHP, the plan must not exceed the maximum family out-of-pocket expenses ($12,900 for 2015). An insurance plan that provides for individual embedded deductibles without an overall maximum out-of-pocket cap could violate that rule. It depends on level of the embedded deductible and the size of the family. If a large family results in the possibility of a family paying more than maximum out-of-pocket expense then the plan is not an HDHP. Given requirements for all health plans to meet the HSA maximum out-of-pocket expenses starting in 2014 this issue should disappear (with grandfathering and some exceptions it may remain for a few years).

> *Example 1.* Peter is covered under a family HDHP with a $2,500 deductible for each family member with full coverage after the deductible is met. The plan does not contain an overall maximum out-of-pocket limit. This plan meets the HDHP maximum out-of-pocket rules for any family with two to five covered individuals ($2,500 × 5 = $12,500). The maximum the family could face is $2,500 times each of the five family members or $12,500 which is below the 2015 out-of-pocket maximum of $12,900. However, the plan is not an HDHP with regard to families larger than five because the maximum out-of-pocket could exceed the limit ($12,900 for 2015).

> *Example 2.* Same facts as above, except the plan includes an umbrella deductible of $10,000. The plan reimburses 100 percent of covered benefits if the family satisfies the $10,000 limit in aggregate, even if no single family member satisfies the $2,500 embedded deductible. This plan satisfies the HDHP maximum out-of-pocket rules.

IRS Notice 2004-50, See Q 21.

Permitted Insurance

62. Are there "permitted" types of insurance that do not cause the loss of HSA eligibility?

Yes. Individuals are allowed to have the following types of coverage without losing eligibility for an HSA:

- Accident insurance

- Dental care

- Vision care

- Long-term care

- Workers Compensation insurance

- Tort liability insurance

- Liability insurance related to property (e.g., automobile insurance)

- Specific illness insurance

- Hospitalization insurance (a fixed amount paid per day)

IRC Sec. 223(c)(3), See also IRS Notice 2004-2, See Q 7, See also IRS PLR 200704010 (lists numerous examples of polices and riders of permitted insurance and preventive care).

63. Does liability insurance coverage impact HSA eligibility?

No. Insurance for tort liability, liability under workers' compensation laws, liability for ownership or use of property, and such other liabilities as the IRS allows will not disqualify you for an HSA.

IRC Sec. 223(c)(3)(A).

64. Does specified disease or illness coverage disqualify an individual for an HSA?

No. The law allows for coverage for specified disease or illness in addition to HDHP coverage without impacting HSA eligibility. Permitted coverage includes: insurance for one or more specific diseases or illnesses, such as cancer, diabetes, asthma or congestive heart failure; insurance paying a fixed amount per day (or other period) for hospitalization; insurance for liabilities incurred under workers' compensation laws; insurance for tort liabilities, and insurance for liabilities relating to ownership or use of property.

Caution: The insurance industry sells insurance that at first glance appears to satisfy the specified disease exception but the actual coverage is not for a disease. Check with the insurance provider concerning compatibility with HDHPs and HSA eligibility.

IRC Sec. 223(c)(3)(B), IRS Notice 2004-50, See Q 8, IRS PLR 200704010.

65. Is supplemental insurance coverage for hospitalization permitted with an HSA?

Yes. Insurance that pays a fixed amount per day of hospitalization is allowed under HSA rules and does not disqualify a person for an HSA. Aflac is a common provider of this type of insurance.

Caution: Supplemental insurance is problematic if it is used to try to cover the deductible amounts.

IRS Notice 2004-50, See Q 9.

66. Does critical illness insurance coverage impact HSA eligibility?

Some critical illness insurance plans are designed to be compatible with HDHPs and HSA eligibility and others are not. The concern is that a critical illness policy may cover items outside of the allowed types of coverage for specified disease, fixed amount per day for hospitalization, or permitted liability coverage. A critical illness policy that is attempting to cover the deductible amount or to pay for medical expenses other than those allowed below the deductible would be problematic. The best approach is to ask the critical illness provider if the plan is compatible with HSA eligibility.

Other Health Plan

Overview

67. What is "other health coverage"?

Individuals are only eligible for an HSA if they are covered by a HDHP and are not covered "under any other health plan" that is not a high deductible plan and which provides coverage for any benefit which is covered by the HDHP. This basically means individuals are not allowed to have "other health coverage" in addition to the HDHP if they want to remain eligible for an HSA. Of course, there are exceptions.

IRC Sec. 223(c)(1)(A)(ii).

68. Are there exceptions to the rule that no other health coverage is allowed?

Yes. There are a number of exceptions to the rule of requiring HDHP coverage to be eligible for an HSA and no other health coverage. Exceptions include:

- **Permitted Insurance.** The HSA rules contain a list of types of insurance that are permitted.

- **Preventive Care.** The HSA rules allow for first-dollar coverage of "preventive care."

- **Post-Deductible Care.** Health coverage that does not begin until after the minimum HDHP deductible limits have been met.

- **Limited-Purpose Care.** Insurance that is limited to dental and vision care is allowed.

The rule for exceptions is important and complex. Please review all the Questions and Answers in this section for a more detail on each of these exceptions.

69. Why does "other health coverage" disqualify someone for an HSA?

The government wants to ensure that only people that really need the benefits of an HSA can open one. That is, people that must pay the large deductibles found in HDHPs. Accordingly, people with double coverage for the benefits found in the HDHP, covered by both an HDHP and another health plan that is not a high deductible plan, are not eligible for an HSA. This rule prevents a person from receiving a large tax break for making an HSA contribution without really needing the HSA to pay for medical expenses because they have other health coverage that will pay for those expenses. There are a lot of exceptions to this rule; but the exceptions hold true to this principle.

Traditional Health Plan and HDHP

70. Are HDHP covered individuals that are also covered by their spouse's traditional insurance eligible for an HSA?

No. The individual would have "other health coverage" that disqualifies the individual for an HSA. This type of double coverage represents the typical example of someone that is not eligible for an HSA due to the "other health coverage" rule.

Example. Dick and Jane are married. Dick's employer provides him with self-only HDHP coverage and contributes $50 per month into each eligible employee's HSA. Jane's employer provides traditional insurance for Jane and her family. Dick is covered under traditional health insurance through Jane's policy. Accordingly, Dick is ineligible for an HSA and he cannot receive the $50 per month contribution into an HSA offered by his employer. In some cases, it may make sense for Jane to drop Dick from her traditional coverage in order for him to receive the employer HSA contributions.

Spouse or Children with Non-qualifying Other Coverage

71. Is a married individual who is otherwise HSA-eligible made ineligible if the individual's spouse has traditional health coverage?

No. The HSA law and rules only look at the eligibility of the individual. A married individual is not made ineligible for an HSA because the individual's spouse is ineligible. Of course, spouses often are covered by the same health policies so if one spouse is ineligible, the other spouse may be ineligible for the same reason.

Caution: If a spouse participates in a medical FSA* that can be used for either spouse's general health expenses, common for companies that offer traditional health insurance, then neither spouse would be eligible for an HSA. This is because both spouses have "other insurance." An exception to this rule exists for limited-purpose FSAs (those that cover vision and dental expenses only), as discussed below.

Example 1. Amy and Pedro are married, under age fifty-five with two dependent children. Amy has a self-only HDHP policy. Pedro has a family traditional insurance policy that covers himself and their two children. Amy is not covered by Pedro's family traditional insurance. Amy remains eligible for an HSA and may contribute the self-only amount.

Example 2. Same as above, except that Amy has a family HDHP policy that covers her and one of her two children. Pedro has a traditional health policy that covers him and their other child. Amy is not covered by Pedro's traditional policy. Amy remains eligible for an HSA and may contribute the family maximum amount.

Example 3. Same as above, except that Amy has a family HDHP that covers her, Pedro and their two children. Pedro also has a family traditional plan that covers Pedro and their two children. Amy is not covered by Pedro's traditional health policy. Amy remains eligible for an HSA and may contribute the family maximum.

Rev. Rul. 2004-25, See Part III: Eligibility – Other Health Plan – Flexible Spending Accounts (Q 73 to Q 80) for details.

72. Is an individual who is otherwise eligible for an HSA made ineligible if the individual's dependent children have traditional health insurance?

No. In determining HSA eligibility, only the individual's coverage matters. The health coverage of a dependent child (or spouse) does not impact an individual's eligibility for an HSA.

Flexible Spending Accounts

73. Does health FSA coverage disqualify an individual for an HSA?

Yes. An individual with general health FSA coverage is not eligible for an HSA. A health FSA is considered another health plan because an individual can use the money in the health FSA for general health expenses.

Note: Exceptions exist for limited-purpose health FSAs and post-deductible health FSAs.

74. Is a medical spending account the same as a health FSA?

Yes. The industry uses a few different names to describe a general medical spending account offered under a Section 125 Cafeteria plan including: Flexible Spending Account (FSA), Medical Flex Plan, Flexible Spending Arrangement, Medical Reimbursement Plan and others. Any plan that provides coverage for general health expenses would disqualify a person for an HSA so the names used are not crucial. An individual that wants to understand whether their plan is a health FSA should ask the provider if the plan is offered through a Section 125 Cafeteria plan.

If the plan is not offered through a Section 125 Cafeteria plan it is likely an HRA. FSAs are often confused with HRAs, a different type of account, but both the FSAs and HRAs are disqualifying "other" health plans (some exceptions apply).

75. Does a spouse's health FSA coverage disqualify an individual for an HSA?

Generally, yes. If the spouse's general health FSA coverage can be used to pay for the individual's medical expenses that makes the individual covered under another health plan and ineligible for an HSA.

Example 1. Jim's receives HDHP coverage through his employer who contributes $100 a month to the HSAs of eligible employees. Jim's wife, however, gets traditional insurance through her company and elected to participate in the company's health FSA. Because Jim's wife can use her FSA to pay Jim's medical expenses, Jim has other health coverage and is not eligible for an HSA. Jim is ineligible to receive the $100 per month contribution into an HSA offered by his employer. Jim's wife can decline to participate in her company's FSA to resolve the issue in future years.

Example 2. Sally works at ABC Company which provides her an HDHP and contributes $1,000 to her HSA. Sally is otherwise eligible for an HSA. Sally's husband works for XYZ Company and has traditional insurance with an option to put money aside in a medical flex plan. Sally's husband decides to defer $500 to the medical flex plan. He uses this money only for HIS medical needs because his wife has an HSA. Sally is not eligible for an HSA and must refuse the $1,000 from the company. Sally's husband could use the $500 flex money for Sally, which means Sally is covered by another health plan making her ineligible for an HSA. If the flex plan actually allows for Sally's husband to restrict usage to only him, that would change the answer.

Rev. Rul. 2004-22.

76. If a health FSA plan document provides that only the employee is covered, is the employee's spouse still disqualified for an HSA?

No. The rule disqualifying an individual when the individual's spouse is covered by a health FSA assumes the health FSA can also be used for the individual. Given the popularity of HSAs and their strong growth, some Section 125 plan documents are being drafted to limit the benefits of the health FSA to the employee or to the employee and the employee's dependents. The Section 125 plan may give the employee the choice of whether or not to cover the spouse. Until the introduction of HSAs, there was no benefit in excluding a spouse from FSA coverage so it was not an option. This answer does not address the issue of modifying the FSA to allow for this, but if the FSA cannot be used for an individual then that individual does not have other health coverage because of that health FSA.

Example. Blondie, Inc. offers traditional insurance for its employees and a general purpose health FSA. Iker is an employee of Blondie, Inc. and elects self-only traditional insurance coverage. Iker is married to Samantha. Samantha is covered under a self-only HDHP and is otherwise eligible for an HSA. Iker and Samantha desire to maximize their tax benefits and pay for as much of their medical expenses as possible through tax deferred accounts.

They decided that the HSA with a higher contribution limit, more flexibility on distribution reasons and no use it or lose it issues was preferable to an FSA. They agree to fully fund Samantha's HSA. However, Iker has some known medical issues and will likely spend at least $2,000 over the next year and combined they will almost certainly spend more than the self-only HSA limit. In addition, they would like to save for the future.

Blondie's health FSA has a new option that allows for an employee to elect "employee only" coverage. This option will exclude Samantha from being able to use Iker's health FSA and that will allow him to contribute up to $2,500 into a health FSA for him. Samantha will remain eligible for an HSA.

77. Can an employee agree not to use an FSA for a spouse in order for the spouse to remain HSA-eligible?

No. The Section 125 plan document itself must provide an option for an employee to exclude a spouse from FSA coverage in order for that spouse to be excluded from FSA coverage.

Example. Tina and Tony are married. Tina is covered by a traditional health plan through her work and also elects coverage under her employer's FSA and defers $1,000 into the FSA. Tony is not covered by Tina's traditional health insurance but instead has a HDHP he obtains through his employer. Tony's employer also contributes $100 each month into its employee's HSAs. Tony would like to receive the $100 into his HSA. The FSA legal document adopted by Tina's employer does not have language in the document allowing for Tina to exclude Tony from coverage. Tony is not eligible for an HSA and cannot receive the $100 employer HSA contributions. Tina cannot resolve this issue by unilaterally stating that she will not use the FSA for Tony. Tina also cannot resolve this problem by entering into an agreement with her employer not to use the funds for Tony. Tina's employer must modify its Section 125 plan document to allow for Tina to exclude Tony.

78. Does mere eligibility to participate in an FSA remove HSA eligibility?

No. In order to lose HSA eligibility, an individual must actually enroll in the health FSA. If an employee chooses not to participate in an employer's health FSA, that individual remains otherwise eligible for an HSA. Participation means that the employee elected to defer a portion of pay into the health FSA or the employee received an employer contribution into the FSA.

Example. Gary works at a company that offers a Section 125 with a health FSA. Each year the company does a benefits enrollment and collects forms regarding participating in the health FSA. Gary does not elect to contribute any money to the health FSA and the employer does not make any contribution on Gary's behalf. Gary is not a participant in the health FSA and remains otherwise eligible for an HSA.

Caution: An individual will also lose HSA eligibility if a spouse elects to participate in a general health FSA and can use the FSA money to pay for that individual's general health expenses, regardless of whether or not the spouse actually does use the FSA for the individual's health expenses.

Rev. Rul. 2004-45, see also IRS Notice 2005-86.

79. Is an employer obligated to warn employees of the impact of FSA coverage on HSA eligibility?

No. There is no direct rule requiring an employer to warn employees about how selecting FSA coverage could impact a spouse's HSA eligibility. Employers certainly want to help employees make informed decisions and are best served by explaining this rule. This is especially true given the rapid increase in HDHP sales.

80. Can an employer allow for employees to coordinate an HSA with an FSA?

Yes. Under certain limited circumstances it is possible for employees to fund an HSA in addition to a health FSA. Integration of these plans must be carefully constructed so that the benefits being reimbursed under the health FSA are permitted under HSA laws. This generally means that FSA is a "limited-purpose" FSA used for dental and vision only (maybe some permissible preventive care items). A post-deductible FSA could also be used in combination with an HSA.

See Part III: Eligibility – Other Health Plan – Limited-Purpose FSA or HRA (Q 91 to Q 93).

Ending FSA Eligibility and Grace Periods

81. Does a zero balance in a health FSA mean an individual is not covered by a health FSA?

Not necessarily. Exhausting an FSA is not the same as ending participation in an FSA. Accordingly, an individual is not eligible for an HSA if the individual is currently part of a general purpose health FSA even if that individual has already used all the money allocated to the FSA for the year.

Example. Health Plans, Inc. offers its employees a health FSA with a grace period. In November 2013, Mark elected to defer $100 a month or $1,200 for the year into the health FSA for 2014. Early in 2014, Mark incurred a large medical expense and exhausted his FSA. In July, 2014, Mark switched insurance to an HDHP. Mark wanted to start an HSA right away. Mark is not eligible for an HSA in July 2014 because he is part of a health FSA. The fact that he exhausted the balance does not matter. He is still paying $100 a month in deferrals and is still within the plan year. Assuming a calendar year plan, Mark would become eligible for an HSA on January 1, 2015 after the FSA plan year ends and Mark has a zero balance at the end of the plan year.

82. How can employers switch from offering a general health FSA to an HSA mid-year?

Employers that change from offering traditional health insurance to HDHPs mid-year generally want to allow employees to start HSA coverage concurrent with HDHP coverage. This result is difficult or impossible to achieve because employee coverage under a general purpose health FSA is not compatible with HSA eligibility.

Employers should complete the term of the health FSA which will allow employees to become HSA-eligible in the next plan year. The health FSA offered under a Section 125 plan is intended to remain in place for a full plan year. Employees commit to a health FSA deferral amount based on that commitment. Changes mid-year intrude on that basic commitment and legal obligation.

The IRS has stated that changing insurance from traditional insurance to an HDHP is not a change that allows FSA participants to change their Section 125 plan elections. Accordingly, employers cannot simply ask employees if they would like to change their health FSA deferral elections mid-year.

This issue is important enough to some employers to pursue more aggressive options. One approach some employers take is to terminate health FSA mid-year for all participants to enable mid-year HSA eligibility for its employees. This approach may run afoul of ERISA requirements. An employer must fulfill its obligations under the Section 125 plan as it promised when employees' made their health FSA deferral elections and employees with balances remaining would lose their health FSA balances under the use-it-or-lose it rules.

Another approach some employers take is to change their general purpose health FSA to a limited-purpose FSA mid-year. The IRS has supported this approach to avoid HSA eligibility problems caused by health FSA grace periods (IRS Notice 2005-86). The IRS, however, limited the change to after the plan-year end. Expanding that approach to a mid-year change is troubling because the employer would not be fulfilling its obligations under the general purpose health FSA as committed to at the time employees made their health FSA deferral elections. An employee may have deferred a substantial amount assuming that the money could be used for general medical expenses and a conversion to a limited-purpose health FSA would limit that use to dental and vision expenses.

Employers are advised to seek professional assistance before pursuing the more aggressive approaches outlined above to ensure compliance with Section 125 plan requirements.

> *Example.* Big Box Store offers a calendar year Section 125 plan with a general purpose health FSA option and no grace period. In late 2013, employees provided Big Box Store with a deferral election form for payroll deferral amounts into the general purpose health FSA for 2014. Effective July 1, 2014, Big Box Store decides to switch its health insurance to an HDHP. It advises employees that elected to participate in the general purpose health FSA that they will have to wait until January 1, 2015 before opening an HSA because the general purpose health FSA offered by Big Box Store will make the employees ineligible until that date. Employees that did not elect to participate in the health FSA will become HSA-eligible on July 1, 2014 (assuming the employee was otherwise eligible).

IRS Notice 2004-50, See Q 60, IRS Notice 2005-86.

83. How do people switch from an FSA to an HSA and gain HSA eligibility as soon as possible?

Employees need to stop participation in the health FSA in order to begin eligibility for an HSA. Most health FSAs run on a one-year basis and do not allow for changes mid-year. Accordingly, an employee will generally have to wait until the next benefits election period for the health FSA and then make sure not to participate in the health FSA for the next year. Assuming a calendar year plan and that the FSA does not have a grace period, an employee can become eligible for an HSA as of January 1. If the heath FSA has a grace period, allows for carryover of unused dollars or is a non-calendar year plan additional rules apply.

84. How does an FSA grace period impact HSA eligibility?

Employees that are currently covered under a general purpose health FSA and want to become eligible for an HSA must stop coverage under the FSA. For a calendar year FSA, employees will generally make the election to stop the FSA late in the year effective for January 1 of the next year. However, health FSAs that allow for grace periods complicate this issue.

Health FSAs with grace periods allow for an employee to incur medical expenses and to turn in receipts for expenses for up to two and half months into the next year (must not extend beyond the fifteenth day of the third calendar month after the end of the immediately preceding plan year). A grace period could be shorter.

Health FSAs can also offer a "run-out period" which can be confused with a grace period. A run-out period is a period of time after the plan year end when participants can submit medical receipts incurred during the plan year. Run-out periods are typically 90 days but are not required to be 90 days. An employee can become HSA-eligible during the run-out period.

Prior to January 1, 2007, HSA law prevented employees from becoming eligible for the HSA until after the expiration of the grace period. The rule now is that if the employee meets either of the following, the employee can become eligible for an HSA beginning in the new plan year (January 1 for calendar year plans):

- The employee had a zero balance in the FSA on the last day of the plan year. This is the most likely reason an individual would meet the new rule.

- The employer amends the FSA to be HSA compatible for all participants (e.g., change to a limited-purpose FSA).

This answer is based on 2007 IRS guidance and remains valid. However, in 2013, the IRS released new rules allowing for the carryover of unused FSA funds to the next year. A carryover or rollover of funds is very similar to a grace period but is more generous in that it allows the funds to be used the entire next year rather than just the limited period that the grace period rules allow. Employers that adopt the new carryover features and employees that are entitled to carryover FSA funds face different rules on gaining HSA eligibility.

Important In 2014, the IRS released new guidance concerning HSA eligibility for employees with FSAs that allow for carryover of unused FSA funds into the next year. The approaches allowed by the IRS for gaining HSA eligibility as of January 1 for the carryover provisions may also work for grace period provisions.

Example 1. For 2014, Tina's Computers, had a calendar year general purpose health FSA with a grace period ending on March 15, 2015. For 2014, Steve elected a salary reduction of $500 in the health FSA. Tina's Computers offers the option of an HDHP with an HSA for 2015. In early December 2014, Steve elects the new HDHP option for 2015 and further elects to defer a portion of his income into an HSA starting with his paychecks in January 2015. Steve exhausted the $500 in his FSA in the first half of 2014 and has a zero balance on December 31, 2014. Steve is eligible for an HSA as of January 1, 2015 even though Tina's Computers offers a grace period with its FSA.

Example 2. Assume the same facts as above, except that Steve still had $100 left in his FSA on December 31, 2014. Steve is not eligible for an HSA until after his grace period expires on March 15, 2015. He cannot start eligibility mid-month so Steve first becomes eligible for an HSA on April 1, 2015 and could open and begin payroll deferral in April of 2015. Under the full contribution rule, he would still be able to contribute the full 2015 HSA limit (assuming he remains HSA-eligible for all of 2015 and 2016), but he has to wait until April 1 to begin funding and could not use his HSA for medical expenses incurred before it was opened.

IRS Notice 2005-86 for pre-2007 rule, IRS Notice 2007-22 for post-2007 rule, See also Part III: Eligibility – Other Health Plan – FSA Carryovers (Q 85 to Q 87).

FSA Carryovers

85. What is an FSA "carryover"?

An FSA "carryover" or "rollover" is when an FSA plan allows employees to rollover or carryover unused FSA funds to the next year rather than face the use it or lose it rule. Historically, an FSA carryover has not been allowed other than the two and one-half month grace period. Now FSAs can allow for a carryover of funds to be used the entire next year.

The IRS released new guidance in 2013 that allows for employees to roll over year-to-year up to $500 in an FSA. Employers must amend their Section 125 Cafeteria plans in order to allow for this rollover and employers are not required to allow for the rollover and could limit the amount to less than $500. Employers are not allowed to increase the amount of the rollover above $500.

If an employee does rollover some or all of the allowed $500, the amount rolled over does not count against the employee's next year FSA contribution limit. Accordingly, an employee rolling over the maximum $500 could still elect to defer $2,500 for the next year (or an amount as adjusted for inflation). The IRS states that "this carryover option provides an alternative to the current grace period rule and administrative relief similar to that rule" so an employer cannot offer both a rollover and a grace period (some transitional relief applies).

IRS Notice 2013-71. See also Part X: Employer Issues – HSAs, FSAs and HRAs Compared (Q 645 to Q 655).

86. If an employee carryovers unused FSA funds, does that disqualify the employee for an HSA the entire next year?

Yes, although good options are available to prevent this result. The general answer is that an employee covered under a general health FSA is not eligible for an HSA because that employee has other disqualifying health plan coverage. This answer remains the same if the only reason the individual has general health FSA coverage is because of a carryover of unused FSA funds.

> *Example.* Late in 2013, Mike elected to defer $100 a month into his employer's health FSA during the 2014 calendar plan year. The FSA plan allows for carryover of unused funds into the next year. By the end of 2014, Mike had spent $1,100 of the $1,200 he had available to him in the health FSA. Accordingly, $100 carried over into the general purpose health FSA for use in 2015. In completing his deferral election for 2015, Mike elected not to make any contributions to the general health FSA as he planned on opening an HSA. Mike will not be eligible for an HSA in 2015 due to his ongoing participation in the general health FSA (even though his only participation was through the $100 carryover). This answer does not change if Mike quickly spends the $100 in 2015. He remains eligible under the plan for the entire 2015 plan year.

87. What options are available to permit HSA eligibility as soon as possible for employees with health FSA coverage that allows for carryover of unused funds?

In 2014 guidance, the IRS outlined three options that will allow employees to gain HSA eligibility on the first day of the new year (assuming a calendar year plan year):

- **Elect to Carryover Balance to Limited-Purpose FSA.** An individual who participates in a general purpose health FSA and elects, for the following year, to participate in an HSA-compatible FSA (limited-purpose FSA) and has any unused amounts from the general purpose health FSA carried over to the HSA-compatible FSA is eligible to contribute to an HSA as of the first day of the new year.

  > *Example.* Jannikan participated in her company's calendar year general purpose health FSA for 2014. The plan allowed for carryover and Jannikan had funds remaining at the end of 2014 available for carryover to 2015. Jannikan elects that the carryover funds instead be put into an HSA-compatible FSA. Jannikan can open her HSA on January 1, 2015 provided Jannikan is otherwise HSA-eligible.

- **Automatic Carryover Balance to Limited-Purpose FSA.** A cafeteria plan that offers both a general purpose health FSA and an HSA-compatible health FSA may automatically treat an individual who elects coverage in an HDHP for the following year as enrolled in the HSA-compatible health FSA and carry over any unused amounts from the general purpose health FSA to the HSA-compatible health FSA for the following year.

- **Waive Carryover Balance.** A Cafeteria plan may provide that if an individual participates in a general purpose health FSA that provides for a carryover of unused amounts, the individual may elect prior to the beginning of the following year to decline or waive the carryover for the following year. In that case, the individual who declines under the terms of the Cafeteria plan may contribute to an HSA the following year (assuming the individual is otherwise HSA-eligible).

  > *Example.* In 2014, Partha participated in his company's calendar year general purpose health FSA. The plan allows for carryover of unused FSA funds. Late in 2014, Partha elects HDHP coverage for 2015 and he will not participate in the general health FSA for 2015. Partha has not use all his FSA funds in 2014 and

is eligible for a carryover of $250. Instead of using those funds in 2015, Partha elects to waive the carry-over feature and forfeits the $250. Partha can open and fund his HSA as of January 1, 2015, assuming he is otherwise eligible.

IRS Memorandum Number 201413005.

Healthcare Reimbursement Account

88. What is a Healthcare Reimbursement Account (HRA)?

An HRA is a tax-deferred plan to pay for medical expenses.

89. Does participation in an HRA make a person ineligible for an HSA?

Yes, unless the HRA meets one of the exceptions: (1) limited-purpose HRA, (2) post-deductible HRA, or (3) retirement HRA.

90. When does participation in a HRA end if a participant has a zero balance?

An individual with a zero balance in a general purpose HRA on the last day of the HRA plan year, does not fail to be an HSA-eligible individual on the first day of the immediately following HRA plan year, so long as (1) effective on the first day of the immediately following HRA plan year, the employee elects to waive participation in the HRA, or (2) effective on or before the first day of the following HRA plan year, the employer terminates the general purpose HRA with respect to all employees, or (3) effective on or before the first day of the following HRA plan year, with respect to all employees, the employer converts the general purpose HRA to an HSA compatible HRA.

IRS Notice 2007-22.

Limited-Purpose FSA or HRA

91. What is a limited-purpose FSA or HRA?

A limited-purpose health FSA means an FSA offered through a Cafeteria plan that only pays or reimburses permitted coverage benefits; such as, vision care, dental, or certain preventive care. A limited-purpose HRA is an HRA that only pays or reimburses permitted coverage benefits; such as, vision care, dental, or certain preventive care. A limited-purpose HRA can also pay for the employee's share of the premiums of an employer-sponsored HDHP.

IRS Notice 2008-59.

92. Are employees with "limited-purpose health FSAs" or limited-purpose HRAs still HSA-eligible?

Yes, a limited-purpose health FSA is an exception to the general rule that an FSA disqualifies an employee for an HSA. The limited-purpose FSA may only cover "permitted" health care expenses. "Permitted" includes coverage for dental and vision as well as other permitted preventative care. In this case an individual could fund both an FSA with pre-tax dollars and still fully fund the HSA, thus maximizing the tax benefits. This scenario requires the employer to offer an FSA that fits the limited-purpose definition. A limited-purpose HRA is also an exception.

> *Example.* Jane runs a small company and wants to enable her employees to defer as much as possible on a tax-favored basis to pay for medical expenses. Jane can offer an HDHP along with payroll deferral to both a limited-purpose FSA and an HSA. Employees could then fully fund the HSA and also fund the FSA. The FSA funds would only be available for vision, dental and very limited other preventive care options.

93. What's the benefit of a limited-purpose FSA if someone is eligible for an HSA?

The benefit of a combination limited-purpose FSA and HSA is more tax-favored savings to pay for health expenses. An HSA can pay for the same dental and vision expenses as the limited-purpose FSA and an HSA allows for an individual to rollover the entire HSA balance so there is no risk of losing any money. Accordingly, for most people the HSA is the better choice and many people in this situation will just open an HSA.

Some people have large medical expenses and the limitation on how much they can contribute to an HSA is not high enough to cover all their qualified medical expenses. Others want to save for possible large medical expenses in the future by maximizing their contributions now. Some will do both simply for the tax breaks. The strategy to maximize tax deductions is to use the limited-purpose FSA for dental and vision and save the HSA for other types of medical expenses or future expenses.

> *Example.* JoAnn's daughter is getting braces next year and she already has a firm idea of the cost: $5,000. JoAnn has built a large balance in her HSA and contributes the maximum every year, but decides to also participate in her employer's limited-purpose FSA for the next year and defer $2,500. She plans to use the limited-purpose FSA to pay her daughter's orthodontic expenses and save her HSA for other medical expenses that she incurs either next year or sometime in the future. With proper planning, she can likely spread the $5,000 orthodontics treatment and expense over two years allowing her to use her FSA to cover the full $5,000 saving her HSA for other expenses (having her daughter start the process in one year and finish in the next).

Post-Deductible FSA or HRA

94. What is a "post-deductible FSA or HRA"?

A post-deductible health FSA or HRA is one that does not pay or reimburse any medical expense incurred before the minimum annual deductible required to meet the HDHP limits is met. A post-deductible health FSA or HRA could set a reimbursement threshold higher than the minimum annual deductible is required to meet the HDHP limits. This means that the employee is facing the full cost of the deductible without the benefit of the post-deductible FSA or HRA. This is important because the HSA rules against "other health coverage" are concerned with someone having another method to pay for the medical costs below the deductible. Since a post-deductible plan does not allow for this, an employee can have a post-deductible FSA or HRA and remain HSA-eligible.

Note: A key point for this is that the deductible for the post-deductible FSA or HRA does not need to match the individual's actual deductible on the HDHP; it just needs to meet the legal limits.

Example 1. Johnson Law Office offers its employees an HDHP with a $3,000 deductible for singles and a $5,000 deductible for families for 2014. Johnson Law Office also offers a post-deductible HRA that pays for employee medical expenses after they reach the legal HDHP limits of $1,250 for singles and $2,500 for families (2014). This approach allows Johnson Law Office to provide employees with a higher deductible HDHP than necessary under the law for HSA eligibility and still cover employees for the expenses after they hit the HDHP legal limit rather than the higher limits on Johnson Law Office's actual plan. Employers may choose this option because the employers can buy the higher deductible coverage for less money and then "self-insure" using the post-deductible FSA/HRA for medical expenses of employees after the HDHP legal deductible is met but before the employers' actual HDHP deductible is met. Employees in this case are eligible for an HSA.

Example 2. Assuming the same facts as the previous example, except that Johnson Law Office offers a post-deductible HRA that pays for employee medical expenses after they reach $2,000 for singles and $4,000 for families. This example uses deductible limits above the 2014 minimum limits for an HDHP ($1,250 for singles and $2,500 for families) and accordingly satisfies the requirement of not reimbursing for medical expenses incurred below the minimum annual deductible for an HDHP. Employees in this case are eligible for an HSA.

IRS Notice 2008-59, See Q 3.

95. Are "post-deductible health FSAs" an exception to the rule of no other health plans concerning HSA eligibility?

Yes. Post-deductible health FSAs are an exception to the general rule that a health FSA disqualifies an individual for an HSA.

96. What expenses are included as part of the deductible for the HDHP when a limited-purpose or post-deductible HRA is in place?

The High Deductible Health Plan must credit qualified medical expenses covered by the plan towards the deductible. For example, if the HDHP does not cover chiropractic care, then the expenses incurred for chiropractic care do not count toward satisfying the HDHP deductible.

Example. Mary and her daughter are covered under a $2,500 deductible family HDHP. The HDHP does not cover vision or dental. Mary's employer also provides a combination limited-purpose and post-deductible HRA. The HRA pays for dental and vision expenses incurred before the $2,500 deductible is met and for any eligible medical expense after the $2,500 deductible is satisfied. During the year, Mary's daughter incurs $2,500 in dental expense. Later in the same year, her daughter incurs a $400 medical expense that would be covered by the HDHP if she had met her deductible. The HRA cannot reimburse Mary the $400 because that is the first $400 that has counted toward her deductible. The $2,500 of dental expenses did not count toward the deductible because the services are not covered by the HDHP. Mary has another $2,100 to spend on covered medical expenses before meeting her HDHP deductible for the year.

IRS Notice 2008-59, See Q 16.

97. Can an employee elect three plans: a post-deductible health FSA, a limited-purpose health FSA, and an HSA?

Yes. These three plans work together and an employee can be covered by both a post-deductible health FSA and a limited-purpose health FSA and remain eligible for an HSA.

Retirement HRA

98. What is a "Retirement HRA"?

A Retirement HRA is an HRA that only pays those medical expenses incurred after retirement. An employer pays money into the plan while the employee is working but the money is not available for use until after retirement.

99. Are Retirement HRAs allowed in combination with HSAs?

Yes. Retirement HRAs are an exception to the rule prohibiting a person from having both an HSA and an HRA. Once an employee actually retires and becomes eligible to use the retirement HRA the individual will lose eligibility for the HSA.

Suspended HRA

100. What is a "suspended HRA"?

A suspended HRA is an HRA that cannot pay or reimburse any medical expenses incurred during the suspension period. The employee would have had to have elected to have the plan suspended prior to the HRA coverage period. When the suspension ends, the person will lose HSA eligibility. The suspended HRA can pay for preventive care and other permitted coverage during the suspension period. A suspended HRA allows an employee to become eligible for an HSA without forfeiting the money in the HRA. The employee cannot access the money while the HRA is suspended but at some point in the future the plan can become active again (at which point the employee will lose HSA eligibility).

101. Are "suspended HRAs" allowed in combination with HSAs?

Yes, a suspended HRA is an exception to the "other health plan" rule.

Non-Medical Cafeteria Plan Benefits

102. Does participation in pre-tax dependent care benefits impact HSA eligibility?

No. Employees are allowed to participate in a dependent care program offered through a Section 125 plan and still remain eligible for an HSA.

103. Does participation in pre-tax parking benefits impact HSA eligibility?

No. Pre-tax parking deferrals do not make employees ineligible for an HSA.

Department of Veterans Affairs (VA) and Indian Health Services (IHS) Coverage

104. Does Department of Veterans Affairs (VA) health coverage disqualify someone for an HSA?

The answer depends on whether or not the veteran has used the service. VA coverage does not disqualify individuals for HSAs provided they have not actually received any benefits from the VA in the preceding three months.

Example. Tyrone is a veteran entitled to VA benefits. Tyrone now works for a business that provides an HDHP and puts $100 per month into eligible employee's HSAs. Tyrone is generally healthy and when he does go to the doctor he uses his company's health plan to select the doctor and pay benefits - not the VA. Tyrone has not sought or received VA benefits in years. Tyrone is eligible for an HSA and will receive the monthly employer contribution because he has not received any benefits from the VA in the preceding three months and he is otherwise eligible for an HSA.

IRS Notice 2004-50, See Q 6.

105. Can a veteran seek preventive care, dental and vision through the VA and remain eligible for an HSA?

Yes. A veteran will remain eligible for an HSA if a veteran only uses the VA health coverage for preventive care (the HSA rules allow for certain types of preventive care services such as well-baby visits, immunizations, weight-loss and tobacco cessation programs) or the veteran only uses the VA health coverage for disregarded coverage (disregarded coverage means coverage for dental, vision, or some limited other exceptions).

IRS Notice 2008-59, See Q 10.

106. Does coverage under the TRICARE disqualify someone for an HSA?

Yes, TRICARE, the health care program for active duty and retired members of the uniformed services, their families and survivors, would be considered an "other health plan" making a person ineligible for an HSA. The TRICARE plan does not currently meet the definition of an HDHP.

IRS Notice 2004-50, See Q 7.

107. Does medical coverage through Indian Health Services (IHS) disqualify individuals for an HSA?

Generally IHS coverage does not disqualify an individual for an HSA provided the individual has not actually received any benefits from the IHS in the preceding three months.

The IHS is a division within the U.S. Department of Health and Human Services. An IHS facility is defined as a facility operated directly by IHS, or by a tribe or tribal organization under the Indian Self-Determination and Education Assistance Act.

If treatment received by the IHS is limited to "permitted coverage," then the receipt of those permitted services does not impact HSA eligibility. This would include dental, vision, and preventive services such as well-baby visits, immunizations, weight-loss and tobacco cessation programs.

IRS Notice 2012-14.

Concierge Medicine

108. Can an individual participate in a physician retainer program (concierge medicine) and retain HSA eligibility?

The answer is heavily dependent upon the facts behind the program. The concern for HSA eligibility is that the physician retainer program is a form of health insurance. If a physician retainer program falls within the definition of "other insurance", it disqualifies a person for an HSA.

A program that charges a one-time fee in exchange for unlimited doctor visits or unlimited communication with a doctor and some other types of medical treatment could be considered "other insurance" disqualifying a person for an HSA. Physicians offering these programs would want to avoid selling "insurance" or potentially face the regulatory burden of complying with state insurance laws. For these reasons and others, the organizations creating these programs are likely trying to avoid becoming insurance. If the retainer program is more of payment just for access to the physician, the patient still pays separate bills for medical services, it is less likely to disqualify the person for an HSA. We may see more IRS guidance on these types of programs as they grow in popularity.

See Part VIII: Distributions — Qualified Medical Expenses — Concierge Medicine (Q 416) for information on whether HSA owners can use HSA funds to pay for concierge medicine.

Miscellaneous

109. Does COBRA continuation coverage impact HSA eligibility?

Employees that separate from service are given an option to continue health coverage though COBRA continuation coverage (Comprehensive Omnibus Budget Reconciliation Act of 1985). The change to COBRA coverage often generates concern regarding what happens to HSA eligibility. Continued eligibility for an HSA depends on whether the COBRA continuation coverage is an HDHP or not. If the COBRA coverage is an HDHP and the other eligibility rules are met, the individual is eligible for an HSA. If the plan is not an HDHP, then the individual is not HSA-eligible.

110. Can an HDHP insured individual enroll in a catastrophic insurance plan (non-HDHP), in addition to the HDHP, and still be eligible for an HSA?

Yes, provided the other health plan has a deductible that is equal to or greater than the minimum HDHP deductibles ($1,300 single and $2,600 family for 2015) then the other policy does not disqualify someone for an HSA.

> *Example.* Carrie is covered under a self-only HDHP that has a lifetime limit of benefits at $1,000,000. Carrie buys a secondary policy that has a $1,000,000 deductible and offers $2,000,000 in benefits. Carrie remains eligible for an HSA because her other health plan is above the HDHP deductible limits.

IRS Notice 2008-59, See Q 8.

111. Does coverage under a mini-med plan disqualify a person for an HSA?

Mini-med plans are generally considered "other health plans" and will disqualify a person for an HSA. Ultimately, it depends on what the mini-med plan covers. If the mini-med is limited to preventive care or disregarded services (dental and vision), then it would not be a disqualifying other plan. Mini-meds are defined as plans that limit the benefit offered by category of service and overall. Generally mini-meds provide coverage up to a relatively low cap (often $2,000 to $5,000 per year). These types of plans are not HDHPs because they do not meet the requirements for maximum out-of-pocket costs and for providing coverage below the HDHP deductible limits.

The Affordable Care Act requirements will phase these plans out over time (some waivers have been granted and it is possible employers may still offer the plans even if the plans do not meet Affordable Care Act requirements).

> *Example.* Tony is covered by an HDHP and also a mini-med. The mini-med provides a fixed amount per day for hospitalization; a fixed amount per office visit with a physician; a fixed amount per outpatient treatment at a hospital; a fixed amount per ambulance use; and coverage for expenses relating to the treatment of a specified list of diseases. Although the fixed amount per day of hospitalization and the specified disease benefits are allowed under HSA rules as "permitted insurance," the other benefits are not allowed and Tony would not be eligible for an HSA because he has "other" health coverage.

IRS Notice 2008-59, See Q 2.

112. Can an employer reimburse employees for medical expenses below the group's HDHP limits?

No. If an employer reimburses for medical expenses before the minimum HDHP limits are met that reimbursement is an "other health plan" and disqualifies the employee for an HSA. This assumes the reimbursement is not for preventive care or disregarded care.

> *Example 1.* An employer offers an HDHP with a $2,000 deductible for self-only HDHP insured employees. The employee pays the first $250 of covered expenses and the employer reimburses the next $1,000 of covered expenses below the deductible. The employee is responsible for the last $750. The $1,000 of employer paid medical expenses is not disregarded coverage and the employees are not eligible for an HSA.

> *Example 2.* In 2014, an employer offers an HDHP with a $4,500 deductible for self-only HDHP covered employees. The employee pays the first $1,250 of covered expenses. The employer reimburses the next $3,250 of covered medical expenses below the deductible. The $3,250 of medical expenses paid or reimbursed by the employer is not a contribution to an HSA and is not disregarded coverage. However, the employee in this case is a qualified employee because the employee is responsible for the minimum annual deductible of $1,250 required under the HSA law for 2014 for self-only HDHP covered employees.

113. Does a company free on-site health clinic disqualify employees for HSAs?

No, provided the employer's clinic meets the specific exception that allows for limited health coverage through an on-site clinic for employees. The clinic cannot provide "significant benefits in the nature of medical care" (in addition to disregarded coverage or preventive care). Permitted services include:

- Physicals

- Immunizations

- Injecting antigens provided by employee

- Providing aspirin/pain relievers and

- Treatment of injuries or accidents that occur at work

> *Example.* A hospital permits its employees to receive care at its facilities for all of their medical needs. For employees without health insurance, the hospital provides medical care at no charge. For employees

who have health insurance, the hospital waives all deductibles and co-pays. The hospital provides significant health care benefits and does not meet the on-site exception and its employees will not be eligible for HSAs.

IRS Notice 2008-59, See Q 11.

114. Does an Employee Assistance Program (EAP) disqualify employees for HSAs?

No. Employers are allowed to offer an EAP program without jeopardizing its employees' HSA eligibility provided the program does not provide "significant benefits in the nature of medical care or treatment."

115. Would these EAP programs be considered "provide significant benefits in the nature of medical care and treatment" and be a health plan and disqualify one from an HSA?

No. The three types of EAP programs below are generally not considered to be a health plan and would not disqualify you for an HSA.

- **Counseling EAP Program.** EAPs designed to provide short-term counseling to identify problems that may impact work performance are generally allowed with an HSA. Issues addressed in this type of EAP program often includes substance abuse, mental health or emotional disorders, financial or legal difficulties and dependent care needs. The benefit consists primarily of free or low-cost confidential short-term counseling to identify an employee's problem that may affect job performance and, when appropriate, referral to an outside organization, facility or program to assist the employee in resolving the problem.

- **Disease Management EAP Program.** EAPs designed for disease management are generally allowed with an HSA. This type of EAP identifies employees and their family members who have, or are at risk for, certain chronic conditions. The program provides evidence-based information, disease specific support, case monitoring and coordination of care (not the actual care). Typical interventions include monitoring laboratory or other test results, telephone contacts or web-based reminders of health care schedules, and providing information to minimize health risks.

- **Wellness EAP Program.** EAPs designed for employee wellness are generally allowed with an HSA. A wellness program provides a wide-range of education and fitness services designed to improve the overall health of the employees and prevent illness. Typical services include education, fitness, sports, and recreation activities, stress management and health screenings.

IRS Notice 2004-50, See Q 11.

116. Does participation in a discount drug card program disqualify people for HSAs?

No. Individuals can participate in a discount drug card and still be eligible for an HSA. The discount card must require the HSA owner to pay the expenses for the medications, albeit at a discounted rate.

Example. ABC Company gives its employees a discount pharmacy card that entitles the employees to a discount ranging from 15 to 50 percent on drugs. ABC Company pays a fixed annual fee for the card, but the employees are required to pay for any drugs actually purchased using the card. This card will not disqualify a person for the HSA.

IRS Notice 2004-50, See Q 10.

117. Does a prescription drug plan disqualify people for an HSA?

An individual can participate in a prescription drug plan, either as part of your HDHP or a separate plan, and remain HSA-eligible provided the plan does not provide benefits until the minimum annual deductible of the HDHP has been met. If the individual can receive benefits before that deductible is met, the individual is not an HSA qualified individual.

IRS Publication 969, p. 4.

118. Can an HDHP provide negotiated discounts for health services and still qualify as an HDHP?

Yes. AN HDHP provider can negotiate discounts with health providers and offer these reduced rates to HSA owners regardless of whether or not the HSA owner has met the deductible. The plan remains an HDHP.

IRS Notice 2004-50, See Q 26.

119. Does Voluntary Employees' Beneficiary Association (VEBA) coverage disqualify a person for an HSA?

Yes. Voluntary Employees' Beneficiary Association (VEBA) accounts are tax-favored accounts that can be used to pay for qualified medical expenses. Accordingly, coverage under a VEBA will generally disqualify individuals for an HSA. A VEBA plan that is limited to dental, vision and allowed preventive care would not disqualify a person for an HSA. It may also be possible to suspend a VEBA so the coverage does not apply for a period of time allowing for HSA contributions.

120. Are there any VEBA plans that will not disqualify an individual for an HSA?

Yes. A VEBA plan that is limited to dental, vision and allowed preventive care would not disqualify a person for an HSA.

Medicare Coverage

121. Does Medicare coverage disqualify a person for an HSA?

Yes. Medicare coverage makes individuals ineligible for an HSA. Most Americans will enroll in Medicare at age sixty-five and lose HSA eligibility.

IRS Notice 2004-50, See Q 2.

122. What types of Medicare coverage end HSA eligibility?

Any Medicare plan coverage makes an individual ineligible including:

- **Medicare Part A** (hospital insurance)

- **Medicare Part B** (medical insurance)

- **Medicare Part C** (Medicare Advantage Plans – run by Medicare-approved private plans that replace Parts A and B and possibly D)

- **Medicare Part D** (prescription drug coverage run by Medicare-approved private insurance companies)

- **Medicare Supplement Insurance** ("Medigap" – sold by private companies to help cover expenses that Medicare does not cover such as copayments, coinsurance, and deductibles)

Medicare Part A is the Medicare plan to focus on for HSA eligibility as the other plan types generally only occur after an individual is entitled to Part A.

IRS Notice 2008-59, See Q 7, IRS Notice 2004-50, See Q 2.

123. Does merely being "eligible for" Medicare without being actually enrolled end HSA eligibility?

No. HSA rules make a distinction between being merely "eligible" for Medicare, in which case individuals do <u>not</u> lose HSA eligibility, and being "entitled" to or "enrolled" in Medicare, in which case individuals are no longer eligible for an HSA. Accordingly, some people that reach age sixty-five and become eligible for Medicare will maintain their HSA eligibility, potentially for many more years, by not enrolling in Medicare.

Caution: When individuals apply for Social Security benefits, the Social Security Administration automatically enrolls them in Medicare Part A, when they sixty-five reach age sixty-five.

IRC Sec. 223(b)(7), IRS Notice 2004-50, See Q 2, IRS Notice 2008-59, See Q 6.

124. Would someone know if they were automatically enrolled in Medicare?

Yes. Medicare sends new enrollees a Medicare Card three months before reaching age sixty-five, therefore individuals should be aware that they are enrolled. Some individuals pro-actively enroll in Medicare Part A but others wait for the Social Security Administration to automatically "enrolls" them when they begin collecting Social Security benefits. Accordingly, anyone receiving Social Security payments over age sixty-five is very likely already enrolled in Medicare Part A and ineligible for an HSA (even if a Medicare Card never arrived).

125. Can an individual stop Medicare Part A coverage and reclaim HSA eligibility?

Yes. A Medicare Part A enrolled individual that now wants to decline or opt out of coverage can do so by contacting the Social Security Administration. Assuming the individual has not begun receiving Social Security checks, opting out will reestablish HSA eligibility.

If the individual has already begun receiving Social Security, in order to opt out the individual must repay the government all money received from Social Security payments plus any money Medicare paid for medical claims. This action will also stop future Social Security payments (the individual can reapply for Social Security which will cause this issue to start anew).

The inability to opt out of Medicare Part A without the impact on Social Security caused enough frustration that Congress considered a bill (that did not pass) to change the law. Suing the government has been unsuccessful: Former Congressman Dick Armey and others lost a lawsuit to opt out of Medicare but keep Social Security benefits.

Hall v. Sebelius, 667 F.3d 1293 (2012).

126. When does an individual lose HSA eligibility because of Medicare coverage?

An individual loses eligibility as of the first day of the month the individual reaches age sixty-five if they enroll in Medicare.

> *Example.* An individual that reaches age sixty-five on July 21 loses eligibility for an HSA as of July 1 if they are enrolled in Medicare. The maximum contribution for that year would be 6/12 (the individual was eligible for the first six months of the year) times the applicable federal limit (remember to include the catch-up amount in the federal limit).

See the Eligibility and Contribution Worksheet for details.

127. Do individuals that continue to work after age sixty-five remain HSA-eligible?

Yes. Many HSA owners continue to work and continue to be covered under HDHP plans well past age sixty-five. The test for HSA eligibility is HDHP coverage plus no other non-permitted health coverage (in addition to other rules). Most people become covered by Medicare at age sixty-five even if they are also covered by an HDHP as well which makes them ineligible for an HSA.

An individual over age sixty-five that works for an employer with twenty or more employees that provides a group HDHP policy could remain HSA-eligible by not enrolling in Medicare by not applying for Social Security benefits (the Social Security Administration automatically enrolls you in Medicare apply for Social Security benefits).

128. Can HSA owners that enroll in Medicare use their HSA to pay for Medicare premiums even though they are no longer HSA-eligible?

Yes. The majority of Americans will start Medicare at age sixty-five and therefore lose eligibility for an HSA. Losing eligibility for an HSA means that the HSA owner cannot contribute new money but does not stop a person with an HSA balance from continuing to use that balance for medical expenses.

Someone age sixty-five or older has a special opportunity to use that money to pay for Medicare premiums. This is an incredible feature of HSAs: the ability to pay for Medicare premiums with pre-tax dollars. However, this feature is only available to Americans that have built up a balance in their HSAs prior to losing eligibility. The Social Security Administration will directly deduct the Medicare premiums from Social Security payments, so an HSA owner can write a check from their HSA payable to his or herself to reimburse for the Medicare the premium paid directly by Social Security.

See Part VIII: Distributions - Insurance — Medicare Premiums (Q 429 to Q 434).

129. When an HSA owner enrolls in Medicare, can a spouse under age sixty-five still contribute?

Yes, provided the spouse is otherwise eligible for an HSA.

Example 1. Dick and Adelle are covered under a family HDHP provided through Dick's employer. Dick reached age sixty-five in July and enrolled in Medicare. Dick has always contributed the family maximum into his HSA, but is no longer eligible. Dick's employer continues to provide the family HDHP and coverage for both Dick and Adelle, but Dick's employer stops his HSA contributions. Adelle, age fifty-eight, can now open an HSA and contribute the family maximum (plus the catch-up since she is over age fifty-five) because she remains covered by a family HDHP. Adelle can use her HSA for Dick's medical expenses but cannot contribute to it.

Example 2. Using the same facts as above, but assuming that when Dick became eligible for Medicare his company dropped his insurance coverage. Adelle buys a self-only HDHP for her insurance for July through December. Adelle remains eligible for an HSA but must calculate a pro-rata contribution amount. She was eligible for the family HSA limit for six months and under the self-only HDHP limit for six months. She will also need to coordinate her family contribution limit with Dick's HSA contributions. She will get the full $1,000 catch-up since she is over age fifty-five.

130. Can an employer make an HSA contribution into an HSA for an employee's spouse?

No. An employer cannot make HSA contributions into the HSA of an employee's spouse and be entitled to the same tax treatment (assuming the spouse is not also an employee). Any pre-tax employer contribution must go into the employee's HSA and not the spouse's. Part of the reason for this is income tax reporting. The IRS matches the individual's SSN and IRS Form W-2 with the IRS Form 5498 from the HSA custodian. The IRS has chosen not to provide for this issue for married couples and allow these type of contributions.

Note: HSA rules allow any person the ability to make an HSA contribution for someone's HSA. Accordingly, an employer can make HSA contributions for non-employees. This type of contribution would not be deductible by the employer as either an employer HSA contribution or an employee pre-tax payroll deferral.

Example. BBB, Inc. offers a pre-tax HSA payroll deferral option for employees. Samantha, an employee of BBB, is over age sixty-five and enrolled in Medicare. Samantha's husband is under age sixty-five and eligible for an HSA. Samantha requests that BBB take money out of her pay pre-tax and contribute it to her husband's HSA. BBB cannot accommodate Samantha's request on a pre-tax basis and could only do so by reporting the contribution as income to Samantha, negating any benefit to her.

IRS Notice 2008-59, See Q 27, IRS Form 5498, IRS Form W-2.

Preventive Care

131. Can an HDHP provide preventive care without a deductible?

Yes. HDHP plans are allowed to provide preventive care services without a deductible or with a lower deductible than the HDHP rules allow for general coverage. This rule supports an overall health objective of allowing people to receive preventive care services without paying or paying at reduced amounts. The Affordable Care Act advances this policy objective even further mandating certain preventive care areas be included in health care where HSA law merely allows its inclusion for first-dollar coverage.

132. What preventive care services are permissible in an HDHP?

The HSA law defining an HDHP provides that "[a] plan shall not fail to be treated as a high deductible health plan by reason of failing to have a deductible for preventative care…except as otherwise provided for by the Secretary." HSA compatible insurance plans, HDHPs, are allowed to offer the following types of preventive services below the deductible (meaning the HDHP can pay for the expenses directly even if the individual is still below their deductible limit for the year).

- Periodic health evaluations, including tests and diagnostic procedures ordered in connection with routine examinations, such as annual physicals

- Routine prenatal and well-child care

- Child and adult immunizations

- Tobacco cessation programs

- Obesity weight-loss programs

- Screening services for the following

  - Cancer

  - Heart and vascular diseases

  - Infectious diseases

  - Mental health conditions

  - Substance abuse

  - Metabolic, nutritional and endocrine conditions

  - Musculoskeletal disorders

  - Obstetric and gynecological conditions

  - Pediatric conditions

  - Vision and hearing disorders

Preventive care does not generally include any service or benefit intended to treat an existing illness, injury, or condition. Allowing an HDHP to pay for these preventive care services below the deductible is not the same as requiring these expenses be paid below the deductible. HSA laws do not require that these expenses be paid below the deductible. This is important because some preventive care items are now required to be paid for below the deductible under the Affordable Care Act.

IRS Notice 2004-23.

133. What are the "safe harbor" screenings permitted under the preventive care exception?

The IRS specifically lists the following "safe harbor" preventive care screening services as allowed for first-dollar coverage under the preventive care exception for HDHPs.

Cancer Screening "Breast Cancer (e.g., mammograms)" "Cervical Cancer (e.g., pap smears)" "Colorectal Cancer (e.g., colonoscopies)" "Prostate Cancer (e.g., PSA tests)" Skin Cancer Oral Cancer Ovarian Cancer Testicular Cancer Thyroid Cancer	**"Metabolic, Nutritional, and Endocrine Conditions Screening"** "Anemia, Iron Deficiency" Dental and Periodontal Disease Diabetes Mellitus Obesity in Adults Thyroid Disease **Musculoskeletal Disorders Screening** Osteoporosis
Heart and Vascular Diseases Screening Abdominal Aortic Aneurysm Carotid Artery Stenosis Coronary Heart Disease Hemoglobinopathies Hypertension Lipid Disorders	**Obstetric and Gynecologic Conditions Screening** Bacterial Vaginosis in Pregnancy Gestational Diabetes Mellitus Home Uterine Activity Monitoring Neural Tube Defects Preeclampsia Rh Incompatibility Rubella Ultrasonography in Pregnancy
Infectious Diseases Screening Bacteriuria Chlamydial Infection Gonorrhea Hepatitis B Virus Infection Hepatitis C Human Immunodeficiency Virus (HIV) Infection Syphilis Tuberculosis Infection	**Pediatric Conditions Screening** Child Developmental Delay Congenital Hypothyroidism Lead Levels in Childhood and Pregnancy Phenylketonuria "Scoliosis, Adolescent Idiopathic"

Mental Health Conditions and Substance Abuse Screening	Vision and Hearing Disorders Screening
Dementia	Glaucoma
Depression	Hearing Impairment in Older Adults
Drug Abuse	Newborn Hearing
Problem Drinking	
Suicide Risk	
Family Violence	

IRS Notice 2004-23.

134. How do the preventive care rules interact with the Affordable Care Act?

The Affordable Health Care Act requires that an HDHP offer some preventive care services without cost-sharing. The definition of "preventive care" is crucial to both the Affordable Care Act and the law that created HSAs. The key for HSAs is that the definitions match.

Fortunately, both laws put preventive care into a special category with the Affordable Care Act requiring preventive care services at zero cost-sharing and the HDHP law allowing preventive care services without cost-sharing.

The IRS-provided important guidance on the definition of preventive care under HSA law in late 2013. The HSA law's definition of preventive care "…also includes services required to be provided as preventive health services by a group health plan or a health insurance issuer offering group or individual health insurance under…" the Affordable Care Act (as implemented under Section 2713 of the Public Health Services Act), and regulations and other administrative guidance.

This interpretation allows for HDHPs to offer the preventive care required under the Affordable Care Act (Section 2713 of the Public Health Services Act) without a deductible and remain HDHPs. This is very welcome guidance for the industry, namely if the Affordable Care Act requires preventive care without a deductible that requirement should not preclude HSA eligibility. The ruling also clarifies that the HSA law's previous definition of preventive care also remains in place and any item that was previously considered preventive care under HSA law remains so.

IRS Notice 2013-57.

135. How do the preventive care rules interact with state law requirements?

With the passage of the Affordable Care Act, state health care laws are undergoing radical change and in many cases are being replaced by federal law. HSA law does not contain any blanket exception to the preventive care requirements to meet a state legal requirement. This is a bit surprising as the law creating Archer Medical Savings Accounts (the predecessor to HSAs) does contain a specific rule that provided if a state law requires certain preventive care that care will not disqualify the plan for compatibility with an MSA. The determination of whether health care that is required by state law to be provided by an HDHP without regard to a deductible is "preventive" care for purposes of the exception for preventive care services under HSA law will be based on guidance issued by the IRS (primarily IRS Notice 2004-23).

IRS Notice 2004-23.

136. Are there situations where preventive care that actually involves some treatment does not violate eligibility rules?

Yes. The rule allowing for preventive care without a deductible also applies treatment of an existing illness, injury or condition in situations where it would be unreasonable or impracticable to perform another procedure to treat the condition as well for any treatment that is ancillary to a preventive care service.

Example. Removal of polyps during a diagnostic colonoscopy is preventive care that can be provided before the deductible is met.

IRS Notice 2004-50, See Q 27.

137. Can an HDHP provide preventive drugs without a deductible?

Yes, in some instances. Drugs or medications are preventive when taken by a person who has developed risk factors for a disease that has not yet manifested itself or not yet become clinically apparent or to prevent the reoccurrence of a disease from which a person has recovered. Also, drugs used to provide preventive services include obesity weight-loss and tobacco cessation programs. The preventive care "safe harbor" exception does not include any service or benefit intended to treat an <u>existing</u> illness, injury or condition.

Example. Treatment using cholesterol-lowering medications to prevent heart disease.

IRS Notice 2004-50, See Q 28.

Dependent on Another Person's Tax Return

138. What is the HSA eligibility rule regarding not being a dependent on someone else's income tax return? If you are a dependent on someone else's income tax return, are you eligible for an HSA?

No. This rule serves primarily to prevent children from opening and funding HSAs. The rule does create some interesting scenarios for adult children.

See Part VIII: Distributions - Expenses of Yourself, Your Spouse, and Your Dependents — Qualifying Relative (Q 476 to Q 477).

139. Is there a minimum age limit for opening an HSA?

No. Although there is no minimum age limit on an HSA or earned income requirement, being a dependent on someone else's tax return disqualifies an individual for an HSA. Most children are dependents on someone else's tax return.

140. What is a "tax dependent"?

For HSA purposes, the definition of "dependent" is important for two purposes:

- you are not eligible for an HSA if eligible to be claimed as a dependent on someone else's tax return and

- you can only use your HSA to pay for the medical expenses of yourself, your spouse and your "dependents."

Both of these rules refer to the same law for the definition (IRC Sec. 152), However, the definitions are slightly different because the second item excludes certain paragraphs. In any case, a spouse is not considered a dependent. The full definition of who qualifies as a dependent is beyond the scope of this answer (see citations below) but without covering all the details, a dependent is someone meeting the following criteria:

- **Child under age nineteen.** The taxpayer's child under the age of nineteen at the end of the tax year who lives at the taxpayer's residence more than half the year.

Note: Special rules apply for divorced parents.

- **Student under age twenty-four.** The taxpayer's child that is a student and under age twenty-four at the end of the tax year living at the taxpayer's residence more than half the year.

- **Disabled Child**. A special rule exists eliminating the age requirement for individuals who are permanently and totally disabled.

- **Qualifying Relative.** A qualifying relative may also be a dependent and this can include "any other person" who lived with the taxpayer all year as a member of the household and for whom the taxpayer provided over half the support for the year. A qualifying relative cannot be a spouse or a qualifying child.

The IRS also provides that you can use your HSA for the medical expense of any person that you could have claimed as a dependent on your return except that: (1) the person filed a joint return, (2) the person had gross income of more than $3,800 or, (3) you, or your spouse if filing jointly, could be claimed as a dependent on someone else's tax return.

See IRC Sec. 223(b)(6), IRC Sec. 223(d)(2), IRC Sec. 151, and IRC Sec. 152, See also IRS Pub 502 and IRS Pub 969.

141. If another taxpayer can claim an individual as an exemption, but does not, can that individual open an HSA?

No. If another taxpayer is entitled to claim an exemption for you, you cannot claim a deduction for an HSA contribution. This is true even if the other person does not actually claim your exemption.

IRS Publication 969.

142. Is a spouse a tax dependent?

No. A spouse is not considered a dependent for HSA purposes.

143. Is a child claimed as a dependent on the parent's tax return eligible for an HSA?

No. A child claimed as a dependent on another person's income tax return is not eligible for an HSA. This rule prevents most children from opening HSAs.

144. Is a college student covered under her parents' HDHP eligible for an HSA?

Yes, if the college student cannot be claimed as a dependent on their parent's tax return. College students under age twenty-four are likely to be claimed as dependents of their parents and ineligible for an HSA. A college student can open his or her own HSA and can contribute up to the family HDHP limit if covered under the parents' family HDHP. The parents would also be able to contribute the family limit. The student and the parents would not need to coordinate family HSA limits such that combined they stayed under the maximum. The downside to this is that the parents cannot use their HSAs to pay for the student's qualified medical expenses because the student would not be a tax dependent (even though still on their insurance).

The Affordable Care Act's requirement that children can remain on the parents' health plan until age twenty-six increases occurrences of this issue happening. A more logical approach would be to take away a non-dependent child's eligibility for an HSA but allow the parents to use their HSAs to fund the child's medical expenses until age twenty-six.

The IRS extended the ability of a parent to use FSA and HRA funds for a child who has not reached age twenty-seven by the end of the taxable year, but this guidance did not extend to HSAs. Congress or the IRS may provide additional guidance on this issue in the future.

> *Example.* Sally's employer provides family HDHP insurance coverage that includes Sally's twenty-five year old son. Sally cannot use her HSA to pay his medical because he cannot be claimed as her dependent. He can open his own HSA and make his own contribution assuming he is otherwise eligible for an HSA. Even better, he can use the family contribution limit ($6,650 for 2015) even though he is not married and has no children. Sally could make a contribution on her son's behalf to his HSA, but he would get the tax deduction, not Sally.

IRS Notice 2010-38.

Timing of Eligibility

145. When does HSA eligibility begin for someone whose HDHP coverage begins mid-year?

Eligibility is determined on a monthly basis and an individual must be eligible on the first day of the month to be considered eligible for that month.

> *Example.* If you otherwise become eligible for an HSA on July 15, your actual eligibility will not occur until August 1 because you were not eligible for an HSA on the first day of July.

IRS Notice 2004-50, See Q 12.

146. How long does an individual need to wait to open an HSA after dropping traditional health insurance coverage?

HSA eligibility is determined monthly so in most cases an individual would only need to wait until the beginning of the next month to become eligible for an HSA. An individual must be covered by an HDHP as of the first day of the month to be eligible for an HSA. Exactly when coverage ends can become complicated, especially for FSAs and HRAs.

> *Example.* Dick and Jane are married. Dick's employer provides him with self-only HDHP coverage and contributes $50 per month into each eligible employee's HSA. Jane's employer provides Jane with traditional insurance for her and her family. Dick is covered under traditional health insurance through Jane's policy. Accordingly, Dick is ineligible for an HSA and he cannot receive the $50 per month into an HSA offered by his employer.

> To avoid this problem, Jane drops Dick from Jane's health insurance coverage at the next enrollment period. Dick is no longer covered by the traditional insurance as of July 1 (his last day of coverage is June 30). Assuming Dick is otherwise eligible for an HSA, Dick can open an HSA on July 1.

See Part III: Eligibility – Other Health Plan – Ending FSA Eligibility and Grace Periods (Q 81 to Q 84).

Loss of HSA Eligibility

147. What are the ramifications when someone loses eligibility for an HSA?

Common reasons people lose HSA eligibility include changing jobs, becoming eligible for Medicare or just switching insurance plans. Some items for HSA owners to consider are listed below:

- **The Money Belongs to the HSA Owner.** The HSA belongs to the HSA owner regardless of whether the HSA owner or the employer made the contribution to the HSA.

- **Use HSA for Qualified Medical Expenses.** The HSA owner can continue to use the HSA for qualified medical expenses even if no longer eligible for an HSA. The HSA owner just cannot add more money. The HSA works to pay co-pays, deductibles, dental and other general medical expenses not covered by insurance, at least until the HSA is exhausted.

- **Use as Retirement fund.** HSA owners can simply let the account grow until they do need it. At age sixty-five, an HSA owner can use the balance for any reason without penalty, but the HSA owner will have to pay income taxes on amounts withdrawn for non-medical expenses.

- **Maximize Contribution or Remove an Excess.** In an HSA owner's final year of HSA eligibility, the HSA owner may want to maximize the HSA contribution. For the 2014 tax year, individuals have until April 15, 2015 to make an HSA contribution. HSA owners can make an HSA contribution even if no longer eligible so long as the HSA owner is making the contribution for when the HSA owner was eligible (assuming the HSA owner makes the HSA contribution prior to the tax due date).

- **Protect the Establishment Date.** HSA owners should consider keeping the HSA open to protect the "establishment date."

> *Example.* Ankur was covered under his company's high deductible health plan and eligible for an HSA from January through June 2014. On July 1, Ankur started work at a new company and lost HSA eligibility. He never made an HSA contribution for 2014. Assuming it's before April 15, 2015, He still can. He can contribute one-half of the federal maximum (because he was only eligible during half of 2014).

The HSA Eligibility and Contribution Worksheet and Testing Period Worksheet provide more details on these calculations and rules.

148. Should HSA owners close their HSAs when they lose eligibility?

A common practice is to keep the HSA open and continue to use it for qualified medical expenses until it is exhausted and then close it.

A tip for the financially savvy: it might make more sense to keep the HSA open to protect the HSA establishment date. The HSA establishment date is the date the HSA owner first opened the HSA. This date is important because HSA owners can use their HSA to pay for any medical expenses incurred after that date. However, if an HSA owner closes his HSA and leaves it closed for more than eighteen months then he has to start all over again and set a new establishment date. To avoid that happening, HSA owners are wise to simply never close the HSA. If an HSA owner can keep it open then the HSA owner can use the HSA in the future to pay for all his unreimbursed medical expenses over the years.

> *Example.* Jim, an HSA owner, was no longer eligible for an HSA starting in January 2011 due to a change of jobs. Jim kept his HSA open with a balance of $2,000. Over the next four years, Jim worked at his new job and spent a lot on health care expenses. Most of these expenses were paid for through his insurance and a flexible spending account his new company offers, but he also incurs medical expenses that are not paid with tax-favored accounts. In the first couple of years he used his HSA to pay those expenses until he worked his HSA balance down to $200. He then stopped using his HSA and simply saved the receipts for the uncovered/non-reimbursed medical expenses since he was not eligible to contribute more to his HSA.
>
> In the fifth year, Jim's employer switches to a HDHP and Jim is once again eligible for an HSA. Jim produces his receipts, adds the unreimbursed ones together and finds that he had $3,000 of unreimbursed medical expenses during the last three years. Jim can contribute $3,000 to his HSA because he is once again eligible and then write himself a check for $3,000 to reimburse himself for the previous year's medical expenses. Using this strategy all of Jim's qualified medical expenses are paid for through tax-favored accounts. If he had closed his HSA shortly after his job change, then these expenses would have been incurred prior to his establishment date and would not have been eligible for reimbursement through the HSA.

149. Does a person need to be HSA-eligible every day of the month to count that month?

A taxpayer has to be eligible on the first day of the month for that month to count for eligibility. A taxpayer losing eligibility during the month may still be able to count that month as an eligible month. However, individuals losing eligibility because they turn sixty-five face a different rule that states when a taxpayer enrolls in Medicare the taxpayer loses eligibility for that month as of the first day of that month. Most health plans run on a monthly basis so losing eligibility mid-month is not common.

IRS Notice 2004-2, See Q 2. IRS Notice 2004-50, See Q 2.

PART IV: ESTABLISHMENT

Overview

150. How is an HSA opened?

Opening an HSA is similar to opening another type of banking or investment account, except that an individual can only open an HSA at an IRS-approved custodian or trustee that offers HSAs. An individual generally must complete an application that asks for contact and personal information as well as requiring the individual to sign a custodial or trust agreement.

The HSA custodial agreement may be separate from any underlying investment held in the HSA so an individual may need to complete additional documentation for the investment selected. For example, an individual may need to sign both an HSA custodial agreement (the legal trust for the HSA) and a separate account agreement for a checking account (the investment held in the HSA).

151. Do HSA owners have to file with the IRS when they open an HSA?

HSA owners do not need to file anything with the IRS at the time the HSA is established, although they will need to reflect HSA contributions and distributions on their federal income tax return. The HSA custodian will send IRS Form 5498-SA, reporting the HSA owner's HSA contribution and by implication that the HSA owner opened an HSA.

IRS Notice 2004-2, See Q 9, IRS Form 5498-SA

152. When can an HSA be opened?

An HSA can be opened at any time of year, as long as the individual is already enrolled in a qualified HDHP. If enrolling through an employer, generally people enroll during the employer's open enrollment period.

153. Where can an individual open an HSA?

An HSA can be established with any approved HSA custodian or trustee. The HSA marketplace is competitive with no shortage of banks, credit unions, insurance companies, mutual fund companies, brokers and other third-party custodian or trustee offering HSA solutions. The requirement that the HSA provider be approved by the IRS as a custodian or trustee limits the market somewhat, but regulated banks and credit unions are automatically approved as is any institution approved to serve as a custodian or trustee for IRAs. Many insurance companies are also automatically approved.

154. Is there a list of approved non-bank HSA custodians and trustees available?

Yes. The IRS publishes a list of non-bank approved HSA custodians and trustees available at http://www.irs.gov/Retirement-Plans/Approved-Nonbank-Trustees-and-Custodians.

155. Does an HSA need to be established with the health insurance company?

No. The HSA can be set-up with any qualified HSA trustee or custodian. Many people are choosing to open their HSAs with a provider that is different from their insurance company to take advantage of lower fees and establish independence in the event that they change insurance.

If an employer is making HSA contributions, the employer could require all employees to open an HSA at a custodian of its choice. The rules allow this to provide some administrative convenience for employers. Individuals may also agree by contract to a certain HSA custodian and that agreement could happen in connection with the purchase of health insurance, but there is no law requiring individuals to open an HSA anywhere in particular.

Custodial or Trust Agreement

156. What is a "custodial account agreement"?

The IRS requires that all HSA custodians and trustees have a custodial or trust agreement signed by HSA owners. This agreement sets forth the legal relationship between the HSA owner and the HSA custodian or trustee. The agreement also contains some of the basic rules of HSAs.

157. Does the IRS provide model HSA forms?

Yes. The IRS provides the IRS Form 5305-B for trust and 5305-C for custodial HSAs. Most custodians use the model form. If the HSA custodian uses the model form it should include "IRS Form 5305-C" near the top of the form.

The IRS model form allows custodians to add additional language beyond the basic language provided by the IRS. Most custodians use the ability to add language to impose additional account terms and further explain the legal relationship between the HSA owner and the custodian (or trustee).

IRS Notice 2004-50, See Q 63, IRS Form 5305-B, IRS Form 5305-C

158. What additional terms do custodians impose in the custodial agreement?

The following lists common areas for additional language in an HSA custodial agreement.

- Definitions section
- Investment limitations
- Restrictions on rollovers
- Voting rights
- Termination provisions
- Removal of custodian

- State law requirements

- Treatment of excess contributions

- Treatment of mistaken distributions

- Distribution procedures (frequency, minimum dollar, etc.)

- Use of debit, credit, or stored value cards

- Prohibited transactions description

- Liability limitations

- Fees language

- Choice of law

- Arbitration clauses

- Notices provisions

- Other clauses

159. What is the difference between a "custodial" HSA and a "trust" HSA?

HSA law treats them with no appreciable difference. The common and legal understanding of the term "custodial" better describes the relationship between the financial institution holding the HSA funds and the HSA owner. The financial institution is reporting to the IRS as to contributions and distributions and serves as an intermediary between the HSA owner and the HSA money. This role of the financial institution is primarily administrative or "custodial" in nature. The law requires a custodian or trustee to provide third party information reporting to the IRS to increase tax compliance.

The term "trust" implies a fiduciary relationship between the HSA owner and the financial institution. Generally, the relationship between an HSA owner and the financial institution serving as either a custodian or a trustee is not a fiduciary relationship. If the HSA is offered through a trust department or an actual fiduciary then the use of the trust agreement may be appropriate.

160. Why do HSA Applications require so much personal information?

HSAs are tax-driven accounts and must be tied to a Social Security Number (or TIN). If the custodian is a regulated bank or credit union, other state and federal banking laws, especially the Patriot Act, likely require the gathering of a fair amount of personal data to ensure the financial institution knows who it is working with and to reduce the chance of fraud.

Multiple HSAs

161. Can HSA owners open more than one HSA?

Yes. There is no restriction on the number of HSAs an HSA owner can open. However, the annual HSA contribution limit applies to all of an HSA owner's HSAs when added together.

162. Can an HSA owner contribute the HSA maximum limit to each of the HSA owner's HSAs?

No. The federal HSA contribution limits apply to all HSAs established by an HSA owner.

> *Example.* Jody's employer makes HSA contributions on Jody's behalf to an HSA in her name at Big Bank. Jody personally banks at Little Bank and would like to open a second HSA at Little Bank. Jody can have two or more open HSAs at the same time. Jody's annual HSA contribution limit applies to all her HSAs so opening multiple HSAs is not an avoidance of HSA contribution limits.

IRS Notice 2004-50, See Q 65.

163. Are there valid reasons to establish more than one HSA?

Yes. The most common reason to have multiple HSAs is to allow for different investment choices and different account features. Another common reason is that an employer requires an HSA be opened at a specific HSA custodian in order to receive employer HSA contributions. An HSA owner may not prefer that particular custodian but keeps the HSA open in order to receive the employer contributions. The HSA owner could then open a separate HSA at a more preferred HSA custodian and periodically transfer HSA funds from the non-preferred HSA custodian to the preferred HSA custodian.

> *Example.* Kelly has an HSA at Sunny Credit Union. Sunny Credit Union offers Kelly the convenience of a debit card and checking for easy access to her money. Kelly appreciates and values that easy access but as her HSA has grown she also wants additional investment options. Kelly opens a second HSA at Growth Mutual Funds and transfers the portion of her HSA balance that she is unlikely to need for qualified medical expenses in the next few years. Growth Mutual Funds places restrictions on distributions making it difficult to use the funds invested at Growth Mutual Funds for day-to-day medical expenses. Kelly benefits from having two HSAs: one to pay qualified medical expenses and a second for investment for future use.

Joint HSAs

164. Are joint HSAs allowed?

No. All HSAs are individual and must be in one person's name and Social Security Number.

IRS Notice 2004-50, See Q 64.

165. If an HSA owner has family HDHP coverage is a joint account allowed?

No. All HSAs are individual accounts. This answer confuses many HSA owners as they specifically enroll in a "family" health plan, review the HSA law to determine the "family" maximum HSA limit and use their HSA for their "family's" medical expenses (spouse and dependents).

166. Why aren't joint HSAs allowed?

Tax reporting is likely a key reason that HSAs (and IRAs) are individual accounts. Congress modeled HSAs using the legal framework for IRAs (Individual Retirement Accounts) which are tied to one person even if a person may be saving for his or her spouse as well. Although the rules <u>could</u> allow for joint or family HSAs, they do not.

Requiring all HSAs to be individual accounts simplifies the tax reporting for the IRS by tying it to one Social Security Number. Employers already tie employer HSA contributions to that same Social Security Number and HSA owners file under their individual Social Security Numbers (although spouses can file joint returns).

167. Does the rule against joint HSAs hurt HSA owners?

No. Most objectives in having a joint HSA can be accomplished with individual HSAs including:

- **Joint Use of HSA Funds.** HSA owners can authorize access via ATM/debit cards, checks or other signature devices on an HSA. This action allows both a spouse and potentially others to directly access the HSA funds for medical expenses.

- **Direct Payment Upon Death.** Joint accounts allow for easier transition in case of a death of one of the account owners, but HSA pay on death rules and the ability of a spouse beneficiary to treat the HSA as his or her own (basically the same treatment as a joint account) reduce this concern.

- **HSA Limits.** The family HDHP limit is not reduced for an individual because they cannot open a joint account so in most instances the HSA limits are not impacted by the rule against joint HSAs. The rules regarding how much HSA owners can contribute is based on whether or not a person has family coverage and also whether or not the person is married. A married person with family coverage must coordinate the maximum family HSA limit with the other spouse (the two spouses' individual HSAs cannot exceed the family limit). This rule does complicate HSAs over joint accounts as in some instances it requires that each spouse open an HSA and then coordinate the combined HSA.

Example. Dorothy and Jim are married and are covered under a family HDHP. Since they cannot open a joint HSA, the custodian suggests that they open an HSA in Dorothy's name and name Jim as an authorized signer. This will allow both Dorothy and Jim to have direct access to the funds in the account.

Dorothy also names Jim as the beneficiary of her HSA. If Dorothy dies, the HSA will become Jim's pursuant to HSA law. Dorothy is covered by a family HDHP and is otherwise HSA-eligible so she can contribute the family HSA limit (the maximum limit of Jim and Dorothy combined if they both opened HSAs and assuming they are both under the age fifty-five). Dorothy will get to claim the income tax deduction for the contribution (which will not matter if they file a joint income tax return).

Establishment Date
Overview
168. What is an "establishment date" and why is it important?

The key point of the establishment date is that HSA owners can use the HSA to pay for all medical expenses incurred <u>after</u> (but not before) that date. The "establishment date" rule allows HSA owners to maximize HSA tax benefits by paying for most qualified medical expenses tax-free through their HSA, even in years when the HSA owners' medical expenses exceed the HSA limits. This assumes that the HSA owners will have some years in which medical expenses are lower. The examples below illustrate the importance of the establishment date in gaining access to HSA funds.

> *Example 1.* Bill is eligible for his first HSA on January 1 but decides to wait to open his account. Prior to opening his HSA, Bill incurs an emergency $2,500 medical bill that he has to pay directly because it is below his deductible amount. Bill cannot use his HSA to pay the bill because he did not establish his HSA prior to the date of the medical expense.

> *Example 2.* Assuming the same facts as above, except that Bill opened his HSA and funded it with just $25 on January 1 when he became eligible for the HSA. Now when Bill incurs the emergency medical expense, he can use his HSA to pay for it because the HSA was established prior to the expense. The fact that the HSA only has $25 merely requires Bill to make an additional HSA contribution to pay the expense.

> *Example 3.* Again assuming the same facts, but Bill incurs a $10,000 dental bill in the same year. He cannot contribute enough to his HSA to cover this large expense because of the federal HSA contribution limits. However, he can pay the expense from other funds, save his receipts, and pay himself back from the HSA in the future as he makes future year HSA contributions. The expense can be carried forward indefinitely. It takes some paperwork and patience, but it's well worth it to get every dollar of tax savings from an HSA.

IRS Notice 2004-50, See Q 40.

When is an HSA Established

169. When is the date that an HSA is established?

The quick answer is the date the HSA owner opens the HSA but ultimately the definition of "established" is controlled by the state law of the HSA owner. This answer can get more complicated if an HSA owner closes and then reopens another HSA.

Funding requirement: A common requirement under state law is that a trust be funded in order to be established. Generally people open their HSA with an initial contribution which meets the funding requirement (the size of the funding should not matter) so meeting a funding requirement generally is not an issue.

Trust agreement: Another likely requirement is the necessity for an agreement showing a trust exists. Whether a signature is required also depends on state law. Completing and signing the IRS Application and Custodial agreement should satisfy a requirement to have an agreement. HSA laws requires that HSA custodians use a formal document for HSA establishment; the IRS Form 5305-C (custodial account form), IRS Form 5305-B (trust account form) or an IRS approved prototype, so a document requirement is not likely to cause any establishment issues. These forms can be found at the IRS website at www.irs.com.

> *Example.* Cole is eligible for an HSA on January 1, so he completes and signs an HSA Application and Custodial Agreement in December at Neighborhood Credit Union in preparation for his upcoming change in insurance to an HDHP. Cole cannot contribute to an HSA prior to being eligible so he left a check asking for it to be deposited on January 1. Since the credit union is not open on January 1, the HSA is established on January 2 under state trust law which provides that a trust is not established until the trust exists and is funded. If there were a system in place to automatically open the HSA or if state law allowed for the placement of the of the funds and signing of the forms into the hands of the custodian to complete the establishment of the trust, then January 1 would be the establishment date.

IRS Notice 2008-59, See Q 39, IRS Form 5305-B, IRS Form 5305-C.

170. Where does one find the HSA establishment date rules in state law?

Each state addresses trust law differently and an attorney in the state familiar with the trust laws is the best place to begin a search. The IRS simply defers to state trust law as to what constitutes an "established" HSA. States are unlikely to have specifically addressed HSA establishment so the proper question is "when is a trust considered established under state law?"

IRS Notice 2008-59, See Q 39.

171. Can an HSA owner "establish" an HSA with a zero balance?

Pursuant to many state laws, the HSA must be funded to be considered "established." Without researching state laws, a conservative approach is for HSA owners to fund the HSA with a small amount to get it "established."

> *Example.* Molly wants to set her establishment date as soon as possible but does not want to commit to any ongoing funding of an HSA. Molly completes and signs a 5305-C HSA Custodial Agreement with an approved HSA custodian and contributes $25 (or some other minimum amount above zero as may be required by the custodian). She has set her establishment date and does not need to commit to additional funding of the HSA. She can use her HSA for any medical expenses incurred after her establishment date and could add money to her HSA after the expense amount is known (assuming she remains eligible for an HSA and has not already contributed the maximum limit for the year).

172. Can the health insurance coverage date serve as the establishment date?

No. The establishment date is the date when an HSA owner opens the HSA, not the date when the HSA owner was eligible to open the HSA (usually the date when HDHP coverage begins).

IRS Notice 2008-59, See Q 40.

173. Can the date an HSA owner becomes eligible for an HSA serve as the establishment date?

No. An HSA owner must be eligible for an HSA in order to establish an HSA, but mere eligibility does not equal establishment. The HSA owner must take the action of opening and funding an HSA with an approved HSA custodian.

174. Does an employer contribution to an HSA set the establishment date?

Generally, yes. In order for an employer to fund an HSA, the employee would have needed to have completed and signed an HSA custodial agreement satisfying a state requirement that the trust be established and the employer's funding would satisfy a state requirement for funding.

Note: As a general practice, employers do not open HSA for employees that fail to open an HSA on their own. However, if an employer did open an HSA for an employee without the employee's signature on the HSA agreement, then a question arises as to whether or not a trust was formed (for states that require a signed trust document).

Example 1. John's employer starts an HDHP and HSA plan for its employees and gives everyone $50 upfront into their HSA to get them started and encourages them to do more through payroll deferral. John opens his HSA to take advantage of the employer's $50 but never puts any more money into the HSA. John later incurs a large medical bill - because he established his HSA by opening it and having the employer's $50 deposited, he can add more to cover it because the expense was incurred after the establishment date.

Example 2. Same example, but John's employer did not offer the $50 so John never set up his HSA. He cannot use his HSA to pay the expense because he never established it. If the medical issue will require more treatment, he should quickly establish the HSA and use his HSA for the future medical expenses.

175. What is the establishment date when an employer requires employees to complete all the HSA agreements two weeks before becoming HSA-eligible?

The first year employers' switch to a combination HDHP and HSA causes some timing issues on getting HSAs established. An employer starting an HDHP and HSA program is well served by having employees complete the HSA paperwork ahead of the actual program's starting date as it takes some time to complete the set-up.

However, the employees are not eligible for an HSA until the HDHP coverage actually begins. A good practice to address this issue is for the custodian to get the HSAs set up on its system and ready to go but not actually "establish" the HSA until the date the employees become eligible. This can be accomplished in many states by waiting to fund the HSAs until the eligibility begins as establishment requires both signing the trust agreement and funding of the trust. Even following this procedure employees may not have debit cards or other access tool for the new HSA until sometime after the HSA is established. The employees' establishment date the date the HSAs were funded or potentially opened on the system (which can occur no earlier than the first day the employees become eligible for an HSA).

Not the First HSA

176. What is the establishment date for someone that used to have an HSA and is now opening a new one?

The establishment date of the new HSA depends on how long ago the original HSA existed. Any later HSA is deemed established the same day the first HSA was established so long as the earlier HSA had a positive balance at any point during the eighteen month period ending on the date of the opening of the new HSA.

Example. Frank opened an HSA on March 1, 2010. On June 15, 2012, he closed it. On November 21, 2013, he opened a new HSA. The second HSA was established within eighteen months of June 15, 2012 so the second HSA is deemed established on March 1, 2010. Frank's establishment date is March 1, 2010 and he can use the HSA for any medical expenses incurred after that date.

IRS Notice 2008-59, See Q 42.

177. Do HSA transfers impact the establishment date?

No. The establishment date stays the same as the date the original HSA was established for HSA owners that move funds to a new HSA custodian via a trustee-to-trustee transfer.

Example. Bill opens an HSA at ABC Bank and has an establishment date of October 30, 2011. In 2014, Bill transfers all the assets in his HSA at ABC Bank to XYZ Credit Union in a trustee-to-trustee transfer. Bill's establishment date for his HSA at XYZ Credit Union remains October 30, 2011.

178. Do HSA rollovers impact the establishment date?

No. Rolling money from one HSA to another does not change the establishment date (provided the rollover is properly completed within the sixty day period and the HSA owner has not completed another rollover within the previous twelve months).

Example. Jim opened his first HSA on January 15, 2008 and has kept it open with a positive balance ever since. In January of this year, he decides to roll it over to a new HSA custodian. Jim completes his rollover within 60 days of the distribution. His establishment date remains January 15, 2008.

IRS Notice 2008-59, See Q 41.

179. Does rolling funds from an Archer MSA to an HSA maintain the Archer MSA establishment date?

Yes. The Archer MSA establishment date is maintained when rolling money from an Archer MSA into an HSA.

Example. Cindy established an Archer MSA on October 17, 2000. In May of 2014, Cindy rolled the entire amount into an HSA. Cindy's establishment date for her HSA is October 17, 2000.

IRS Notice 2008-59, See Q 41.

Tracking

180. Who is responsible for tracking the Establishment Date?

The HSA owner is responsible for knowing and tracking the establishment date.

181. Does the HSA custodian know the establishment date of its HSAs?

Maybe. If an HSA owner first opened the HSA at the current HSA custodian, the custodian can probably help determine the establishment date. With rollovers and transfers to new custodians, or after the opening and closing of multiple HSAs, this becomes difficult or impossible for the HSA custodian to know the establishment date. The HSA owner, not the custodian, is responsible to know the establishment date.

In the case of a dispute between the HSA owner and the IRS the HSA custodian's records will be crucial to determine what the establishment date really is. The IRS will want to see when the HSA application was signed (the first one), when was money deposited and possibly when the HSA was placed on the custodian's system.

Authorized Signer

Overview

182. What is an authorized signer?

An authorized signer is someone designated by the HSA owner to sign for distributions from the HSA.

IRS Notice 2008-59, See Q 29.

183. What powers does an authorized signer have?

An authorized signer's power can vary depending upon the contractual language. Generally an authorized signer's powers will be limited to taking distributions from the HSA. Included could be a debit card issued in the authorized signer's name, checks issued in the authorized signer's name, an Automated Teller Machine (ATM) card issued in the authorized signer's name, access to electronic bill pay systems, or other access methods.

An authorized signer generally can also make contributions to the HSA because anyone, whether they are an authorized signer or not, can generally make contributions to another person's HSA (from a practical perspective only employers and maybe family members tend to do so).

184. Does an authorized signer have the same rights on the HSA as the HSA owner?

No. Although the level of authority granted an authorized signer will vary depending upon the HSA custodian or trustee, generally an authorized signer cannot do any of the following:

- Add or change beneficiaries

- Change investment selections

- Transfer or rollover HSA funds to a new custodian or trustee

- Change account profile information

- Add new authorized signers

- Perform other functions limited by agreement to the HSA owner

185. Is having "power of attorney" the same as being an authorized signer?

No. Generally a power of attorney over an HSA will give more control over the HSA than being an authorized signer. However, both the power of attorney and the authorized signer rules are governed by the document signed granting that power. A careful review of the power of attorney is necessary to determine what level of authority the holder has over an HSA. A general power of attorney will likely provide all of the authority that the HSA owner would have. Authorized signers generally have more limited authority.

186. Is having an authorized signer the same as having a joint HSA?

No. HSAs are not joint account and adding an authorized signer to an HSA does not make it joint. The HSA is still in one person's name and Social Security Number as required by law.

187. If an authorized signer is over age fifty-five; but the HSA owner is not, can the authorized signer's age be used to make a catch-up contribution?

No. The HSA owner's age is the age used to determine eligibility for a catch-up contribution.

188. Is an authorized signer also the beneficiary?

No. An authorized signer is not the designated beneficiary in the event of death of the HSA owner. The same person can be named as both an authorized signer and a death beneficiary.

Example. Yunqing and Steve are married. Steve has an HSA and names Yunqing as an authorized signer. Steve would also like Yunqing to get the HSA if he dies. He names Yunqing as a designated beneficiary as well.

Who Can Serve

189. Can an HSA owner's spouse serve as an authorized signer?

Yes. Most HSA custodians allow for "authorized signers" on an HSA and as such, a spouse can be named as an authorized signer to sign for distributions from the HSA.

Example. Pete and Kathy are covered under a family HDHP. Kathy can be an authorized signer and write checks and have a debit card issued in her name to spend funds from an has that Pete opens.

190. Can an HSA owner name a child as an authorized signer?

Yes, a child can serve as an authorized signer provided the custodian accepts the authorized signer.

Example. Matthew can complete a form authorizing his nineteen year old son to be signer on his HSA to enable him to pay for qualified medical expenses.

191. Do HSA laws require a minimum age to serve as an authorized signer?

No. HSA laws do not put an age requirement on authorized signers, but general contract law may prevent minors from serving as authorized signers. In some states, depending on the status of the minor, medical services may fit within an exception allowing them to enter into contracts, but most HSA custodians will likely deny minors the ability to serve as authorized signers to avoid legal issues. Also, many medical service providers will question a signature of a minor. Generally, authorized signers must be eighteen years old to avoid the legal capacity issue presented by minors serving in the role of an authorized signer.

192. Can an HSA owner name a nanny or grandparent as an authorized signer?

Yes. Authorized signers can be anyone and are not limited to a spouse. The person will have the power to take distributions from the HSA so HSA owners are advised to only grant authorized signer status to trusted individuals.

Example. Bill employs a non-related nanny to provide child care to his children. Bill can grant authorization for his nanny to serve as an authorized signer of checks and a debit card for the HSA for the children. The nanny cannot use the HSA for her own medical expenses on a tax-free basis as she is not Bill's spouse or dependent.

IRS Notice 2008-59, See Q 29.

193. Can a spouse covered by traditional health insurance and not eligible for an HSA serve as an authorized signer?

Yes, an authorized signer does not need to be eligible for the HSA.

194. Can an HSA owner name more than one authorized signer?

Yes. HSA owners can name as many authorized signers as they want unless the HSA custodian limits the number of authorized signers.

195. Can spouses list each other as authorized signers?

Yes, spouses can be authorized signers on each other's accounts.

Custodian Control

196. Does an HSA custodian have to allow authorized signers?

No. Custodians are not required to accept authorized signers for HSAs, although most do as it is a convenience for HSA owners.

If authorized signers are not allowed, although it creates an inconvenience for the HSA owner, there are options. The HSA owner can still use the HSA for a spouse or dependent's medical expenses by simply have to signing the check or debit card instead of an authorized signer. Alternatively, if the HSA owner is not available, they can reimburse the other person from the HSA for the expense.

197. Is an HSA custodian required to accept a particular authorized signer?

No. HSA custodians need to approve an authorized signer and may refuse to do so. A minor child will likely not be approved given capacity issues to sign legal agreements and individuals with improper financial experience or records may be denied.

Designation of Beneficiary
(see also Death Distributions)

198. May an HSA owner designate a beneficiary?

Yes. An HSA is a payable on death account meaning that designated beneficiaries will get the money directly from the HSA custodian without having to wait for probate.

199. May an HSA owner designate more than one beneficiary?

Yes. Most HSA custodians will allow HSA owners to name more than one beneficiary and allow the HSA owner to split the HSA either equally or based on a percentage.

200. May an HSA owner name contingent beneficiaries?

Yes, an HSA owner can name contingent beneficiaries to receive the money in the situation where the primary beneficiaries pre-decease the HSA owner.

201. Do HSA owners have to name beneficiaries?

No. HSA owners do not have to name a beneficiary for the HSA.

202. What if an HSA owner fails to name a beneficiary?

The HSA funds will pass to the HSA owner's estate.

203. Can HSA owners change beneficiary designations?

Yes. HSA owners can generally change a beneficiary designation at any time by completing a change of beneficiary form.

204. Should an HSA owner name a child or a spouse as the beneficiary?

Spouses are the only beneficiaries that are allowed to continue to use the HSA as an HSA after the HSA owner dies. For this reason, it makes more sense to name a spouse. Children must close the HSA and pay taxes on the amount distributed. Many factors must be considered before naming a beneficiary.

205. Can a trust serve as the beneficiary of an HSA?

Yes. There are tax implications of naming a trust as a beneficiary so HSA owners desiring to do so should first seek tax advice.

NOTE: A risk of naming a trust over a spouse is the possible loss of a spouse beneficiary's ability to treat the HSA as his or her own. If the HSA owner's spouse is the ultimate beneficiary of the trust, the spouse may lose the ability to continue to use the HSA as an HSA because the HSA owner named a trust as the beneficiary rather than the spouse directly (only spouse beneficiaries are allowed to treat the HSA as their own). In some circumstances for Individual Retirement Accounts the IRS has allowed the ability to "look through" the trust at the ultimate beneficiary. Although IRS rulings for IRAs do not apply to HSAs, this same ability may be available for HSA spouse beneficiaries of trusts.

Investments

206. What are the HSA investment options?

HSAs enjoy the same investment choices as Individual Retirement Accounts. Theoretically, HSA owners can invest in a wide range of assets inside an HSA. In practice, most or perhaps all HSA custodians limit investment choices. HSA dollars are often placed in checking accounts, Certificates of Deposit, money markets accounts; or less frequently, stocks, bonds and mutual funds.

IRC Sec. 223(d)(1)(C), IRS Notice 2004-50, See Q 66.

207. Are there limitations on HSA investment options?

Yes. There are actually few limitations on investment choices, but HSAs may not be invested in collectibles. This includes works of art, antiques, metals (some exceptions involving platinum, gold and silver coins and bullion), gems, stamps, coins, alcoholic beverages, or other tangible personal property (specified by the IRS in guidance on IRC Sec. 408(m)). HSAs may not be invested in life insurance contracts and HSAs cannot be commingled with other property except in a common investment fund. You have to open your HSA with an approved HSA custodian so finding one that allows for your investment choice is vital.

IRC Sec. 223(d)(1)(C), IRC Sec. 408(m), IRS Notice 2004-50, See Q 66, See Q. 217.

208. Why do most HSA custodians offer only checking accounts as investment options?

HSAs are designed to be used for day-to-day medical expenses and HSA owners often contribute monthly. A checking account that allows for frequent contributions and distributions works well for the manner many HSA owners view and use HSAs. A checking account allows the HSA owner easy access to their HSA through checks, a debit/ATM card, and often online banking. As an HSA balance grows, an HSA owner is more likely to seek out longer-term, higher yielding investment choices. As the industry as a whole has grown, more and more providers are expanding their investment choices and that trend will likely continue.

209. Are HSAs FDIC insured?

The HSA is FDIC insured if the assets are held in Federal Deposit Insurance Corporation (FDIC) insured investments offered through an FDIC insured institution.

Since FDIC insured banks are automatically approved to serve as HSA custodians and that those institutions generally offer FDIC insured checking accounts for HSAs, many HSAs are FDIC insured. The FDIC explains as follows:

> "An HSA, like any other deposit, is insured based on who owns the funds and whether beneficiaries have been named. If a depositor opens an HSA and names beneficiaries either in the HSA agreement or in the bank's records, the FDIC would insure the deposit under the Revocable Trust Account ownership category. If a depositor opens an HSA and does not name any beneficiaries, the FDIC would insure the deposit under the Single Account ownership category."

FDIC Brochure: Your Insured Deposits.

210. Are HSAs invested at credit unions insured?

Yes, if an HSA owner places funds at a credit union insured by the National Credit Union Administration (NCUA) through the National Credit Union Share Insurance Fund (NCUSIF) offering NCUSIF insured investments.

211. Do HSAs qualify for the increased FDIC limits of certain retirement plans?

No. The FDIC provides increased and separate insurance coverage for certain retirement accounts. HSAs are not considered retirement accounts and are not entitled to this special treatment.

212. Can an HSA invest in gold or other precious metals?

Yes, but only certain types and it must be held in the "physical possession" of the HSA custodian/trustee. The rules allow for specific gold, silver, and platinum coins and bullion of the same materials meeting certain standards. As an example, the American Eagle gold and silver coins qualify. Most HSA custodians refuse to accept gold or silver as an investment. Allowing for these specific precious metals is an exception to the general rule prohibiting collectibles in an HSA.

IRC Sec. 408(m).

213. Is the HSA account and the investment account the same?

No. An HSA is a legal agreement between the HSA owner and the HSA custodian setting forth the terms of the HSA (the IRS is also involved because the agreement must be based on an IRS model form or be separately approved by the IRS).

The investment choice is separate and will generally require the HSA owner to sign another legal agreement setting forth the terms and conditions of that investment. For instance, if an HSA owner selects a checking account as the investment, the HSA owner will have to sign a separate account agreement for the checking account unless the HSA custodian has combined the HSA custodial account agreement and the checking account agreement into one document.

214. Are there prohibited investments?

Yes, HSA owners are not allowed to invest in an asset resulting in a prohibited transition. Prohibited transactions generally result from self-dealing, such as an HSA owner selling his or her HSA an asset the HSA owner currently owns outside of the HSA.

See Part IX: Tax Issues – Prohibited Transactions (Q 543 to Q 557).

215. Are collectables prohibited as investments?

Yes. There are actually few limitations on investment choices, but HSAs may not be invested in collectibles. This includes works of art, antiques, metals (see exceptions above), gems, stamps, coins (see exceptions above), alcoholic beverages, or other tangible personal property (specified by the IRS in guidance on IRC Sec. 408(m)). HSAs may not be invested in life insurance contracts and HSAs cannot be commingled with other property except in a common investment fund.

IRC Sec. 408(m).

216. Does the IRS "approve" investments?

No, the law does set forth rules on permissible and non-permissible investments, but HSA owners are advised to keep a cautious lookout for investment firms selling "IRS Approved Investments for an HSA." Financial product sales people have used the pitch "IRS Approved" to put a veneer of credibility and safety to investments that may be fraudulent or higher risk than desired. Historically this has occurred in the IRA market but as HSAs grow the pitches will be directed at HSA owners as well. The laws for investments in IRAs and HSAs are virtually identical. One example of this was selling ostrich farming as an IRA investment. The investment may very well be "permissible" as an HSA investment, but the IRS does not "approve" or "sanction" such investments.

The IRS published that it does not:

- Review or approve investments

- Endorse any investments

- Advise people on how to invest their IRAs

- Issue any statement that an investment in an IRA is protected because a particular trustee or custodian has been approved by the IRS

The IRS included an example of a fraudulent sales pitch:

"This investment has been approved for your IRA. You can use your IRA for this investment by filling out the forms in the attached information package, and our agent will take care of the rest. This has been reviewed by the government (or IRS). This investment is so safe you can use it for your IRA. Only certain investments are approved for IRAs."

IRS Publication 3125.

217. How do brokerage accounts within an HSA work?

HSA custodians enjoy great flexibility in designing a brokerage account for an HSA. This answer explains some of the common elements of these programs driven by the HSA legal framework. An HSA is a trust or custodial account that can hold many different types of assets, including, both FDIC insured investments and others. An HSA custodian can allow those varying investments to be held in one custodial HSA such that an HSA owner may have a money market account, mutual funds, and stocks all held under one HSA umbrella custodial account. HSA owners are allowed to select the investments provided the custodian allows for the investment selection. The rules allow for self-directed trading so long as the HSA brokerage program is structured properly.

An HSA custodian needs to have rules in place that prevent HSA law violations. This would include that there <u>cannot</u> be a method for the HSA owner to contribute to the HSA or take a distribution from the HSA without the HSA custodian being aware of the transaction. This usually requires that the investments held in the HSA are titled something to the effect of: "First National Bank as Custodian for John Doe's HSA." Also, HSA laws do not allow for losing more money than the amount invested so any investment choices that allow for losses greater than the amount invested cannot be allowed. For example, margin accounts are not allowed (or at least not without a lot of rules to ensure that the HSA can cover any losses incurred with assets held inside the HSA).

Paying brokerage fees and costs can also be somewhat problematic in HSAs. Some types banking fees can be paid outside of the HSA, although fees directly associated with the cost of the investment must be paid with HSA assets. This is generally desired as it allows for an HSA owner to use pre-tax money to pay the fees, but it's also required as it could become a prohibited transaction to have the fees paid outside of the HSA.

PART V: CONTRIBUTIONS

Overview

218. What are the general HSA contribution rules?

Listed below are the key issues for HSA contributions.

- **Eligibility.** Individuals must be eligible for an HSA to make an HSA contribution.

- **Contribution Source.** HSA rules are flexible as to who can make a contribution for an individual and allow for anyone to make an HSA contribution for an individual.

- **Contribution Limits.** HSA contributions are limited. The amount is based on whether an individual has self-only HDHP coverage or family HDHP coverage, the individual's age, and the individual's months of HSA eligibility during a tax year. The limit is an overall limit for HSA contributions from all sources except rollovers and transfers.

- **Contribution Timing.** HSA contributions cannot be made any sooner than the beginning of the taxable year (January 1 for most people) and no later than the tax filing date (April 15 for most people).

- **Special Spousal Rules.** Spouses face a few special rules with the most important one requiring that spouses coordinate their contributions and not exceed the family HSA limit if one spouse, or both, have family HDHP coverage. Another special rule for spouses is if one spouse has family HDHP coverage both spouses are deemed to have family HDHP coverage.

219. Can HSA contributions be made in-kind or must it be in cash?

HSA contributions must be made in cash (cash, check, money order, etc.). Cash contributions include contributions made by employers through payroll deferral or directly. Individuals cannot contribute stock or other property to an HSA. HSA owners may transfer HSA assets between HSA custodians in-kind if the HSA custodians allow in-kind transfers.

> *Example 1.* Cienna owns 100 shares of XYZ stock worth $3,000 and would like to contribute that stock to her HSA and claim a $3,000 HSA contribution deduction on her income tax return. This is not allowed even though she could contribute $3,000 cash to her HSA and then use the cash to purchase the stock within her HSA.

> *Example 2.* Samantha holds 100 shares of XYZ stock in her HSA at Bank One. She would like to transfer the assets in her HSA at Bank One to a new HSA at Bank Two. Provided the two custodians allow for in-kind transfers of securities this is permissible under the law.

IRS Notice 2004-2, See Q 17.

220. How do HSA owners make additional contributions?

HSA contributions are generally made either through an employer or directly with an HSA custodian. If an HSA owner's employer allows for pre-tax payroll deferral, the HSA owner should contact the employer to start or change periodic HSA contributions. If the HSA owner makes contribution directly, the HSA owner simply contacts the HSA custodian to make an additional contribution.

Most HSA custodians offer an HSA contribution form that will collect the basic information necessary to correctly report an HSA contribution. Information needed is generally the HSA owner's name, an account number or other verifying information, the dollar amount of the contribution and the year of the contribution. Some contributions can be made for the current year or the previous year (if between January 1 and April 15) designating the year of the contribution is a key piece of information.

221. FSAs are now limited to $2,500, does that rule apply to HSAs?

No. The Affordable Care Act limited Flexible Spending Account (FSA) contributions to $2,500 starting in 2013, but that law does not apply to HSAs.

Who Can Contribute

222. Can any person make HSA contributions for an HSA owner?

Yes. Any person may make an HSA contribution for any other person including family members, employers, even neighbors and strangers. Whether or not the contributor or the HSA owner gets the tax break depends on the relationship. Employers generally do get a deduction for HSA contributions and spouses that file joint return get the benefit of each other's contributions. If someone other than an employer or spouse makes an HSA contribution on behalf of the HSA owner, the HSA owner gets the HSA deduction, not the person who contributed.

IRS Notice 2004-50, See Q 29.

223. Can parents make HSA contributions for minor children?

No. Minor children are not eligible for HSAs because they can be claimed on someone else's tax return. Accordingly, parents generally cannot make HSA contributions for their children.

However, if a child is no longer eligible to be claimed on the parents' (or someone else's) tax return, and the child is eligible for and HSA, then the parents could make an HSA contribution for their child. The rule for who can make a contribution on someone's behalf is very broad: anyone can make a contribution into anyone's HSA. The child receiving the HSA contribution would be entitled to the HSA deduction, not the parent making the HSA contribution.

224. If someone other than the HSA owner makes an HSA contribution, does the HSA owner get the tax break?

Yes. The HSA owner gets the tax break, not the person making the contribution. Employer HSA contributions work a bit differently where both the employer and the employee get tax benefits.

Note: If a spouse makes a contribution for his or her spouse and together they file a joint tax return, both spouses are essentially getting the same tax break.

Example. Jill's parents made a $2,000 HSA contribution for Jill, an HSA-eligible individual. Jill has a very low income and cannot afford to make any HSA contribution on her own. Jill's parents are high income earners and would greatly benefit from the HSA tax deduction. Jill not her parents, will be able to deduct the $2,000 on her personal income tax return (given her low income this deduction is less valuable to her than it would be to her parents).

IRS Notice 2004-2, See Q 19. See Employer Issues — Employer Contributions.

225. If an employer contributes to an HSA can the employee add more funds?

Yes. HSA owners may fully fund an HSA up to the contribution limit. If an employer only partially funds the HSA, the employee can contribute the difference up to the limit.

HSA Limits

226. What are the HSA limits for 2014 and 2015?

The maximum an HSA owner can contribute to an HSA is set by law and is referred to as the "HSA limits." The HSA limits are adjusted each year for inflation and depend on whether the HSA owner has self-only HDHP coverage or family HDHP coverage. Individuals who are age fifty-five and over may make additional catch-up contributions of up to $1,000 (this number does not adjust for inflation).

Caution: The HSA limits represent the maximum full-year HSA contributions. A particular individual's limit may be lower if the individual was not eligible for the entire year.

HSA Limits		
TYPE	**2014**	**2015**
Individual	$3,300	$3,350
Family	$6,550	$6,650
Catch-up (age 55+)	$1,000	$1,000

227. What are the HSA limits for past years?

HSA LIMITS											
TYPE	**2004***	**2005***	**2006***	**2007**	**2008**	**2009**	**2010**	**2011**	**2012**	**2013**	**2014**	**2015**
Individual	$2,600	$2,650	$2,700	$2,850	$2,900	$3,000	$3,050	$3,050	$3,100	$3,250	$3,300	$3,350
Family	$5,150	$5,250	$5,450	$5,650	$5,800	$5,950	$6,150	$6,150	$6,250	$6,450	$6,550	$6,650
Catch-up (age 55+)	$500	$600	$700	$800	$900	$1,000	$1,000	$1,000	$1,000	$1,000	$1,000	$1,000
HDHP-Min Single	$1,000	$1,000	$1,050	$1,100	$1,100	$1,150	$1,200	$1,200	$1,200	$1,250	$1,250	$1,300
HDHP-Min Family	$2,000	$2,000	$2,100	$2,200	$2,200	$2,300	$2,400	$2,400	$2,400	$2,500	$2,500	$2,600
HDHP-Max Single	$5,000	$5,100	$5,250	$5,500	$5,600	$5,800	$5,950	$5,950	$6,050	$6,250	$6,350	$6,450
HDHP-Max Family	$10,000	$10,200	$10,500	$11,000	$11,200	$11,600	$11,900	$11,900	$12,100	$12,500	$12,700	$12,900

*Lesser of HDHP deductible or stated limit

This chart includes the HSA limits for the definition of High Deductible Health Plan as well.

228. When does the IRS announce the inflation adjusted HSA limits each year?

The Secretary of the Treasury must publish the adjusted HSA limits no later than June 1 of the preceding year (June 1, 2014 for 2015 HSA limits). To do this, the Secretary of the Treasury uses the Consumer Price Index for a twelve month period ending March 31.

Prior to 2008, the law required the use of a twelve month period ending August 31. The change allowed more time for HSA providers to update brochures and forms and HSA owners more time to plan for the next year.

IRC Sec. 223(g).

229. Are the HSA limits rounded?

Yes, the HSA limits are rounded to the nearest $50.

IRC Sec. 223 (g)(2).

230. Is the family HSA limit twice the single limit?

No. The self-only (single) HSA limit times two will approximate the family limit but how the numbers are adjusted for inflation causes the numbers to fluctuate within $50.

Looking back over the life of HSAs, a married couple each contributing the single HSA limit would have yielded an extra $50 deposit in seven of the twelve years HSAs have existed (2004, 2005, 2007, 2009, 2013, 2014, and 2015); married couples contributing the family limit would have gained an extra $50 in four out of twelve years (2006, 2010, 2011, and 2012); and the numbers were even in one year (2008). For 2015 the numbers are $3,350 for self-only (or $6,700 for two self-only contributions) versus $6,650 for one family contribution.

231. Are after-tax HSA contributions allowed above the HSA limits?

No. HSA owners are not allowed to make non-deductible HSA contributions and cannot contribute more than the HSA limits.

Calculating Contribution Amount

232. How much can an HSA owner contribute to an HSA?

The simple answer is $3,350 for 2015 ($3,300 for 2014) for HSA-eligible individuals covered by self-only HDHPs and $6,650 for 2015 ($6,550 for 2014) for individuals with family HDHP coverage. Additionally, there is a $1,000 catch-up contribution amount allowed for those over age fifty-five.

The simple answer is inadequate because it ignores the issue of eligibility throughout the year. The amount an individual can contribute depends on the following factors.

- **HSA Maximums for the Year.** The HSA maximum limits are adjusted each year for inflation.

- **Self-Only or Family HDHP Coverage.** The HSA maximum depends on whether the individual had self-only HDHP coverage or family HDHP coverage.

- **Age.** Individuals over age fifty-five are entitled to take advantage of a catch-up contribution.

- **First Day of Eligibility – Eligibility on December 1.** Individuals that become eligible before December 1 of the year and who remain eligible on December 1, can take advantage of the "full contribution rule." December 1 is the key date for most taxpayers, if a taxpayer's tax year does not end in December, then the first day of the last month of the tax year is the key date.

- **Last Day of Eligibility – Not Eligible on December 1.** If an individual's last day of eligibility falls in the calendar year and the individual is not eligible on December 1 (calendar year taxpayer), the individual will need to reduce the HSA contribution amount using the "sum-of-the-months" rule.

- **First Day of the Month.** Eligibility is tied to whether the person was eligible as of the first day of a month.

See the HSA Eligibility and Contribution Worksheet

233. Are the HSA contribution rules different for full year eligibility versus partial year eligibility?

Yes. The HSA maximum contribution depends upon an individual's HSA eligibility throughout the year.

- **Eligible the Entire Year.** If an individual is eligible the entire year, which means the individual maintained HSA eligibility for every day from January 1 through December 1 (eligibility is determined by eligibility as of the first day of the month), that individual can contribute up to the HSA limits for the year

- **Eligible for Part of the Year – Not Including December 1.** If an individual is eligible for only part of the year and is not eligible on December 1 of the year, the individual is subject to the "sum-of-the-months" calculation to determine how much that individual can contribute. The sum of the month's calculation requires the individual to determine eligibility on a month-by-month basis and only contribute a pro-rata amount of the federal maximum HSA limit. See the sum-of-the-months Calculation Table in the HSA Eligibility and Contribution Worksheet.

- **Eligible for Part of the Year – Including December 1.** If an individual became eligible for an HSA at some point during the year between January 1 and December 1, and the individual remained eligible on December 1, then that individual qualifies for the "full contribution rule." The full contribution rule allows an individual to make a full HSA contribution, up to the federal limits for the year, even though the individual was only eligible for part of the year. The key to the full contribution rule is that the individual was eligible on December 1 (or the first day of your last month of your tax year for a non-calendar year taxpayer). However, an individual that takes advantage of the full contribution rule must maintain HSA eligibility for a testing period. If the individual fails to maintain eligibility for a testing period, then a portion of the amount contributed is subject to taxation plus a 10 percent penalty. The testing period begins on December 1 and runs through December 31 of the next year.

Note: The rules above assume a calendar year taxpayer. If an individual uses a fiscal year for their individual taxes (rare) then replace the December 1 date above with the first day of the last month of the fiscal tax year.

Note: Individuals that are eligible on December 1 but then lose eligibility later the same month are technically eligible for the full contribution rule but the individual will fail the testing period. Individuals in this position should follow the sum-of-the-months rules to avoid testing period penalties.

234. When does the "sum-of-the-months" rule apply versus the full contribution rule?

Every year HSA owners need to calculate how much they can contribute to their HSAs by using either the full contribution rule or the sum-of-the-months rule. Basically, anyone that loses HSA eligibility mid-year is covered by the sum-of-the-months rule and anyone that gains HSA eligibility mid-year is covered by the full contribution rule, assuming the person remains eligible on December 1. This simple manner of viewing it can lead to wrong results for individuals that gain and lose eligibility multiple times. If a person is eligible every month of the year, the full contribution rule applies, but the two calculation methods yield the same results.

The rule is a bit more confusing in that it focuses on whether or not the individual was eligible as of the first day of the last month of their tax year (December 1 for calendar year taxpayers) rather than when an individual gained or lost HSA eligibility. Anyone not eligible on the first day of the last month of the tax year is subject to the sum-of-the-months rule and anyone that is eligible on that date is subject to the full contribution rule.

A common situation where the sum-of-the-months rule applies is for people that switch from HDHP coverage to traditional insurance. A person switching to traditional health insurance mid-year will not be eligible for an HSA as of December 1 and therefore is not eligible for the full contribution rule.

A common situation where the full contribution rule applies is for people that switch from traditional health insurance to HDHP coverage mid-year.

The sum-of-the-months rule should also be followed by HSA owners that are eligible on December 1 (the first day of the last month of the tax year), but know that they will fail their testing period. In this situation, if the HSA owners use the sum-of-the-months rule they will not owe any taxes or penalties for failing the testing period.

Example 1. Steve had been contributing to an HSA for years through his company's payroll deferral. He switched jobs and his new company enrolled him in its traditional health insurance as of March 1 and lost eligibility for an HSA. Steve will not be eligible on December 1, the first day of the last month of his tax year so he is subject to the sum-of-the-months rule to calculate his HSA maximum. He can contribute 2/12 of the HSA limit for the year because he was only eligible for two months of the year (January and February).

Example 2. Sam's company switched from traditional insurance to a HSA-eligible HDHP on October 1. He remained eligible for the HDHP and an HSA from October 1 through December 1. Sam, a calendar year taxpayer, can take advantage of the full contribution rule because he was eligible on December 1 so he can make a full year's HSA contribution.

Example 3. Stewart works at the same company as Sam from the previous example. Stewart will turn sixty-five next year and enroll in Medicare and lose HSA eligibility. Technically, Stewart is subject to the full contribution rule and could make a full year's contribution but because he knows he will lose eligibility the next year he should use the sum-of-the-months calculation instead. Stewart will fail the testing period which requires him to remain HSA-eligible through December 31 of the next year. He will owe taxes and penalties on any amount he contributed above the sum-of-the-months' calculation method for failing to meet the testing period.

"Sum-of-the-months" Rule

235. What is the "sum-of-the-months" rule?

The "sum-of-the-months" rule is used to calculate how much an individual can contribute to an HSA when the individual was not eligible on December 1 (or the first day of the last month of the tax year for a non-calendar year taxpayer). The sum-of-the-months calculation results in a pro-rated amount of the HSA limit based how many months an individual is HSA-eligible. This rule generally applies to individuals that were eligible for an HSA for part of the year but then lost eligibility and remained ineligible for the rest of the year. The rule requires individuals to review their HSA eligibility month-by-month and calculate how much they can contribute by adding up the monthly amounts to obtain an annual amount.

236. How do the calculations work using the "sum of the months" method?

The chart below provides a method to calculate an individual's HSA contribution limit using the sum-of-the-months' method. This chart applies to HSA owners that were eligible for an HSA only part of the year and that part did not include the first day of the last month of the tax year - December 1 for most people.

	Sum of the Months Contribution Worksheet	Individual	Family
A	**Federal Limit** (Choose individual or family column based on whether you have self-only or family HDHP coverage	$3,300 (2014) $3,350 (2015)	$6,550 (2014) $6,650 (2015)
B	**Catch-Up Contribution** – Add $1,000 if over 55[1]		
C	**Add A + B** = Total Federal Limit		
D	**Divide C by 12** = Monthly Contribution Eligibility		
E	**Insert # of Months** you were eligible for an HSA in the Year[2]		
F	**Multiply D × E** = Total Eligible Amount Based on Sum of the Months		

[1] If both you and your spouse are age 55 or over an HSA eligible (e.g. not enrolled in Medicare), you each get a catch-up contribution. You cannot contribute two catch-up contributions into the same HSA, you must make them into each spouse's respective HSA.
[2] HSA contribution amounts are determined on a monthly basis and then aggregated. To determine how much you may contribute, you must determine the number of months you were covered by a HDHP and otherwise eligible. Count months that you were eligible as of the first day of that month and every day in that month.

Example. Jim was covered by a self-only HDHP and eligible for an HSA in 2014 but turned sixty-five on July 2, 2014, and enrolled in Medicare. Jim lost eligibility for an HSA as of July 1, 2014 therefore being eligible for six months of 2014. The federal HSA limit for Jim is $4,300 ($3,300 single limit plus a $1,000 catch-up). Accordingly, Jim's calculation is 6/12 × $4,300 = $2,150. Jim's maximum contribution for 2014 is $2,150. The chart below assists in the calculation.

	Sum of the Months Contribution Worksheet	**Individual**	**Family**
A	**Federal Limit** (Choose individual or family column based on whether you have self-only or family HDHP coverage	$3,300 (2014) $3,350 (2015)	$6,550 (2014) $6,650 (2015)
B	**Catch-Up Contribution** – Add $1,000 if over 55[1]	$1,000	
C	**Add A + B** = Total Federal Limit	$4,300	
D	**Divide C by 12** = Monthly Contribution Eligibility	$358.33	
E	**Insert # of Months** you were eligible for an HSA in the Year[2]	6	
F	**Multiply D × E** = Total Eligible Amount Based on Sum of the Months	$2,150	

[1] If both you and your spouse are age 55 or over an HSA eligible (e.g. not enrolled in Medicare), you each get a catch-up contribution. You cannot contribute two catch-up contributions into the same HSA, you must make them into each spouse's respective HSA.
[2] HSA contribution amounts are determined on a monthly basis and then aggregated. To determine how much you may contribute, you must determine the number of months you were covered by a HDHP and otherwise eligible. Count months that you were eligible as of the first day of that month and every day in that month.

Full Contribution Rule

237. What is the "full contribution" or "last month" rule?

The "full contribution rule" allows individuals to contribute up to the maximum HSA limit for the year if they were eligible for the HSA as late as December 1 of the year. The actual rule is if they were HSA-eligible on the first day of the last month of their tax year. Most people are calendar year taxpayers making December 1 the key date. For a calendar year taxpayer, anyone that becomes eligible for an HSA between January 1 and December 1 and remains eligible on December 1 can contribute the maximum HSA limit. Basically, a person eligible for an HSA on December 1 of the year is treated as if that person were eligible for the entire year with one important caveat. The person is subject to a testing period and must remain HSA-eligible for that testing period or face taxes and penalties.

Example. Sophia, age 45, started family HDHP coverage on December 1, 2014 and became eligible for an HSA on that date. Under the full contribution rule, she could contribute up to $6,550 for 2014 even though she was only eligible for one month. Sophia will be subject to a testing period and could face taxes and penalties if she fails to remain eligible for an HSA during the testing period.

238. Why did Congress create the full contribution rule?

Congress created the full contribution rule a few years after HSAs were introduced to address the situation of a person starting HDHP coverage late in the year and then facing a large medical expense right away. Prior to 2007, individuals that started their HSA eligibility mid-year could not make a full year's HSA contribution. Instead, they were required to multiply the number of HSA-eligible months times the applicable federal limit (single or family) and divide by twelve (number of months in a year) to determine the maximum HSA contribution (the "sum-of-the-months rule").

A person could face a situation where the insurance deductible is very high but the HSA contribution limit is very low because the insurance coverage started late in the year. Not many Americans liked the sum-of-the-months rule or the math that went along with it. Congress changed the law to allow for full contributions by individuals that have HDHP coverage on the first day of the last month of their tax year. Congress also imposed a testing period to avoid abuses of this rule.

> *Example.* In October 2006, Barbara first became eligible for an HSA when her employer switched to HDHP insurance. Under the law in place at the time Barbara's maximum HSA contribution was determined using the sum-of-the-months calculation (a pro-rata amount of the yearly contribution). Barbara was only eligible from October through December so she could only contribute 3/12 of the yearly limit. Her insurance deductible greatly exceeded her HSA contribution limit. To correct this problem, Congress created the full contribution rule which if in place would have allowed Barbara to make a full HSA contribution even though she was only eligible the last three months of the year.

See the Testing Period Worksheet.

239. If an HSA owner loses the first three months of HSA eligibility in a calendar year due to FSA grace period, can that HSA owner still contribute the HSA maximum limit?

Under the full contribution rule, if the HSA owner will be eligible on December 1, 2015, the HSA owner can make a full contribution for 2015 ($3,350 for single and $6,650 for family plus a $1,000 catch-up if over fifty-five) even though the HSA owner was not eligible January through April of 2015.

See Part III: Eligibility – Other Heath Plan – Ending FSA Eligibility and Grace Periods (Q 81 to Q 84) for more information on the grace period.

240. If an HSA owner is only eligible for an HSA from January through June, can the HSA take advantage of the full contribution rule?

No. An HSA owner must be eligible on December 1 to take advantage of the full contribution rule (or the first day of the last month of the tax year for non-calendar year taxpayers). The HSA owner in this case is subject to the sum-of-the-months rule.

Family versus Single Coverage

241. What is family HDHP coverage or self-only coverage?

Family coverage is any coverage that is not self-only coverage. Self-only coverage is coverage for only one individual. Family coverage is for one individual plus at least one other individual.

IRS Notice 2004-50, See Q 13.

242. How does an HSA owner know if family or single health coverage applies?

HSA owners must determine whether they are covered under a self-only HDHP or a family HDHP in order to determine the HSA contribution limit. A family HDHP is a plan that covers the HSA owner and at least one other person. In other words, a family plan is any plan that is not a self-only plan. The extra person could be a spouse, a child or another dependent. The other individual does not need to be eligible for an HSA in order for the HSA owner to make the full contribution.

> *Example.* Sam has a family HDHP because it covers himself and his dependent son. His son is also covered by his spouse's traditional health insurance coverage. Sam has family HDHP coverage and can contribute up to the family limit. Sam can use the money in the HSA for himself, his spouse and his son regardless of the fact that they are not eligible for the HSA.

243. What is the contribution limit if both spouses are covered by self-only HDHPs?

An individual covered by a self-only HDHP is entitled to the self-only HSA limit. In the situation where each spouse has self-only HDHP coverage, then each spouse is entitled to contribute the self-only HSA limit.

If one spouse had family HDHP coverage then both would be deemed to family HDHP coverage. The self-only coverage HSA limit is approximately one-half of the family limit so the difference between self-only HSA contributions for both spouses or making a family HSA limit contribution does not matter significantly (the two numbers vary by $50 in most years).

> *Example.* Shauna and Bill each had self-only HDHP coverage in 2015. They each opened an HSA and contributed the self-only HDHP maximum of $3,350 for a combined HSA contribution and deduction of $6,700. If one of the two had family HDHP coverage then their combined maximum would have been the 2015 family limit of $6,650 ($50 less).

244. Can a couple with two self-only HDHPs combine their HSA contribution into one HSA?

No. Two spouses with self-only HDHPs must open two HSAs to reach the maximum HSA limit. Only someone covered under a family HDHP is entitled to make the larger family HSA contribution.

The answer is frustrating to couples that want just one HSA to keep their financial lives as simple as possible and to avoid extra fees. The answer can also limit a couple's flexibility in deferring income through payroll at work or otherwise. There is not an obvious government policy advantage in preventing a couple from combining two self-only contribution limits so perhaps this rule will change in the future.

> *Example.* Kari and Chris are married and are each covered by self-only HDHPs and otherwise eligible for HSAs. They want to maximize their HSA contributions by each contributing the self-only HSA limit to an HSA ($3,350 each for 2015). They would prefer to open just one HSA to simplify matters, But HSAs are individual accounts and they are each subject to the self-only HSA limit and can each only contribute that amount. They are not allowed to combine contributions.

245. What is the contribution limit if one spouse has family coverage and the other spouse has self-only coverage?

The family limit applies and the spouses can split the amount as they agree.

IRS Notice 2008-59, See Q 18. See Contributions – Married Couples.

246. What is the contribution limit if each spouse has family coverage that does not cover the other spouse?

The family limit applies and the spouses can split the amount as they agree.

> *Example.* Shane and Shelly each have family HDHP coverage. Shane's HDHP covers Shane and his kids. Shelly's HDHP covers Shelly and her kids. Together Shane and Shelly can contribute the family HSA limit and can divide that limit between them as they wish.

IRS Notice 2008-59, See Q 19.

247. Can a spouse with self-only coverage contribute the family maximum if her husband has family HDHP coverage?

Yes. The rules provide that if one spouse has family coverage they are both deemed to have family coverage. Accordingly, a spouse covered under a self-only HDHP policy but married to a person with a family policy will be deemed to have family coverage and can contribute the family limit This must be coordinated with the other spouse.

IRS Notice 2008-59, See Q 18. See Contributions – Married Couples.

Mid-Year Change In HDHP Coverage Type

248. Does the family limit rule apply to an HSA owner who changes from a self-only HDHP to family HDHP coverage prior to December 1?

Yes. The full contribution rule applies using the higher family HSA limit. However, an HSA owner in this situation will be subject to the testing period and a failure of the testing period could be costly if most of the months of the year were self-only coverage or no eligibility.

See Part VII: Testing Period (Q 355 to Q 388). See also the Testing Period Worksheet.

249. Does the self-only limit rule apply if an HSA owner changes from family HDHP to self-only HDHP coverage?

Yes. The full contribution rule applies at the lower self-only HSA limit. However, an HSA owner in this situation can take advantage of the larger sum-of-the-months rule to get a larger HSA contribution without concern over failing the testing period, provided the HSA owner does not contribute more than the sum-of-the-months method allows.

> *Example.* Jim and Jill, both under age fifty-five, are married and had family HDHP coverage for January through June 2014. In July, Jill started a new job and switched insurance and Jim changed his family HDHP policy to a self-only HDHP policy. Jim remained HSA-eligible with self-only HDHP coverage through the end of the year. Jim would like to contribute the maximum allowed to his HSA (Jill is not making any HSA

contribution). His full contribution rule maximum amount is $3,300, the self-only limit for 2014. His sum-of-the-months maximum contribution amount is 6/12 of the family limit to cover the first six months of the year or $3,275 ($6,550 × 6/12) plus 6/12 of the self-only limit or $1,650 ($3,300 × 6/12). His total limit is $4,925. If he fails his testing period, he will not owe any taxes or penalties for this failure for a contribution up to $4,925.

Catch-Up Contributions

250. What is a catch-up contribution?

Eligible individuals who are over age fifty-five are allowed to make an additional "catch-up" contribution to their HSAs. The catch-up contribution is $1,000 and does not adjust for inflation.

251. Does the catch-up contribution amount increase for inflation like the other HSA limits?

No. The catch-up amount is set by law at $1,000. The amount did increase for the first five years after HSAs were introduced by a set increment of $100 per year and was not based on inflation. Starting in 2009 and years subsequent, the catch-up remains at $1,000 and does not increase for inflation or otherwise.

HSA CATCH-UP LIMITS	
Year	2011
2004	$500
2005	$600
2006	$700
2007	$800
2008	$900
2009 and after	$1,000

IRS Notice 2008-59, See Q 23.

252. Are catch-up contributions determined pro-rata?

There are two different aspects of the catch-up contribution: one is determined pro-rata, the other is not.

- **Catch-Up Limit Not Pro-Rata Based on When HSA Owner Turns fifty-five.** The catch-up amount is not treated pro-rata based on when the HSA owner turns fifty-five during the year. As long as the HSA owner's fifty-fifth birthday is on or before the last day of the year, the HSA owner is considered age fifty-five and can increase the HSA limit by the $1,000 catch-up amount.

  Example. Peter turned fifty-five on December 31, 2015. His catch-up contribution for 2015 is $1,000.

- **Catch-Up Limit Is Pro-Rata Based on Months of Eligibility.** HSA owners do need to reduce the catch-up contribution limit on a pro-rata basis when the HSA owner was not eligible for the full twelve months of the year and is subject to the sum-of-the-months rule. However, HSA owners subject to the full contribution rule (eligible on December 1) do not need to reduce the catch-up amount but are subject to the testing period rules.

Example 1. Jim was covered under a self-only HDHP and eligible for an HSA from January 1 through March 31, 2014. Jim turned fifty-five on December 31, 2014. Jim's maximum HSA contribution for 2014 is determined using the sum-of-the-months calculation method. Jim was eligible for three of the twelve months so he can contribute 3/12 of his otherwise yearly limit. The 2014 limit for self-only HDHP coverage is $3,300 and he would add the $1,000 for the catch-up because he turns fifty-five in 2014 to get a maximum of $4,300. His maximum is 3/12 of that amount or $1,075. Isolating just the catch-up amount he gets 3/12 of $1,000 for the catch-up amount or $300 out of the possible $1,000 catch-up amount.

Example 2. Dorothy turned fifty-five in June 2014. Dorothy is covered under a family HDHP and was eligible for an HSA from January 1 through December 31, 2014. Dorothy can make a full $1,000 catch-up contribution because she is eligible all year.

Example 3. Marge turned fifty-five in June 2014. Marge first became eligible for an HSA on December 1, 2014. Marge contributed her HSA maximum including the full $1,000 catch-up contribution for 2014. She is allowed to do that because she is subject to the full contribution rule and does not need to pro-rate the $1,000. However, she is subject to a testing period. The testing period requires Marge to remain eligible for an HSA from December 1, 2014 through December 31, 2015 to avoid paying taxes and a penalty on the amount of her overage (the difference between her "sum-of-the-months" amount and her "full contribution rule" amount).

See the HSA Eligibility and Contribution Worksheet and the Testing Period Worksheet for details.

253. Can both spouses make a catch-up contribution?

Yes, if both spouses are age fifty-five or older. However, the catch-up amount cannot be combined and put into one HSA. Each spouse must open an HSA and put the catch-up amount into his or her own respective HSA.

254. Can a husband and wife combine catch-up contributions into one HSA?

No. The HSA rules require that each spouse contribute the catch-up amount into his or her respective HSA. One spouse cannot make two catch-up contributions into the same HSA.

IRS Notice 2008-59, See Q 23.

255. Can a spouse over age fifty-five elect to put the catch-up contribution into the other spouse's HSA?

No. The catch-up amount must go into the HSA of the person over age fifty-five, entitled to the catch-up, and otherwise eligible for an HSA.

Example. Nikki and Bob are married. Nikki has family HDHP coverage through her work that also covers Bob. Nikki has contributed the family maximum HSA limit through payroll deferral into her HSA for several years. Bob is older than Nikki and just turned fifty-five. Because Nikki is under age fifty-five, she cannot increase her payroll deferral by $1000 to get the catch-up amount. In order to get the extra $1,000, Bob must open an HSA and contribute the $1,000 catch-up amount because he is the spouse over age fifty-five.

IRS Notice 2008-59, See Q 23.

256. Can HSA owners make a catch-up contribution before their fifty-fifth birthday, but in the same year they will turn fifty-five?

Yes. HSA owners do not need to wait until their actual fifty-fifth birthday to contribute the catch-up amount. HSA owners do need to turn fifty-five prior to the end of the tax year of the contribution.

Note: If the HSA owner loses eligibility prior to the end of the year, then the HSA owner will only be able to contribute a pro-rated amount of both the normal HSA contribution limit and the catch-up amount.

Example. Claudia turns fifty-five in November 2014. Claudia plans ahead and makes her full HSA contribution on January 1 each year because she likes to maximize the tax-deferred earning potential. On January 1, 2014, Claudia can contribute her maximum HSA contribution based on self-only or family coverage plus the $1,000 catch-up contribution.

257. Are HSA owners over the age of sixty-five eligible for the catch-up contribution?

Yes. Any eligible individual over the age fifty-five is also eligible to make the $1,000 catch-up contribution. Some early IRS materials stated that the catch-up was available for individuals age fifty-five to sixty-five. The IRS did this because most people enroll in Medicare at age sixty-five and lose eligibility for an HSA. Individuals that do not enroll in Medicare, however, are entitled to continue to make the catch-up contribution. The IRS issued corrections for the materials that stated otherwise.

IRS Notice 2004-50, See Q 3.

Married Couples
Overview

258. Are there special rules for married couples with HSAs?

Yes. HSA law provides special treatment for spouses in the following areas:

- **Tax-Free Distributions.** An HSA owner can use his or her HSA tax-free to pay the qualified medical expenses of spouses

- **Beneficiary Treatment.** A spouse beneficiary can treat the HSA as his or her own upon the death of the HSA owner

- **Divorce Transfer.** An HSA owner can transfer assets into an HSA of former spouse in the case of a divorce

- **Estate Tax Treatment.** If a spouse is named as the beneficiary of the HSA, the treatment of the HSA may change for estate tax purposes

- **Family HDHP Treatment.** Spouses covered under a family HDHP are capped at the combined HSA family limit. Also, if one spouse has a family HDHP, then both spouses are deemed to have family HDHPs.

- **Child of Former Spouse.** An HSA owner can use the HSA to pay for medical expenses of his or her child that is claimed as a tax dependent by a former spouse (this rule is helpful in cases of divorce and legal separation).

259. What does "deemed" family coverage mean?

The law for HSAs provides a special rule that if one spouse has family coverage both spouses are deemed to have family coverage. This rule prevents a couple from doubling up HSA contributions by making both a self-only HSA contribution plus a family HSA contribution.

> *Example.* Lee and Tina are married with two kids. Lee is covered by a family HDHP that also covers his kids but not his wife. Tina is covered by a self-only HDHP. Both Lee and Tina are otherwise eligible for HSAs. Lee wants to contribute the family HSA limit because he is covered by a family HDHP. Tina wants to contribute the self-only HSA limit because she is eligible and covered by a self-only HDHP and not covered by a family HDHP. This plan does not work because of the "deemed" family coverage rule. Tina is deemed to have family coverage because her husband has family coverage. Lee and Tina must coordinate their family HSA contributions not to exceed the HSA family limit on a combined basis.

IRC Sec. 223(b)(5).

260. Does a couple's tax filing status matter?

No. The combined limited of a married couple where one or both of the spouses have family HDHP coverage is the family HSA limit. This is true regardless of whether the couple files jointly or separately.

How to Split the HSA Contribution

261. Are there exceptions as to how a married couple can split their HSA contribution?

Yes. A married couple can divide the family HSA limit using any method they want with the following exceptions.

- **Eligibility Required.** Both spouses must be eligible for an HSA to make an HSA contribution. If only one spouse is eligible for an HSA then that spouse must make the full HSA contribution. In some cases this means forfeiting HSA contributions. For example, an employer may offer to give employees HSA contributions but the employee is ineligible. That employee could not direct the employer to give the money to his or her spouse not employed by that company.

- **Catch-Up Amount Cannot Be Split.** An individual cannot put a catch-up contribution into their spouse's HSA. This means an HSA owner cannot exceed the HSA limit plus one catch-up contribution in one HSA and that's only possible if the HSA owner is eligible and over fifty-five.

- **Family HDHP Coverage.** Splitting the HSA contribution amount between spouses only becomes an issue when one spouse or both have family HDHP coverage. If neither spouse has family coverage then there is nothing to split. If each spouse has self-only HDHP coverage than each spouse can contribute the self-only HSA limit. If one spouse has family coverage then both are deemed to have family coverage.

A common choice is to put the entire HSA contribution into one spouse's HSA as that limits the added complexity of having multiple accounts and potential banking fees.

> *Example.* For 2015, Mr. and Mrs. Smith are both eligible for an HSA and are both covered under family HDHPs. Mr. Smith is fifty-eight and Mrs. Smith is fifty-three. Mr. Smith could open an HSA and put all $7,650 in his HSA ($6,650 family limit plus his $1,000 catch-up) or both Mr. Smith and Mrs. could open HSAs and split the contribution with Mr. Smith contributing $4,300 and Mrs. Smith contributing $3,350. Or, Mrs. Smith could contribute $6,650 and Mr. Smith $1,000. The $6,650 represents the highest amount that could go into Mrs. Smith's HSA as she is under age fifty-five and the $1,000 catch-up must go into Mr. Smith's HSA. Once Mrs. Smith reaches age fifty-five, she will have to open an HSA of her own to get her $1,000 catch-up contribution.

IRS Publication 969, p. 6, IRS Notice 2004-2, See Q 17, IRS Notice 2004-50, See Q 33.

262. How are contributions between spouses divided in the event of divorce?

In the year of the divorce, spouses need to allocate their HSA contributions between the two spouses per agreement for the months while married. For the months after the divorce, each spouse is entitled to his or her own contribution.

> *Example.* Julie and John are under age fifty-five, married and have family HDHP coverage. In March 2014, they divorce. Julie continues to have family HDHP coverage for herself and her children while John changes to self-only HDHP coverage on April 1. They will need to agree on how to split the combined maximum contribution for the months of marriage is $1,637.50 ($6,550 × 3/12).

> John's additional contribution limit for his nine months of self-only HDHP coverage is $2,512.50 ($3,330 × 9/12). John could contribute and report on his IRS Form 8889 up to $2,512.50 plus the amount he agrees to with Julie of the shared $1,637.50.

> Julie's additional contribution amount for her nine months of family coverage is $4,912.50 ($6,550 × 9/12). Julie would reflect on the IRS Form 8889 the $4,912.50 plus the amount she agrees to with John as her share of the shared $1,637.50.

> Julie benefits from the full contribution rule. She has family coverage on December 1, 2014 and she can contribute the greater of the amount calculated with John or the family limit of $6,550. Accordingly, Julie can contribute the full $6,550 even if she allocated a portion or all of the $1,637.50 to John (this may make it easier for them to agree to the split). However, Julie will be subject to a testing period and if she fails the testing period more of an allocation for her shared amount with John would reduce her taxes and penalties.

IRS Instructions for IRS Form 8889, IRS Form 8889.

263. Can one spouse contribute the self-only HSA limit and the other the family HSA limit?

No. If one spouse has family HDHP coverage both spouses are deemed to have family coverage. This prevents a married couple from getting a larger HSA contribution than the family maximum for the year.

Example. In 2015 Sam and Sally were married and both under age fifty-five. Sam was covered under a family HDHP and Sally was covered under a self-only HDHP. Sam and Sally's combined HSA limit for the year is $6,650, the family limit for 2015, because Sally is deemed to have family coverage.

264. What is the contribution limit if the HSA owner has family HDHP coverage but the only other person on the family coverage, a spouse, also has traditional health insurance?

An eligible person with family HDHP coverage can contribute the family HSA maximum ($6,650 for 2015) plus a catch-up if over fifty-five. That answer does not change if other people covered by the family HDHP have other health coverage.

IRS Notice 2004-50, See Q 32.

265. Can employers combine HSA contributions for spouses that work together?

No. All HSA accounts are individual accounts. Each employer's HSA contribution for an employee must be deposited into that employee's HSA and cannot be combined. This statement is assuming pre-tax HSA contributions. Employers and employees have more freedom for after-tax HSA contributions. There are a few different situations where this could be an issue:

- **Employer Contribution.** Assume a married couple, a husband and wife, both work for the same employer. The husband's family HDHP policy covers himself and his wife. The employer makes a $200 per month comparable HSA contribution for each employee enrolled in the family HDHP $200 and $100 per month for each employee enrolled in a single HDHP $100. The comparability rules allow the employer to make the $200 contribution for the husband only in this case (because he got the insurance through the employer) or the employer can elect to give the funding to all employees that have family HDHP coverage (not just those that have the HDHP coverage offered through the company). If the employer elects to give the $200 to all eligible employees, then the husband and the wife would each be entitled to the $200. In that case, $200 must go into the husband's HSA and the other $200 must go into his wife's HSA. These amounts cannot be combined and contributed to one of the HSAs.

  If each spouse elects single HDHP coverage through the employer, then the employer must give each spouse $100 month into the HSA. The spouses cannot combine this contribution: it must go into their respective HSAs.

- **Payroll Deferral.** Pre-tax HSA payroll deferrals through a Cafeteria plan must go into the HSA of the person doing the deferral. An employer cannot take money out of one employee's pay and put it into another employee's HSA.

Example. Yunqing turned sixty-five in 2014 and is no longer eligible for an HSA. In 2015, she wants to have her employer take money out of her pay pre-tax pursuant to her employer's Cafeteria plan and contribute it to her husband's HSA. Her husband is under sixty-five and eligible for an HSA. She cannot do this. Her payroll deferral contributions must go into her HSA and as she is no longer eligible for an HSA she cannot payroll defer.

Impact on Eligibility

266. Does one spouse's traditional insurance coverage impact the other spouse's HSA eligibility?

Generally, no. As long the traditional insurance does not cover both spouses, the fact that an HSA owner's spouse has traditional insurance coverage does not impact on the HSA owner's eligibility. The HSA owner cannot be covered by traditional health insurance or have "other coverage."

See Part III: Eligibility – Other Health Plan – Spouse or Children with Non-qualifying Other Coverage (Q 71 to Q 72).

267. Does a dependent child's traditional insurance coverage impact an individuals' HSA eligibility?

Generally, no. The fact that an HSA owner's dependent children have other health coverage does not impact the HSA owner's HSA eligibility. Furthermore, if the HSA owner has family HDHP coverage (the children are doubled covered by both an HDHP and traditional insurance), the HSA owner can contribute the family HSA limit.

> *Example.* Mayuuri has a family HDHP that covers herself and her two children. The children are also covered through her former spouse's traditional health insurance policy giving the kids double health coverage. Mayuuri is HSA-eligible and may contribute the family maximum amount. She can use her HSA for herself and her children.

IRS Notice 2008-59, See Q 12. See Part III: Eligibility – Other Health Plan – Spouse or Children with Non-qualifying Other Coverage (Q 71 to Q 72).

268. When an HSA owner enrolls in Medicare but keeps family HDHP coverage can a younger spouse open an HSA and contribute the family HSA limit?

If a married couple has a family HDHP, the couple can decide how to allocate the HSA family limit. If one of the spouses is not eligible for an HSA, but the other spouse is, then it makes sense to put the full family contribution into the eligible spouse's HSA. Once the money is in the HSA, it can be used for either spouse's medical expenses.

> *Example.* Staci and Evan are married and are covered under the same family HDHP. Evan has contributed the family HSA limit to his HSA plus a catch-up contribution for the last five years. Although eligible, Staci does not have an HSA. Evan turns sixty-five in June of this year and will become entitled to Medicare. This will be the last year Evan can make an HSA contribution and he is only entitled to a pro-rata amount this year (half the full contribution because he will only be eligible for half the year). Evan and Staci decide that for this year she will open an HSA and contribute the family HSA limit. She is under fifty-five and not entitled to the catch-up contribution. Evan will also make a contribution to his HSA this year of one-half of his catch-up amount for the year or $500. Evan and Staci could adjust the amounts that go into his HSA versus hers but in no case can Evan contribute more than one-half the HSA family limit for the year plus one-half the catch-up limit. Given this limitation, they decided to put the full family amount in Staci's new HSA except for Evan's catch-up amount.

269. When an HSA owner enrolls in Medicare and his or her spouse switches to a self-only HDHP plan, how does this impact the HSA contribution?

Calculating the maximum HSA contribution can be challenging for spouses that switch from family HDHP coverage to self-only coverage for one spouse. The spouse that switches from family to self-only must do a pro-rata calculation to determine the maximum. This means that spouse will get to make a contribution using the family limit for the number of months covered by the family plan and the single limit for the number of months under the single limit. The $1,000 catch-up is not impacted by this calculation.

> *Example.* Dick and Jane are married and have been covered under a family HDHP for years with Dick contributing the maximum HSA contribution plus one catch-up amount for years. Jane does not have an HSA. Dick enrolls in Medicare in August of 2015 and loses HSA eligibility. Jane, age sixty, changes to a self-only HDHP effective August 1, 2015. Neither Dick nor Jane has made any 2015 HSA contributions.

> Dick's maximum contribution for 2015 is 7/12 of the full year's contribution because he will only be eligible for seven months of the year (January – July). This amount is $4,462.50 ($6,650 family limit plus $1,000 catch-up × 7/12).

> Jane's maximum contribution for 2015 is also $4,462.50 for the first seven months of the year plus her self-only coverage for the next five months (August – December) of $1,812.50 ($3,350 + $1,000 × 5/12). Her total is $6,275.00.

> Another method to arrive at this total is she gets 7/12 of the family limit, $3,879.17; plus 5/12 of the self-only limit, $1,395.83; or $5,275.00 added together. Add in the $1,000 catch-up to arrive at a limit of $6,275.00.

> These calculations provide the maximum that can go into each spouse's respective HSA, but still leaves a lot of room open for how to do that. Jane will have to open an HSA for the family to get the maximum. One simple split is just to have Jane put her full maximum in her HSA: $6,275. This takes all the contribution away from Dick, except his catch-up amount of $700 (7/12 of the $1,000 catch-up) that he puts in his HSA. Combined they get $6,975.

Timing of Contributions

270. Is there a deadline to make an HSA contribution?

Yes. Individuals have until their tax filing due date to make an HSA contribution. For most (but not all) taxpayers, the filing due date is April 15.

IRS Notice 2004-2, See Q 22.

271. Do tax due date extensions allow for extra time to make an HSA contribution?

No. Tax extensions do not provide extra time to make an HSA contribution.

IRS Notice 2004-2, See Q 22.

272. Can an HSA owner fully fund an HSA early in the year?

Yes. HSA owners can fully fund an HSA as early as January 1 if they are eligible on that date (for calendar year taxpayers). Although eligibility for an HSA is determined on a monthly basis, HSA owners do not need to wait until they have earned eligibility for a month to make a contribution. If an HSA owner fully contributes and later loses HSA eligibility, the HSA owner may need to complete a return of an excess contribution to correct the problem.

Example. Zelda's employer implemented HDHP coverage effective January 1, 2015. Zelda contributed $6,650 (the 2015 family limit) on January 15, 2015. This is permissible as Zelda can fully fund her HSA for 2015 as early as January 1, 2015. If she loses HSA eligibility during 2015, she will have to correct an excess contribution caused by her over-contribution.

273. What's the earliest an individual can make an HSA contribution?

An HSA owner cannot make an HSA contribution for a year prior to the beginning of the year. For calendar year taxpayers that date is January 1.

Example. Xi, a calendar year taxpayer, wants to fully fund his HSA for both 2014 and 2015 in late 2014 by writing one large check. He cannot do that because it's too early to fund for 2015. If he waits until January 1, 2015, he can fund for both 2014 in 2015 at the same time because he has until April 15, 2015 to fund for 2014 and he can fund for 2015 between January 1, 2015 and April 15, 2016.

274. Can individuals make HSA contributions after they lose eligibility for an HSA?

Yes. HSA owners can make HSA contributions even if no longer eligible if they are making the contribution(s) for a period when they were eligible. This ability ends on the tax due date as that is the last date to make an HSA contribution for a year that included some months of eligibility.

Example. Jeremy was eligible for an HSA from January 1, 2015 through October 31, 2015. On November 1 he changed insurance to a non-HSA compatible plan. Jeremy never made any contributions for 2015. In January of 2016, Jeremy's accountant suggested he make a 2015 HSA contribution. Jeremy made a pro-rata contribution of 10/12 of a full year's limit because he was only eligible for ten months of the year. Jeremy could make that 2015 contribution in 2016 prior to his tax filing due date (April 15, 2016). This answer would be the same regardless of whether Jeremy had to open a new HSA or contribute to an existing one.

IRS Notice 2008-59, See Q 20. See the Eligibility & Contribution Worksheet.

275. Can an individual make an HSA contribution after enrolling in Medicare if the individual did not maximize the HSA contribution prior to enrolling?

Yes, for one last year. Taxpayers have until April 15 of the year following the tax year to make an HSA contribution. Taxpayers can still make an HSA contribution even if no longer eligible for an HSA as long as they are making a contribution for a period when they were eligible.

Example. Jim turned sixty-five on July 4, 2014 and enrolled in Medicare losing eligibility for an HSA. Jim was eligible for an HSA under self-only HDHP coverage from January through June 2014 but did not make any HSA contributions and never opened an HSA. Jim can still open and make an HSA contribution and he has until April 15, 2015 to do so. The amount Jim can contribute for 2014 is reduced because he was not eligible for the full year.

Jim can contribute up to $6/12 \times \$3,300$ (2014 self-only limit) = $1,650. Jim can also contribute a pro-rated amount of the catch-up contribution, $6/12 \times \$1,000$ (2014 catch-up limit) = $500. These contributions total $2,150 for 2014.

276. How do HSA owners know how much they contributed last year?

HSA owners' personal records should have information regarding how much they contributed. The HSA contribution amount will be reflected on HSA statements provided by the custodian and may also be available online. HSA owners will receive an IRS Form 5498-SA with the annual HSA contribution amount, but that is not required to be provided to the HSA owner until after tax returns are due. Some HSA custodians send the 5498-SA early (generally sent late January or early February) and in that case HSA owners would have the information in time for taxes (these custodians must send an updated 5498-SA if the HSA owner makes a contribution between January 1 and April 15 for the previous tax year). HSA owners that made their contributions through an employer can look at the IRS Form W-2, see Box 12 with a Code "W."

IRS Form W-2, IRS Form 5498-SA.

277. Can HSA owners wait to contribute until they have a known medical expense?

Yes, provided that the HSA owner has opened the HSA (to set the establishment date), remains eligible for an HSA (necessary to put more money into an HSA) and has not yet contributed the maximum limit for the year. Some HSA owners prefer to keep their HSA balance low and only fund the HSA when they know they will need the money. This approach may result in lost tax benefits as individuals have a limited period of time to contribute to an HSA for a particular tax year. Also this approach will not result in the building of a balance in the HSA over time to cover larger expenses. However, for individuals tight on funds this approach will allow for minimizing the HSA cost while still getting the tax benefits.

> *Example.* Susan is struggling financially and is eligible for an HSA. She opened an HSA with a $50 deposit to set her establishment date but had hoped not to put any more money into the HSA. Mid-year, Susan incurred a $250 dental bill. After she got the bill, she made a $250 contribution to her HSA and then used her HSA to pay the bill. She plans to do this for all her medical expenses - wait until she knows the cost before contributing to her HSA. This approach works within HSA laws and allows Susan to get the full tax breaks she needs for her medical expenses but also allows her to limit her HSA contributions for only known medical expenses.

IRS Notice 2008-58.

Archer MSA Contributions

278. What is an Archer MSA?

An Archer Medical Savings Account (MSA) is a tax-exempt trust or custodial account that individuals set up to pay qualified medical expenses. The Archer MSA is the predecessor for HSAs and has been largely replaced with HSAs.

IRS Publication 969.

279. What are the fundamental differences between HSAs and MSAs?

Some of the fundamental differences include:

- **MSAs Limited to Employers of Fifty Employees or Fewer.** MSAs were only available to small employers, including self-employed. With some exceptions, large employers and individuals are not allowed to have MSAs.

- **Different Contribution Limits.** MSAs do not share contribution limits with HSAs instead using a percentage of the deductible to set the limits

- **Very Limited Eligibility.** MSAs were experimental with a four year sunset after which no new MSAs could be established (except for new employees of groups that are grandfathered in). We are past that sunset date so you need to either already have an MSA or work for an MSA participating employer to open an MSA.

280. Does an Archer MSA contribution impact how much an HSA owner can contribute to an HSA?

Yes. Archer MSA contributions reduce the HSA limit.

IRC Sec. 223(b)(4)(A).

281. Does a spouse's contribution to an Archer MSA reduce an HSA owner's HSA limit?

Yes. Archer MSA contributions made by a spouse reduce the HSA limit for the year.

IRC Sec. 223(b)(5)(B)(1).

Excess Contributions

282. What is an "excess contribution?"

An "excess contribution" occurs when an HSA owner contributes more than the allowable limits to an HSA during a single tax year. The law defines an excess contribution as when an HSA owner puts more money into an HSA than the HSA owner can deduct, or if an employer is contributing for the HSA owner, the contribution exceeds what the employer can exclude from income for HSA contributions.

283. What types of contributions count in determining whether there is an excess contribution?

Most types of contributions count toward an HSA owner's total HSA limit each year. This includes: (1) contributions made directly by the HSA owner, (2) employer contributions, (3) employee payroll deferral contributions, (4) contributions made by others on the owner's behalf, and (5) IRA to HSA qualified funding distributions.

IRC Sec. 223(f)(3).

284. What types of contributions do not count in determining whether there is an excess contribution?

Some contributions do not count: (1) HSA transfer contributions from another HSA or MSA (including transfers from a spouse due to death or divorce), (2) HSA rollover contributions from another HSA or MSA, (3) FSA and HRA direct transfers (no longer allowed), and (4) contributions that are the return of mistaken distributions.

IRC Sec. 223(f)(3).

285. How do HSA owners fix excess contributions?

HSA owners need to correct the excess by removing the excess and in some cases the earnings on the excess. HSA owners can do this either before or after their tax filing due date with different results.

- **Corrected by the Tax Deadline, Including Extensions.** If an HSA owner corrects the mistake by his or her tax filing due, the HSA owner does not owe a penalty or tax on the amount of the excess contribution returned. HSA owners that discover and correct excesses prior to their tax due date are in a much better position than those discovering the mistake after their tax due date. HSA owners should take the following steps to correct the excess prior to the tax filing due date.

  - **Remove Excess.** The HSA owner should complete a distribution form (or the appropriate form provided by the HSA custodian) and request the return of an "excess contribution" and mark that the return was "corrected before the tax filing due date." HSA custodians report the return of excesses differently depending upon whether they were corrected before or after the tax due date. The return of the excess amount is not subject to the 20 percent penalty for non-qualified withdrawals nor the 6 percent penalty for excess distributions returned after the tax due date.

  - **Do Not Claim HSA Deduction on Excess Amount.** The HSA owner cannot claim an HSA deduction for the amount returned as an excess. The HSA owner never should have contributed the excess amount and cannot get the benefit of an HSA deduction for the amount.

  - **Remove Earnings.** The HSA owner must also remove any earnings that accrued while the excess contribution was held in the HSA. The earnings are any interest paid on the amount of the excess; or if the HSA held stocks, bonds or mutual funds, the amount of appreciation in value. The HSA owner will owe taxes on the earnings and must report the earnings as "other income" on the income tax return in the year the earnings are withdrawn. The earnings are not subject to the 20 percent non-qualified withdrawal penalty nor the 6 percent excess contribution penalty. The earnings are generally very small and this is not a significant tax issue for most people. The IRS, however, has its own method for calculating earnings and the earnings are sometimes different than expected and more complicated to compute than expected.

- **Corrected After the Tax Filing Deadline.** If the HSA owner waits until after his or her tax-filing due date, plus extensions, to correct an excess, the HSA owner will owe a penalty of 6 percent of the amount of the excess per year until the excess is corrected. The following steps illustrate how to correct excesses after the tax filing due date.

  - **Remove Excess.** The HSA owner completes a distribution/excess form provided by the HSA custodian requesting the return of an excess contribution and marking it as "an excess returned after the tax filing due date." HSA custodians report the return of excesses differently depending upon whether they were corrected before or after the tax due date. The distribution will be subject to taxes and potentially the 20 percent penalty unless an exception applies. See the "Alternative Approach" below for a potentially better method to fix the excess.

o **Pay 6 percent Penalty – File IRS Form 5329.** The HSA owner pays a 6 percent penalty per year on the excess amount that has remained in the HSA. The HSA owner uses the IRS Form 5329 to do this (the IRS Form 5329 provides a calculation that adjusts for some distributions from the HSA).

o **Earnings Remain in the HSA.** HSA owners that correct an excess after the tax-filing due date do not need to calculate or remove earnings.

o **Alternative Approach: Use Excess for Future HSA Contributions.** Rather than removing an excess, an HSA owner can use the excess amount as a current year's HSA contribution provided the excess amount is less than the HSA maximum contribution limit for the year (minus any HSA contributions already made). This approach does not allow the HSA owner to avoid the 6 percent penalty but does allow the HSA owner to avoid taxes on the distribution.

• **Special Rule – Amend Tax Return within six months.** An HSA owner may be able to amend his or her tax return if the tax return was timely filed and the HSA owner discovered the excess later. This special rule provides a method for an HSA owner to avoid the 6 percent penalty. The rules that provided for this are the following.

o **File Amended Return within six months.** The HSA owner must file an amended return within six (6) months after the due date of his or her tax return, excluding extensions.

o **Write Special Language on Return.** The HSA owner needs to write on the top of the return "Filed pursuant to section 301.9100-2" this amendment process provides for an automatic extension and the HSA owner should then include an explanation of the withdrawal.

o **Remove Excess.** The HSA owner needs to remove the excess amount from the HSA. The HSA owner also needs to report any earnings from the excess on the amended tax return.

o **Make Changes on Return.** The HSA owner makes all necessary changes on the amended return.

Example 1. Jim, had self-only HDHP insurance coverage in 2014, but mistakenly believed he could contribute the family contribution amount. He contributed $6,550 for 2014. His accountant discovered the mistake when doing his taxes for 2014. The accountant told Jim he needs to remove $3,250 from his HSA ($6,550-$3,300 limit for Jim = $3,250 excess contribution). Jim needs to request a distribution of the $3,250, plus the $30 earnings on that amount (the earnings amount depends on the circumstances). If Jim corrects his mistake by taking a distribution of $3,280 ($3,250 in excess plus $30 in earnings) prior to his tax filing due date (April 15, 2015), he will not owe taxes or penalties on the $3,250. Jim will have to include the $30 of earnings as "other income" on his 2015 tax return and pay taxes on that amount. Jim will not owe a penalty on the $30. Jim cannot take a deduction for the $3,250 as an HSA contribution.

Example 2. Harry turned sixty-five on July 15, 2014 and enrolled in Medicare. Harry contributed what he thought was his maximum for the year: $3,300 + $1,000 as a catch-up for a total of $4,300. Harry actually over-contributed. Harry was only eligible for an HSA from January through June or six months of the year. His maximum limit for 2014 was $6/12 \times \$4,300 = \$2,150$. Harry must remove $2,150 as an excess ($4,300 contributed less maximum of $2,150 = excess of $2,150). Harry did not discover his 2014 excess until early 2016, too late to correct before his tax due date. Harry has to remove the excess and will owe a 6 percent penalty ($2,150 $\times$ .06 = $129) provided the excess is returned before his 2015 tax due date (if not corrected the penalty would increase to 12 percent because another 6 percent penalty would be added). Harry cannot use the return of the excess as a current year HSA contribution because he is no longer eligible for an HSA. Harry will have to pay taxes on the amount of the excess distributed but not the 20 percent penalty because he is over sixty-five.

Example 3. Sari first became eligible for an HSA on December 1, 2013 when she started her self-only HDHP coverage. In January of 2014, she contributed $3,250 to her HSA for 2013 using the full contribution rule. In October of 2014, she changed jobs and lost her eligibility for an HSA. Sari failed her testing period and will owe taxes and penalty on the amount she "over" contributed, $2,979.16 ($3,250 contributed minus her "sum-of-the-months" amount for 2014 of $270.83 = $2,979.16 overage base for tax and penalty). This over-contribution is not an excess contribution and is not treated as an excess contribution. This is a testing period failure and is treated entirely differently. The $2,979.16 remains in her HSA. If she removes the amount as an excess, she will owe taxes and penalties twice on the same amount. See Part VII: Testing Period.

IRS Notice 2004-2, See Q 23, IRS Form 5329.

286. What is the penalty for an excess contribution?

If an HSA owner removes an excess contribution prior to his or her tax-filing due date, including extensions, there is no penalty on the return of the excess amount. An HSA owner may be able to get more time by filing an amended return. An HSA owner will have to pay a penalty on the amount if the HSA owner fails to remove the amount by the tax due date. The penalty is 6 percent per year until removed or used as a future year's contribution.

287. How do HSA owners calculate earnings on an excess contribution?

The rules for calculating earnings on an excess are complicated. The general idea is that HSA owners have to remove a pro-rata share of the earnings on the assets in the HSA during the period the HSA held the excess contribution. This makes sense because if an HSA owner were allowed to leave the earnings in the HSA, the HSA owner would be rewarded for making the mistake (rewarded by earning tax-deferred earnings on the amount of the excess).

The IRS created a special formula for calculating earnings on an excess contribution.

$$\text{Earnings on Excess} = \text{Excess contribution} \times \frac{(\text{Adjusted Closing Balance} - \text{Adjusted Opening Balance})}{\text{Adjusted Opening Balance}}$$

- **Earnings on Excess.** This is the amount that must be returned as "earnings" in addition to the amount of the actual excess contribution

- **Excess Contribution.** This is the amount of the excess that is being returned (not including the earnings that this formula is calculating)

- **Adjusted Opening Balance.** The adjusted opening balance is the fair market value of the HSA at the beginning of the computation period (the period immediately prior to when the excess contribution was made) plus any amount of any contributions or transfers, including the contribution that is being distributed as the return of an excess

- **Adjusted Closing Balance.** The adjusted closing balance is the fair market value of the HSA at the end of the computation period (the period immediately prior to the removal of the excess contribution) plus the amount of any distributions or transfers made during the contribution period (i.e., the HSA owner needs to add back any distributions or transfers)

- **Additional Rules.**

  o   When an HSA is not normally valued on a daily basis, the fair market value of the asset at the beginning of the computation period is deemed to be the most recent, regularly determined, fair market value of the asset, as of a date that coincides with or precedes the first day of the computation period

  o   In the case of an HSA that has received more than one regular contribution for a particular taxable year, the last regular contribution made to the HSA for the year is deemed to be the contribution that is distributed as a returned excess contribution

  o   In the case of an individual with more than one HSA, the net income calculation is performed only on the HSA containing the excess contribution being returned and that HSA must distribute the excess contribution

Example. On May 1, 2014, when her HSA contains $4,800, Petra makes a $4,300 regular contribution to her HSA. Petra is covered under a self-only HDHP and her annual limit is $3,300. Petra misunderstood the catch-up rules and believed she was eligible for the catch-up contribution, but at only fifty years old she was not eligible for the catch-up. Petra requested a return of an excess contribution of $1,000.

To determine the earnings on the $1,000, Petra needs to know her adjusted account opening balance. Her account opening balance is the balance immediately before the contribution that caused the excess. That amount is $4,800 in this example. She then needs to "adjust" it by adding in any contributions, including the $4,300 contribution that caused the excess. In this example that is the only adjustment so the adjusted balance is $9,100 ($4,800 + $4,300 = $9,100).

Her adjusted closing balance is her balance when she requests the distribution of the excess. She would need to ask her HSA custodian for this value or possibly look online if the account is valued daily. For this example that is $9,150. No other distributions have been made or she would have to adjust the balance for those distributions. Then she uses the formula below to determine her earnings on the excess were $5.46. Petra needs to include the $5.46 as "other income" on her income tax return.

$$\text{Earnings (excess amount)} = \$1,000 \times \frac{(\$9,150\,(\text{Adjusted Closing Balance}) - \$9,100\,(\text{Adjusted Opening Balance}))}{\$9,100\,(\text{Adjusted Opening Balance})}$$

$$\text{Earnings on Excess} = \$1,000 \times \frac{(\$9,150 - \$9,100)}{\$9,150} = \$5,46$$

Treas. Reg. §1.408-11, IRS Notice 2004-50, See Q 35.

288. How are earnings calculated if an HSA owner only made one HSA contribution and no distributions?

If an HSA owner made only one contribution to the HSA and took no distributions then the return of the entire balance will constitute a return of the earnings attributable to the excess. If the amount of the total balance is larger than the contribution amount, the difference is the earnings. Given low current interest rates and generally low contribution amounts, there are often very small or even no earnings attributable to an excess HSA contribution. If the amount remaining is less than the original contribution due to banking fees or loss on an investment, removal of the entire amount satisfies the rules.

289. Can the earnings be a negative amount?

Yes. The IRS formula can result in negative or zero earnings. If that's the case, the HSA owner will not have to include any earnings as "other income" on his or her tax return.

290. If an HSA owner corrects the excess after the tax filing due date do earnings need to be calculated and removed?

No. HSA owners that correct the excess contribution after the tax filing due date do not need to remove earnings. The HSA owner owes a 6 percent penalty per year of the excess.

291. Can an HSA owner use the excess contribution rules to fix other problems or to change her mind about making a contribution?

No. HSA owners cannot elect to treat an amount as an excess unless it really is an excess contribution. HSA owners that do so will have the distribution deemed a withdrawal for a non-medical purpose and the amount will be includable in gross income.

IRS Notice 2004-50, See Q 36.

292. How is an excess corrected when the HSA owner already spent the money?

If an HSA owner has an excess, the amount of the excess must be removed. If there is not enough money in the HSA to remove the excess, the HSA owner must first contribute that amount. If the HSA is eligible for an HSA and is still under the annual HSA contribution limit it may work to make a regular HSA contribution. If the HSA owner is no longer eligible for an HSA (common with excesses), then the HSA owner will need to use the rules allowing for the return of a mistaken distribution to first get funds into the HSA and then take those funds back out immediately as the return of an excess contribution.

> *Example.* Tony was eligible for an HSA for the first three months of 2014 under self-only HDHP coverage and had a 2014 HSA limit of $825. When Tony first started his HSA he contributed $2,000 believing he was going to remain eligible the entire year. Tony also faced a medical issue early in the year and spent $1,500 of the $2,000 in his HSA on qualified medical expenses. Later in the same year, Tony switched to traditional health insurance and learned about his maximum limit of $825. To correct this excess he must remove the $1,175 plus earnings by his tax filing due date. He only had $500 remaining in his HSA and cannot contribute more as he is no longer eligible. He can return to his HSA $625 of the money he took out for qualified medical expenses as the return of mistaken distributions. He mistakenly thought he could use an HSA to pay the medial expenses, but he could not because he did not have enough HSA money to do so (provided the custodian allows for the return of mistaken distributions). After the $625 is put back into his HSA, he will have sufficient funds to correct the excess ($625 returned + $500 remaining balance = $1,175 the amount of the excess to be returned). If Tony had earning on the excess amount then he would need to remove the earnings as well by returning a bit more money as the return of a mistaken distribution.

293. Does an employer correct the employee's IRS Form W-2 if it accidently contributes an excess amount and does not remove it as an employer?

No. Generally, an employer will document all HSA contributions in Box 12 of the employee's W-2 with a Code W. This includes excess contributions.

The employer could adjust the Form W-2 to show the amount in Box 1 of the W-2 as taxable income or the individual will have to report it as "other income" on the individual's tax return. There is an exception to this rule when an employer recoups HSA contributions.

IRS Publication 969. See Part X: Employer Issues — Recoupment, Form W-2 (Q 630 to Q 644).

PART VI: TRANSFERS AND ROLLOVERS

Overview

294. What is an HSA rollover or transfer?

A rollover or transfer is a method to move money already in an HSA to a different HSA custodian or trustee.

- **Rollover.** A rollover is when an HSA owner takes a distribution from an HSA and contributes it to a new HSA custodian within sixty days. An HSA owner can accomplish a rollover using a variety of techniques but each involve taking a distribution from the HSA of some or all of the funds and then moving those funds to a new HSA custodian. One method to complete a rollover is for HSA owners to write a check from the HSA to themselves. The HSA owner then deposits the check into a personal checking account, and then writes a check from the personal checking account in the same amount to the new HSA custodian for deposit into the new HSA (or an existing HSA). HSA owners may use the rollover approach to move all their HSA money from one HSA provider to another. In this case, the HSA owner would notify the current HSA provider that they are closing the HSA.

  The current HSA custodian reports the HSA distribution as a normal distribution on the IRS Form 1099-SA, meaning the HSA owner will owe taxes plus a 20 percent penalty on the amount unless rolled into a new HSA custodian or trustee within sixty days (or the amount distributed is used for qualified medical expenses). The HSA owner must tell the new HSA custodian or trustee that the HSA owner is completing a "rollover" in order for the tax reporting to be done correctly. HSA owners are only allowed to do a rollover once every twelve months.

- **Transfer.** A transfer is when an HSA owner moves money from a current HSA custodian or trustee to a new HSA custodian or trustee without taking a distribution of the funds. The money moves directly in a "trustee-to-trustee transfer." This is the preferable method to move HSA funds as there is no 60 day limit (although a transfer should occur in less than 60 days anyway) and HSA owners are not limited to one transfer per twelve month period. Plus, because the HSA owner never gains direct access to the funds, the two HSA custodians are not required to do any extra IRS reporting on the transaction. Less reporting means less chance for mistakes. A transfer also generally involves less hassle for the HSA owner as a transfer requires the two custodians work together to move the money rather than the HSA owner acting as the go between.

Form 1099-SA.

295. Does a rollover or transfer contribution count as part of the total HSA contribution limit for a year?

No. A rollover or transfer of an HSA to a new HSA is not included when calculating how much an HSA owner can contribute for the year. A properly completed rollover and transfer is also not taxable or penalized.

Note: An IRA funding of an HSA does count against the HSA limit for the year (qualified HSA funding distribution). IRA funding of an HSA is often referred to as a "transfer" or even "rollover" from an IRA to an HSA and this can lead to confusion in this area.

See Part XI: Transfers and Rollovers – IRA to HSA for the detailed rules.

296. Is a rollover or transfer contribution deductible?

No. In a rollover or transfer HSA owners are just moving HSA funds from one HSA custodian or trustee to another and they already got the tax deduction when they first contributed the money.

297. Can an HSA owner complete a rollover or transfer even if no longer eligible for an HSA?

Yes. You do not need to be currently eligible for an HSA to move your existing HSA balance to a new HSA custodian or trustee. You can open a new HSA at a new HSA custodian to receive funds from an HSA rollover or transfer even if you are no longer eligible for an HSA.

IRS Notice 2008-59, See Q 21.

298. Are in-kind transfers of assets allowed?

Yes, provided that both the current HSA custodian and the new HSA custodian permit in-kind transfers. In-kind transfers of assets are often not allowed by HSA custodians because many HSA custodians limit investment offerings. For example, a bank custodian is unlikely to allow an HSA owner to transfer a bank issued Certificate of Deposit or checking account to a new HSA custodian. Transfers of publically traded stocks and mutual funds are more likely. As brokerage becomes more popular in HSAs, in-kind transfers will likely become more common.

> *Example.* John holds Big Company stock in his HSA at Bank One. He would like to transfer his HSA to Bank Two. The law allows for John to move the shares of Big Company from Bank One to Bank Two, provided the custodians also allow for it. As actual physical stock certificates are no longer used, the transaction to move the stock basically involves moving the electronic records for the stock and Bank Two takes over the recordkeeping for the stock. If the custodians do not allow for this then John may need to liquidate his shares of Big Company, transfer the cash, and then buy Big Company stock again with the new custodian incurring some additional transaction cost and time out of the market.

IRS Notice 2004-2, See Q 24.

299. Can an individual rollover or transfer a part of their HSA?

Yes. HSA owners can choose the amount they want to rollover or transfer.

Example. Bob has an HSA that has grown in balance to $100,000. He is very unlikely to use a large part of that for current medical expenses and wants to transfer the bulk of the money to an HSA custodian that offers longer term investment choices but also wants to keep his current HSA for day-to-day medical expenses. He can request a trustee-to-trustee transfer of the amount he desires to be moved to a new HSA.

Rollovers

Overview

300. What are the basic rollover rules?

An HSA owner must complete a rollover from one custodian or trustee to another within sixty days and may only complete one rollover per twelve month period.

301. Why would an HSA owner want to change custodians?

HSA owners desire to change custodians for many reasons including: (1) better investment options, (2) higher interest rate, (3) lower fees, (4) greater convenience, and (5) better service.

302. Why would an HSA owner choose to rollover HSA funds instead of transfer the funds?

Transferring HSA funds is generally preferred because transfers are not limited to one per year, transfers are not subject to a sixty-day time period and transfers are completed by the HSA custodians generally removing some administrative hassle for the HSA owner.

There are a number of instances when rolling over funds may be desired including: (1) The HSA owner may want to keep the new HSA custodian a secret from the current HSA custodian, (2) The HSA owner may know they want to change custodians but have not yet picked the new custodian (possibly someone moving to a new city or an HSA owner that closes a current HSA in moment of frustration with the current custodian), (3) The HSA owner may want to use the funds during the sixty-day rollover window (not sanctioned by the spirit of the law) (4) The HSA owner may be better able to control the timing of a rollover versus a transfer and desire a rollover for that reason. There are other reasons as well, but generally, transfer is a better choice than a rollover.

Sixty-Day Rule

303. How long does an HSA owner have to complete a rollover?

HSA owners have sixty-days to complete an HSA rollover.

Example. Sonja takes a distribution of all the remaining funds in her HSA and closes her HSA. She has sixty-days from the date of this transaction to open a new HSA and roll the money into the new HSA.

Failure to do so will result in the amount distributed being subject to taxes and penalties and eliminate the possibility of it being rolled over.

IRS Notice 2004-50, See Q 56.

One Per Twelve Month Rule

304. How frequently can HSA owners rollover HSA funds?

An HSA owner may complete only one rollover contribution during a twelve-month period.

> *Example*. Amanda's employer contributes $250 a month into her HSA at Deep Lake Bank. Amanda is not happy with Deep Lake Bank because of poor service and she wants to roll the money to a new HSA custodian. The employer will only make its contributions to Deep Lake Bank. Amanda cannot rollover the HSA funds contributed on a monthly basis different HSA custodian or trustee because HSA owners are allowed only one rollover per twelve month period. Amanda can either use transfers (unlimited) or perform one rollover per year.

IRS Notice 2004-50, See Q 56.

Rollover of the Balance

305. Is a "rollover" the same as "rolling over" an HSA balance year to year?

No. These terms describe two different HSA actions. The term "rollover" is used to indicate the process of moving HSA money from one HSA custodian to another and is allowed once during a twelve month period. The term "rolling over" is used to indicate how an HSA balance is carried forward from one year to the next (HSAs do not have the use it or lose it rule). These are two different items and not related. The term "rollover" is also used to describe moving money from an IRA to an HSA, another separate legal event.

306. Are there any limits on the amount an HSA owner can carry over to subsequent years?

No. There are no limits and the entire balance can be carried over from year to year. Some people are beginning to build very large balances in their HSAs that will provide a fund for future medical expenses, or if the person remains exceptionally healthy, can be used for general retirement.

See Part VIII: Distributions — Age Sixty-Five Distributions.

Transfers

Overview

307. What are the basic rules for completing an HSA transfer?

A transfer is a process of moving money from one HSA custodian or trustee to another. The process is often called a "trustee-to-trustee" transfer. A transfer must take place between the two custodians or trustees involved and the HSA owner cannot obtain access to the funds. Not having access to the funds is critical for a successful transfer.

The IRS uses HSA custodians as trusted third-party information reporting entities and the IRS is not too concerned with a transaction that keeps the money out of the hands of the HSA owner because no taxable event is occurring. According, the IRS does not require any special reporting for transfers and removes the sixty-day period and one per twelve month rules applicable to rollovers.

An HSA owner can generally request a transfer either by approaching the HSA custodian currently holding the HSA funds or approaching the HSA custodian that will receive the funds. Both custodians should have a form for the HSA owner to complete authorizing the transfer and collecting the information necessary to complete the transfer.

Often the HSA custodian receiving the funds is in a better position to assist as its form will contain clear instructions to the current HSA custodian on how and where to send the funds. After the forms are completed the two custodians work together directly to facilitate the transfer using the signed forms as authorization.

The best procedure is for the HSA custodian with the funds to send the funds electronically to the new HSA custodian or to write a check to the new HSA custodian and mail it directly to the new HSA custodian. Generally the check is made payable to "ABC Bank as custodian for John Doe's HSA" or something to that effect.

308. Are HSA owners limited in the number of transfers per year?

No, there is no limit on the number of HSA-to-HSA transfers per year.

IRS Notice 2004-50, See Q 57.

309. Is there a sixty-day time limit to complete transfers?

No. There is no sixty-day time limit for HSA transfers.

310. How long does a transfer typically take to complete?

There is no set timeframe for how long a transfer takes to complete and there is lot of variance in the industry. Transfers typically take longer than HSA owners expect and two weeks is not uncommon.

311. Can an HSA owner hand carry a transfer check to the new custodian?

Probably. A properly completed trustee-to-trustee transfer requires that the transaction take place between HSA custodians and trustees without the HSA owner obtaining the ability to access the funds. Giving the HSA owner a check arguably gives the HSA owner the ability to negotiate the check. However, a check that is properly made payable to the new HSA custodian or trustee is not negotiable by the HSA owner and therefore would not violate this rule.

This answer is supported by a history of allowing IRA to IRA transfers with hand-carried checks and the IRS allows IRA to HSA qualified funding distribution to occur in this manner (the IRA to HSA funding is reported by both the HSA and IRA custodians so this is not a direct comparison).

The better practice is for the current HSA custodian to deliver the funds directly to the new HSA custodian and avoid allowing the HSA owner to hand carry the check.

To Spouses

312. Are spouses allowed to transfer HSAs assets to each other?

No (not generally). Death and divorce are only two instances when one spouse can transfer or rollover funds in an HSA in their name to an HSA in their spouse's name.

> *Example.* Bob and Jane each have HSAs and would like to consolidate their two HSAs to one now that they are married. Bob and Jane cannot transfer their HSAs to the other and also cannot set up a joint HSA. If they want just one HSA, they can make future contributions into just one HSA and then use the other HSA first to reduce the balance and eventually close the HSA. Note: Bob and Jane may want two HSAs again when they are over age fifty-five to take advantage of the catch-up contribution which must go into each respective spouse's HSA.

See Part VIII: Distributions – Death Distributions for details on transfer to spouse due to death.

313. Can a spouse beneficiary rollover or transfer funds to a new HSA?

Yes. After the death of an HSA owner, the HSA becomes the HSA of the surviving spouse named as a beneficiary. The surviving spouse can roll or transfer the HSA to a new HSA custodian or trustee. The sixty-day rule to complete the rollover and the one rollover per twelve months limit apply. The spouse can transfer the money to a new HSA without restrictions as to time or number.

314. Can an HSA owner transfer HSA funds to a spouse due to a divorce?

Yes. Divorce is an exception to the general rule prohibiting a spouse from transferring assets to the other spouse's HSA. The transfer must be pursuant to a divorce decree or separation agreement. If those conditions are met, the transaction is handled as a trustee-to-trustee transfer. Neither spouse pays taxes or penalties based on the transfer itself. The receiving spouse can use the HSA for qualified medical expenses tax-free or for any reason subject to taxes and penalties.

315. Can a divorce decree authorize the division of an HSA?

Yes, all or a portion of an HSA can be transferred to a spouse pursuant to a divorce decree or legal separation agreement.

Custodian Limitations

316. Can an HSA custodian limit the availability of transfers and rollovers?

No. The law permits the HSA owner to move HSA funds via rollover and transfer and the custodian cannot restrict that. However, if an HSA owner has to break the term of an investment account; for example a one-year Certificate of Deposit or a mutual fund with an early withdrawal fee, the HSA owner will have to pay those fees. The HSA owner may face other fees for transferring or rolling over funds as well (e.g., brokerage fees to sell investments, account closing fee, etc.). These fees are not likely considered a restriction on the ability to transfer or roll funds.

IRS Notice 2004-50, See Q 78.

317. Can an HSA custodian refuse to accept rollover or transferred HSA funds?

Yes. Although the law allows for HSA rollovers and transfers, it does not require HSA custodians to automatically accept any rollovers and transfers.

IRS Notice 2004-50, See Q 79.

MSA

318. Can Archer MSA owners rollover MSA funds into an HSA?

Yes. MSA owners can roll MSA funds into an HSA (basically change it from an MSA to an HSA). Once completed, the account will be subject to the rules for HSAs rather than MSAs. HSA rules are generally more favorable than MSA rules so the transfer will be a positive for most people, but MSA owners should review the rules prior to making this decision.

IRS Notice 2004-2, See Q 24.

IRA to HSA

Overview

319. Can an individual move IRA money into an HSA?

The law allows individuals a one-time transfer of IRA assets to fund an HSA provided: (1) they are eligible for an HSA, (2) they have a permitted IRA with sufficient funds, (3) they have not already completed an IRA to HSA funding distribution, and (4) the names and Social Security numbers are the same on the IRA and HSA. The amount transferred may not exceed the amount of one year's HSA contribution limit. The technical term for this transaction is a "qualified HSA funding distribution," not "transfer."

IRS Notice 2008-51, See the IRA to HSA Worksheet.

320. How much money can an HSA owner move from the IRA to the HSA?

The annual HSA federal contribution limit is the maximum amount HSA owners can take from an IRA and put into an HSA. The IRA to HSA funding is not in addition to other HSA contributions. Accordingly, an HSA owner needs to coordinate the IRA to HSA funding along with any employer contribution, payroll deferral, or other direct HSA contributions for the year to make sure the combined amount does not exceed the federal limit for that year.

Example. Bob is considering using his one-time IRA to HSA funding option. Bob is eligible for a family HSA limit but not the catch-up because he is under age fifty-five. At this point late in the year, Bob already deferred $50 per month in 2014 ($600) and his employer contributed $100 per month ($1,200) for a total of $1,800 already contributed. That leaves Bob up to $4,750 to fund with his IRA ($6,550 2014 HSA limit − $1,800 already contributed = $4,750 remaining).

321. What's the benefit of funding an HSA with an IRA?

Basically, this option is important for HSA owners that need another source of funds for their HSAs. A person facing large medical expenses prior to having the time to build up an HSA balance is a candidate for funding an HSA with an IRA. IRAs and HSAs are creations of the tax code and the main reason to complete an IRA to HSA funding should be tax-driven. In addition, this rule gives taxpayers a method to avoid paying taxes and penalties on an IRA distribution necessary to pay medical expenses.

> *Example.* Desmond started a $5,000 deductible family HDHP with plans to contribute $100 a month to an HSA to build up a balance to be used for his health expenses below the deductible. Unfortunately, Desmond incurred a large health expense right away requiring the immediate need for him to pay the full $5,000 deductible. He had little money in the HSA, nor did he have any other savings except his IRA. Taking advantage of the IRA to HSA funding option allows Desmond to use pre-tax dollars to pay for his medical expenses tax-free and penalty-free. He is able to avoid the normal IRA tax and penalty for premature distributions.

322. Why are HSA owners allowed to fund with IRAs?

The law gives HSA owners an additional source of funds for their HSAs outside of their current income and non-tax favored savings. Congress addressed a common concern among new HSA enrollees; the new enrollee starts the HDHP coverage without adequate current financial resources to fund an HSA. A common approach is for HSA owners to establish automatic payments into the HSA on a monthly or other periodic basis in order to adequately fund the HSA to pay ongoing and future medical expenses.

This plan works for most taxpayers. Taxpayers that face a large medical expense early in the life of the HSA prior to accumulating a sufficient reserve could face the situation of a large medical expense that is below or at the level of the deductible without the funds to pay the expense. Their IRA now provides another source of funds. Funding with an IRA, however, is not meant to be an ongoing solution to find HSA funding (taking retirement funding for health funding) so the rules only allow taxpayers to do this once in a lifetime. The law imposes restrictions on the ability to fund an HSA with an IRA and the tax advantages are not as positive as some taxpayers first assume.

323. Is it a good idea to move money from an IRA to an HSA?

Whether an HSA owner should move money from an IRA to an HSA depends on the HSA owner's personal circumstances and the HSA owner should check with a tax or legal advisor. As a general guide, the HSA is arguably a better spot for money than an IRA from a tax perspective. The key difference is that the HSA can be used to pay for medical expenses tax-free and the IRA cannot. So given the choice of having the same amount of money in a traditional deductible IRA or an HSA, many would choose the HSA. Even this basic difference requires closer examination because HSA rules require you wait until age sixty-five to take distributions for non-medical expenses and may provide reduced investment choices or higher fees.

Moving money from a Roth IRA or non-deductible traditional IRA makes the choice harder because Roth IRA contributions can be withdrawn tax and penalty-free. The decision to move money from an IRA must be made only after a careful review of both the circumstances and the law to determine if it is appropriate.

324. Should new HSA owners without savings use their IRA to fund their HSA?

New enrollees to HDHPs are often intimidated by the large deductible they potentially face. A rational response to this potential liability for some taxpayers is the desire to fund the HSA fully by taking advantage of the IRA funding law. This may be a mistake. The IRA funding is an once-in-a-lifetime option that may be worth saving. Also, the IRA to HSA transfer prevents the possibility of getting a tax deduction for both the HSA and the IRA.

Another option that works for some is to begin funding the HSA with periodic payments and hope that they experience low health care costs during the early months or years of the plan. An attraction of this approach is that the taxpayer can change his or her mind at any point. If the taxpayer does experience large medical expenses, the taxpayer can take a qualified HSA funding distribution from the IRA at that time. Of course, the taxpayer will have to reduce the amount of the IRA funding by any contributions already made thus limiting the maximum potential benefit of the law.

This option is also somewhat more attractive to taxpayers when they understand that an HSA allows for taxpayers to pay medical expenses from other sources and then reimburse themselves later when the HSA has sufficient funds.

> *Example.* Assume a taxpayer enrolled in a $5,000 deductible family HDHP on August 1, 2014, and immediately began deferring $100 per month to her HSA. In November 2014, the taxpayer contracts a rare disease and incurs a medical expense exceeding the deductible on the plan. The taxpayer is responsible for $5,000, her deductible amount. Assume her HSA balance is $300. One option she can take is to pay $300 of the expense from her HSA and pay the remaining $4,700 from other sources. Assume she pays the $4,700 from a sinking fund she started to buy a new car. She is continuing to fund the HSA at a rate of $100 per month and she can use those payments to reimburse herself for the $4,700. She can simply write herself a check each month from her HSA or she can wait until she has sufficient funds ($4,700/100 = 47 months) and just write one check. Although that's almost four years, she is allowed to carry forward this unreimbursed expense indefinitely. More likely, she will increase her HSA deferral amount.
>
> Another option is to ask the health care provider to allow for payments. This option often works for both the HSA owner and the health care service provider. A commitment to fund from an HSA receiving regular payroll deferrals provides an additional level of security to the health care provider that they will get paid and the automatic savings feature also simplifies the payments for the HSA owner.
>
> Assuming the taxpayer has an IRA, another option would be to use the once-in-a-lifetime option to fund the HSA with an IRA. In this case, because she already contributed $300 to an HSA her HSA limit for an IRA to HSA qualified funding distribution is reduced by $300.

Procedures

325. Is an HSA qualified funding distribution a rollover or a transfer?

Both. Taking money out of an IRA to fund an HSA is called an "HSA qualified funding distribution" and is a hybrid of both rollovers and transfers. The IRA to HSA is similar to a transfer because the money must move as a trustee-to-trustee transfer meaning the taxpayer cannot control the funds directly. The IRA to HSA money movement is like a rollover because both sides of the transaction are reporting to the IRS (1099-R for the IRA and 5498-SA for the HSA). Transfers are normally not reported.

Also, similar to a trustee-to-trustee transfer the money must not be accessible by the IRA/HSA owner. This rule prohibits a taxpayer from moving the funds as a rollover (taking a normal or pre-mature distribution from the IRA and then contributing that amount into an HSA within 60 days).

326. What is the procedure for moving money from an IRA to an HSA?

The money must move directly between the IRA custodian and the HSA custodian. This means that the HSA owner cannot gain direct access to the funds. Generally the HSA qualified funding distribution occurs by the IRA custodian working directly with the HSA custodian to send the funds directly. Most HSA custodians will provide a special form for this purpose (usually called a "transfer" or "rollover" form).

> *Example.* Rob want to take an HSA qualified funding distribution from his IRA to fund his HSA. He goes to his HSA custodian and obtains a transfer form with a spot for completing this type of transaction (his IRA custodian would also likely provide forms). The form will ask for: (1) the IRA custodian's name and contact information, (2) identifying features of the IRA (account number), (3) the dollar amount requested for movement, and (4) more general and account related information. Rob completes and signs the form and gives it to his HSA custodian. His HSA custodian will then forward the form to his IRA custodian. The IRA custodian will verify the information and work directly with the HSA custodian to send the funds directly (electronically or via check sent to the HSA custodian).

327. Can the HSA owner hand carry a check from the IRA custodian to complete an IRA to HSA funding?

Yes. The check must be made payable to the HSA custodian in order to meet the HSA qualified funding distribution rules. The taxpayer cannot be given direct access to the funds.

Tip: General practice is for the IRA custodian to make the check payable to the HSA custodian or trustee for the benefit of the HSA owner and then send the check directly to the HSA custodian. This relieves the taxpayer of the burden of conveying the check and eliminates one potential channel for mistake or fraud.

IRS Notice 2008-51.

Timing

328. What is deadline for an IRA to HSA qualified funding distribution?

Individuals must complete IRA to HSA qualified funding distributions during the same taxable year. IRA to HSA funding transactions occur in the year that the qualified HSA funding transaction took place.

This rule prevents a taxpayer from making an HSA contribution for the prior tax year using an IRA for funding. HSA owners are given more time to make other types of HSA contributions (April 15 of the next year for most filers). Taxpayers wishing to complete a qualified HSA funding distribution from their IRA will need to plan in advance to complete the transaction prior to tax year end. For many taxpayers it will work to simply fund for the next year if they miss the end of the year deadline.

> *Example*. Richard became eligible for an HSA on January 1, 2014 but never opened an HSA. In January 2015, Richard would like to use his once-in-a-lifetime IRA to HSA funding option to fund his HSA for 2014. He cannot do so as that distribution would have had to have been completed by December 31, 2014. Richard may decide to fund for 2014 with another source and use his one-time IRA to HSA funding for 2015.

329. Does an HSA owner have until April 15 to complete an IRA to HSA funding transaction?

No. The HSA owner must complete a qualified HSA funding distribution from an IRA in the taxable year of the HSA contribution. The rules that allow for calendar year HSA contributions to be made as late as April 15 of the next year do not apply to IRA funding. No deemed distribution dates are allowed.

> *Example*. JoAnn first became eligible for an HSA in 2014, but she never opened an HSA because of her tight financial position. Early in 2015 she incurred a large medical expense and she now wants to make a full 2014 HSA contribution. Her only source of funds is her IRA. It's too late. She cannot make a 2014 HSA contribution using an HSA qualified funding distribution from her IRA because it's already 2015 and she cannot "deem" the distribution to occur in 2014. She could still make a 2014 HSA contribution using other methods as taxpayers are given until April 15, 2015 to fund for 2014. Assuming JoAnn will remain eligible for an HSA in 2015, she could choose to use her once-in-a-lifetime IRA to HSA funding option to make her 2015 HSA contribution.

Tax Treatment
330. What is the tax impact of moving money from an IRA to an HSA?

HSA owners are not allowed to deduct the amount moved from an IRA to an HSA. This makes sense because the distribution from the IRA is treated as a "qualified HSA funding distribution" and is not subject to taxes or penalty (if an early withdrawal). HSA owners do not pay taxes on the IRA distribution therefore they do not get to claim that tax deduction for the subsequent HSA contribution.

Essentially HSA owners are trading one tax-favored account — the IRA, for another — the HSA. Financial planners generally advise individuals to maximize their tax-favored accounts. With that goal in mind, a common recommendation would be to keep an IRA as is and fund an HSA with other funds to maximize contributions to tax deferred accounts. By using other funds, the HSA owner will get a federal income tax deduction for the HSA contribution and protect the IRA for the future. The IRA to HSA funding option will generally appeal to individuals that do not have other funds available.

> *Example*. Bob takes a $6,550 qualified funding distribution from his IRA to fund his HSA for 2014. He will not be allowed to deduct that $6,550 on line 25 of the IRS Form 1040 where HSA contributions are generally deducted. Nor will he otherwise be able to deduct the amount. The $6,550 distribution from the IRA will not be subject to taxes or penalties.

Caution: This question assumes a traditional deductible IRA. Nondeductible IRAs and Roth IRAs have different tax consequences.

IRS Form 1040.

331. What is the tax consequence of moving money from a Roth IRA to an HSA?

The tax situation becomes more complicated if an individual moves money from a Roth IRA or a non-deductible traditional IRA with a basis. For the purposes of an IRA, "basis" is the amount in an IRA that is not subject to taxes when it is distributed because it never received an income tax deduction when initially contributed.

All contributions to Roth IRAs are after-tax and have basis. The earnings in a Roth IRA or non-deductible traditional IRA are tax-deferred, meaning the earnings grow federal income tax-free until distributed. The IRA to HSA rules allow the entire basis to stay with the IRA where it can be recovered at the time of distribution from the IRA. No basis transfers to the HSA.

This is very favorable treatment, albeit a bit complex to track. If an individual does not have enough non-basis money in an IRA and still chooses to move the money into the HSA, the individual will lose the basis in that amount moved into the HSA. The individual should seek professional tax guidance because losing basis could have serious tax consequences.

In limited circumstances, it may make sense to move funds with basis into an HSA. For example, if someone is facing a large medical bill with no other method to pay it, the transferred IRA money will very quickly be used to pay medical bills from the HSA. The basis issue in this case becomes somewhat moot as the money will not be taxed anyway because it is used to pay a qualified medical expense. A person in this position may be just as well served taking the money directly from the Roth IRA and using it to pay medical expenses. Individuals are allowed to take non-qualified distributions from a Roth IRA without tax or penalty so long as no earnings are returned (the return of basis following Roth IRA basis recovery rules).

332. What is "basis" and how does it relate to IRA funding of HSAs?

Deductible traditional IRAs and HSAs have no basis. This means all the money in them is subject to taxation when taken out. Roth IRAs and non-deductible traditional IRAs have basis. This occurs when the contributions made to the IRAs were not tax deductible. This amount is called basis. When the IRA owner takes a distribution of the basis (non-deductible contributions), the IRA owner does not have to pay taxes on the return of the basis. Earnings, however, in a non-deductible IRA or a Roth IRA grow tax-deferred. The earnings are subject to taxation when withdrawn (not necessarily taxed if the Roth IRA owner meets the rules to avoid taxation).

How does the IRS know whether an IRA owner is withdrawing basis or taxable earnings? The IRS asks the IRA owner on the income tax return.

The IRA qualified distributions to an HSA allows basis to remain in the IRA and not be transferred to the HSA. This is favorable in the sense that the IRA rules allow an IRA owner to take basis out tax-free. The HSA rules do not allow for basis to remain in an HSA — all dollars are taxable. Accordingly, an IRA owner would not want to transfer basis dollars from an IRA to an HSA (there are exceptions to this — if the person really needs the money for a medical expense it might make sense to transfer the basis because HSA distributions for medical expenses are tax-free anyway and the IRA distribution to fund the HSA avoids early withdrawal penalties).

> *Example.* Bill contributed $2,000 to his Roth IRA ten years ago. It is now worth $5,000 ($3,000 in earnings). He wants to complete a qualified funding distribution from his IRA to his HSA. He can move up to $3,000 without transferring any basis because the rules allow any basis to remain in the IRA (rather than requiring a pro-rata amount of basis and non-basis dollars like the IRS generally does). If he moves all $5,000, he will lose his $2,000 in basis. Note: He would need to have family HDHP coverage to move all $5,000 as this amount exceeds the individual HSA limits.

IRS Notice 2008-51.

333. Does an IRA to HSA funding distribution work for an IRA owner that is taking substantially equal period distributions from the IRA?

No. An IRA to HSA qualified funding distribution is generally not a good option for an IRA owner that is taking a series of substantially equal periodic payments from an IRA (a method to avoid the early withdrawal penalty from an IRA). A qualified HSA funding distribution from an IRA that modifies the series of substantially equal periodic payments will result in the recapture rules applying to the payments made in the series prior to the qualified HSA funding distribution. This rule will prevent most taxpayers that are in engaged in a series of substantially equal periodic payments from moving those IRA funds to an HSA.

IRS Notice 2008-51.

Testing Period

334. Does a "testing period" apply to money moved from an IRA to an HSA?

If an HSA owner moves money from an IRA to an HSA, the HSA owner will be subject to a testing period. The HSA owner must maintain HSA eligibility for the twelve months following the transaction. The HSA owner must retain eligibility for the HSA for a period beginning on the first day of the month of the qualified funding distribution and ending on the last day of the twelfth month following that month.

The rule prevents a taxpayer from enrolling in an HDHP on December first, making a full HSA contribution using the full contribution and IRA funding rules, and then switching back to traditional insurance the next month.

> *Example 1.* If an individual moves money from an IRA to an HSA on November 1, 2014, the testing period will begin on November 1, 2014 and ends on November 30, 2015. The individual must remain eligible for the HSA that entire period or the amount of the IRA moved to the HSA is subject to taxation and a 10 percent penalty. If the individual loses HSA eligibility due to death or disability, he or she will still pass the test.

> *Example 2.* If an individual moves money from an IRA to an HSA on August 5, 2014, the testing period will begin on August 1, 2014 and end on August 31, 2015. The individual must remain eligible

for the HSA that entire period or the amount of the IRA to HSA funding is subject to taxation and a 10 percent penalty.

See Part VII: Testing Period – IRA to HSA Testing Period. See also the HSA Testing Period Worksheet.

Types of IRAs Allowed

335. What types of IRAs are permitted for funding an HSA?

Only certain types of IRAs are permitted:

- Traditional IRAs (both deductible and non-deductible)

- Roth IRAs

- SEP IRAs (see limitation below)

- SIMPLE IRAs (see limitation below)

SEP and SIMPLE IRAs are only permitted if they are not ongoing plans. Ongoing plans are plans that continue to receive employer contributions. A SEP or SIMPLE is considered to be ongoing if an employer contribution is made for the plan year ending with or within the IRA owner's taxable year in which the qualified HSA funding distribution would be made. This provision essentially recognizes the fact that a non-active SEP or SIMPLE is a traditional IRA. The feature that distinguishes them as a SEP or a SIMPLE is the contributions coming into the accounts and if that is not happening then they are basically IRAs.

336. Can money be moved from a 403(b) into an HSA?

Not directly. In some cases a 403(b) can be rolled into an IRA. If a person first rolls the 403(b) into a traditional IRA, then as a next step the person can move the money from the IRA to the HSA.

337. Can an individual fund an HSA with an inherited IRA?

Yes. The IRA rules generally allow a beneficiary of an IRA to maintain the IRA for a number of years after the death of the IRA owner. These rules are complex in themselves and a non-spouse IRA beneficiary is subject to required minimum distributions. A spouse beneficiary enjoys more flexibility but will face required distributions at some point as well. In the case of IRAs, a non-spouse beneficiary cannot move the assets in an inherited IRA into the non-spouse beneficiary's own IRA. A spouse can treat the inherited IRA as his or her own IRA.

For HSAs, the IRS rules allow non-spouse beneficiaries, as well as spouse beneficiaries, the ability to move an inherited IRA into the beneficiary's own HSA. This is a favorable approach for non-spouse beneficiaries, given that the IRS also allows the distribution from the inherited IRA to count toward the required minimum distribution for the year. This provides an attractive avenue to avoid taxation and meet the required minimum distribution from an inherited HSA.

Example. Bill dies leaving his traditional IRA to his son, Junior. Junior elected to receive payments from Bill's IRA over the Junior's life expectancy to meet the required minimum distribution requirements for the inherited IRA. Assume Junior is eligible for an HSA and Junior decides to engage in a qualified HSA funding distribution from the inherited IRA to his HSA. Assume further that Junior has not taken a distribution for the taxable year and the IRA has a current balance of $1,500. Junior may take a distribution of the full $1,500 as a qualified HSA funding distribution and place the entire $1,500 in his HSA assuming he is eligible, below his HSA limit for the year and has not previously completed an IRA to HSA funding distribution. Junior's required minimum distribution for the year is considered met because the $1,500 counts towards the required minimum for the year.

338. Can an individual move money from an inherited SEP into an HSA?

Possibly. A SEP is just an IRA if it has not received any SEP contributions in the previous two years, in which case the IRA to HSA rules apply.

339. Can an individual fund an HSA with a 401(k)?

No. Qualified HSA funding distributions are not permitted from a 401(k) plan to an HSA.

Although a full review of the rules for moving funds from a 401(k) plan to an IRA are beyond the scope of this answer, some taxpayers could move money to an IRA from a 401(k) and then move the money to an HSA. This extra step is relatively painless for someone with an existing IRA that offers a money market or equivalent cash type investment. A person that must first establish an IRA for the sole purpose of using it as a conduit to fund the HSA will face a bit more complexity. IRA custodians often have some rules built into their IRA investments that penalize early withdrawals or early closings of an IRA.

340. Can individuals fund an HSA with a spouse's IRA?

No. A qualified HSA funding distributions cannot be taken from one spouse's IRA and contributed to the other spouse's HSA. The situation where one spouse has assets in an IRA and the other spouse has the HSA creates a challenge. The IRA assets cannot be changed from one spouse to the other, absent death of the IRA owner or a divorce.

Often both spouses are eligible for an HSA. The solution in that case is for the IRA owning spouse to establish an HSA and complete the IRA to HSA funding transaction. This may result in both spouses maintaining HSAs, but that is result is perfectly permissible and is sometimes necessary. This issue is sometimes frustrating to taxpayers that view the HSA and to a lesser extent the IRA as joint assets. The law treats both the IRA and the HSA as individual accounts owned by one person.

A spouse receiving the other spouse's IRA through divorce or death, could move that money into his or her HSA. In that case, the receiving spouse becomes the IRA owner and as the IRA owner can move the money to an HSA.

IRC Sec. 408(d)(9)(B).

Once-in-a-Lifetime
341. What is the "once-in-a-lifetime" rule?

HSA owners are only allowed to move money from their IRA to their HSA (HSA qualified funding distribution) one time during their lifetime.

342. Why is only one IRA to HSA funding allowed in a lifetime?

Congress established the IRA funding rule as more of an emergency measure to cover larger medical expenses before an HSA owner has time to build up a balance. The rule is not meant to be a year-to-year funding mechanism. Limiting the IRA to HSA funding to once-in-a-lifetime assures that taxpayers will not abuse the rule by moving funds annually from IRAs to HSAs.

343. Who is responsible for tracking the once-in-a-lifetime requirement?

The HSA owner bears the burden of ensuring that not more than one IRA to HSA qualified funding distribution occurs. An HSA custodian has no responsibility to track this and practically speaking is not able to track it because an HSA owner could complete a second IRA to HSA funding transaction at another financial institution.

344. What are the consequences for completing a second IRA to HSA funding transaction?

The second transaction will be treated as a taxable distribution from the IRA subject to the 10 percent penalty for early withdrawals from IRAs. The individual can claim the amount contributed to the HSA as a deduction assuming the individual is otherwise eligible for the HSA.

> *Example.* Assume a taxpayer enrolled in a family HDHP on August 1, 2013 and completed a qualified HSA funding distribution from his IRA to fund his HSA also on August 1, 2013. On January 1, 2014, the taxpayer took a second qualified HSA funding distribution in the amount of $6,550 (2014 HSA limit) due to a misunderstanding of the rules. The second IRA distribution does not meet the requirements for a qualified HSA funding distribution because it violates the once-per-lifetime rule and is subject to taxes and penalties. The subsequent contribution to the HSA, however, is permissible assuming the taxpayer remains eligible for the HSA and the amount is within the limits. The taxpayer can take a deduction for the HSA contribution on the taxpayer's income tax return.

345. Can an individual combine two or more smaller IRAs to reach the HSA limit?

No. Taxpayers are limited to one IRA funding distribution in a lifetime and moving multiple smaller IRAs to achieve the full HSA limit is not allowed. A taxpayer can accomplish the same objective by first consolidating smaller IRAs to achieve the same result.

> *Example.* Brittany wants to complete a one-time IRA to HSA funding distribution in the amount of $6,550 (2014 family limit). She has two IRAs: (1) at Bank One with a balance of $2,500 and (2) at Bank Two with a balance of $5,000. She can request a trustee-to-trustee transfer of the money at Bank One to be transferred to her IRA at Bank Two (or vice versa). After she has consolidated the IRAs she can complete her one-time IRA to HSA funding distribution.

346. Is there an exception for a second IRA to HSA funding when switching from self-only HDHP to family? What happens if the switch is from family HDHP to self-only HDHP?

Yes, an individual can complete a second IRA to HSA funding if the individual switches from single HDHP coverage to family HDHP coverage within the same tax year of the first

IRA to HSA funding transaction. In this case, the individual is allowed one additional IRA to HSA funding transfer to increase the contribution amount up to the family HDHP limit. Surprisingly, the IRS grants relief in the reverse situation as well, allowing taxpayers to retain larger family HDHP limit contributions if they switch back to single HDHP coverage.

> *Example 1. Second Allowed IRA Funding.* Assume a taxpayer started a single HDHP on August 1, 2014. On August 2, the taxpayer took a $3,300 qualified HSA funding distribution from his IRA and contributed it to his HSA. On Oct 1, the taxpayer changed to family HDHP coverage. The taxpayer then took a second qualified HSA funding distribution from his IRA on Oct 15 for an additional $3,250. This is permissible under the exception for a second qualified HSA funding distribution if the taxpayer changes from single to family HDHP coverage in the same taxable year.

> *Example 2. Family HDHP Change to Single HDHP.* Assume a taxpayer starts a family HDHP on August 1, 2014 and immediately moved $6,550 from his IRA to his HSA. If that taxpayer changes to single HDHP coverage in November 2014, the individual does not need to pay taxes or penalties so long as he met the contribution limitations in place at the time of the IRA to HSA transaction and meets the testing period.

Tax Reporting

347. How are IRA to HSA qualified funding distributions reported to the IRS?

The IRA distribution is called a "HSA Qualified Funding Distribution" and is reported as a normal (over age 59½) or premature (under age 59½) distribution on the IRS Form 1099-R. The corresponding HSA contribution is reported in Box 2 of the IRS Form 5498-SA as a regular HSA contribution. HSA custodians report the contribution the same as an employer or individual HSA contribution.

IRS Form 1099-R, Form 5498-SA.

348. How do taxpayers report the IRA funding on their individual income tax returns?

The IRS requires taxpayers to file IRS Form 8889 to sort out HSA contributions and Line 10 of that form requires the taxpayer to list qualified HSA funding distributions from an IRA. Taxpayers cannot deduct the amount on line 25 of the IRS Form 1040 as an HSA contribution.

The IRA custodian will generate a 1099-R that is important for individual's tax return. The IRS double checks that the person is being honest by comparing the IRS Form 8889, IRS Form 1099-R from the IRA, and the IRS Form 5498-SA from the HSA.

IRS Form 8889, Form 1040, IRS Form 5498-SA, Form 1099-R.

349. How does the HSA custodian report contributions coming from IRAs?

IRA funding distributions to HSAs are reported by the HSA custodian as regular HSA contributions. The IRA to HSA contribution is treated by the HSA custodian the same as employer or individual contributions.

350. Is the IRA custodian required to withhold for income taxes for an HSA qualified funding distribution?

A qualified HSA funding distribution is not subject to income tax withholding under IRC Sec. 3405 because the IRA owner is deemed to have opted out of withholding.

IRS Notice 2008-51, p. 12, IRC Sec. 3405.

FSA and HRA Rollovers to an HSA

351. What are FSAs and HRAs?

A Flexible Spending Account (FSA) or Medical FSA is an account used to pay for qualified medical expenses on a tax-favored basis. An FSA is part of a Section 125 Cafeteria plan that allows for employees to defer a portion of their income pre-tax. An FSA operates in much the same manner as an HSA but the FSA has a $2,500 maximum contribution and any remaining balance does not roll over from year-to-year.

A Healthcare Reimbursement Account (HRA) is similar to an FSA but the rules are more flexible for an HRA.

See the HSA, FSA, HRA Comparison Chart. See also Part Three: Eligibility — Other Health Plan — Flexible Spending Accounts and Healthcare Reimbursement Accounts.

352. Can employees move money from an FSA or HRA into an HSA?

No. The rule allowing money to move from an FSA or HRA to an HSA expired in 2012.

353. Prior to the sunset of the rule, did an FSA to an HSA transaction count towards the HSA limit?

No. Money moved from FSAs to HSAs did not count against the maximum HSA limits for the year.

Caution: IRA to HSA money movements DO count against the federal maximum for the year.

---

354. What were the rules for an employer that wanted to allow employees to roll an FSA into an HSA?

The rules for FSA or HRA rollovers were tough to meet and accordingly even when this option was possible, it was not common for an employer to allow it. An employer that wanted to allow its employees to roll over money from an FSA or HRA into an HSA must have met the following:

- **FSA/HRA Plan Amendment Required.** In order to roll money from an FSA or HRA into an HSA, the business must have amended its HRA or FSA plan prior to the end of the year to allow for the rollover the following year.

- **Employee Election Required.** The employees that wanted to complete the rollover must have elected to do so and must not have had a previous FSA or HRA to HSA rollover from that particular FSA or HRA.

- **Maximum Rollover Calculation Required.** The amount rolled from an FSA or HRA into an HSA could not exceed the lesser of (1) the balance in the FSA or HRA on September 21, 2006 or, (2) the amount as of the date of the distribution. Individuals that started their job after September 21, 2006 were not eligible for a rollover from the new job because they would have had a zero balance in that employer's FSA or HRA as of September 21, 2006. This maximum amount is not related and not tied to the HSA annual limit.

- **Employees Must Have Been HSA Eligible.** In order to do a rollover, the individual must have been otherwise eligible for an HSA. The individual would also be subject to a testing period.

- **No Additional Payments from FSA or HRA.** The FSA or HRA must not have made any payments to the employee after the last day of the plan year. The individual must have had a zero balance in the FSA or HRA.

- **No Previous FSA or HRA Rollover.** An employee is only allowed one FSA or HRA rollover per particular health FSA or HRA.

- **Funds Transferred Within 2½ Months.** The funds must have been rolled over within two and half months after the end of the plan year.

- **Additional Rules.** The rules get more complex, particularly around grace periods, fiscal year plans, expenses incurred but not yet claimed, and coverage by a FSA or HRA but with a zero balance.

Example. Top Toys had a calendar year general purpose health FSA with a grace period ending March 15. Top Toys offered its employees an HDHP option starting January 1, 2011. Top Toys amended its FSA to allow for qualified HSA distributions (rollovers to an HSA) and the amendment states that employees that elect an HSA rollover may not submit any additional claims after December 31, 2011, regardless of when the claim was incurred.

Jim, an employee of Top Toys, had an FSA balance of $950 on September 21, 2006 and a balance of $700 on December 31, 2010. Jim elected HDHP coverage and requested an FSA to HSA rollover of the $700 remaining in his FSA. Top Toys completes that transfer on or before March 15, 2011 as required.

IRS Notice 2007-22, Example 2.

PART VII: TESTING PERIODS

Overview

355. What is a "testing period" for HSAs?

A testing period is a special rule that requires HSA owners in some circumstances to maintain their HSA eligibility for a period of time after making an HSA contribution.

Congress created the testing period rules when it passed a law allowing HSA owners to fully fund an HSA up to the IRS limits for a year even if they were not HSA-eligible for the full year (the full contribution rule). This rule replaced the sum-of-the-months rule for some HSA owners that limited HSA contributions to a pro-rata amount of the IRS maximum based on the number of months a person was eligible for an HSA. The testing period is designed to prevent someone from making a larger HSA contribution under the new rule than they could have under the previous pro-rata rule and then switching to a traditional health insurance plan during the testing period. Basically, the testing period serves to plug a potential loophole.

HSA owners who do not maintain their eligibility for the HSA must pay taxes and penalties.

See the Testing Period Worksheet. See also IRS Notice 2008-52.

356. When do the testing period rules apply?

The testing period rules apply in two circumstances:

(1) **Eligible on December 1.** HSA owners that were eligible on December 1 of the tax year must meet a testing period. This includes people that just started their HSA eligibility on December 1 as well as someone that started eligibility on or after January 1 and remained eligible on December 1. It does not include someone that was eligible for part of the year not including December 1. The December 1 date is for calendar year taxpayers. For non-calendar year taxpayers, the key date is the first day of the last month of their tax year.

(2) **IRA Funding of an HSA.** An HSA owner using an IRA to fund his or her HSA must meet a testing period.

Any calendar-year taxpayer who makes a regular HSA contribution and remains eligible on December 1 is subject to a testing period. Or, anyone who completes an HSA qualified funding distribution from an IRA, is also subject to the testing period rules. This means that most participants in an HSA, those who make contributions every year and remain eligible year after year, are subject to the testing period rules.

Example 1. Claudia first became eligible for an HSA on August 1, 2014 and remained eligible as of December 1, 2014. Claudia is subject to the testing period rules because she was eligible on December 1.

Example 2. Rod first became eligible for an HSA on August 1, 2014 but he changed jobs and lost eligibility as of November 1, 2014. Rod did not complete an IRA funding of his HSA. Rod was not eligible on December 1 and the testing period rules do not apply to Rod.

Example 3. Assume the same facts as above, except Rod did complete an IRA funding of his HSA on October 1, 2014. Rod is subject to the testing period rules for IRA funding of HSAs and will fail the test.

357. How long is the testing period?

The testing period for regular HSA contributions runs from December 1 of the year of the HSA contribution until December 31 of the following year (calendar year taxpayers only). For HSA qualified funding distributions from an IRA, the testing period runs from the month of the rollover until the last day of the twelfth month following that month (i.e., thirteen months counting the month of the rollover).

Example 1. Tia, who was eligible for an HSA from February 1 through December 31, 2013, made a full year regular HSA contribution in November of 2013. Her regular contribution testing period runs from December 1, 2013 to December 31, 2014.

Example 2. Tia also completed a qualified funding distribution from her IRA and contributed the money to her HSA on November 15, 2013. Her qualified funding testing period for this contribution runs from November 1, 2013 through November 30, 2014.

Example 3. Carlos enrolled in his company's family HDHP as of October 1, 2013 and made a full year's HSA contribution at that time. Carlos still remained eligible under the family HDHP on December 1, 2013. Carlos's regular contribution testing period runs from December 1, 2013 until December 31, 2014.

358. Why does the testing period exist?

In 2006, Congress created three new and advantageous rules for HSAs: (1) the full contribution rule, (2) the qualified funding distribution rule from IRAs to HSAs, and (3) the qualified funding distribution rule for FSAs and HRAs to HSAs (this third rule sunset at the end of 2011 and is no longer available). These rules often allow HSA owners to make larger HSA contributions than was possible prior to 2007.

The full contribution rule is the most common of these rules and it allows new HSA owners to make a full year's HSA contributions even if they were eligible only part of the year. Prior to the creation of the full contribution rule, individuals had to do a pro-rata calculation to determine how much they could contribute to their HSA. For example, an individual first becoming eligible on December 1 would only be able to contribute 1/12 of the full limit (because they were only eligible 1/12 of the year). That individual, however, may have faced a deductible much larger than that amount. The full contribution rule was meant to aid individuals that were switching to HDHPs and HSAs for the long term, not to help someone contribute a lot to an HSA only to switch to traditional health insurance shortly after the contribution.

Overshadowed by the positive changes was the creation of the testing period. Congress wanted to limit the benefits of the larger HSA contributions to only those HSA owners that retain HSA eligibility for a testing period. The testing period stops the potential abuse of using the full contribution rule then changing to traditional insurance, albeit by adding a fair amount of complexity to the HSA rules. HSA owners that fail the testing period are basically being pushed back into the pre-2007 rule for all HSA owners – the sum-of-the-months method.

359. What is a calendar year taxpayer versus a non-calendar year taxpayer?

Most taxpayers use a calendar-year and this book assumes taxpayers are using a calendar year. Individuals generally must adopt a calendar year as their tax year. Most individuals file based on a calendar year the first time they file and would need IRS permission to change. An individual can adopt a fiscal year, provided that the individual maintains her or his records and books on the basis of the adopted fiscal year.

IRS Pub. 538.

360. Is the testing period based on a calendar or fiscal year?

The testing period is computed on a calendar year for calendar year taxpayers for regular contributions (December 1 through December 31 of the next year) and runs for a thirteen month period for HSA qualified funding distributions from IRAs.

361. Who is responsible to track the testing period?

The HSA owner is responsible to understand the testing period rules, track the testing period and report any failures of the testing period. Neither the HSA custodian nor an employer bears any responsibility for tracking the testing period.

Failed Testing Period

362. How does an HSA owner fail the testing period?

HSA owners fail the testing period by not remaining HSA-eligible for their testing period.

> *Example.* Carlos enrolled in his company's family HDHP as of October 1, 2013. Carlos still remained eligible under the family HDHP on December 1, 2013. Carlos's testing period runs from December 1, 2013 until December 31, 2014. On July 1, 2014, Carlos loses his job and drops all his health insurance. He failed his testing period by not remaining eligible for an HSA from December 1, 2013 through December 31, 2014. Carlos must pay taxes and a penalty.

363. Do HSA owners fail the testing period if they remain covered by an HDHP but lose HSA eligibility for a different reason?

Although the most common reason to lose HSA eligibility is a change in insurance coverage, other events can also cause someone to become ineligible for an HSA. These events also cause a failed testing period.

> *Example.* Mary Jo, age sixty-four, first became eligible for an HSA on December 1, 2013, under a self-only HDHP and she contributed $3,250 to her HSA for 2013. In 2014, Mary Jo turned sixty-five and enrolled in Medicare. She remained covered under her self-only HDHP but lost HSA eligibility because of her Medicare coverage. She failed her testing period and must pay taxes and penalties.

With better knowledge and planning she would have known to only contribute 1/12 of the 2013 limit, or $270.83, because she should have anticipated enrolling in Medicare in 2014. If she had limited her contribution amount to $270.83 she would still have been subject to the testing period, would still have failed the testing period, but would not owe any taxes or penalties. See examples of calculating the penalty.

364. If an HSA owner changes type of HDHP coverage (from self-only to family or vice versa) does that cause a failure in the testing period?

No. If an HSA owner changes from self-only HDHP coverage to family HDHP coverage or from family HDHP coverage to self-only during the testing period, the HSA owner will still pass the testing period. This assumes the HSA owner remains otherwise eligible for an HSA.

Example. Maria enrolled in a family HDHP effective December 1, 2013 and contributed the family maximum of $6,450 in December of 2013. In July of 2014, she switched to self-only HDHP coverage. This change occurred during her testing period. Maria remained covered under the self-only HDHP until December 31, 2014. Maria passes her testing period.

Calculating the Amount to Base Penalties

365. How are taxes and penalties calculated for a failed testing period?

HSA owners that fail to meet the testing period must calculate the amount of an HSA contribution they could have made under the sum-of-the-months rule and then compare that amount to their actual contribution. If their actual contribution is larger, the HSA owner will owe taxes and penalties on the difference. The sum-of-the-months calculation determines the amount that a taxpayer would have been allowed to contribute under the pre-2007 law and a failed testing period essentially results in a taxpayer having to return to that potentially lower contribution amount.

Accordingly, HSA owners that fail the testing period first need to calculate their sum-of-the months' amount. The chart below is designed to assist HSA owners in the calculation (the IRS provides a different chart method to calculate the same number illustrated in the next question). Please note that this chart is for regular HSA contributions only and is not for IRA funding of an HSA.

	Sum of the Months Contribution Worksheet	Individual	Family
A	Enter Total Amount Actually Contributed to HSA for Tax Year[1]		
B	Federal Limit (this limit changes every year for inflation).	$3,300 (2014) $3,350 (2015)	$6,550 (2014) $6,650 (2015)
C	Catch-Up Contribution (if between ages 55-65 add $1,000)		
D	Add B + C = Total Federal Limit		

	Sum of the Months Contribution Worksheet	Individual	Family
E	Divide D by 12 = Monthly Contribution Eligibility		
F	Insert # of Months Eligible in the Year[2]		
G	Multiply E × F = Total Eligible Amount Based on Sum of Months		
H	Subtract G from A = Base for Taxes & Penalty[3]		

[1] This includes all employer and individual contributions – not HSA to HSA rollover or transfer amounts.
[2] HSA contribution amounts are determined on a monthly basis and then aggregated. To determine how much you may contribute, you must determine the number of months you were covered by a HDHP and otherwise eligible as of the first day of that month.
[3] If zero or negative, no taxes or penalty owed. If a positive number, you owe taxes and a 10% penalty on this amount. File IRS Form 8889. You should leave this amount in the HSA and use if for eligible medical expenses. De not take out as the return of an excess contribution or you may owe additional taxes and penalties on that distribution as well.

Example. Leleja first became eligible for an HSA on December 1, 2013 and she contributed $3,250, the maximum HSA limit for 2013 under the full contribution rule. In April of 2014, she changed her job and lost eligibility for an HSA. Her testing period runs from December 1, 2013 to December 31, 2014 so she failed the testing period. The chart calculates her base for taxes and penalties. She has to pay income taxes and a 10 percent penalty on $2,979.16 (penalty of $298).

	Sum of the Months Contribution Worksheet	Individual	Family
A	Enter Total Amount Actually Contributed to HSA for Tax Year[1]	$3,250	
B	Federal Limit (this limit changes every year for inflation).	$3,250 (2013)	$6,450 (2013)
C	Catch-Up Contribution (if between ages 55-65 add $1,000)	$0	
D	Add B + C = Total Federal Limit	$3,250	
E	Divide D by 12 = Monthly Contribution Eligibility	$270.83	
F	Insert # of Months Eligible in the Year[2]	1	
G	Multiply E × F = Total Eligible Amount Based on Sum of Months	$270.83	
H	Subtract G from A = Base for Taxes & Penalty[3]	$2,979.16	

[1] This includes all employer and individual contributions – not HSA to HSA rollover or transfer amounts.
[2] HSA contribution amounts are determined on a monthly basis and then aggregated. To determine how much you may contribute, you must determine the number of months you were covered by a HDHP and otherwise eligible as of the first day of that month.
[3] If zero or negative, no taxes or penalty owed. If a positive number, you owe taxes and a 10% penalty on this amount. File IRS Form 8889. You should leave this amount in the HSA and use if for eligible medical expenses. De not take out as the return of an excess contribution or you may owe additional taxes and penalties on that distribution as well.

366. How is the failed testing period calculation performed when the HSA owner had both self-only and family HDHP coverage?

The calculation is performed the same as other testing period failures: the HSA owner must compare the sum-of-the-months' calculation to the actual calculation and pay taxes and penalties on the difference. The calculation is more complex because in order to calculate the sum-of-the-months' amount, some months will be calculated using the family limit and others will be calculated using the self-only limit.

Example. Erica, age thirty-nine, had self-only HDHP coverage on January 1, 2013. Erica changed to family HDHP coverage on November 1, 2013. Because Erica had family HDHP coverage on December 1, she was eligible to contribute up to the 2013 family HSA maximum of $6,450 under the full contribution rule. Erica contributed the full $6,450.

Erica is subject to a testing period that runs from December 1, 2013 until December 31, 2014. In March of 2014, Erica changed jobs and lost her eligibility for an HSA. She failed her testing period.

Erica must calculate her maximum contribution amount under the sum-of-the-months' method and compare it to her actual contribution ($6,450) to determine her taxes and penalty. Erica was eligible under a self-only HDHP from January through the end of October or ten months of the year. For each of these months, she was eligible to contribute 1/12 of the self-only limit of $3,250 for 2013 for a total eligible contribution of $2,708.33 (10 × $270.83 the monthly eligible amount). She was also eligible under a family HDHP for the two months of November and December for an additional contribution amount of $1,075 (2/12 × $6,450 = $1,075). Her combined limit for the self-only months, $2,708.33, plus the family months, $1,075, equals her sum-of-the-months' limit of $3,783.33.

She then takes her actual contribution and subtracts her sum-of-the-months calculated amount to get her base for taxes and penalties: $6,450 (actual contribution) - $3,783.33 (sum-of-the-months) = $2,666.67. She owes income taxes plus a 10 percent penalty on $2,666.67 for failing her testing period.

The IRS encourages the use of a chart method to calculate this number as illustrated below.

IRS Chart to Determine Sum-of-the-months Contribution Amount for this Example

January	$3,250
February	$3,250
March	$3,250
April	$3,250
May	$3,250
June	$3,250
July	$3,250
August	$3,250
September	$3,250
October	$3,250
November	$6,450
December	$6,450
$45,400 ÷ 12 = $3,783.33	

IRS Publication 969.

367. How does the calculation work when an HSA owner had both family and self-only coverage during the year but had self-only coverage on December 1?

The same rules as the question above apply. The reason this question is separated is that the full contribution rule requires the HSA to review what type of plan coverage is in place as of December 1 (for calendar year taxpayers). If self-only coverage is in place as of December 1, then the self-only limit applies. A person in this situation is less likely to face taxes or penalties for failure to meet the testing period because the months of family coverage will increase the contribution limit and the self-only coverage in place as of December 1 will limit the amount of the contribution. An individual in this situation is more likely to face an excess contribution than penalties for a failed testing period. The full contribution generally increases the amount a person can contribute to an HSA over the sum-of-the-months method however, in this situation the full contribution rule results in a lower total than the sum-of-the-months method.

> *Example.* Pete enrolled in a family HDHP on January 1, 2013 and was a qualified individual on that date. He immediately contributed the full $6,450 HSA limit for the year anticipating that he would be covered the full year. Pete changed to self-only HDHP coverage on September 1, 2013. Pete's sum-of-the-months contribution limit is 8/12 × $6,450 (2013 family limit) + 4/12 × $3,250 (2013 self-only limit) = $5,383.33. Pete's full contribution rule limit is the self-only limit of $3,250 because he was covered by self-only coverage as of December 1, 2013. Pete can contribute the greater of his sum-of-the-months limit ($5,383.33) or his full contribution rule limit ($3,250). Pete must remove $1,066.67 from his HSA as the return of an excess contribution by April 15, 2014 ($6,450 − $5,383.33). This is an excess contribution issue, not a failed testing period issue.

> If Pete also fails his testing period by not remaining eligible from December 1, 2013 through December 31, 2014, he will not face any additional taxes or penalties. His sum-of-the-months' amount is $5,383.33 and his contribution amount was $5,383.33 after he corrected the excess.

Penalties

368. What is the penalty for failure to meet the testing period?

The penalty is ten percent of the amount of over contribution (the difference between the amount contributed and the sum-of-the-months calculated amount). Plus, the HSA owner owes federal and possible state income taxes on that amount.

369. Did the penalty for failure to meet the testing period increase to 20 percent?

No. Although the penalty for non-eligible medical expense distributions increased to 20 percent under the Affordable Care Act, the failed testing period penalty remains at 10 percent.

370. Are disability and death exceptions to the testing period penalty?

If the failure to remain HSA-eligible while under a testing period for the HSA results from death or disability of the HSA owner, then the HSA owner essentially passes the test because no taxes or penalties are owed. This exception applies to both the full contribution year testing and to IRA to HSA funding testing periods. The HSA owner is not subject to taxes or the 10 percent penalty that applies to testing period failures.

IRC Sec. 223(b)(8)(B)(ii). See also IRS Pub 969.

371. Is obtaining age sixty-five an exception to the testing period penalty?

No. Although sixty-five year olds do not incur the 20 percent penalty for non-medical distributions, they do still incur the 10 percent penalty for failing to meet the testing period. Turning sixty-five and enrolling in Medicare is actually a likely triggering event for many

HSA owners to fail their testing period. Individuals knowing they are turning sixty-five and will enroll in Medicare should prepare for failing the testing period by only contributing the sum-of-the-months' amount.

372. Does a failed testing period result in additional state taxes?

Whether an HSA owner owes additional state income taxes, and potentially a state penalty, depends on state law. If the HSA owner originally got a state income tax deduction for the HSA contribution, the HSA owner will likely owe state taxes on the amount calculated (many states use federal tax deductions as a method to determine state income tax deductions).

373. How do HSA owners actually pay the taxes and penalties for a failed testing period?

HSA owners pay the tax and penalty on IRS Form 8889, Part III. This form is a required attachment to the IRS Form 1040 series for HSAs owners in any year an HSA owner makes a contribution or takes a distribution so most HSA owners are filing this form anyway and will just need to complete the additional section.

IRS Form 8889, Part III, IRS Form 1040.

Failed Testing Period and Excess Contributions Compared

374. Is failing the testing period the same as making an excess contribution?

No. HSA owners must be careful in not confusing failed testing periods and excess contributions. A failed testing period results from not remaining eligible for the testing period. An excess contribution results from contributing more than the HSA limits allow. The full contribution rule increases the HSA limits for individuals eligible on December 1. The increased limits under the full testing period are used for individuals' eligible on December 1 for the purposes of determining whether an excess contribution occurred or not.

A key reason to get the distinction between excesses and testing period failures correct is the very different tax treatment. The base amount calculated for taxes and penalties due to a failed testing period must remain in the HSA. This is counter-intuitive for most people and especially for HSA custodians. The IRS has trained the industry over the years that if someone puts too much money into an HSA (or IRA), they need to take it out (excesses are removed). Not in this case. The overage amount remains in the HSA.

> *Example 1.* Sara enrolled in a self-only HDHP and was eligible for an HSA starting May 1, 2013. She contributed her federal HSA maximum amount of $3,250 on May 1. Sara remained eligible on December 1, 2013, the start of her testing period. Sara does not have an excess because she contributed her maximum HSA limit – not an excess over that maximum. On February 1, 2014, Sara started work at a new company, received traditional health insurance coverage, and lost HSA eligibility. Sara failed her testing period because she did not remain eligible until December 31, 2014.
>
> Sara must calculate her 2013 HSA contribution using the sum-of-the-months' formula and compare that to what she contributed. The sum-of-the-months' formula amount is $2,166.66 (Sara was eligible for

eight months of the year × $3,250 divided by 12 = $2,166.66). Sara then subtracts the $2,166.66 from her actual contribution of $3,250 to get $1,083.33. Sara must pay taxes and a 10 percent penalty on that amount. She leaves the $1,083.33 in the HSA and does not treat it as an excess contribution. To avoid future taxes and penalties she can use this money for qualified medical expenses.

Example 2. Assume the same facts as above except that Sara mistakenly believes the $1,083.33 was an excess contribution and she removed the $1,083.33 from her HSA as the return of an excess contribution. In addition to having to pay taxes and a 10 percent penalty on the $1,083.33 for failing the testing period, she will also have to pay taxes and a 20 percent penalty on the same $1,083.33 again for taking money out of an HSA for a non-eligible medical expense.

Example 3. Assume the same facts as the first example, except that Sara lost her HSA eligibility November 1, 2013. She is no longer subject to the testing period because it only applies to people eligible as of December 1. Instead she must calculate her contribution amount using the sum-of-the-months' method. She was eligible for six months of the year (May-October) so she gets half the annual limit or $1,625 (6 x $3,250 ÷ 12 = $1,625). She actually contributed $3,250 so she must remove $1,625 ($3,250 actual contribution –$1,625 Sara's limit) as the return of an excess contribution prior to April 15, 2014.

375. How is an HSA owner taxed when the HSA owner fails a testing period and then tries to correct it by removing it as an excess?

Failing the testing period does not result in an excess contribution. Testing period rules and excess contribution rules are different. It is easy to confuse the two, but the tax consequences of confusion can be severe.

An HSA owner that treated a failed testing period as an excess contribution, will owe taxes and penalties twice. Once for failing the testing period (taxes plus a 10 percent penalty) and a second time for a non-eligible distribution (taxes plus a 20 percent penalty). An HSA owner that is disabled or dead is granted an exception. HSA owners over sixty-five or meeting another exception to the 20 percent distribution from the HSA can avoid the HSA penalty, but not the income taxes.

IRS Notice 2008-52 Example 9, IRS Notice 2004-50, See Q 36.

Reporting

376. How do custodians report failed testing periods?

Interestingly, the HSA custodian does not report a failed testing period. The HSA owner owes taxes and penalties on the amount that the HSA owner contributed that were more than the testing period calculation allowed. The HSA owner pays the tax and penalty on his or her income tax return without any reporting or action by the HSA custodian. The "overage" amount remains in the HSA and is available for use for qualified medical expenses (or otherwise).

If an HSA owner tries to correct the failed testing period by assuming the amount is an excess (a very logical, albeit wrong, assumption), the HSA owner will have to pay a double tax and penalty (once for failing the testing period and a second time for taking money out of the HSA for a non-eligible medical expense because that's what the return of the excess will be treated as).

377. Does the custodian have any responsibility regarding the testing period?

No. The HSA custodian does not have any responsibility regarding the testing period. From a customer service prospective, HSA custodians are likely to make educational information available regarding the testing period, but HSA custodians are not in a position to know an individual's ongoing eligibility for an HSA.

The HSA owner, not the HSA custodian, is responsible for meeting the testing period and paying the taxes and penalties for a testing period failure. Given the complication of the testing period rules and the burden falling on the taxpayer, this is likely an area with high noncompliance.

IRA to HSA Testing Period
Overview

378. Is there a separate testing period for IRA to HSA money movements?

Yes, if an individual moves money from an Individual Retirement Account (IRA) a different testing period applies.

379. What is the testing period for IRA to HSA funding?

The testing period starts in the month in which the contribution is completed and ends on the last day of the thirteenth month following. The IRS instructions to the Form 8889 state it in another manner: "[t]he testing period begins with the last month of your tax year and ends on the last day of the twelfth month following that month."

> *Example.* A person that moved money from an IRA to an HSA on May 17, 2014 has a testing period that starts May 1, 2014 and ends May 31, 2015. Failure to remain eligible during the testing period results in taxes and penalties on the amount moved. This test is separate from the test for regular HSA contributions.

IRS Form 8889.

380. What is the testing period if an IRA to HSA funding transaction starts in one month and finishes in the next month?

The IRS guidance on when the testing period starts for an HSA qualified funding distribution simply references when the transaction is "made." In practice, the process of requesting an HSA qualified funding distribution from an IRA can take some time. Generally, the HSA owner will complete a transfer/rollover request form with the HSA custodian properly documenting that the HSA owner requests an HSA qualified funding distribution from the IRA. The HSA custodian will forward that completed and signed form to the IRA custodian. The IRA custodian will generally accept that form or may require that the HSA/IRA owner complete its own form. After accepting the form, the IRA custodian will prepare a check and forward the check to the HSA custodian (or directly move the money electronically or in another acceptable fashion). If an individual starts this process near the end of one month, it may very well not be completed until the next month. This leaves a question as to when the testing period starts. Although the rules do not directly address this issue, a logical conclusion is that an HSA qualified funding distribution is "made" when it is completed with the funds arriving at the HSA custodian.

> *Example.* Jessica approached her HSA custodian on March 25 regarding how to accomplish moving money from her IRA to her HSA. Jessica's HSA custodian provided Jessica a transfer/rollover form that it uses for these transactions and works with Jessica to properly complete and sign the form. Jessica completes and signs the form on March 25 and leaves it with her HSA custodian. Her HSA custodian forwards the form to Jessica's IRA custodian on March 26. Jessica's IRA custodian is located in another state and does not receive the request until March 29. The IRA custodian puts the request into its work flow and prepares and mails a check to the HSA custodian on April 2. The HSA custodian receives the check on April 5 and deposits it into Jessica's HSA. A logical interpretation of the rules is that Jessica's testing period runs from April 1 through April 30 of the next year. The HSA qualified funding distribution was "made" on April 5, the date the funds arrived at the HSA custodian completing the transaction.

Failed Testing Period

381. What happens when an HSA owner fails the IRA to HSA testing period?

An HSA owner's failure to maintain the testing period results in the amount of the qualified HSA funding distribution being included in income and subject to the 10 percent penalty (the amount moved from the IRA to the HSA). The money now in the HSA remains in the HSA.

An exception exists if the failure is due to disability or death. Any earnings attributable to the qualified HSA funding distribution are not subject to taxation or the penalty.

Caution: If an HSA owner fails the testing period, the money remains in the HSA and is not distributed in connection with the failed test.

> *Example.* Nate, age forty-five, is a qualified individual with family HDHP coverage as of January 1, 2014 and remains eligible through December 31, 2014. Nate's maximum HSA contribution limit for 2014 is $6,550 (the legal 2014 HSA limit). On April 2, 2014, Nate completes a direct trustee-to-trustee transfer (HSA qualified funding distribution) of $5,000 from his IRA to his HSA. The $5,000 is an HSA qualified funding distribution and is not subject to the normal early withdrawal penalty or taxes. Nate's testing period for the IRA to HSA funding runs from April 1, 2014 through April 30, 2015. Nate ceases to be HSA-eligible as of January 1, 2015. Nate must include the $5,000 in his gross income plus pay an additional 10 percent tax ($500) for failure to meet the testing period.

382. Do HSA owners have to amend their tax return for a failed testing period?

No. The taxes and penalties are owed in the current calendar year so HSA owners are not required to amend the tax return for the year they made the HSA contribution.

See IRS Form 8889.

383. What happens when HSA owner completes two IRA to HSA qualified funding distributions and then fails the testing period?

In limited circumstances a taxpayer could complete two HSA qualified funding distributions from IRAs (a change from self-only HDHP to family HDHP in the year of the qualified

HSA funding distribution). In this case, it's possible that the HSA owner could pass the testing period for one of the funding transactions and not the other.

> *Example – Application of Testing Period*. Juan enrolled in a self-only HDHP on March 1, 2013. On April 20, 2013 Juan completed a qualified HSA funding distribution of $3,250 to fund his HSA. On August 1, Juan switches to a family HDHP and completes a second qualified HSA Funding distribution of another $3,200 ($6,450 family limit – $3,250 already contributed = $3,200) on August 2. The first qualified HSA funding distribution has a testing period that runs from April 1, 2013 to April 30, 2014. The second qualified HSA funding distribution has a testing period that runs from August 1, 2013 through August 31, 2014. The two tests are separate and the Juan could pass one and fail the other.

> *Example – Failed Test*. Assume now that Juan enrolled in a traditional health plan on May 20, 2014. Juan met the testing period for the first qualified HSA funding distribution that ran from April 1, 2013 to April 30, 2014. This contribution is not subject to tax or penalty under the testing period rules. The second qualified HSA funding distribution testing period ran from August 1 through August 31 and Juan failed to remain HSA-eligible during this entire period and failed the test. Juan must include in income the $3,200 from the second qualified HSA funding distribution in income plus pay a 10 percent penalty of $320.

See Testing Period FAQs for more detail. IRC Sec. 408(d)(9)(D), IRC Sec. 408(d)(1) or (2), and IRC Sec. 72(t)), IRS Notice 2008-51.

Interaction of IRA Funding and Full Contribution Rule

384. Can the two different testing periods ever interact with each other?

Yes. The two testing periods are separate but in limited circumstances the two testing periods can interact.

385. What happens when an HSA owner funds the HSA both directly and with an IRA and then fails the testing period for the regular contribution?

Although the tests generally run separately with no interaction, in some limited circumstances special rules apply. Special rules apply when a taxpayer makes both regular HSA contributions under the full contribution rule and engages in a qualified HSA funding distribution from an IRA and fails one or both of the tests. This is unusual because often individuals that do a HSA qualified funding from an IRA take full advantage of the once-in-a-lifetime opportunity by fully funding with the IRA and not also contributing cash separately to the HSA. However, an may have contributed some money or otherwise the HSA owner make HSA contributions.

In the case where both types of funding do occur, there is an additional step added to determine the amount of tax or penalty: a comparison between the actual cash contribution and the amount calculated. The taxpayer only pays a tax and penalty on the lesser of: (1) the amount that would otherwise be included under the sum-of-the-months calculation compared to the actual contribution, and (2) the amount of contributions to the HSA for the taxable year other than the amount contributed through qualified HSA funding distributions. This rule is a bit confusing and best shown through the examples below.

> *Example 1. Fails Full Contribution Rule Testing Period*. Greg, age twenty-five, enrolled in a family HDHP and was HSA-eligible as of July 1, 2013 and remained eligible on December 1, 2013. Greg took a $4,000 qualified HSA funding distribution from the IRA on July 15 to fund the HSA. Also on July 15, Greg contributed

$2,450 as a regular HSA contribution to reach the $6,450 federal HSA 2013 maximum, taking advantage of the full contribution rule.

Greg's testing period for the qualified HSA funding distribution runs from July 1, 2013, through July 31, 2014. The testing period for the regular contribution runs from December 1, 2013, through December 31, 2014. Assume Greg ceases to be HSA-eligible on August 15, 2014. Greg met the testing period for the IRA to HSA funding, but failed the testing period for the regular contribution.

To determine the tax and penalty owed for the testing period failure, Greg must first calculate the sum-of-the-months amount for 2013: 6 (months of eligibility) × $6,450 (maximum family HDHP limit)/12 (number of months in a year) = $3,225.

Without a special rule, the tax and penalty base amount would be $3,225 ($6,450 (amount contributed) − $3,225 (Sum-of-the-months) = $3,225). The special rule takes the $3,225 calculation and compares it to the amount actually contributed in cash (not counting the IRA funding) or $2,450. The taxpayer only pays taxes and penalties on the lesser of the two, or $2,450 in this case (10 percent of $245):

The answer makes sense as Greg passed the test for the IRA funding and should not have to pay taxes or penalties on that amount.

Example 2. Fails Full Contribution Rule Testing Period. Assume the same facts as above except that Greg only took $1,000 from his IRA as an HSA qualified funding distribution and made an additional cash contribution of $5,450 to reach the full HSA limit of $6,450 for 2013.

Greg runs the same calculations as the first example to arrive at a sum-of-the-months' contribution limit of $3,225. The normal rule would have the taxpayer pay tax and penalty on the difference between the amount actually contributed and the sum-of-the-months method (if smaller) or $6,450−$3,225 = $3,225.

The special rule requires the taxpayer to pay the tax on the lesser of the $3,225 calculated amount or the actual cash contribution made $5,450 in this case (not including the IRA to HSA contribution). The $3,225 is less and that is the amount Greg must include in taxes and pay a penalty of $322.50 (10 percent).

Example 3. Fails Both Testing Periods. Assume the same facts as example 1 above, except that Greg loses HSA eligibility as of January 1, 2014 and fails both testing periods. In this case, the $4,000 HSA qualified funding distribution failed the testing period and must be included in income and subject to the 10 percent penalty for failure to meet the testing period ($400).

The $2,450 cash contribution also failed the testing period. Greg must calculate his sum-of-the-months contribution amount which he already did in example 2: $3,225. Greg normally would have to pay taxes and the 10 percent penalty on the difference between his actual contribution $6,450 less his sum-of-the-months calculated amount $3,225 = $3,225. However, for this special calculation, Greg only needs to pay tax and penalty of the lesser of the sum of the month's calculated amount or the actual cash amount contributed $2,450. In this case, Greg owes the tax and penalty on the base amount of $2,450.

The end result is that he pays taxes and penalties on the full amount he contributed.

386. Is it possible to pass the regular HSA contribution testing period and fail the IRA to HSA funding testing period?

No. IRA funding of HSA must be completed in the taxable year. For a calendar year taxpayer that means the last date it could be done is December 31. The testing period for the IRA funding would run from December 1 through December 31 of the next year. That is the same testing as regular contributions for a tax year.

Excess Contribution from IRA to HSA Funding

387. What happens if an HSA owner exceeds the HSA limits when funding with an IRA?

HSA owners are only allowed to complete an HSA qualified funding distribution up to their HSA maximum for the year. If the HSA owner exceeds the maximum, then the amount over the limit will be taxable and penalized as an early withdrawal from their IRA (generally fully taxed and subject to a penalty if under age 59½ and no other exception applies).

The HSA owner must also remove the excess amount from the HSA as the return of an excess contribution prior to their tax filing due date or face additional taxes and penalties.

> *Example*. Bri, age forty-seven, first became eligible for an HSA on January 1, 2014 under family HDHP coverage. Bri's HSA limit for 2014 is $6,550. Bri misunderstands the rules and completes an IRA funding of her HSA in the amount of $10,000. For her 2014 taxes, Bri must include $3,450 ($10,000–$6,550) in her gross income as a taxable distribution. She will also be subject to the 10 percent early withdrawal penalty for individuals taking IRA withdrawals before the age of 59½. Further, she needs to contact her HSA custodian and request the removal of the excess $3,450 from her HSA prior to her April 15, 2015 tax due date (plus extensions).

IRS Notice 2008-51, Example 9.

388. If an HSA owner's contribution exceeds the HSA limits does that result in a failed testing period?

No. If an HSA owner contributes more than the HSA limit for the year, the HSA owner must remove the excess amount. This is different than failing the testing period.

> *Example*. Betty had self-only HDHP coverage and was otherwise HSA-eligible for January through June, 2014. She contributed $3,300, the federal HSA maximum for Betty. She is not eligible for the full contribution rule because she was not eligible on December 1, 2014 and she is not subject to the testing period rule also because she was not eligible on December 1. Her HSA limit is half the annual limit using the sum-of-the-months' calculation or $1,650.

Betty must remove the $1,650 as the return of an excess contribution from her HSA by April 15, 2015 or face a 6 percent penalty per year the excess remains in the HSA. If she does remove the excess timely, she will not owe taxes or penalties on the amount of the excess. She will owe taxes and penalties on any earnings the excess amount generated while held in the HSA.

PART VIII: DISTRIBUTIONS

Overview

389. What are the basic distribution rules for HSAs?

HSAs are designed to pay for qualified medical expenses of the HSA owner, the HSA owner's spouse, and the HSA owner's tax dependents (generally children) tax-free and penalty-free. These expenses must be "qualified" to get this special treatment and include medical expenses incurred before the insurance deductible is met, co-payments, prescription drugs, dental, vision, and much more.

HSA owners enjoy a great deal of control as to how and when HSA funds are spent. HSA owners can use current HSA funds to pay for current medical expenses, save for future medical expenses and even reimburse for past medical expenses incurred after the HSA establishment date. The HSA owner, the spouse or dependents do not need to be currently eligible to contribute to an HSA in order to use HSA funds on qualified medical expenses.

Most HSA custodians provide checks, debit cards, online banking or other tools to give HSA owners direct control over their HSA distributions. There is no requirement that HSA custodians or employers check to see if distributions are used for qualified medical expenses. The IRS could possibly ask the HSA owner for proof of a medical expense so individuals need to save medical receipts in their tax files.

There are no required mandatory distributions from an HSA although an HSA owner can begin to use the funds for general retirement at age sixty-five without penalty although income taxes apply.

There are many special rules, exceptions, and details that make HSA distributions more complicated than this general overview implies, but generally HSAs are used to pay for medical expenses.

390. What are the different types of HSA distributions and how are they treated for tax purposes?

HSA rules provide for a variety of types of distributions with different tax treatment depending on why the distribution occurred. These types of distributions fall into three categories for tax treatment: (1) tax-free and penalty-free, (2) subject to taxes but no penalty, and (3) subject to taxes and penalty.

Tax Consequence	HSA Distribution Reason
Tax-Free and Penalty-Free	Eligible medical expenses
	Long-term care insurance
	COBRA health insurance premiums
	Health insurance premiums while receiving unemployment compensation
	Health insurance premiums after age 65
	Medicare premiums for individuals enrolled in Medicare (but no Medigap)
	Rollovers and transfers to new HSA

Taxable But No Penalty	Made after age 65
	Death distributions
	Disability distributions
Taxable and Penalized	Other distributions are taxable and subject to a 20% penalty.

Qualified Medical Expenses
Overview
391. What are qualified medical expenses?

Qualified medical expenses include: most normal medical care, co-pays, prescription drugs, dental care, and eye care. HSA owners that use an HSA for non-qualified medical expense will owe taxes and a 20 percent penalty applies unless another exception applies.

IRS Publication 502 provides a good definition of a qualified medical expense.

"Medical expenses are the costs of diagnosis, cure, mitigation, treatment, or prevention of disease, and the costs for treatments affecting any part or function of the body. These expenses include payments for legal medical services rendered by physicians, surgeons, dentists, and other medical practitioners. They include the costs of equipment, supplies, and diagnostic devices needed for these purposes.

Medical care expenses must be primarily to alleviate or prevent a physical or mental defect or illness. They do not include expenses that are merely beneficial to general health, such as vitamins or a vacation."

This definition can often lead to questions without certain answers. Publication 502 proceeds to provide a lot of additional detail and examples applying the above definition.

392. Is there a difference between "qualified" medical expenses and "eligible" medical expenses?

This book uses the terms "qualified" and "eligible" interchangeable, although the HSA law uses the word "qualified."

IRC Secs. 223(d)(2)(A) and 219(d).

393. Is there a list of all qualified medical expenses?

IRS Publication 502 provides the most detailed list from a government source. Although comprehensive, Publication 502's list is not exhaustive. Also, some medical expenses may be qualified for some people and not others depending on the facts and circumstances. Below is a list put together from IRS Publication 502 and industry best practices.

Medical Expense	Eligible	Note
Abortion	Yes	Must be a legal abortion
Acne Treatment	Maybe	Prescription required if medicine. Doctor visit covered.
Acupuncture	Yes	
Airfare	Maybe	See Transportation in Pub 502.
Alcoholism	Yes	Inpatient treatment for addiction. Transportation to AA meetings.
Allergy Medicines	Maybe	Prescription required.
Allergy Products	Maybe	Medical need. Excess cost over normal product only.
Alternative Medicine	Yes	Must be treating a specific medical condition.
Ambulance	Yes	
Annual Physical	Yes	
Antacids	Maybe	Must get prescription.
Artificial Limb	Yes	
Artificial Teeth	Yes	Not for cosmetic only.
Aspirin	Maybe	Must get prescription.
Asthma Medicines	Maybe	Must get prescription.
Baby Sitting	No	Even if necessary to attend to medical treatment.
Bandages	Yes	
Birth Control Pills	Yes	
Blood Pressure Monitor	Yes	
Blood Storage	Maybe	Temporary storage for known procedure likely applies.
Blood Sugar Test Kit	Yes	
Blood Tests	Yes	
Body Scan	Yes	
Bottled Water	No	
Braille Books	Yes	
Breast Pump/Supplies	Yes	
Breast Reconstruction	Yes	
Capital Expenses	Maybe	See Pub 502 for details. For expense above normal cost.
Car – Modifications	Yes	The extra cost to make car accessible if medically necessary.
Carpal Tunnel Brace	Yes	For example, a wrist brace.
Christian Science	Yes	Fees to Christian Science practitioners for medical care.
COBRA Premiums	Yes	See Pub 969 for limiting rules.
Cold Medicines	Maybe	Must get prescription.
Cold/Hot Pack	Yes	If for medical care.
Condoms	Yes	

Contact Lenses	Yes	Plus contact lenses cleaning supplies and solutions.
Contraceptives	Yes	
Controlled Substances	No	
Cosmetic Surgery	No	Unless arising from an accident or congenital abnormality.
Cosmetics	No	
Counseling	Maybe	Covered for medical purposes: psychological, etc.
CPR Class	No	
Crutches	Yes	Buy or rent.
Dancing Lessons	No	
Dental Floss	No	
Dental Treatment	Yes	Most dental – not cosmetic
Dentures	Yes	Plus cleaners.
Dermatologist	Yes	
Diabetic Supplies	Yes	
Diagnostic Devices	Yes	
Diaper Service	No	
Diarrhea Medicine	Maybe	Must get prescription.
Diet Foods	No	Some food exceptions.
Doctor's Fees	Yes	Not otherwise paid by insurance, FSA or HRA.
Drug Addiction	Yes	Inpatient treatment.
Drugs	Yes	If prescription obtained.
Electrolysis Hair Rem.	No	See Cosmetic Surgery.
Ergonomic Chair	Maybe	Must be doctor recommended. Only increased cost allowed.
Exercise Equipment	No	Possible exceptions.
Eye Exam	Yes	
Eye Surgery	Yes	Includes laser eye surgery.
Eyeglasses	Yes	
Facial Tissues	No	
Fertility Enhancement	Yes	
Finance Charge	No	
First Aid Supplies	Yes	
Flu Shot	Yes	
Funeral Expenses	No	
Guide Dog	Yes	Including maintenance costs (food, vet, etc.).
Gynecologist	Yes	
Hair Transplant	No	See Cosmetic Surgery.
Health Club Dues	No	

Health Institute	Yes	If prescribed by a doctor with statement of necessity.
Hearing Aids	Yes	Including batteries and repair.
Home Improvements	Maybe	See Capital Expenses
Homeopathic Care	Yes	
Homeopathic Medicine	Maybe	If used to treat specific illness.
Household Help	No	But see Nursing Services
Humidifier	Maybe	If used to treat specific illness. Doctor Recommended.
Illegal Treatments	No	
Immunizations	Yes	
Imported Medicines	Maybe	Must be legally imported.
Insurance Premiums	Limited	See Pub 969.
Laboratory Fees	Yes	
Lactation Expenses	Yes	See Breast Pump.
Lead-Based Paint Fix	Yes	If child has or had lead poisoning. Rules apply. See Pub 502.
Legal Fees	Yes	If necessary to authorize treatment for mental illness. Limited.
Lodging	Yes	Many rules and limitations apply – see Pub 502.
Long-term Care Ins.	Yes	Dollar limits apply.
Marijuana	No	Even if prescribed and legal in your state.
Maternity Clothes	No	
Mattress	Maybe	If medically necessary and only cost difference – see capital.
Meals	Limited	In hospital. Very limited.
Medical Alert Bracelet	Yes	
Medical Conference	Yes	If conference concerns chronic illness. Limited.
Medical Info. Plan	Yes	Plan to keep medical information available.
Medicare Premiums	Yes	Not Medigap.
Medicines	Maybe	If prescribed.
Medigap Premiums	No	
Nonprescription Drugs	Maybe	Must get prescription.
Nursing Home	Yes	If for medical care.
Nursing Services	Yes	Medical services only – see Pub 502 for details.
Nutritional Supp.	Maybe	No, unless practitioner recommended for specific condition.
Operations	Yes	Unless cosmetic or otherwise unnecessary.
Optometrist	Yes	
Orthopedic Shoes	Limited	Medically necessary and only extra cost can be paid from HSA.
Orthopedist	Yes	
Orthotic Inserts	Yes	

Osteopath	Yes	
Out-of-Network	Yes	
Oxygen	Yes	For a medical condition.
Personal Use Items	No	
Physical Examination	Yes	
Pregnancy Test Kit	Yes	
Prosthesis	Yes	
Psychiatric Care	Yes	
Psychoanalysis	Yes	
Psychologist	Yes	
Sleep Aids	Maybe	Prescription required.
Smoking Cessation	Limited	Classes. Nicotine gum or patches require prescription.
Special Education	Maybe	See Pub 502 for details.
Special Home	Yes	Intellectually and developmentally disabled if necessary.
Splints	Yes	
Sterilization	Yes	
Sunglasses	Maybe	Prescription glasses only.
Sunscreen	Maybe	If high enough SPF.
Surgery	Yes	See Operations.
Swimming Lessons	No	
Teeth Whitening	No	
Telephone	Maybe	If necessary for hearing disability.
Television	Maybe	If necessary, pay for the part that displays the audio (subtitles).
Therapy	Yes	
Thermometers	Yes	
Transplants	Yes	See Pub 502 for details.
Transportation	Limited	See Pub 502 for details.
Trips	Limited	See Pub 502 for details.
Vasectomy	Yes	
Veterinary Fees	No	But See Guide Dogs.
Vision Surgery	Yes	
Weight-Loss Program	Limited	But See Guide Dogs.
Wheelchair	Yes	
Wig	Yes	If physician advised after disease caused hair loss.
X-Ray	Yes	

394. Do HSAs follow the same rules as FSAs and HRAs as to what is a qualified medical expense?

Generally, yes. The same IRS guidance on qualified medical expense, IRS Publication 502, applies to HSAs, FSAs and HRAs with some key differences outlined below. IRS Publication 502 serves as a starting point to determine whether an expense is qualified or not and is not the ending point as the facts and circumstances matter.

- **Insurance Premiums.** HSAs allow for the purchase of insurance premiums in some cases in a manner different than FSAs and HRAs

- **Death Distributions.** HSA assets pass to named beneficiaries in the case of death of the HSA owner with a special rule that spouses can treat it as their own

- **Timing of Distributions.** HSAs are more flexible on the timing of distributions

- **Distributions for General Expenses.** HSAs can be used for non-qualified medical expenses if the HSA owner is willing to pay taxes and penalties

- **Age sixty-five Distributions.** At age sixty-five HSA owners can use the HSA for any reason penalty-free

- **Rollovers/Transfers.** HSAs allow for an HSA owner to move the funds to a new custodian at the HSA owner's discretion

Caution: Employers can further restrict the definition of a qualified medical expense for FSAs and HRAs, but not HSAs.

IRC Sec. 213(d).

Prescription Drugs/Medications

395. What is a prescription drug?

A prescription drug is a licensed medication or biological that requires a prescription for its dispensing. Under HSA rules an HSA owner may use his or her HSA to pay for over-the-counter drugs so long as the HSA owner obtains a "prescription" even if the drug is available without a prescription.

For HSAs, a "prescription" means a written or electronic order for a medicine or drug that meets the legal requirements in the state in which the medical expense is incurred and that is issued by an individual who is legally authorized to issue prescriptions in that state.

IRS Notice 2010-59, IRC Sec. 213(d)(3).

396. Is medical marijuana qualified with a prescription?

No. Marijuana is a banned substance under federal law. Even if the taxpayer lives in a state that has legalized marijuana and the taxpayer has a valid prescription, the HSA owner cannot use the HSA to pay for the marijuana.

397. Are prescription drugs from Canada qualified?

Generally, no. Individuals cannot buy prescription drugs from another country and import them into the U.S. because that process is usually illegal - although though many people do it. If an HSA owner buys drugs from Canada in violation of U.S. law, the HSA owner cannot use the HSA to pay for them.

If an HSA owner buys a legally imported foreign prescription drug then it is an eligible medical expense (this would include drugs bought legally in the U.S. but were produced overseas or are produced by foreign drug companies).

An HSA owner can include the cost of a prescribed drug that is both purchased and consumed in another country provided the drug is legal in both U.S. and the foreign country.

IRS Publication 502.

Over the Counter Drugs

398. Are over-the-counter drugs qualified?

Generally, no. The Affordable Care Act eliminated over-the-counter drugs as a qualified medical expense starting in 2011. HSA owners now need a prescription for a drug in order for the drug to qualify as a qualified medical expense. Insulin is an exception to this rule.

Note: If an HSA owner gets a prescription for an over-the-counter drug, then the HSA owner can use an HSA for the expense.

> *Example.* Tamara feels sick and generally buys an over-the-counter drug for her cold symptoms. The over-the-counter cold medicine does not meet the qualified medical expense rules unless Tamara gets a prescription for the over-the-counter drug from her doctor. She will not need to show the prescription to buy the over-the-counter drug but will need to save it in case of an IRS audit (some medical debit card companies may require an HSA owner to show the prescription at the point of purchase in order to use the HSA debit card to pay for then purchase).

399. Are over-the-counter drugs purchased prior to 2011 still eligible?

Yes. Prior to 2011, over-the-counter drugs were qualified medical expenses. HSA owners that paid for otherwise unreimbursed over-the-counter drug expense from before 2011 and after their HSA establishment date, can use an HSA to reimburse for those expenses.

IRS Notice 2010-59.

400. Can medical professionals prescribe over-the-counter drugs?

Yes. The professional that writes a prescription must be authorized by the state to issue prescriptions and the prescription must meet the legal definition of prescription for the state in which the medical expense is incurred.

IRS Notice 2010-59.

401. Is a doctor recommendation for an over-the-counter drug the same as a prescription?

No. "Prescription" means a written or electronic order for a medicine or drug that meets the legal requirements of a prescription in the state in which the medical expense is incurred and that is issued by an individual who is legally authorized to issue a prescription in that state.

IRS Notice 2010-59.

402. Is insulin a qualified medical expense?

Yes. HSA owners can buy insulin as a qualified medical expense without a prescription. This is an exception to the general rule making over-the-counter drugs ineligible. Furthermore, blood sugar kits would not require a doctor's prescription as the kit is not a drug and would qualify as meeting the definition of medical care for a diabetic.

403. Are over-the-counter weight-loss supplements qualified expenses?

No. Weight-loss supplements used for general health are not qualified medical expenses. HSA owners also cannot include the cost of diet food or beverages in medical expenses because the diet food and beverages substitute for what is normally consumed to satisfy nutritional needs.

HSA owners can include the cost of special food if: (1) the food does not satisfy normal nutritional needs, (2) the food alleviates or treats an illness, and (3) the need for the food is substantiated by a physician. The substantiation by a physician should include a written prescription or order.

IRS Publication 502.

404. Are nutritional supplements qualified medical expenses?

Generally nutritional supplements are not qualified medical expenses because they are generally taken to improve general health. If the nutritional supplements are recommended by a medical practitioner as treatment for a specific medical condition diagnosed by a doctor, then they may be qualified.

IRS Publication 502.

405. Are vitamins qualified medical expenses?

The IRS provides that:

> "You cannot include in medical expenses the cost of nutritional supplements, vitamins, herbal supplements, 'natural medicines,' etc. unless they are recommended by a medical practitioner for a specific medical condition diagnosed by a physician. Otherwise, these items are taken to maintain your ordinary good health and are not for medical care."

This quote is meant as a general prohibition on using your HSA to pay for vitamins and nutritional supplements. The language of "unless they are recommended…" creates an opening for HSA use. Given that over-the-counter drugs are not qualified medical expenses without a prescription and that vitamins are likely considered over-the-counter drugs, an HSA owner planning to use his or her HSA to pay for vitamins should get a doctor's prescription.

IRA Publication 502.

Over the Counter Non-Drug Items
406. Are non-drug over-the-counter items, such as bandages, qualified?

Yes. Although over-the-counter drugs are not qualified medical expenses, over-the-counter items that are not medicines still qualify. Any non-drug over-the-counter items must meet the definition of medical care. The definition includes expenses for the diagnosis, cure, mitigation, treatment or prevention of disease, or for the purpose of affecting any structure or function of the body. This may include items such as crutches, bandages, and blood pressure monitors.

However, expenses for items that are merely beneficial to the general health of an individual, such as a piece of exercise equipment, are not expenses for medical care.

Rev Ruling 2010-23.

407. Is a breast pump a qualified medical expense?

Yes. In 2011, the IRS announced that breast pumps are a qualified medical expense and can be purchased tax-free using an HSA. This changed the industry position prior to this announcement of only allowing breast pumps in case of medical necessity. The IRS's rationale for this is that breast pumps are "for the purpose of affecting a structure or function of the body of the lactating woman."

IRS Announcement 2011-14, IRS Publication 502.

General Health
408. Are gym or health club memberships qualified?

No. The IRS specifically provides the following:

> "[y]ou cannot include in medical expenses health club dues or amounts paid to improve one's general health or to relieve physical or mental discomfort not related to a particular medical condition. You cannot include in medical expenses the cost of membership in any club organized for business, pleasure, recreation, or other social purpose."

There is a small opening in this language to interpret that gym memberships are allowed as qualified medical expenses. Qualified medical expenses include items necessary to cure, mitigate, treat or prevent disease and the costs for treatments affecting any part or function of the body.

Linking the gym membership to the cure or treatment of a specific ailment or disease rather than general health is the key to wiggling through this narrow interpretation that may allow an HSA owner to use an HSA to pay the fees. Faced with an IRS challenge, an HSA owner will want as much evidence of that link as possible. A clear statement from a doctor that the membership is necessary to treat a specific medical condition is the base of that support. Using a gym connected to a health care institution that is clearly established to address specific health issues rather than serving as a health club for general health would further support the argument that it's allowed.

An HSA owner using a gym under the guidance of a medical professional located in a medical facility for the specific purpose of therapy to recover from a specific injury would likely be able to use the HSA to pay for those expenses. The medical provider may bill the patient for the health care, not the gym services, eliminating this issue as the direct health care expense for therapy would be qualified. In fact, even the IRS states that you can include "separate fees" charged at a health club for weight-loss if "it is a treatment for a specific disease diagnosed by a physician (such as obesity, hypertension, or heart disease)." Accordingly, separate charges for more specific services may be allowed.

Conservatively, and for the vast majority of HSA owners that also belong to health clubs, health club memberships address general health and should not be included in medical distributions from HSAs.

IRS Publication 502.

409. Is a weight-loss program a qualified medical expense?

HSA owners cannot include as a qualified medical expense the cost of a weight-loss program if the purpose of the weight-loss is the improvement of appearance, general health, or sense of well-being. HSA owners cannot include payments to lose weight unless the weight-loss is a treatment for a specific disease diagnosed by a physician (such as obesity, hypertension, or heart disease). If the weight-loss treatment is not for a specific disease diagnosed by a physician, the HSA owner cannot include either the fees paid for membership in a weight reduction group or fees for attendance at period meetings.

IRS Publication 502.

410. Are family planning expenses, such as, childbirth classes qualified?

Most general health expenses are not covered. A family planning class or other expense is likely to fall within that category. However, there is an exception for HSA owners that are already pregnant as well an exception for most medical expenses related to infertility.

Expenses for childbirth classes are reimbursable, but are limited to expenses incurred by the mother-to-be. Expenses incurred by a "coach," even if that is the father-to-be, are not qualified. To qualify as medical care, the classes must address specific medical issues, such as labor, delivery procedures, breathing techniques and nursing.

411. Are stress reduction classes qualified?

Stress reduction items, including gym memberships, yoga classes, vacations, massages, and more are generally not qualified medical expenses because they are designed to improve general health rather than curing a particular illness or condition. Items that are medically necessary for a particular condition can usually be included.

> *Example*. A massage because of a muscle that atrophied due to an illness or accident would be qualified in contrast to a massage for relaxation that would generally not be qualified even if needed to reduce stress.

> General health items such as eating better foods and taking classes to improve general health and fitness are usually not covered. If the stress reduction is medically necessary, as opposed to just good for your general health, then it may be qualified. A well-documented tax file would include a doctor's letter stating that the classes are medically necessary to treat a specific condition.

412. Are personal care items, such as a toothbrush, qualified?

No. HSA owners cannot use their HSA for personal care items such as a toothbrush, toothpaste, soap, antibacterial wipes, etc. If in order to accommodate a medical condition, an HSA owner must spend more for these items than normal, the HSA owner may be able to include the difference in cost as a qualified medical expense.

Travel

413. Are travel, meal and lodging expenses qualified?

Yes. HSA owners can include the cost of travel as qualified medical expenses <u>if the transportation and trip are primarily for and essential to medical care</u>. This can include the cost of tickets for bus, taxi, train, plane or ambulance. HSA owners can also include the out-of-pocket costs for car expenses such as gas and oil, parking and tolls. HSA owners cannot include depreciation, insurance, general repair or maintenance. HSA owners that do not want to calculate actual expenses, can use a standard mileage rate of 23.5 cents (2014).

HSA owners cannot include: (1) going to and from work, even if a medical condition requires an unusual means of transportation, (2) travel for purely personal reasons to another city for an operation or other medical care, (3) travel that is merely for the general improvement of one's health, and (4) the costs of operating a specially equipped car for other than medical reasons.

An HSA owner can include costs for trips that are primarily for and essential to medical care. If an HSA owner is staying at a hospital or similar institution, the HSA owner can include the cost of meals and lodging.

If the HSA owner is not staying at a hospital, the HSA owner can include up to $50 for each night for each person for lodging provided the following conditions are met.

- The lodging is primarily for and essential to medical care

- The medical care is provided by a doctor in a licensed hospital or in a medical care facility related to, or the equivalent of, a licensed hospital

- The lodging is not lavish or extravagant under the circumstances

- There is no significant element of personal pleasure, recreation, or vacation in the travel away from home

For example, if a parent is traveling with a sick child, up to $100 per night can be included as qualified medical expenses. An HSA owner cannot include the cost of meals if not staying at a hospital that serves the meals as part of inpatient care.

HSA owners cannot include in medical expenses a trip or vacation taken merely for a change of environment, improvement of morale, or general improvement of health, even if the trip is made on the advice of a doctor.

IRS Publication 502.

414. Are mileage costs to visit a doctor qualified?

Yes. An HSA owner can use an HSA to pay actual out-of-pocket expenses (including tolls and parking) for using his or her own car for transportation to a medical facility (including picking up medicine) or can use a standard mileage rate (23.5 cents for 2014). HSA owners should keep a mileage log to track miles in case of an IRS audit.

415. Are procedures performed outside of the U.S. qualified?

Yes, provided the procedures are otherwise qualified medical expenses and the care is legal in the foreign country and in the U.S. This allows for HSA owners to save money by having medical procedures performed abroad.

Concierge Medicine
416. Can an HSA owner use an HSA to pay "concierge medicine" fees?

The IRS does not directly answer whether you can use an HSA to pay for concierge medicine programs (also called "physician retainer programs" and "boutique medicine"). IRS general guidance provides that you can use your HSA to pay for the prevention or alleviation of a physical or mental defect or illness and not for general health. Whether concierge medicine programs provide treatment for medical treatment or general health is heavily dependent on how the program works. Ultimately, the HSA owner will need to decide with the help of their tax adviser. Some variations on the programs include:

- **Cash for Care Programs.** Some of these programs are more designed around the doctor not accepting insurance payments. If these programs simply charge fees assuming cash payment, they work very well for HSA owners. Of course, an HSA owner can use his or her HSA to pay for qualified medical expenses billed by a doctor who does not accept medical insurance.

- **Retainer Fee/Amenities Program.** This type of program charges an annual fee for access to a specific physician or physician group. Amenity items could include seeing a physician that has a limited number of patients, getting access twenty-four hours a day/seven days a week to that physician, and same-day or quick appointments. When you actually see the physician you or your medical insurance are still charged separately for that visit. These amenities are not likely to be considered qualified medical expenses as they relate to access not treatment. There is some room for debate on this interpretation and certainly some concierge service providers are stating that you can use your HSA to pay their fees because the fee is part of the medical service, but the conservative answer is that these amenities are not qualified medical expenses.

- **Hybrid Programs.** Concierge medicine is an emerging area with a wide-variety of program offerings. One common hybrid offering is to provide the retainer/ amenities program but also provide one physical included in the annual retainer fee. In this case, a portion of the fee is a qualified medical expense, the cost of the physical (and other included eligible medical services). If the program provides an itemized invoice (or you can find out the costs), you can use your HSA to pay for the annual physical but not the fee for access. There is also a potential timing issue with how these programs work and to be conservative you are best off paying the program fee with non-HSA dollars and then reimbursing yourself for the cost of the annual physical out of your HSA after you receive the physical.

- **Insurance Programs.** Some of the programs operate more like insurance where you pay an upfront fee for an unlimited number of doctor visits/contacts and for limited (or unlimited) additional diagnostic and other services included. You generally cannot buy insurance with your HSA, so if the concierge medical program is considered insurance, you cannot use your HSA to pay for it (you will also likely lose your eligibility for an HSA). Note: In limited circumstances, you can use your HSA to pay for health insurance.

- **Pre-Paid Medical Programs**. Another approach to concierge medicine is closer to a pre-paid medical services model. You buy a package of services that includes a set number of visits and other medical services. Rather than paying separately, you buy a package. Assuming the services provided under this program are all qualified medical expenses you could use your HSA to pay for those expenses. Given uncertainly on how the rules for these services work the conservative approach would be to pay the program fee from non-HSA funds and then reimburse yourself from your HSA for the fair market value of each medical service received. If you do not take advantage of the all the medical services in the package you may not be able to reimburse yourself for the full cost of the package.

See Part III: Eligibility – Other Health Plan – Concierge Medicine.

Cosmetic Procedures

417. Is cosmetic surgery a qualified medical expense?

Generally, cosmetic surgery is not qualified. This includes any procedure that is directed at improving the patient's appearance and does not meaningfully promote the "proper function of the body or prevent or treat illness or disease." You can use your HSA for cosmetic surgery that is necessary to improve a deformity arising from a congenital abnormality, a personal injury resulting from an accident or trauma, or a disfiguring disease.

Example. Beth undergoes surgery that removes a breast as part of treatment for cancer. She pays a surgeon to reconstruct the breast. The surgery to reconstruct the breast corrects a deformity directly related to the disease. The cost of the surgery is an eligible medical expense.

IRS Publication 502.

418. Are hair transplants or hair removal through electrolysis qualified?

No. HSA owners cannot include the cost of hair transplants or for other hair loss treatment if the purpose is cosmetic, but it may be covered if it is to address a specific medical condition.

Capital Expenditures

419. Are capital expenditures, such as installing an entrance ramp, qualified?

Yes. Capital expenditures can be qualified medical expenses if the main purpose is medical care for the HSA owner, the HSA owner's spouse, or the HSA owner's dependent. The cost of permanent improvements that increase the value of your property may only partially be included as a qualified medical expense. The cost of the improvement is reduced by the increase in the value of the property. The difference is the medical expense. If the value of the property is not increased by the improvement, the entire cost is included as a medical expense. Examples of the types of capital expenditures that could be qualified medical expenses include:

- Constructing entrance or exit ramps for your home

- Widening doorways at entrances or exists in your home

- Widening or otherwise modifying hallways and interior doorways

- Installing railing, support bars, or other modifications to bathrooms

- Lowering or modifying kitchen cabinets and equipment

- Moving or modifying electrical outlets and fixtures

- Installing porch lifts and other forms of lifts (elevators generally add value to the home)

- Modifying fire alarms, smoke detectors, and other warning systems

- Modifying stairways

- Adding handrails or grab bars anywhere

- Modifying hardware on doors

- Modifying areas in front of entrance and exit doorways

- Grading the ground to provide access to the residence

Only reasonable costs to accommodate a home to a disabled condition are considered medical care. Additional costs for the personal motives, such as for architectural or aesthetic reasons, are not medical expenses.

IRS Publication 502.

420. Are capital expenses for non-home related expenses allowed?

Some non-home related capital expenses may also be allowed if necessary to treat or cure a specific ailment or disease. This may include improvements to a car, a workstation (a standing desk), or personal item (improved toothbrush).

> *Example.* Jane's doctor informs Jane that she needs to buy a specially designed bed to accommodate her medical condition. The bed is necessary to treat a specific medical issue and is not an improvement for general health. The doctor provides Jane a letter explaining the necessity. Jane buys the special bed for $3,000 which is $2,000 more than a normal non-modified bed would cost. Jane can use her HSA to pay for the additional expense of $2,000.

Age Sixty-five Distributions

421. What changes occur for an HSA owner at age sixty-five?

At age sixty-five three key changes occur for HSA owners:

(1)   **Penalty Free Withdrawals.** At age sixty-five, HSA owners are eligible to take money out of an HSA for any reason without incurring the 20 percent penalty for non-qualified medical expenses.

(2)   **Pay for Health Insurance Premiums.** At age sixty-five, HSA owners can use an HSA to pay for some insurance premiums. *See HSA Distributions - Insurance Premiums.*

(3)   **Loss of HSA Eligibility.** At age sixty-five, most Americans lose HSA eligibility because they begin Medicare.

422. At age Sixty-five, can an owner of an HSA take money out for any reason?

Yes. At age sixty-five an HSA owner can take penalty-free distributions from the HSA for any reason. In order to be tax-free the distribution must be for a qualified medical expense. Given that Medicare does not cover all of a person's medical expenses and that Medicare charges a premium that can be paid for with HSA funds tax-free, it makes sense for most HSA owners after the age of sixty-five to only use their HSA for qualified medical expenses. This will ensure they get the maximum tax benefits from their HSA.

> *Example.* Bill is sixty-six years old and wants to take $1,500 out of his HSA to pay for general retirement expenses (not eligible medical expense). Bill will not have to pay the 20 percent penalty for non-eligible HSA withdrawals because he is over age sixty-five, but he will have to pay income taxes on the distribution. If instead Bill saves the $1,500 in his HSA he can use it tax-free and penalty-free for qualified medical expenses. If Bill anticipates future medical expenses exceeding the value of his HSA, Bill is likely better off saving his HSA for qualified medical expenses rather than using it for general retirement expenses.

IRC Sec. 223(f)(4)(C).

423. Does an HSA provide for age 59½ distributions similar to an IRA and a 401(k)?

No. The comparable age for HSAs is sixty-five, not 59½. After age sixty-five, an HSA can take money out of the HSA and use it for general retirement expenses.

Similar to deductible IRAs and traditional 401(k)s (Roth accounts work differently), HSA contributions are made pre-tax or are tax-deductible and enjoy tax-free earnings as long as the money remains in the HSA. This is an attractive feature for taxpayers for all of these plans. Unlike IRAs and 401(k)s, the HSA allows for tax-free distributions for medical purposes. Given this difference, HSA owners are well advised to use the HSA first for qualified medical expenses and use other funds for general retirement. Given the high cost of medical care and the limits on how much individuals can contribute to HSAs, using HSAs for general retirement is likely to be an exception to the general rule of using the funds for medical expenses. This is especially true because at age sixty-five, HSA owners can use their HSA to pay for some health insurance premiums, including Medicare, tax-free.

424. Why is age sixty-five used for HSAs?

HSA law links the age for penalty-free distributions for any reason to Section 1811 of the Social Security Act. That section currently uses the age sixty-five.

Insurance

425. Are health insurance premiums qualified?

No. The general answer is that HSAs cannot be used to pay for health insurance premiums. However, there are a number of important exceptions. HSA owners can use their HSA tax-free and penalty-free to pay for the following:

- **Long-Term Care Insurance.** Subject to dollar limitations, an HSA owner can use an HSA to pay for long-term care insurance

- **COBRA.** An HSA owner can use his or her HSA to pay for health coverage purchased through a COBRA continuation plan (generally offered by employers when you separate from service)

- **Unemployment.** Payment of premiums for health insurance coverage while receiving unemployment compensation under a federal or state law is allowed as a tax-free distribution from an HSA

- **Age sixty-five.** Payment for Medicare premiums (other than Medigap) and other health care coverage for HSA owners over age sixty-five and over is allowed

IRS Publication 969, pp. 8-9.

426. Can HSA owners use the HSA to pay for health insurance premiums of a spouse or dependent?

HSA owners can use their HSA to pay for health insurance premiums of their spouse or dependents in the case when the spouse or dependents are: (1) receiving health care continuation coverage through COBRA, or (2) are receiving unemployment compensation through a federal or state program. If the HSA owner is not age sixty-five, the HSA owner cannot use the HSA to pay for the Medicare premiums of a spouse who is over sixty-five.

IRS Publication 969, IRS Notice 2008-59, See Q 32.

COBRA Premiums

427. Are COBRA health insurance premiums qualified?

Yes. Health insurance expenses that are paid through COBRA (Consolidated Omnibus Budget Reconciliation Act) are considered qualified medical expenses and are an exception to the general rule that you cannot use an HSA to pay for insurance premiums.

> *Example.* Mia just lost her job and is eligible for COBRA continuation of her health coverage. The premium is expensive. Fortunately Mia regularly contributed to an HSA and has built up a large HSA balance. She can use her HSA to pay for the COBRA health continuation coverage premium tax-free and penalty-free from her HSA.

428. Can a spouse pay for the other spouse's COBRA continuation coverage premiums with an HSA?

Yes. The expense also must have been incurred after the establishment date.

Medicare Premiums

429. Can an HSA owner over age sixty-five pay for Medicare premiums with an HSA?

An HSA owner can use an HSA to pay for the following:

- **Medicare Part A** (hospital insurance)

- **Medicare Part B** (medical insurance)

- **Medicare Part C** (Medicare Advantage Plans – run by Medicare-approved private plans that replace Parts A and B and possibly D)

- **Medicare Part D** (prescription drug coverage run by Medicare-approved private insurance companies)

- **Employee Health Plan.** The employee share of premiums for employer-sponsored health care including premiums for employee-sponsored retiree health care

IRS Notice 2004-2, See Q 28, IRS Notice 2008-59, See Q 30.

430. Can an HSA owner over age sixty-five pay for Medigap insurance premiums with an HSA?

No. An HSA owner cannot use his or her HSA to pay for Medigap insurance premiums. Medigap is Medicare Supplement Insurance, sold by private companies to help cover expenses that Medicare does not cover such as copayments, coinsurance and deductibles.

IRS Notice 2004-2, See Q 28, IRS Notice 2008-59, See Q 30.

431. Medicare automatically deducts its premium from the Social Security payment so how can an HSA owner use an HSA to pay it?

The HSA owner can reimburse for the cost that is automatically deducted from Social Security by writing a check from the HSA, using an ATM or otherwise. This reimbursement can occur monthly or as desired.

IRS Notice 2004-50, See Q 46.

432. Can an HSA owner use an HSA to pay for Medicare premiums of a spouse?

Yes, if the HSA owner has obtained the age sixty-five, Medicare premiums are qualified medical expenses. If the HSA owner has not obtained sixty-five years of age, then the HSA owner cannot use his or her HSA to pay the Medicare premiums of his or her spouse.

IRS Notice 2008-59, See Q 31.

433. Are Medicare Part D premiums qualified?

Yes. If an HSA owner has attained age sixty-five, premiums for Medicare Part D for the HSA owner, the HSA owner's spouse, or the HSA owner's dependents are qualified medical expenses.

See IRS Notice 2004-2, Q 27 and IRS Notice 2004-50, Q 45.

434. Can an HSA owner use an HSA to pay for health insurance premiums and still claim the health coverage tax credit?

No.

Long-Term Care Premiums

435. Are long-term care insurance premiums qualified?

Yes, HSA distributions used to pay for long-term care insurance premiums qualify as a tax-free, penalty-free distribution in limited amounts. The amount allowed is based on age and adjusted for inflation each year. For 2014, the numbers are:

2014 Long Term Care Limitations for HSA	
Attained Age Before Close of Taxable Year	**Amount You Can Take from HSA**
40 years old or less	$370
Older than 40 but not more than 50 (not 51 yet)	$700
Older than 50 but not more than 60 (not 61 yet)	$1,400
Older than 60 but not more than 70 (not 71 yet)	$3.720
Older than 70 (71 or older)	$4,660

Example. In 2014, Joan, age forty-one, pays a premium of $1,500 for a qualified long-term care insurance contract. The limit for 2014 for her age is $700. Joan can use her HSA to reimburse herself for $700 of the $1,500 premiums. The rest must be paid for outside of the HSA or by taking a taxable distribution from the HSA.

See Revenue Code 213(d) (10), IRS Notice 2004-50, See Q 42.

436. Are long-term care insurance premiums qualified even if the HSA owner contributes through a Section 125 plan?

Yes. Section 125 law provides that the plan shall not include any product which is advertised, marketed or offered as long-term care insurance. However, the IRS has interpreted this favorably for HSAs. Where an HSA that is offered under a Cafeteria plan pays or reimburses individuals for qualified long-term care insurance premiums, section 125(f) is not applicable because it is the HSA and not the long-term care insurance that is offered under the Cafeteria plan.

> *Example.* Bo funds his HSA through a Section 125 Cafeteria plan at work. Bo buys a qualified long-term care insurance policy and wants to use his HSA to pay for premium, up to the allowable limit based on his age and the tax year. Bo can use his HSA to pay for the qualified long-term care insurance tax-free and penalty-free.

IRS Notice 2004-50, See Q 41.

437. Can an HSA owner pay for a spouse's long-term care insurance?

Yes. The HSA law provides that an HSA owner can use the HSA to pay for long-term care premiums and does not provide any language limiting this exception to only the HSA owner's long-term care insurance premiums.

IRS Publication 969 has caused some concern over this answer since a conservative reading of that publication may lead to the opposite answer. Publication 969 states that an HSA owner can use an HSA to pay for a spouse's health insurance if that spouse is receiving continuation coverage under COBRA or if the spouse is receiving unemployment compensation pursuant to state or federal law. The lack of a similar statement for long-term care insurance causes this confusion.

IRC Sec. 223(d)(2)(C)(ii), IRS Publication 969.

Health Premiums and Unemployment Compensation
438. Are health insurance premiums qualified for someone that is unemployed?

Yes, if the HSA owner is currently receiving unemployment benefits (and not just eligible to receive) offered through a state or federal program.

439. Can an employed HSA owner use an HSA to pay a health insurance premium of an unemployed spouse?

Yes, if the spouse is receiving unemployment compensation. Although insurance payments are generally not allowed, an exception exists for people receiving unemployment compensation pursuant to a state or federal law. This exception applies to the HSA owner, the HSA owner's spouse and the HSA owner's dependents.

IRS Notice 2008-59, See Q 33.

440. Can an employed HSA owner use an HSA to pay for an unemployed dependent's health insurance premiums?

Yes, if the dependent is receiving unemployment compensation. Although insurance payments are generally not allowed, an exception exists for people receiving unemployment compensation pursuant to a state or federal law. This exception applies to the HSA owner, the HSA owner's spouse and the HSA owner's dependents.

IRS Notice 2008-59, See Q 33.

Other Insurance Issues

441. Should HSA owners show their health insurance cards for medical services even if they are paying the full expense themselves with their HSA?

Yes. Some HSA owners make a logical but potentially expensive error in not using their medical insurance cards for HSA purchases. Even though HSA owners have to pay for the full medical expense when they are still below their deductible, they should show their insurance card to benefit from any discount the insurance carrier may have negotiated with the provider. Also, if an HSA owner shows an insurance card the insurance carrier can track the expense against the deductible. Neither of these reasons may apply in a particular circumstance, but it's relatively easy to show the card and the worst case scenario in showing the card is that the provider says it does not need it or want it.

442. How does an insurance company track the deductible when expenses are paid with an HSA?

This is a concern among HSA owners and a valid one because the HSA owner will be paying for the medical expenses below the deductible amount. HSA custodians generally do not share medical purchase information with the insurance company. Accordingly, for the HSA owner to get credit for a medical purchase towards the deductible, the HSA owner must show both the medical insurance card. Showing the medical insurance card should alert the insurance company of the expense in cases when the expense would be covered by insurance except that the HSA owner is still below the deductible.

In any case, an HSA owner should save all medical receipts. If an HSA owner is close to or exceeds the deductible, the HSA owner should pull out these receipts and review each one against the insurance policy to see whether it qualifies for the deductible and whether the insurance company is aware of the expense or not.

443. Does an HSA owner benefit from insurance company negotiated discounts on medical services?

Yes. Even if the HSA owner has to pay for the expense, one of the benefits of having health insurance is that the health insurance provides negotiated discounts with medical providers. An insurance company has likely negotiated substantial discounts off medical procedures from the list price. Showing an insurance card entitles the HSA owner to the negotiated discounts as well as providing the insurance company a record of the medical spending for deductible purposes.

HSA owners may even try a bit of negotiating themselves for some services. In some cases, individuals paying cash are able to negotiate better discounts than the insurance provider.

Death Distributions
Overview
444. What happens to an HSA when the HSA owner dies?

HSA owners are allowed to name beneficiaries on the HSA and the named beneficiaries will receive any funds in the HSA upon death of the HSA owner. HSAs are payable on death which means that the HSA custodian can pay the beneficiary without waiting for the estate to complete probate. If the HSA owner fails to name a beneficiary, the money in the HSA will pass according to a will or state law.

445. Can HSA beneficiaries continue to use the HSA as an HSA?

Yes, if the beneficiary is a spouse.

- **Spouse Beneficiaries.** A spouse beneficiary treats the HSA as his or her own. Basically, the HSA becomes the spouse's HSA and the spouse can continue to use the HSA as an HSA. The surviving spouse will not owe taxes or penalties on the HSA provided the spouse uses the HSA for qualified medical expenses. The surviving spouse does need to contact the HSA custodian to make some account changes.

- **Non-Spouse Beneficiaries.** Non-spouse beneficiaries are not entitled to use the HSA and must take a full distribution in the year of death. Non-spouse beneficiaries will have to pay income taxes on the HSA amount they receive, but they will not have to pay the 20 percent penalty for non-eligible distributions from an HSA.

IRS Notice 2004-2, See Q 32.

446. Is it better to name a spouse than a non-spouse as beneficiary for an HSA?

Spouses get more favorable tax treatment than non-spouses as beneficiaries for HSAs. In that regard, it makes more sense for an HSA owner to name a spouse given a choice. Whomever an HSA owner names, however, will get the HSA assets after the HSA owner passes away. A non-spouse beneficiary will have to pay taxes on the amount and will not be able to use it tax-free for qualified medical expenses as a spouse could.

447. Can the beneficiary of an HSA use the HSA to pay for the deceased HSA owner's remaining medical expenses?

Yes. A beneficiary can use the deceased HSA owner's HSA to pay for the deceased HSA owner's medical bills incurred prior to death. The beneficiary must pay the expenses within one year of the date of the HSA owner's death. The beneficiary will not have to include the amount used to pay for the deceased HSA owner's medical expenses in income.

IRC Sec. 223(f)(8)(B)(ii)(I), IRS Notice 2004-2, See Q 32.

448. What procedures should a beneficiary follow to request the HSA funds after the death of the HSA owner?

Policies vary according to state law and HSA custodial practices. Generally, a beneficiary must provide the HSA custodian with a copy of the official death certificate as well as personal identification. HSA custodians will most likely require a signature on a distribution form authorizing the distribution of the funds.

449. What if the HSA appreciated in value from the date of the death until the distribution?

For a spouse beneficiary, the additional earnings become part of the surviving spouse's HSA with no additional action required.

For a non-spouse beneficiary, the additional earnings after the date of death must be included as taxable income. The entire HSA balance is also treated as taxable income so this point is only important because the earnings are handled differently. The earnings are taxed as "other income" on the non-spouse beneficiary's income tax return.

The HSA custodian is required to provide a 1099-SA reflecting the death distribution and that form will notify the beneficiary of any earnings on the HSA post the date of death. The earnings number is not a separate line, you have to look at the "gross distribution" in Box 1 and compare it to the "FMV on date of death" amount in Box 4. If the gross exceeds the fair market value on the date of death, then the difference is earnings.

Spouse Beneficiaries

450. Can a spouse beneficiary transfer the HSA assets to a different HSA?

Yes, a spouse beneficiary of an HSA becomes the HSA owner. The spouse beneficiary will have all the rights of a normal HSA owner, including the right to rollover or transfer the money to a new HSA custodian.

> *Example.* John dies leaving his HSA to his wife, Stacy. Stacy already has an HSA at another custodian and wants to combine the money in John's HSA with her HSA. She can do that. She will need to work with the two custodians to facilitate the transfer.

Non-Spouse Beneficiaries

451. Can a non-spouse beneficiary keep the money in the HSA for five years after death?

No. Non-spouse beneficiaries must remove the money and are not entitled to leave the money in the HSA. A five-year period is occasionally mentioned because Individual Retirement Account (IRA) non-spouse beneficiaries are allowed to keep the assets in an IRA for an additional five years after death (along with other options not available to HSA non-spouse beneficiaries).

452. What happens when the HSA owner fails to name a beneficiary?

If an HSA owner fails to name a beneficiary on an HSA, the assets become part of the HSA owner's estate. The value of the HSA is included in taxes on the final income tax return.

The remaining money in the HSA will still pass to the HSA owner's heirs indirectly through a will or according to state law if there is no will (or possibly through another trust established by the HSA owner prior to death).

453. What happens if the HSA owner names her estate as the beneficiary?

The estate includes the HSA balance in taxable income of the deceased HSA owner for the last taxable year of the HSA owner.

IRC Sec. 223(f)(8)(B)(i)(II).

454. How do non-spouse beneficiaries pay the taxes on an inherited HSA?

The non-spouse beneficiary must complete the IRS Form 8889 and attach it to the federal income tax return. This form calculates the taxes owed. The surviving beneficiary writes "Death of HSA account beneficiary" across the top of the form to explain why the non-spouse beneficiary now suddenly has an HSA (this language is a bit disconcerting as it's not the beneficiary's death the statement is referring to but the death of the HSA owner which the IRS calls the "account beneficiary"). The taxable amount is included in the non-spouse beneficiary's income in the taxable year which includes the date of the death of the HSA owner.

If the non-spouse beneficiary also has his or her own HSA and already files IRS Form 8889 (or the person happens to be the beneficiary of more than one HSA in the same year), then the non-spouse beneficiary must file separate Form 8889s for each HSA along with a controlling Form 8889 that combines the amounts on the separate Form 8889s.

IRS Form 8889.

455. When does the non-spouse beneficiary have to claim the HSA?

A non-spouse beneficiary should close the HSA in the year of death.

456. What if a non-spouse beneficiary does not close the HSA in the year of the death?

The non-spouse beneficiary must include the income for the year of the death even if the distribution did not occur until a later year.

Instructions to IRS Form 1099-SA.

Timing of Distributions

457. Can HSA owners withdraw HSA assets at any time?

Yes, however, if the funds are withdrawn for any expense other than a qualified medical expense, the IRS will impose a 20 percent penalty tax. After the HSA owner reaches age sixty-five, the HSA owner can withdraw the funds without penalty but the amounts withdrawn will be taxable as ordinary income.

458. Does the HSA owner control the timing and amount on HSA distributions?

Yes. The HSA owner controls the HSA and distributions from the HSA.

459. Are HSAs subject to mandatory distributions at age 70½, similar to IRAs?

No, HSA do not have mandatory distributions.

460. Do HSA owners have to reimburse themselves for medical expenses paid out-of-pocket in the same year as the expense is incurred?

No, HSA owners have their entire lifetime to reimburse themselves from their HSA. As long as the HSA owner established the HSA prior to the time the expense was incurred, the HSA remained open, and the expense is not otherwise reimbursed, an HSA owner can reimburse for a qualified medical expense even years later.

> *Example.* In 2012, Sara established her HSA. Throughout the rest of 2012 and for the years 2013, and 2014 she visited the doctor, dentist and optometrist a number of times each year. Each time she used her personal credit card to pay these bills. She can reimburse herself for these expenses from her HSA at any time – even years later. She does need to prove she is reimbursing for qualified medical expenses that were not otherwise paid for through insurance or tax-deferred accounts. The passage of time may make that more difficult, but good receipts and record keeping will satisfy a potential IRS audit.

IRS Notice 2004-50, See Q 40.

461. Can an HSA owner use the HSA for qualified medical expenses even if the HSA owner is no longer eligible for an HSA?

Yes.

> *Example.* Pete was covered by an HDHP and contributed to an HSA for a few years. He recently switched to traditional insurance and is no longer eligible for an HSA. Pete can continue to use his remaining HSA funds to pay for qualified medical expenses not covered by his insurance (co-pays, deductible amounts, prescription drugs, and more).

IRS Notice 2004-2, See Q 29.

462. Is it a good financial strategy to save HSA money and use other funds to pay for medical expenses?

Although this is not generally how HSAs are designed to work, some careful tax planners do save their HSA dollars rather than spend them. The advantages to this approach are:

- **Tax Deferred Earnings.** Money in an HSA is protected from taxes and that includes any earnings in the HSA. Accordingly, it makes sense to keep as much money as possible protected from taxes by maintaining money in the HSA and using after-tax accounts to pay for qualified medical expenses.

- **Emergency Fund.** This approach is even better when you consider that the HSA can serve as an emergency fund. If an HSA owner uses after-tax funds to pay for medical expenses rather than the HSA, but saves all medical receipts, the HSA owner can reimburse himself for those previously unreimbursed expenses simply by writing himself a check from his HSA. For this to work the medical expenses could not have been paid by another health plan or the taxpayer cannot have claimed the medical expenses as itemized deductions on the individual's income tax return.

Example. Steve established his HSA in 2010 and has spent $10,000 on qualified medical expenses since then. He did not use his HSA to pay for those expenses and instead paid with after-tax dollars from his general savings account. Steve has diligently saved all his medical receipts. Steve now needs money unrelated to health care spending. He can write himself a check for $10,000 from his HSA tax-free and penalty-free to reimburse himself for the previously unreimbursed medical expenses. By keeping the money in the HSA for the years before needing it he was able to keep the money earning interest (or other earnings growth) tax-free.

463. What happens if an HSA owner's medical expenses exceed the HSA balance?

An HSA owner in this situation has a few options.

- **Contribute More to HSA.** HSA owners can make sure they have maximized their HSA contribution for the year and contribute more if still below the limit. Remember, HSA owners have until their tax filing due date (generally April 15) of the next year to make an HSA contribution. This means that between January 1 and April 15 of the year, calendar year taxpayers potentially have two different years of HSA contributions to consider.

- **Pay with Other Funds – Reimburse in Future Years.** HSA owners can pay the medical expense with after-tax savings (a general savings account), a credit card, a loan or otherwise. The HSA owner would save the unreimbursed medical receipts and reimburse for those receipts with future HSA contributions.

Example. Bill incurs a dental bill for $10,000 which is more than the $6,100 he has in his HSA and more than he can contribute to his HSA. He pays $6,000 of the medical bill with his HSA. He pays the other $4,000 contribution with personal savings. The next year when he can contribute more to his HSA, he makes a $4,000 HSA (below his family limit) and then immediately writes himself a check from his HSA to reimburse himself for the $4,000 he paid with other non-tax favored funds the previous year.

- **Ask for Payment Plan.** A medical provider may be willing to delay the billing if the provider understands that the HSA owner will have additional funds available in an HSA in the future time period.

Example. Bill incurs a medical bill of $3,000 related to an accident. He does not have enough money in his HSA and although he is below his HSA limit does not have any money outside of the HSA either. His employer is making a $100 a month contribution to Bill's HSA. Bill works out a payment plan with the medical provider to pay the $100 per month to the provider until the bill is paid in full.

- **Pay with Other Funds and Deduct on Tax Return.** Medical expenses not paid from the HSA or otherwise by a health plan, are eligible to be deducted on a personal income tax return subject to a 10 percent floor (7.5 percent for individuals aged sixty-five and over). This means a person can deduct medical expenses only after the expenses exceed 10 percent of a person's income. That is a high threshold to reach, but people with large medical expenses may be able to use this deduction. Important: HSA owners cannot claim a deduction for medical expenses and also use their HSA for the same expense (no double dipping).

Documentation for Medical Expenses

464. Do HSA owners have to save receipts for medical expenses paid with the HSA?

Yes, the individual who establishes the HSA is required to maintain a record of the expenses sufficient to demonstrate that the distributions were for qualified medical expenses.

465. What types of records do HSA owners have to save?

The receipts should show the amount paid, a description of the service/item purchased, the date, and the name of the service/item provider.

HSA owners must keep records sufficient to show that:

- The distributions were exclusively to pay or reimburse qualified medical expenses

- The qualified medical expenses had not been previously paid or reimbursed from another source and

- The medical expenses had not been taken as an itemized deduction in any year

IRS Publication 969, p. 9.

466. Are there any special documentation requirements for older medical expenses?

HSA owners must keep records sufficient to later show that the distributions were exclusively to pay for or reimburse for qualified medical expenses. HSA owners must also be prepared to show that the expenses were not previously paid or reimbursed from another source and that the medical expenses were not itemized on their tax return as a deductible medical expense.

An HSA owner should also be prepared to show that the HSA was established prior to the date of the medical expenses and that the HSA remained open on the day of the medical expenses (or the HSA owner otherwise meets the establishment date rules).

IRS Notice 2004-50, See Q 40.

467. Do HSA owners send copies of medical receipts to the IRS or employers?

No. HSA owners should save their medical receipts with their tax information in case of an IRS audit or information request. HSA owners do not need to send them to the IRS, unless specifically requested by the IRS as part of an audit or other request. HSA owners are also not required to send copies to an employer.

468. Do HSA owners need to send copies of medical receipts to their HSA custodian?

No. HSA custodians are not required to check the eligibility of medical expenses and do not need to see your receipts. Some custodians may verify receipts as an additional service, but it is not usual and not required under law.

Coordination with Other Plans

469. Can an HSA owner use an HSA to pay for a qualified medical expense that insurance also covered?

No. HSA owners cannot use an HSA to pay for qualified medical expenses that were paid for through insurance or other tax-deferred plans.

> *Example.* Jamie's health insurance covers the cost of a flu shot provided the insured gets the shot and submits a receipt. Jamie goes to the doctor for the flu shot and uses his HSA to pay for the shot (a flu shot is a qualified medical expense). Jamie then submits the same receipt for reimbursement from his insurance company. If the insurance company pays for the expense, Jamie's use of his HSA to pay for the expense is inappropriate and he will have to return the funds to his HSA as the return of a mistaken distribution or face taxes and penalties.

470. Can an HSA owner itemize medical expenses that were paid with an HSA?

No. An HSA owner cannot double count: an HSA owner cannot use his or her HSA to pay for a medical expense and then claim that same expense as an itemized deduction on an income tax return.

471. Can an HSA owner use both an HSA and a limited-purpose FSA to pay for a large expense?

HSA owners are not allowed to reimburse or pay for the same medical expense twice with tax-favored dollars. An HSA owner could pay for a large dental bill using part limited-purpose FSA funds and part HSA funds.

> *Example.* Tony's daughter is having orthodontia work done that costs $3,000. Tony's employer offers a limited-purpose FSA and Tony deferred $2,000 into the plan in anticipation of this orthodontia work. He also has an HSA. Tony pays for the orthodontia work with $2,000 from his limited-purpose FSA and $1,000 from his HSA. This is permissible.

> Later, Tony reads that he can reimburse himself from his HSA for qualified medical expenses he paid with funds outside his HSA. He now wants to write a check to himself for $2,000 from his HSA to reimburse for the orthodontia work not paid through the HSA. Although the advice he got is usually correct, it does not apply to Tony because he paid the $2,000 with his limited-purpose FSA, another health plan. He is not eligible to reimburse himself for that $2,000.

472. How do HSA owners know they are not being overcharged?

One of the benefits and responsibilities of having an HSA is choosing medical treatments and providers. HSA owners struggle to know whether or not they are paying a fair price, in part because of the complexity of medical bills. For large or complex bills, billing review services exist. These services will review a medical bill and then negotiate a discount based on cost data.

473. Can an HSA owner reimburse for an expense paid for by a personal credit card?

Yes. If an HSA owner paid a qualified medical expense with after-tax dollars from a personal checking account, personal credit card, or just cash, then the HSA owner can reimburse for the expense from the HSA.

HSA owners cannot "double dip" and get two tax benefits for the same eligible medical expense. If the HSA owner itemized the expense on her income tax return, insurance covered the expense or she used another tax-favored account to pay the expense, then she cannot also use her HSA to pay the expense.

Penalties

474. What is the penalty for taking a non-qualified HSA distribution?

The penalty is 20 percent plus the distribution is taxable.

> *Example.* Jim, age thirty-five, has $4,000 in his HSA and writes a check to himself of that amount to pay for a vacation to Europe. In that case, Jim must include the $4,000 as taxable income on his income tax return and pay a penalty of $800 ($4,000 x 20 percent).

475. How do HSA owners pay the penalty?

HSA owners pay the penalty on IRS Form 8889, which is an attachment to the IRS Form 1040 Individual Income Tax Return.

IRS Form 8889, IRS Form 1040.

Expenses of Yourself, Your Spouse, and Your Dependents
Overview
476. Whose medical expenses are qualified for tax-free HSA distributions?

HSA owners can use funds in their HSA to pay for the qualified medical expenses of themselves, their spouse and their dependents.

IRS Publication 969.

477. Can HSA owners use HSA funds to pay for their medical expenses after they lose HSA eligibly?

Yes. HSA owners can use HSA funds to pay for their qualified medical expenses tax-free and penalty-free regardless of whether or not they are currently eligible to contribute more to an HSA. This rule is a key reason to build as large of a balance as possible in an HSA to cover future medical expenses even if future HSA eligibility is lost.

Spouses

478. Who is considered a spouse?

Who is considered a spouse is determined by state law. Generally, individuals who enter into a legal marriage are considered "spouses."

See Part VIII: Distributions - Domestic Partners and Same-Sex Marriages.

479. Can HSA owners use HSA funds to pay for a spouse's medical expenses if the spouse is not eligible for an HSA?

Yes, HSA owners can use their HSA to pay a spouse's qualified expenses. However, if the HSA owner has self-only HDHP coverage, the most the HSA owner can contribute is the HSA limit for singles and that may mean the HSA owner will not have enough money in the HSA to cover a spouse's medical expenses as well as their own.

480. Does the income tax filing status of a couple impact HSA usage?

No. An HSA owner can use his or her HSA to pay for the medical expenses of a spouse regardless of whether the couple files jointly or separately.

Dependents

481. Who is a dependent?

Determining whether a person can be claimed as a dependent on a tax return can be complex and impacts an individual's tax situation beyond just HSA considerations. A basic answer is that a dependent must be either: (1) a qualifying child, or (2) a qualifying relative. The dependent must be a U.S. citizen or national or a resident of the United States, Canada, or Mexico. A special exception exists for adopted children.

The general rule requiring that dependents earn less than $3,950 (2014) does not apply for HSAs.

IRS Publication 502.

Children

482. Who qualifies as a child dependent?

Any natural child, stepchild, foster child, or adopted child that: (1) shares the same home as the HSA owner who for more than one-half of the taxable year, (2) does not provide more than one-half of his or her own support for the year, and (3) meets one of the following age requirements.

- **Under Age nineteen.** The child was under age nineteen. This means the child did not turn 19 during the calendar-year (for calendar-year taxpayers). The child must also have been younger than the HSA owner and the HSA owner's spouse if filing jointly.

- **Under Age twenty-four and a Student**. The child is under age twenty-four (did not turn twenty-four during the tax year) and is a full-time student. The child must also have been younger than the HSA owner and the HSA owner's spouse if filing jointly.

- **Any Age If Disabled**. A child of any age that is permanently and totally disabled.

A child could also be a "qualifying relative" if the above definition is not met.

See Part VIII: Distributions - Expenses of Yourself, Your Spouse, and Your Dependents – Qualifying Relative.

483. Can HSA owners use their HSA to pay the medical expenses of adult children (up to age twenty-six) added to their insurance pursuant to the Affordable Care Act rules?

Maybe. HSA owners can use their HSA for expenses of their dependent children (this means tax dependents). Dependents includes children but generally not children over nineteen (or twenty-four if in school). If the HSA owner cannot claim the child as a dependent, then the HSA owner cannot use the HSA to pay for the child's medical expenses. In that case, the child could open their own HSA.

> *Example.* Sally's employer provides family HDHP insurance coverage that includes Sally's twenty-five year old son. Sally cannot use her HSA to pay the medical expenses of her twenty-five year old son because he is not her dependent. Her son can open his own HSA and make his own contribution. This is because he is covered under a family HDHP, is not a dependent on someone else's tax return, and is otherwise eligible for an HSA. Even better, he can use the family contribution limit ($6,650 for 2015) even though he is not married and has no children. Sally could make a contribution on her son's behalf to his HSA, but he would get the tax deduction.

484. Why can an employee use an FSA or HRA for children up to age twenty-six but not an HSA?

The IRS released guidance that allows the use FSA or HRA funds to reimburse for medical care of a child up to age twenty-six even if that child is not a dependent of the parent(s). The child must not obtain age twenty-seven in the year of the reimbursement. This guidance does not extend to HSAs.

> *Example.* Global, Inc. provides health coverage for its employees and their families, including children who have not yet reached age twenty-six. For 2014, Global provides coverage to Carol and Carol's son, Earl. Earl will attain age twenty-six on November 15, 2014. During 2014, Earl is not a full-time student. Earl is not a dependent of Carol. Carol can use her FSA to pay for Earl's qualified medical expenses until Earl's birthday on November 15, 2014. Earl loses coverage on his birthday because the plan documents provides for coverage only until age twenty-six.

IRS Notice 2010-38.

485. Can HSA owners use HSA funds for a child not covered by the HSA owner's health insurance?

Yes, an HSA owner can use the HSA for the HSA owner, a spouse and any dependents regardless of whether any of them are eligible for an HSA. To contribute money to an HSA, a person must be eligible for an HSA. To use the money in an HSA, the person using the HSA money does not need to be eligible for an HSA (but must be the HSA owner, a spouse of the HSA owner or a dependent of the HSA owner).

> *Example.* John is covered by a family HDHP that also covers his young son. John's wife is not covered by the HDHP and is separately insured through traditional insurance. John can contribute the family HSA limit and use his HSA to pay for the non-covered medical expenses of his wife (co-pays, up to her deductible, dental, vision, etc.) even though she is not covered by the HDHP.

IRS Notice 2004-50, See Q 37.

486. Can HSA owners use an HSA to pay the medical expenses of a child that is claimed as a dependent by a former spouse?

Yes. A special exception allows for this. A parent can use his or her HSA to pay for medical expenses of his or her child if child is claimed as a dependent on the former spouse's tax return. The child is treated as a dependent of both parents. This same rule applies for parents who are separated under a written separation agreement or living apart for the last six months of the year.

The child must be in the custody of both of the parents for more than half the year and must have received over half his or her support from his or her parents.

> *Example.* Bill and Jane were married and are the parents of Billy but are now divorced.. Jane claims Billy as a tax dependent on her income tax return. Bill has an HSA and would like to use his HSA to pay for Billy's medical expenses. Bill can do so even though Billy is not claimed as his dependent because of the special rule that he can use his HSA to pay the medical expenses of his child if that child is claimed as a dependent of his former spouse.

IRS Notice 2008-59, See Q 34.

Qualifying Relative

487. Who is a qualifying relative?

A qualifying relative is a person:

- Who is your:

  o Son, daughter, stepchild, or foster child, or a descendant of any of them (for example a grandchild)

  o Brother, sister, half-brother, half-sister, or a son or daughter of any of them

  o Father, mother, or an ancestor or sibling of either of them (for example, your grandmother, grandfather, aunt, or uncle)

  o Stepbrother, stepsister, stepfather, stepmother, son-in-law, daughter-in-law, father-in-law, mother-in-law, brother-in-law, or sister-in-law, or

  o Any other person (other than your spouse) who lived with you all year as a member of you household if your relationship did not violate local law

- Who was not a qualifying child, and

- For whom you provided over half of the support

IRS Publication 502.

Domestic Partners and Same-Sex Marriages

488. Did the Supreme Court's 2013 ruling that the Defense of Marriage Act is unconstitutional impact HSAs?

Yes, the ruling changes HSAs for legally married same-sex couples. The Defense of Marriage Act (DOMA) defined marriage as between one man and one women and accordingly did not grant same-sex couples the same rights as opposite sex couples under federal law. Prior to the Supreme Court's ruling, same-sex couples could not get the benefits afforded "spouses" under HSA law.

HSA law provides special treatment for spouses in the following areas:

- **Tax-Free Distributions.** An HSA owner can use his or her HSA tax-free to pay the qualified medical expenses of spouses

- **Beneficiary Treatment.** A spouse beneficiary can treat the HSA as his or her own upon the death of the HSA owner

- **Divorce Transfer.** An HSA owner can transfer assets into an HSA of former spouse in the case of a divorce

- **Estate Tax Treatment.** If a spouse is named as the beneficiary of the HSA, the treatment of the HSA may change for estate tax purposes

- **Family HDHP Treatment.** Spouses covered under a family HDHP are capped at the combined HSA family limit. Also, if one spouse has a family HDHP, then both spouses are deemed to have family HDHPs. This rule closes a loophole that allowed each partner in a same-sex couple to contribute the family HSA maximum in certain circumstances.

- **Child of Former Spouse.** An HSA owner can use the HSA to pay for medical expenses of his or her child that is claimed as a tax dependent by a former spouse (this is helpful in cases of divorce and legal separation)

489. Are same-sex couples always considered spouses?

No. Same-sex couples that are legally married and recognized by the state law as "spouses" can take advantage of the special treatment for spouses under HSA law. Check your state law to determine if your state recognizes same-sex marriage..

490. Is a domestic partnership or civil union the same as marriage?

No. The IRS states that for federal tax purposes the term "spouse" does not include "registered domestic partnerships, civil unions, or other similar formal relationships recognized under state law that are not denominated as a marriage under that state's law…"This is true for same-sex and opposite sex relationships. "Spouse" is the key word for HSA laws but "marriage" is generally the state classification that results in couples becoming "spouses."

Rev. Rul. 2013-17.

491. What is the rule for a legal same-sex marriage where the couple now lives in a state that does now allow same-sex marriages?

For federal tax purposes, a legal marriage is recognized assuming it was validly entered into in a state whose laws authorize same-sex marriages.

492. What is the effective date for the changes for same-sex spouses?

Although The Supreme Court declared the Defense of Marriage Act unconstitutional on June 6, 2013 but there remains uncertainly as to what this means from a timing perspective for HSAs. The IRS, the key regulatory authority for HSAs, released guidance on the impact of the change stating that the rules released in its guidance are prospective from September 16, 2013.

The same guidance added that affected taxpayers may retroactively apply the new rules in some cases. This includes filing amended returns to take advantage of tax benefits so long as the deadline for filing amended returns has not expired (generally three years). The IRS is also providing retroactive relief for benefit programs; including salary deferrals to Section 125 plans. At the time of this writing the exact nature of that relief is uncertain and the IRS promised more guidance on the retroactive application of this rule.

From an HSA perspective, a retroactive application could be favorable in a situation where an HSA owner was legally married to a same-sex spouse that incurred medical expenses and desired to use the HSA owner's HSA to pay those expenses. Under DOMA, the HSA owner could not use his or her HSA to pay the medical expenses of that partner but now they can. If still within the time period to amend the tax return, the HSA owner could likely reimburse himself or herself for those expenses paid outside of the HSA with HSA funds (assuming the medical expenses were not otherwise paid for with tax-favored dollars and that the couple was legally married on the date the medical expense were incurred). This could result in a situation where both individuals were able to contribute the maximum family HSA contribution prior to the law change and now be able to use both HSAs for both spouses after the law change. This early interpretation may change as we learn more from future IRS releases.

IRS Rev. Rul. 2013-17.

493. Can an HSA owner use an HSA to pay the medical expenses for a same-sex spouse?

Yes, provided the couple was married in a state that legally recognizes same-sex marriages. The unconstitutional federal Defense of Marriage Act no longer limits HSA law's use of the word "spouse" to mean only an opposite sex spouse.

494. Can HSA owners use HSA funds to pay medical expenses of domestic partners?

No. HSA owners can only use their HSAs to pay for the medical expenses of their spouses or their dependents. If a domestic partner meets the IRS requirements as a dependent (IRS Code Sec. 152), then the HSA owner can use his or her HSA for a domestic partner's medical expenses. Meeting the definition of a "dependent" is difficult for non-children. If the HSA owner's state recognizes same-sex marriages with the result being that the domestic partners are considered "spouses" (married), rather than domestic partners (or are spouses in addition to being domestic partners), then the HSA owner can use an HSA to pay for qualified medical expenses of a spouse.

IRC Sec. 152.

495. Can an HSA owner contribute the family HSA limit if the only other person on the family HDHP is a domestic partner or same-sex spouse?

Yes, in order to contribute the family HSA limit ($6,550 for 2014); an HSA owner must be covered by a family HDHP (covers the HSA owner and at least one other person). If that other person is a domestic partner, then the HSA owner has a family HDHP and can contribute the family limit if otherwise eligible for an HSA.

The rule is pretty straight-forward in this area and to get the family contribution limit you simply need to be covered under a family HDHP meaning the HSA owner and at least one other person be on the plan. That other person could be a spouse (same-sex or not), domestic partner (same sex or not), child or potentially someone else allowed on a family HDHP. The difference between same-sex domestic partners and same-sex married couples is significant for contributions, see the following question and for distributions.

See Part VIII: Distributions - Domestic Partners and Same-Sex Marriages.

496. Does the rule requiring married couples to coordinate their maximum family HSA contribution apply to domestic partners and same-sex spouses?

One potential downside for same-sex couples is that the Supreme Court's ruling striking down the Defense of Marriage Act closed a loophole. HSA law caps spouses' combined HSA contributions to the family limit ($6,550 for 2015) if one or both spouses had family HDHP coverage. Same-sex couples avoided that cap when they were not considered spouses and could each potentially contribute the maximum limit if they were covered under a family HDHP (i.e., they could each contribute $6,550 for 2014).

Spouses are subject to a couple of special rules in this regard: (1) if either spouse has family HDHP coverage both spouses are deemed to have family HDHP coverage and (2) combined the spouses cannot exceed the family HDHP limit.

Whether the loophole is still available to same-sex couples depends on whether or not the couple is legally married under state law.

Example 1. Todd and Adam are domestic partners and are not considered spouses under their state's laws. Todd's employer provides HDHP coverage for Todd and his domestic partner. Todd enrolls in a family HDHP through his employer that covers only Todd and Adam. Todd and Adam are both otherwise eligible for an HSA. Adam is not Todd's dependent (or vice versa). Todd contributes $6,550 to his own HSA for 2014. Adam also contributes $6,550 to his own HSA. Combined they get $13,100 of deductions for HSA contributions. An opposite-sex married couple would only get one $6,550 HSA contribution. Todd cannot use his HSA to cover Adam's medical expenses and Adam cannot use his HSA to pay for Todd's expenses (whereas married couples are able to use their HSA to cover each other's expenses).

Example 2. Using the same facts as the previous example, except that Todd and Adam are same-sex spouses married in a state that allows that status. Todd contributes $6,550 to his HSA for 2014. Adam cannot also contribute to his HSA. Combined married couples must coordinate their HSA contributions not to exceed the federal limit and because Todd contributed the full amount there is no limit left for Adam to contribute to an HSA. Todd can use his HSA to cover Adam's medical expenses.

Mistaken Distributions

497. What happens when HSA owners use their HSA by mistake?

HSA owners that mistakenly take distributions from their HSAs have an opportunity to fix the mistake through special rules for the return of mistaken distributions.

The HSA owner had to have made the mistake due to a reasonable cause and be able to support that with *clear and convincing* evidence. The HSA owner must repay the mistaken distribution amount to the HSA prior to the tax filing due date for the year the HSA owner knew or should have known of the mistake. Custodians generally provide a special spot on a form for this purpose. Failure to notify the HSA custodian as to the reason for the contribution (i.e., a return of mistaken distribution) will result in incorrect IRS reporting. HSA custodians are not required to accept the return. In that case, the HSA owner would have to pay taxes plus a 20 percent penalty on the amount of the mistaken distribution.

Example 1. Jane goes to the doctor and receives a bill for $100. She promptly pays the bill through her HSA. Later, the medical provider sends Jane a check reimbursing her for the $100 stating that the doctor visit was fully covered by her insurance as preventive care. Jane, can now return $100 to the HSA as the return of a mistaken distribution. She does not need to endorse the actual check she received from the medical provider (although she could do that) and can instead deposit the reimbursement check and write a personal check to make the HSA contribution for the return of a mistaken distribution.

Example 2. Juan goes to a restaurant with his family and accidently pays the bill with his HSA debit card (it looks similar to his other cards and he was distracted by his daughter's temper tantrum). He later discovers the mistake and can return the amount spent as the return of a mistaken distribution.

IRS Notice 2004-50, See Q 38.

498. Does the HSA owner need to provide "clear and convincing evidence" to the HSA custodian and the IRS in the case of the return of a mistaken distribution?

Yes. The HSA owner needs to provide clear and convincing evidence to the IRS, if audited. The custodian can rely on the representation of the HSA owner that the distribution was a reasonable mistake supported by evidence. The custodian will not generally ask for clear and convincing evidence but instead will rely on the HSA owner's signature on a form attesting to the fact that the mistake was made and evidence is available.

499. How do HSA owners correct mistaken distributions on their income tax returns?

No. HSA owners generally do not report the mistaken distribution on their income tax return and the HSA owner correspondingly also does not report the return of the amount to the HSA.

If the mistaken distribution is corrected in the same year as it's made, then no reporting is necessary. HSA owners should make sure their HSA custodian understands that that the contribution is the *return of a mistaken distribution*. The HSA custodian will not include the original mistaken distribution as a distribution on the 1099-SA or the return of the money as a contribution on the IRS Form 5498-SA. If the custodian already filed the 1099-SA, it will need to do a corrected 1099-SA.

> *Example.* Duane mistakenly takes out $100 from his HSA to pay for a medical expense that is subsequently reimbursed by his health insurance. He returns the $100 to his HSA custodian as the return of a mistaken distribution. The HSA custodian accepts the $100 and places it in the HSA but does not include the $100 in the category of contributions that will show on the IRS Form 5498-SA. The HSA custodian also must reduce Duane's distribution amount for the purposes of the 1099-SA by $100. Duane does not report the $100 as a contribution or as a distribution on his IRS Form 1040 income tax return.

IRS Form 5498-SA, IRS Form 1099-SA.

Miscellaneous

500. Can an HSA owner use HSA funds to reimburse for garnished wages due to unpaid medical bills?

Yes, if the expenses were otherwise qualified and no additional fees are included in the garnishment. An HSA owner can use his HSA to pay for medical expenses incurred after the establishment date of the HSA. The date that the actual medical services were received and billed is the key date, not the date of the garnishment.

> *Example.* In 2010, Bill opens an HSA and funds it. He continues to hold this HSA today. In 2011, Bill received medical treatment that qualified as a qualified medical expense. However, Bill got into a dispute over the bill and refused to pay a portion of the bill amounting to $2,000. In 2014, the medical provider successfully sued him for that $2,000 and is now garnishing his wages.

> Bill is eligible to use his HSA for the $2,000 in medical expenses because the $2,000 was a legitimate medical expense in 2011, after his establishment date. His receipt for the original medical expense is his proof for tax purposes. Accordingly, if his wages are garnished by $2,000, he could write a check to himself from his HSA to re-pay himself the $2,000 because the expense was qualified. He cannot pay for any additional items that might be garnished. If the garnishment includes interest, legal fees, court fees, penalties, etc., those additional expenses are generally not qualified medical expenses.

501. How are banking fees, such as ATM or annual fees, treated for tax purposes?

Banking fees may be deducted directly from the HSA and not reported as a distribution. This is a good deal for the HSA owner because it allows the individual to pay banking fees tax-free.

In order to have money in the HSA, the money would have been reported as an HSA contribution going into the HSA counting against the federal maximum HSA limit.

Individuals that want to maximize their HSA contribution amount can pay HSA banking fees separately and outside of the HSA. In that case, the fee is not counted as a contribution or a distribution because it is not in the HSA. The individual may be able to deduct the expense as a banking fee on their tax return. From a practical perspective, this would be difficult to do for ATM fees so it may make more sense to require that those fees be deducted from the HSA.

IRS Notice 2008-59, See Q 43.

PART IX: TAX ISSUES

Overview

502. Are there tax benefits to making an HSA contribution?

Yes. HSA owners making an HSA contribution enjoy a number of tax benefits.

- **Federal Income Tax Deduction.** HSA contributions reduce an HSA owner's income for federal income tax purposes.

- **State Income Tax Deduction.** Most states with income taxes allow HSA owners to reduce the state taxable income by the amount of the HSA contribution.

- **Payroll Tax Avoidance.** HSA owners receiving HSA contributions pre-tax through an employer, either employer contributions or employee payroll deferral through a Section 125 plan, also avoid Social Security taxes, Medicare taxes (together with Social Security referred to as FICA), federal unemployment taxes (FUTA), Railroad Retirement Act taxes, and in most cases state unemployment taxes (SUTA).

- **Tax Deferred Earnings Growth.** Any interest, dividends or other appreciation of the assets in an HSA grow tax-deferred while in the HSA.

- **Tax-free Distributions.** HSA owners that use the HSA for qualified medical expenses enjoy tax-free distributions. This is a better deal than traditional IRA or 401(k)s because those plans are only tax-deferred, not tax-free (although Roth IRAs/401(k)s distributions are tax-free, contributions made to Roth accounts are not tax deductible).

503. Do HSAs qualify for state income tax deductions?

Yes (with exceptions). Most states allow for a state income tax deduction for HSA contributions. California, New Jersey and Alabama are the only states with income taxes that do not allow a state income tax deduction for an HSA contribution. All other states have either passed specific legislation allowing HSA deductions for state income tax purposes, have conforming legislation where the federal deductions flow through at the state level, or do not have a state income tax.

504. Do HSA owners have to itemize in order to claim an HSA deduction?

No. HSA contributions are deductible on the individual tax return whether or not the HSA owner itemizes. HSA contributions are an "above-the-line" deduction.

505. Are employer contributions subject to payroll taxes?

No. Employer-made comparable contributions to eligible employees' HSAs on a pre-tax basis are not subject to payroll taxes. Employee HSA pre-tax payroll deferral contributions made pursuant to a Section 125 plan are also not subject to payroll taxes. Employer contributions made after-tax are subject to payroll taxes. Employee direct contributions do not get the benefit of avoiding payroll taxes.

Payroll taxes include: Federal Insurance Contributions Act (FICA), Federal Unemployment Tax Act (FUTA), and the Railroad Retirement Tax Act. FICA includes both Social Security (6.2 percent for both the employer and the employee) and Medicare (1.45 percent for both the employer and the employee). Most states also allow for pre-tax treatment to avoid state unemployment taxes. At a certain income, taxpayers no longer pay Social Security taxes or federal unemployment so the benefit of avoiding taxes on these may not apply.

IRS Notice 2004-2, See Q 20.

Tax Savings

506. How much do HSA owners save in taxes?

The answer depends on a number of factors concerning the HSA owner and the type of HSA contribution: (1) the marginal federal tax rate, (2) the marginal state income tax rate, (3) the size of the HSA contribution, (4) whether or not an employer-made the HSA contribution pre-tax, and (5) a number of other factors too nuanced to list here. For an estimate of tax savings, an HSA owner can use the following chart.

		HSA Tax Savings Calculator[1]	
	A	HSA Contribution Amount	
Federal Income Savings	B	Federal Income Tax Rate	
	C	Estimated Federal Income Tax Savings (Multiply A x B)	
State Income Savings	D	State Income Tax Rate[2]	
	E	Estimated State Income Tax Savings (Multiply A x D)	
Payroll Taxes Savings	F	Payroll Tax Savings, If applicable (7.65%)[3]	
	G	Estimated Payroll Tax Savings[3] (Multiply A x F)	
	H	Estimated Income Tax Savings (Add C + E + G)	

[1]This chart only provides an estimate and your actual savings may differ. The chart does not factor in potential FUTA and SUTA savings.
[2]AL, CA, and NJ do not allow HSA deductions.
[3]You only avoid payroll taxes for pre-tax employer contributions, including pre-tax payroll deferral. The 7.65% reflected in the chart assumes employee savings of FICA at 6.2% (only up to $117,000 for 2014) and an additional 1.45% for Medicare. Add .9% for a Medicare surtax for income above $200,000 for single filers and $250,000 for joint filers. Employer payroll tax savings are in addition to the employee savings.

Example. Jim is in the 28 percent federal income tax bracket and the 6 percent state income tax bracket in a state that grants HSAs deductibility. Jim deferred $554.16 per month to his HSA in 2015 ($6,650 over the year), pre-tax through his company's Section 125 plan (this is treated as an employer contribution that avoids payroll taxes). The chart below illustrates his tax savings by making the HSA contributions.

		HSA Tax Savings Calculator[1]	
Federal Income Savings	A	HSA Contribution Amount	$6,650
	B	Federal Income Tax Rate	28%
	C	Estimated Federal Income Tax Savings (Multiply A x B)	$1,862
State Income Savings	D	State Income Tax Rate[2]	6%
	E	Estimated State Income Tax Savings (Multiply A x D)	$399
Payroll Taxes Savings	F	Payroll Tax Savings, If applicable (7.65%)[3]	7.65%
	G	Estimated Payroll Tax Savings[3] (Multiply A x F)	$508.73
	H	Estimated Income Tax Savings (Add C + E + G)	$2,769.73

[1]This chart only provides an estimate and your actual savings may differ. The chart does not factor in potential FUTA and SUTA savings.
[2]AL, CA, and NJ do not allow HSA deductions.
[3]You only avoid payroll taxes for pre-tax employer contributions, including pre-tax payroll deferral. The 7.65% reflected in the chart assumes employee savings of FICA at 6.2% (only up to $117,000 for 2014) and an additional 1.45% for Medicare. Add .9% for a Medicare surtax for income above $200,000 for single filers and $250,000 for joint filers. Employer payroll tax savings are in addition to the employee savings.

507. What are the federal income tax brackets?

The table below provides the marginal federal income tax rates.

2014 Federal Tax Table				
Single	Married Filing Jointly	Married Filing Separately	Head of House-hold	Tax Rate
$0 to $9,075	$0 to $18,150	$0 to $9,075	$0 to $12,950	10%
$9,975-$36,900	$18,150-$73,800	$9,075-$36,900	$12,950-$49,400	15%
$36,900-$89,350	$73,800-$148,850	$36,900-$74,425	$49,,400-$125,550	25%
$89,350-$186,350	$148,850-$226,850	$74,425-$113,425	$125,550-$206,600	28%
$186,350-$405,100	$226,850-$405,100	$113,425-$202,550	$206,600-$405,100	33%
$405,100-$406,750	$405,100-$457,600	$202,550-$228,800	$405,100-$432,200	35%
Over $406,750	Over $457,600	Over $228,800	Over $432,200	39.6%

Claiming the HSA Deduction

508. How do HSA owners actually claim the tax benefit?

HSA owners that make HSA contributions on their own rather than tax-free through an employer, take their HSA deduction when they file their federal income tax return. HSA contributions are tax deductible as an "above-the-line" deduction found on line 25 of the

IRS Form 1040. "Above-the-line" means that the taxpayer gets the benefit of the deduction even if the taxpayer takes the standard deduction and does not itemize. Unlike other deductions, such as IRA and Roth IRA contributions, no income limits apply so even high income people can take advantage of the HSA deduction. HSA owners must also file IRS Form 8889 as an attachment to their income tax return. Tax preparation software generally does that for taxpayers.

Pre-tax employer contributions, including pre-tax employee payroll deferral, are not deductible on line 25 because the employer already reduced the taxpayer's income by the amount of the HSA contribution. Business owners may face different tax treatment.

IRS Form 1040, IRS Form 8889.

509. How do HSA owners claim HSA deductions for employer-made HSA contributions?

Employers report the HSA contribution on the IRS Form W-2 as not being taxable so the deduction happens automatically. Employer pre-tax HSA contributions or employee payroll deferral HSA contributions through a Section 125 plan are not deductible on an individual's income tax return. The contributions are not deductible because they were never included in income. This is good news for HSA owners because the HSA owner already has gotten the tax benefit as well as saved payroll taxes (FICA and FUTA).

IRS Form W-2.

510. How does an HSA owner know if an employer HSA contribution was made pre-tax?

To verify the status of an HSA contribution as pre-tax, an HSA owner should look at Box 12 of the IRS Form W-2. Pre-tax employer contributions are reflected in Box 12 with a Code "W" next to it. This number will include both employer pre-tax and employee payroll deferral pre-tax HSA contributions. Even though the contribution was made pre-tax, HSA owners are still required to complete IRS Form 8889 and include it as an attachment to their income tax return.

Note: Special rules apply to sole proprietors, partners in a partnership (and LLC members), and more than 2 percent owners of S-corporations.

IRS Form W-2, IRS Form 8889.

Tax Deadline

511. What is the deadline to make an HSA contribution?

HSA owners have until their tax filing due date, without extensions, to make HSA contributions. For taxpayers with an April 15, 2015 tax due date, the last date they can make a 2015 HSA contribution is April 15, 2016. An HSA custodian may require a slightly earlier date to ensure that it properly reports the contribution. HSA owners should make sure to mark on the HSA contribution form the year the contribution is for (e.g., 2014 or 2015) as HSA owners can make contributions for two different years from January 1 to April 15 (or for non-calendar year filers the taxpayer's tax due date).

> *Example.* John became eligible for an HSA on January 1, 2014 but never opened an HSA. In March of 2015, when he was still eligible for an HSA he decided to fully fund his HSA for both 2014 and 2015. He can make a $6,550 HSA contribution for 2014, as it's still before his April 15, 2015 tax filing due date for 2014. Plus he can make another $6,650 HSA contribution for 2015. He can make a 2014 contribution at any point between January 1, 2014 and his tax filing due date for 2014 (April 15, 2015). He can contribute a total contribution of $13,200, potentially on the same day. He should instruct his HSA custodian that $6,550 is for 2014 and $6,650 is for 2015 to ensure proper tax reporting and to avoid a potential excess contribution.

Earnings

512. What is the tax treatment on interest, dividends, and other earnings in an HSA?

Earnings in an HSA are not includable in gross income while held in the HSA. The "buildup" is not taxable unless distributed for a non-qualified reason.

IRS Notice 2004-2, See Q 21.

Attachment of HSAs

513. Can the IRS levy an HSA?

The federal HSA laws do not provide any special exemption from a levy for HSAs -- however, it is state law that determines whether or not the HSA may be levied.

The IRS has issued a memorandum (IRS Memorandum 200927019) that states if an HSA is levied, the HSA owner will owe the 20 percent penalty tax for the amount levied unless the HSA owner meets an exception (is over sixty-five, disabled or dead).

IRS Memorandum 200927019.

514. Is an HSA exempt from bankruptcy?

Uncertain. This is still an emerging area of case law, but one court found that HSAs are not excluded from the property of the estate (not exempt from bankruptcy). The debtor argued that it did not constitute property of the estate because it is part of a health insurance plan regulated by the state. The court disagreed and found it to be a simple trust account.

In re Leitch, 494 B.R. 918, 2013 WL 3722091 (8th Cir. B.A.P. (Minn).

515. Can an HSA be garnished?

Uncertain. Garnishment orders must be issued by a court and the court should review whether or not an HSA can be garnished prior to issuing the order. The answer is not certain because it will be decided state-by-state and states have generally not passed HSA specific laws answering this question. This leaves the issue to the courts. Absent special protection, HSAs can be garnished.

There is a possibility that some states will protect HSAs from garnishment either with special legislation or because HSAs fall within an existing definition of a protected category, such as retirement or health plans. HSAs are generally not ERISA plans so legislation that protects ERISA plans from garnishment will generally not protect HSAs.

516. Can an HSA be escheated to the state?

Yes. Whether and how funds would be escheated depends on state law. Escheat laws provide that states take control of unclaimed or abandoned property. Dormant or inactive HSAs would likely fall into unclaimed property after the state's period for dormancy is met (states struggling to balance their budgets have decreased the dormancy periods to periods as short as three). Dormancy generally is defined as an account with no activity and mailed statements to an address have been returned for the dormancy period (a special letter warning of the escheatment may also be required under state law). After meeting the dormancy requirements the HSA custodian needs to forward the funds to the state. The HSA owner could reclaim the funds by connecting directly with the state.

Note: The escheatment rules are more likely to impact HSAs than other types of accounts given the long-term nature of the savings and with employer-made contributions some individuals may wrongly assume they lose the money when they separate from service.

Withholding for Taxes

517. Is an HSA distribution subject to income tax withholding?

No. Because HSAs are generally used tax-free to pay for qualified medical expenses no withholding is required for distributions from HSAs. HSA owners may be liable for taxes and penalties on HSA distributions and should increase their income tax withholding through their employer or through quarterly estimated withholding if necessary.

518. Can an HSA custodian withhold for income taxes?

No. Although generally the IRS encourages taxpayers to withhold on taxable distributions, the IRS Form 1099-SA does not provide a spot for the custodian to report the amount withheld. Without a system in place to properly report the amount withheld it is not possible for an HSA custodian to do so. Taxpayers can do their own withholding by adjusting their salary withholding (employee can ask to revise the IRS Form W-4) or by increasing their estimated income tax withholding payments (IRS Form-ES).

IRS Form 1099-SA, IRS Form W-4, IRS Form-ES.

Tax Forms Required

519. What IRS forms are necessary for HSA owners to prepare and file income tax returns?

HSAs provide fantastic tax benefits but the IRS checks to make sure individuals follow the rules. The HSA owner's role in this process is to attach IRS Form 8889 to the income tax return for any year the HSA owner took a distribution or made a contribution to an HSA. Tax preparation software (e.g., TurboTax) should generate the IRS Form 8889 automatically based on the taxpayer answering HSA questions in the software's system or by inputting information from an IRS Form 1099-SA. The following are the key forms for HSAs owners in preparation of an income tax return.

- **IRS Form 1040.** There are different versions of the 1040 that work for HSAs, but line 25 of the 1040 is the line where an HSA owner takes a deduction for an individual HSA contribution (not employer pre-tax HSA contributions). The 1040EZ is not available for HSA owners that need to report HSA contributions or distributions. A taxable HSA distribution is also reported on line 21 of the 1040 with the entry "HSA." If a 20 percent penalty is also owed, that is reported on line 60, ("other taxes"), on the 1040.

- **IRS Form 8889.** This is an attachment to an HSA owners' income tax return that follows a step-by-step review of HSA owner's HSA contributions, distributions, and for additional taxes or penalties owed.

- **IRS Form 1099-SA.** The HSA custodian sends HSA owners and the IRS the 1099-SA early in the year to document HSA distributions. HSA owners must use the IRS Form 1099-SA to complete an income tax return.

- **IRS Form 5498-SA.** The IRS Form 5498-SA documents an HSA owner's total yearly contributions to an HSA (including rollovers). An HSA custodian must send this form to the HSA owner and to the IRS. The form is not due to the HSA owner or the IRS until after the tax filing due date. That's because HSA owners have until their tax filing due date to make a contribution for the year so an HSA custodian does not necessarily know the HSA owner's HSA contributions for the year until after the tax due date. Accordingly, HSA owners need to know their HSA contribution information from their own records (non-tax statements from the HSA custodian, IRS Form W-2 from the employer, or personal records). Some HSA custodians provide the report early in the year and then update it if the HSA owner makes a prior to the April 15 deadline for the prior year.

- **IRS Form W-2.** An IRS Form W-2 from an employer will show employer pre-tax HSA contributions as well as pre-tax payroll deferral contributions HSA owners made to an HSA in Box 12 with a Code W.

- **IRS Form 5329.** The IRS Form 5329 is only necessary if the HSA owner owes a penalty for making an excess contribution to an HSA. In that case, the HSA owner files this form as an attachment to the income tax return.

IRS Form 1040, IRS Form 1040-EZ, IRS Form 1099-SA, IRS Form 5498-SA, IRS Form 8889, IRS Form W-2, IRS Form 5329.

520. What tax forms are required if an HSA owner only used the HSA for qualified medical expenses and did not make any HSA contributions?

Distributions for qualified medical expenses are tax-free but the IRS still requires some reporting. The HSA custodian generates a 1099-SA that shows the amount of any distribution the HSA owner took during the year. The custodian sends the 1099-SA to both the IRS and the HSA owner. The HSA owner needs to reflect that distribution on the IRS Form 1040 tax return and complete IRS Form 8889. Form 8889 is required for both HSA contributions and distributions. If the distribution is for qualified medical expenses, it will not be taxable income.

IRS Form 1099-SA, IRS Form 8889, IRS Form 1040.

521. Are any tax forms required if an HSA owner has an HSA but does not make a contribution or take a distribution during the tax year?

No. The IRS Form 8889 is not required in a year where an HSA owner did not make any HSA contributions or take any HSA distributions. The HSA owner would not receive an IRS Form 1099-SA. The HSA owner (and the IRS) would still receive an IRS Form 5498-SA stating the Fair Market Value of the HSA but no special reporting is required.

IRS Form 1099-SA, IRS Form 8889, IRS Form 5498-SA.

522. Can an HSA owner file using the IRS Form 1040EZ?

No. The IRS Form 1040EZ is not available as an option for HSAs owners that made an HSA contribution or took an HSA distribution during the year.

IRS Form 1040-EZ.

Tax Reporting
IRS Form 8889

523. What is IRS Form 8889 and how is it used?

IRS Form 8889 is a schedule that HSA owners need to attach to their federal income tax returns. HSA owners must file a Form 8889 each year they make an HSA contribution or take an HSA distribution. The form reviews HSA contributions for the year in Part I, HSA distributions in Part II, and additional taxes for failing the testing period in Part III.

- **Contributions - Part I.** The upper part of the form, Part I, determines the deduction amount for line 25 on the 1040. The form separates employer contributions that were pre-tax from those deductible on line 25. Generally contributions made through employers are not taxable income on the Form W-2 and therefore are not deductible on the 1040. Contributions that HSA owners make on their own, outside of an employer, are deductible on the 1040. The form also checks to make sure the taxpayer is eligible for an HSA and that the taxpayer did not exceed the federal HSA limits. The form reviews factors like family versus single health coverage, the HSA owner's age for catch-up contributions, and whether a spouse also has an HSA.

- **Distributions - Part II.** The lower part of the form, Part II, validates that HSA distributions were used for qualified medical expenses. The IRS Form 1099-SA combines qualified and non-qualified distributions. Line 15 is the key. HSA owners must write the dollar amount of their eligible medical expense distributions from the HSA on this line. For many HSA owners this number will match the 1099-SA total distribution because the HSA owner only used the HSA to pay for qualified medical expenses. If not, the HSA owner may have to pay taxes plus add a 20 percent penalty for the non-eligible distributions.

- **Income and Additional Tax for Failure to Maintain HDHP Coverage – Part III.** The last section of the form, Part III, is on a second page, and is used to determine any additional tax and penalty owed for failure to maintain the testing period required under the full contribution rule or for IRA to HSA funding of an HSA. Most HSA owners will not need to complete this section as it only applies if the HSA owner failed a testing period.

IRS Form 8889, IRS Form 1040, IRS Form W-2, IRS Form 1099-SA.

524. Is the IRS Form 8889 filed for prohibited transactions?

Yes, if the HSA owner engages in a prohibited transaction, the HSA ceases to be an HSA as of January 1 of the year of the prohibited transaction. The HSA owner must include the full Fair Market Value of the HSA as taxable income on line 14a and will be subject to the 20 percent additional penalty for non-eligible medical distributions.

If the HSA owner used the HSA as security for a loan, then the HSA owner must include the value of the assets used as security for a loan as income on line 21 of IRS Form 1040 or IRS Form 1040NR.

Instructions for IRS Form 8889, IRS Form 8889.

525. Is the IRS Form 8889 filed to report failed testing periods?

Yes, HSA owners need to file IRS Form 8889, Part III, for a failure to maintain an HSA during the testing period.

Instructions for IRS Form 8889, IRS Form 8889.

526. Are beneficiaries of HSAs required to file the IRS Form 8889?

Yes. Individuals that are named as beneficiaries on an HSA and inherit an HSA must file the IRS Form 8889. A spouse beneficiary treats the HSA as his or her own and simply files the Form 8889 as though the HSA belongs to the surviving spouse (as it does).

If a non-spouse beneficiary inherits the money, the HSA ceases to be an HSA and the beneficiary must specially complete the IRS Form 8889.

Completing the IRS Form 8889 in the case of a non-spouse beneficiary:

- On the beneficiary's Form 8889, the beneficiary writes "Death of HSA account beneficiary." (The "beneficiary" refers to the HSA owner (the account beneficiary) and not the designated beneficiary.)

- Enter the designated beneficiaries name and Social Security Number on the top of the form in the spots provided

- Skip Part I

- On line 14, enter the fair market value of the HSA as of the date of death

- On line 15, for a beneficiary other than an estate, enter qualified medical expenses incurred by the HSA owner before the date of death that the beneficiary paid within one year after the date of death

- Finally, complete the rest of Part II of the form

If a beneficiary also has an HSA or is a beneficiary of more than one person's HSA, then the beneficiary must complete one Form 8889 for each HSA and mark the forms on the top as "statement." The beneficiary must also complete a controlling Form 8889 that consolidates the data from the other forms. The controlling form is placed in front of the statement Form 8889s in a paper filing.

IRS Form 8889.

IRS Form W-2

527. Are HSA contributions reported on the IRS Form W-2?

Yes, if the contributions were made pre-tax by the employer. Pre-tax employer contributions, both HSA payroll deferral through a Section 125 plan and employer HSA comparable contributions are reported in Box 12 of the IRS Form W-2 with a Code W. If an employer makes both types of contributions the amounts are combined in Box 12.

See Employer Issues — Employer Contributions — Reporting, IRS Form W-2

IRS Form 5498-SA

528. What is an IRS Form 5498-SA - Contribution Report?

IRS Form 5498-SA is a form that HSA custodians must send to the HSA owner and the IRS each year. The main purpose of this form is to inform the IRS how much the HSA owner contributed to the HSA. The IRS then uses this to check to make sure the HSA owner does not claim an HSA deduction above the amount of the HSA contribution. HSA owners may not get this form until after tax season (required by June 1) because the IRS wants custodians to record all tax year HSA contributions, including those made as late as April 15 of the following year. Accordingly, think of this form as an IRS tool to check on HSA owners; it's not to help HSA owners complete their tax return as it's often sent after the tax return is due.

☐ CORRECTED (if checked)			
TRUSTEE'S name, street address, city or town, state or province, country, ZIP or foreign postal code, and telephone number	1 Employee or self-employed person's Archer MSA contributions made in 2014 and 2015 for 2014 $	OMB No. 1545-1518 2014 Form **5498-SA**	**HSA, Archer MSA, or Medicare Advantage MSA Information**
	2 Total contributions made in 2014 $		
TRUSTEE'S federal identification number PARTICIPANT'S social security number	3 Total HSA or Archer MSA contributions made in 2015 for 2014 $		**Copy B**
PARTICIPANT'S name	4 Rollover contributions $	5 Fair market value of HSA, Archer MSA, or MA MSA $	**For Participant**
Street address (including apt. no.)	6 HSA ☐ Archer MSA ☐		The information in boxes 1 through 6 is being furnished to the Internal Revenue Service.
City or town, state or province, country, and ZIP or foreign postal code	MA MSA ☐		
Account number (see instructions)			

Form **5498-SA**   (keep for your records)   www.irs.gov/form5498sa   Department of the Treasury - Internal Revenue Service

IRS Form 5498-SA.

529. What information gets sent to the IRS on the IRS Form 5498?

The form only contains six boxes of information other than the contact information. For the tax year 2014, the 5498-SA boxes reflect the following.

- **Box 1. Archer MSA Contributions.** This box is only used for an employee or self-employed person's Archer MSA contributions made in 2014 and 2015 for 2014.

- **Box 2. Total HSA Contributions.** This box is used to reflect the total HSA or Archer MSA contributions made in 2014. This includes any contributions made in 2015 for 2014. This includes IRA to HSA funding contributions. This box includes HSA owner contributions, employee payroll deferral and employer contributions. This box does not reflect HSA to HSA rollovers and transfers.

- **Box 3. Total HSA or Archer MSA Contributions Made in 2015 for 2014.** This box reflects the total HSA or Archer MSA contributions made in 2015 for 2014.

- **Box 4. Rollover Contributions.** This box reflects money rolled over from another HSA or Archer MSA received in 2014.

- **Box 5. Fair Market Value.** This box reflects the HSAs Fair Market Value as of December 31, 2014.

- **Box 6. Check Box.** This box is a checkbox to reflect the type of account: HSA, Archer MSA, or MA MSA.

2014 IRS Instructions for Forms 1099-SA and 5498-SA, IRS Form 5498-SA.

530. Is the HSA custodian required to include an account number?

No, the HSA custodian is not required to include an account number on the IRS Form 5498-SA, unless the HSA custodian is filing multiple form 5498-SAs for the HSA owner due to multiple HSAs. The IRS encourages HSA custodians to include an account number on all Form 5498-SAs.

IRS Form 5498-SA.

531. When is the IRS Form 5498-SA sent?

HSA custodians must provide the form to both the IRS and the HSA owner by May 31 each year (May 31, 2016 for 2015). HSA custodians may send a Fair Market Value (FMV) report by the end of January (January 31, 2016 for the 2015 tax year) showing 2015 contributions and the December 31 FMV.

If a custodian provides the earlier FMV report and no additional contributions were made for the taxable year after the report was sent, then the custodian is not required to send the HSA owner the 5498-SA in May. The HSA custodian must still send the 5498-SA to the IRS as it reports the FMV of the HSA. A custodian selecting this approach must designate on the FMV report which information is being provided to the IRS (the December 31, FMV in this case).

IRS Form 5498-SA.

532. Are transfers and rollover contributions reported?

No. HSA custodians do not report HSA to HSA transfers on the IRS Form 5498-SA not is an Archer MSA transfer into an HSA reported. However, a rollover from one HSA to another HSA is reported in Box 4 of the Form 5498-SA. IRA to HSA funding distributions are also reported in Box 2 of the Form 5498-SA. The terms "rollover," "transfer," and "HSA funding distribution" can cause confusion.

See Part VI: Transfers and Rollovers for details, IRS Form 5498-SA.

533. What IRS reporting is required if an HSA is closed during the year?

Generally, if an HSA owner takes a total distribution during the year and makes no contributions during the year, the HSA custodian is not required to generate an IRS Form 5498-SA. The custodian will have to generate an IRS Form 1099-SA documenting the distribution details.

If the HSA owner did make a contribution during the year, then the custodian will be required to generate a Form 5498-SA even though the account is closed to reflect the contributions made for the tax year prior to the closure.

IRS Form 5498-SA, IRS Form 1099-SA.

534. How are death distributions reported for IRS Form 5498-SA purposes?

The reporting rules are different depending upon whether or not a spouse is the beneficiary.

- **Spouse Beneficiary.** If a spouse is the beneficiary, the HSA becomes the HSA of the spouse. The HSA custodian changes the personal account information over to the name, Social Security Number and other personal data of the spouse. The custodian will generate an IRS Form 5498-SA to the surviving spouse and none will generate for the deceased HSA owner. If the custodian generates a FMV Report in January that can serve as meeting the participant half of the contribution reporting if no contributions were made to the account by either the deceased HSA owner prior to death or by the surviving spouse after acquiring the HSA.

- **Non-Spouse Beneficiary.** If a non-spouse beneficiary is named then the HSA ceases to be an HSA. The custodian would generate a final Form 5498-SA showing the FMV and any contributions made for the final tax year prior to the HSA owner's death.

IRS Form 5498-SA.

IRS Form 1099-SA

535. What is the IRS Form 1099-SA - Distribution Report?

HSA custodians are required to send an IRS Form1099-SA to the HSA owner and the IRS each year the HSA owner takes a distribution from an HSA. The purpose of this form is to give the IRS a report showing the amount the HSA owner took out of the HSA for the year so it can check for proper tax treatment.

The use of the 1099 series of forms can cause confusion to HSA owners that correlate a 1099 form to miscellaneous income. The 1099 series is also used for IRA distributions and that is likely the reason the IRS used a 1099 for HSAs. Receipt of a IRS Form 1099 generally means a taxpayer has taxable income, but in the case of an HSA that might not be the case. If all the distributions reflected on the 1099-SA correspond to qualified medical expenses then no taxes are owed.

The IRS requires the HSA custodian to "code" the transactions into categories that may have different tax treatment. Most HSA distributions are "normal" or "Code 1" distributions. These distributions include both qualified medical expenses (a doctor visit) and most non-qualified medical expenses (a car muffler). Many people are surprised that the qualified and non-qualified distributions are lumped together. The IRS looks to the HSA owner to clarify the distributions on the IRS Form 8889.

Other codes include: excess (Code 2), disability (Code 3), and death distribution (Code 4 or 6). If all HSA distributions were for qualified medical expenses the HSA owner will not owe any taxes or penalties.

IRS Form 1099-SA, IRS 5498-SA.

536. What are the IRS distribution codes for the IRS Form 1099-SA?

The IRS requires the HSA custodian to determine the appropriate code for all HSA distributions. The vast majority of HSA distributions are normal distributions (Code 1). The other codes are used much less frequently. The codes include:

- **Code 1 – Normal Distributions**. Custodians use this code for both qualified medical expenses and other distributions when no other code applies.

- **Code 2 – Excess Contributions**. Custodians use this code for the return of excess contributions to HSA owners (when the HSA owner contributed a larger amount than allowed under the law).

- **Code 3 – Disability.** Custodians use this code if the HSA owner was disabled. Disabled HSA owners are not subject to the 20 percent penalty for non-eligible medical expense withdrawals.

- **Code 4 – Death Distributions.** Custodians use this code for payments to an HSA owner's estate in the year of death or the year after the year of death. Custodians use this code for payments to beneficiaries in the year of the death. See Code 6 for non-estate distributions.

- **Code 5. Prohibited Transaction.** Custodians use this code to report a prohibited transaction.

- **Code 6 – Death Distribution.** HSA custodians use this code to report payments to a non-spouse beneficiary after the year of death. Custodians do not use Code 4 or 6 for spouse beneficiaries because the HSA just becomes their own.

IRS 1099-SA.

537. What are the boxes on an IRS Form 1099-SA?

The boxes are as followings:

- **Box 1. Gross Distribution.** This box includes the total amount of the distribution. The custodian will combine multiple distributions made in the same year with the same code. In the case of the return of an excess contribution, the gross amount includes any earnings on the excess which is also reported in Box 2. A negative return cannot be reported in Box 1. Direct returns to an employer are also not included. *See Employer Issues - Recoupment.*

- **Box 2. Earning on Excess Contributions.** The custodian enters the total earnings distributed with any excess HSA contribution returned by the tax due date.

- **Box 3. Distribution Code.** The custodian reports the distribution code in this box.

- **Box 4. FMV on Date of Death.** The custodian enters the Fair Market Value on the date of death of the HSA.

- **Box 5. Checkbox.** The form provides a checkbox to indicate if the distribution was from an HSA, Archer MSA or MA MSA.

IRS Form 1099-SA.

538. How are the return of mistaken distributions reported?

Mistaken distributions are corrected internally by the custodian. They are not reported as contributions (the return) or distributions (the mistake). The distribution is not taxable or penalized. If the mistaken distribution is corrected after the 1099-SA was already sent reflecting the amount distributed, then the custodian would need to file a corrected 1099-SA (if it agreed to correct the mistake).

IRS Form 1099-SA.

539. How are distributions to beneficiaries of HSA reported on the IRS Form 1099-SA?

Distributions that occur after the date of death of the HSA owner are reported on the IRS Form 1099-SA in several different manners depending upon whether the beneficiary was a spouse or non-spouse and depending upon when the distribution is made.

- **Spouse Beneficiaries.** A spouse beneficiary treats the HSA as his or her own. This generally involves the HSA Custodian changing the name and Social Security Number on the HSA to the surviving spouse or transferring the assets into an HSA of the surviving spouse. Note: a custodian will generally require the surviving spouse to sign the application/custodian agreement and receive proper disclosures for the investment/banking account.

A spouse beneficiary in this case does not need to be eligible to open an HSA to receive HSA assets via transfer from a deceased spouse's HSA. If the name and Social Security number are changed on the existing HSA, then the surviving spouse will simply receive the 1099-SA and 5498-SA that otherwise would have gone to the deceased HSA owner.

If the surviving spouse opens a new HSA to receive the funds, then the custodian will likely send a 1099-SA and 5498-SA to the deceased HSA owner for the original HSA and to the surviving spouse for the newly created HSA. Assuming the surviving spouse is reporting one last joint return, separating the accounts and obtaining additional IRS forms will not change the tax situation and should not cause any issues.

- **Non-Spouse Beneficiaries.** If the designated beneficiary is not the spouse, the HSA ceases to be an HSA as of the date of the HSA owner's death. If the distribution occurs in the year of death to a non-spouse beneficiary, the HSA custodian uses a Code 4 in Box 3 of the 1099-SA. The same code is used for payments to the HSA owner's estate in the year of the death. The IRS also uses Code 4 for payments to estates after the year of the death. The HSA custodian reports the Fair Market Value of the HSA as of the date of death in Box 4 and the gross distribution in Box 1 (this may be larger than the fair market value if the account has accrued interest or earnings from the date of death to the date of distribution).

  If the custodian does not learn of the death of the HSA owner until after the year of the death, the custodian uses Code 6 in Box 3 for payments to non-spouse beneficiaries other than the estate (Code 4 is used for payments to the estate).

The 1099-SA is issued in the name and Social Security number of the designated beneficiary not the deceased HSA owner.

IRS Form 1099-SA, IRS Form 5498-SA.

540. What if an HSA owner has two different types of distributions during the same tax year?

If an HSA owner takes out distributions with different tax codes, then the custodian must generate multiple IRS Form 1099-SA reports.

IRS Form 1099-SA.

IRS Form 5329

541. What is the IRS Form 5329?

The IRS Form 5329 is used to pay additional taxes on tax-favored accounts. For HSAs, the form is used to pay the tax for failure to correct an excess contribution by the tax-filing due date.

IRS Form 5329.

542. When must the IRS Form 5329 be filed?

The IRS Form 5329 is usually filed with the income tax return but can be filed separately. HSA owners failing to remove an excess contribution in a timely fashion must file the IRS Form 5329.

Instructions for IRS Form 5329. See also Instructions for IRS Form 8889, IRS Form 5329.

Prohibited Transactions
Overview
543. What is a prohibited transaction?

HSA rules prohibit certain types of transactions and apply severe consequences for engaging in a transaction that is prohibited. For most HSA owners the likelihood of engaging in a prohibited transaction is very low and the prohibited transaction rules are not a concern. Some examples of transactions that are prohibited include:

- Sale, exchange, or leasing of property between the HSA owner and the HSA

- Lending of money between the HSA owner and the HSA

- Furnishing of goods, services, or facilities between the HSA owner and the HSA

- Transfer to or use by the HSA owner, or for the HSA owner's benefit, of any assets of the HSA (this does not mean taking a distribution from the HSA for qualified or non-qualified reasons)

A prohibited transaction also occurs if any of the above occur with another disqualified person (other than the HSA owner). The consequence for violating these rules is that the HSA is deemed fully distributed and ceases to be an HSA as well as having penalties apply.

> *Example.* Jane owns 100 shares of privately held stock that does not have an active market. Jane would like to sell these shares to her HSA for $100 a share or $10,000. Jane views this as a good investment for her HSA. The HSA rules do not allow this type of transaction because she is selling property she owns to her HSA. Jane could buy 100 shares of the stock from an arm's-length third party (someone she is not affiliated with) in her HSA, she simply cannot buy it from herself.

IRS Publication 969, p. 9, IRC Sec. 4975, IRS Notice 2004-50, See Q 68.

544. Why are certain transactions prohibited?

The types of transactions that are prohibited generally relate to self-dealing (or dealing with an insider or relative) and provide an opportunity for tax fraud. The law and IRS rules essentially prohibit the types of transactions that allow the opportunity for fraud regardless of whether or not any tax fraud is actually involved.

> *Example.* Bill owns a piece of real estate. The actual value of the real estate is difficult to determine but Bill has it appraised for $50,000 and sells it to his HSA for $50,000 (real estate as an asset held inside an

HSA is legally possible but not practical). This act alone is a prohibited transaction because it is self-dealing, but this example continues to illustrate why.

Later that year, Bill sells the land while it is in the HSA for $150,000. The $100,000 profit is tax-free because it is now protected by the HSA. Bill was able to get a large gain transferred into his HSA where it is not taxed. The possibility for this type of abuse is why the IRS prohibits these types of transactions.

The risk of abuse is also true even if the facts are reversed. Assume the same facts as above, but Bill sells the land for $5,000 (rather than $150,000) while it's in the HSA. He has now used tax-favored assets, his HSA, to pay for a real estate loss that he may not have been able to deduct.

To prevent any gamesmanship for tax advantage is why the IRS prohibits certain types of transactions.

545. Do the class prohibited transaction exemptions for IRA owners apply to HSAs?

No. The class exemptions for IRAs do not apply to HSAs.

DOL FAB 2006-02, See Q 10.

Disqualified Persons

546. Who are disqualified persons for prohibited transaction purposes?

The full definition of a disqualified person is beyond the scope of this book and requires professional guidance. The HSA owner is a disqualified person both because the HSA owner is a fiduciary to the plan and because HSA law provides that the HSA owner cannot engage in prohibited transactions (see IRC Sec. 223(e)(2) which refers to IRC Sec. 408(e) that states the individual cannot engage in these prohibited transactions).

Other than the HSA owner, the disqualified persons most likely to result in a prohibited transaction with an HSA include:

- A fiduciary (the HSA owner is one example of a fiduciary to the HSA)

- A person providing services to the plan (the HSA custodian or trustee)

- An employer any of whose employees are covered by the plan

- An employee organization any of whose members are covered by the plan

- A member of the family of the fiduciary, service provider or employer (family members include spouse, ancestor, lineal descendants and any spouse of a lineal descendant)

Example. Owen owns shares of stock in a privately held company. Owen sells the stock to his wife's HSA. This act is a prohibited transaction because his wife is a disqualified person and the transaction is a sale or exchange between the HSA and a disqualified person.

IRC Secs. 223(e)(2) and 408(e).

Buying and Selling Assets

547. Can HSA owners sell stock they own outside of their HSAs to their HSAs?

No, the prohibited transaction rules prevent HSA owners from directly selling any assets they already own to their HSAs. Plus, new HSA contributions must be in cash. HSA owners could transfer assets in-kind, including stock, from one HSA to another HSA.

548. Can HSA owners buy assets, such as stock, from their HSAs?

No, the prohibited transaction rules prevent HSA owners from buying assets held in their HSAs.

> *Example.* Segun owns 1,000 shares of a privately held security in his HSA. He believes the stock to be a good investment but it does not have a large market and he is struggling to sell the stock for what he believes it is worth. He has large medical expenses and needs his HSA to cover those expenses so he needs to liquidate his 1,000 shares of stock to pay his medical expenses. If he purchases the 1,000 shares himself and pays his HSA what he could have gotten from another buyer (the "fair market value"), he has engaged in a prohibited transaction.

Borrowing and Lending

549. If an HSA Owner borrows funds from his or her HSA, is that a prohibited transaction?

Yes. A loan or an extension of credit between an HSA owner and a "disqualified person" is a prohibited transaction. The HSA owner is a disqualified person for their own HSA. Although generally not allowed by HSA custodians, it would be legal for an HSA owner to lend money to an unrelated third-party in an arm's length transaction.

> *Example.* Mary needs a loan to start a business and has built up a large balance in her HSA. She would like to borrow that money to start her business and pay her HSA a better rate of interest than she is currently earning. Mary considers this a "win-win" scenario as she gets money for her business and increases her HSA savings at the same time. This transaction is not allowed and is a prohibited transaction. An HSA owner cannot borrow money from her HSA.

IRS Notice 2008-59, See Q 35.

550. Can an HSA owner pledge an HSA for security for a loan?

No, pledging an HSA as security for a loan is considered a prohibited transaction.

> *Example.* Pam has an HSA at Z Bank. Z Bank extends Pam a line-of-credit unrelated to the HSA but Z Bank asks Pam to pledge her HSA as collateral for the extension of credit. This is a prohibited transaction.

IRS Notice 2008-59, See Q 37.

551. Can an HSA custodian loan money to an HSA owner's HSA?

No. An HSA custodian is a "disqualified person" and any extension of credit between the HSA and the custodian is a prohibited transaction.

Example. Jim has an HSA with Four Corners Bank. Jim enters into an overdraft protection program for his HSA checking account with Four Corners Bank. The agreement provides that if Jim overdrafts his HSA, Four Corners will automatically extend credit for the amount overdrawn and will charge interest on the amount borrowed. This is a prohibited transaction and destroys the HSA.

IRS Notice 2008-59, See Q 36.

552. Can an HSA custodian offer a line-of-credit to an HSA owner that is not secured by the HSA?

Yes, provided the HSA is not security for the loan and is not directly tied to the loan. The HSA owner could even direct money from the HSA to be used to pay for the line-of-credit, for example for medical expenses paid with the line of credit and now being reimbursed from the HSA. How the accounts are structured is important as any extension of credit to the HSA or pledging of the HSA as security for a loan will cause a prohibited transaction.

Example. Jim has an HSA with Four Corners Bank. Jim also has a line of credit with Four Corners Bank. The line of credit is separate from the HSA and not secured by the HSA. The line of credit is not a prohibited transaction.

IRS Notice 2008-59, See Q 36. See also DOL FAB 2006-02, See Q 12.

Custodial Issues

553. Can an HSA custodian earn 12b-1 fees from a third party fund provider for HSA investments?

The HSA custodian is a disqualified party so any receipt of compensation from a third party is potentially problematic. The compensation should be disclosed to the HSA owner.

554. Can an HSA custodian offer a free personal checking account to anyone that opens an HSA?

Probably not. Offering an inducement to an HSA owner given outside the HSA for an action inside the HSA or for opening an HSA would most likely constitute a prohibited transaction. The exact facts of the situation and more guidance is necessary to answer this question with certainty. For example, if all customers are offered free personal checking then offering free checking to HSA owners would not constitute a prohibited transaction. The prohibited transaction rules are in place to prevent the possibility of tax fraud. Giving inducements outside of the HSA hold the potential for tax fraud; the rules prevent these situations even in the absence of any fraud.

Example. ABC Bank charges $10 per month for a personal checking account. To encourage its HSA customers to open personal checking accounts and to encourage its personal checking account customers to open HSAs, ABC Bank waives the fee for anyone that opens an HSA with ABC Bank as the custodian. This arrangement is likely a prohibited transaction (although the DOL could issue an exemption for this situation as it may not hold any potential for fraud).

To make the situation even more likely to be prohibited and to clarify the potential for abuse, assume ABC Bank gives anyone that opens an HSA with it, a monthly payment of $10 outside the HSA (arguably the same as waiving a $10 monthly fee). This arrangement is essentially allowing an HSA owner to use tax-favored money in the HSA to earn a monthly amount outside of the HSA without all the restrictions imposed on HSAs (money must be spent on qualified medical expenses or a penalty applies).

555. Can an HSA custodian provide a cash incentive to open an HSA?

Yes, provided the cash is deposited into the HSA. If the cash incentive is paid directly to the HSA owner, outside of the HSA, it is likely a prohibited transaction as the "sale or exchange of property." The facts and circumstances regarding cash incentives matter and it's important to structure the arrangement properly.

The HSA custodian is a disqualified person under the prohibited transaction rules. However, giving a cash incentive into the HSA is not a sale or exchange nor is it the transfer of assets in the plan.

DOL Advisory Opinion 2004-09A, DOL FAB 2006-02, See Q 11.

556. Do custodians face a penalty for prohibited transactions?

Yes. HSA custodians potentially can be fined under the prohibited transaction rules. Unlike the HSA owner whose consequence is generally the destruction of the HSA, the HSA custodian faces the more traditional prohibited transaction penalty of 15 percent of the amount involved.

IRC Sec. 4975.

Consequences

557. What happens to HSA owners that engage in prohibited transactions?

The HSA ceases to be an HSA as of the first day of the calendar year the HSA owner engaged in the prohibited transaction. The assets in the HSA are deemed distributed to the HSA owner and the HSA owner will owe appropriate taxes plus penalties. This treatment will result in full taxation plus, in most cases, a 20 percent penalty for not using the HSA distribution for qualified medical expenses (or meeting another exception). The additional tax of 15 percent for prohibited transactions does not apply provided the HSA ceases to be an HSA as of the date required.

IRS Notice 2008-59, See Q 38.

PART X: EMPLOYER ISSUES

Overview

558. What is an employer HSA program?

The terms "employer HSA," "employer HSA program," or "group HSA" are not legally defined terms but instead refer to when an employer makes HSA contributions on a pre-tax basis to employees' individual HSAs. Special rules apply to employers in this situation. All HSAs are individual accounts, but when pre-tax employer contributions are involved different rules may apply.

559. Do special HSA laws apply if an employer offers employees "HSA" qualified health insurance (HDHPs)?

Many insurance companies sell health insurance with the term "HSA" in the policy description. Although insurance companies do this to promote the fact that the plan is an HDHP necessary to qualify for an HSA, the description can cause confusion for employers and employees. Health insurance and HSAs are two different products. Employers that offer HDHPs to employees or health insurance with term "HSA" in the title or description are not automatically subject to any additional laws regarding HSAs. The HDHP product is insurance and HSA laws only apply when an employer is involved in the HSA plan as well as the insurance. Employers offering insurance to employees are subject to a whole host of federal and state laws, the most significant being the Affordable Care Act. If an employer that offers HDHP insurance decides to also make a pre-tax HSA employer contribution or allow for employees to made pre-tax payroll deferral HSA contributions then special HSA rules apply.

560. When do HSA laws apply to employers?

Employers need to adhere to HSA laws when the employer makes pre-tax contributions into an HSA of an employee. Accordingly, the employer HSA group level rules can apply even if an employer has only one employee that receives an HSA contribution. Conversely, an employer with many employees with HSAs is not subject to the HSA group rules provided the employer only allows after-tax payroll contributions into HSAs or no HSA contributions at all. The employer group rules refer to special rules for employers. Employers also often assist in educating their employees on HSA laws that apply to the employee and this educational process often occurs regardless of whether the employer is subject to employer group HSA rules or not.

Benefits of HDHP and HSA

561. What are the advantages to an employer of offering an HDHP and HSA combination?

The benefits of offering employees an HDHP and HSA vary dramatically depending upon the circumstances. A major strength of offering an HSA program is flexibility. Employers can be very generous and fully fund an HSA and also pay for the HDHP coverage. Alternatively, employers can also use the flexibility of the HSA to allow for the employer to reduce its involvement in benefits and put more responsibility onto the employee. Generally, employers switch to HDHPs and HSAs to save money on the health insurance premiums (or to reduce the rate of increase) and to embrace the concept of consumer driven healthcare. The list below elaborates on strengths of HDHPs and HSAs.

- **Lower Premiums.** HDHPs, with their high deductibles, are usually less expensive than traditional insurance

- **Consumer Driven Healthcare.** Many employers believe in the concept of consumer driven healthcare. If an employer makes employees responsible for the relatively high deductible, the employees may be more careful and inquisitive into their health care purchases. Combining this with an HSA where employees can keep unused money increases employees' desire to use health care dollars as if they were their own money – because it is their own money

- **Lower Administration Burden.** Given the individual account nature of HSAs, much of the administrative burden for HSAs is switched from the employer (or paid third-party administrator) to the employee and the HSA custodian as compared to health FSAs and HRAs. This increased burden on the employee comes with significant perks: more control over how and when the money is spent, increased privacy, and better ability to add money to the HSA outside of the employer.

- **Tax Deductibility at Employee Level.** The ability of employees to make their own HSA contributions directly and still get a tax deduction is advantageous. Although it is better for employees to contribute through an employer, an employee can make contributions directly. An employer may not offer pre-tax payroll deferral or it may be too late for an employee to defer. For example, an employee that decides to maximize his prior year HSA contribution in April as he is filing his taxes can still do so by making an HSA contribution directly with the HSA custodian.

- **HSA Eligibility.** Becoming eligible for an HSA is a benefit that also stands on its own. Although not all employees will embrace HSAs, savvy employees that understand the benefits of HSAs will value a program that enables them to have an HSA.

562. What are the tax benefits when an employer makes the HSA contributions?

Employers that make pre-tax HSA contributions maximize the tax benefits for their employees and the business. The main tax benefit for employees, the HSA owners, is the income tax exclusion. HSA owners get this deduction regardless of whether the company makes the contribution pre-tax, or post-tax or whether the employee makes the contribution directly.

The additional tax savings from employer pre-tax contributions come from payroll taxes: Social Security, Medicare (together with Social Security referred to as FICA), Federal Unemployment Tax (FUTA), and possibly State Unemployment Tax (SUTA). Both employer-direct contributions and pre-tax payroll deferral HSA contributions avoid payroll taxes. The savings achieved by avoiding payroll taxes are worth some effort. FICA is 6.2 percent up to $117,000 of income on the employer side and another 6.2 percent for the employee side (2014). Medicare is an additional 1.45 percent for both the employer and the employee on all income. Plus, the Affordable Care Act introduced an additional 0.9 percent Medicare tax for incomes over $200,000 for individual filers and $250,000 for joint filers. The FUTA tax is relatively small and only the employer pays it (generally 0.8 percent on the first $7,000), but there may be savings for state unemployment taxes as well.

Tax	Avoidance	
	Pre-Tax Employer	Employee On Own
Federal Income Tax	√	√
State Income Tax*	√	√
FICA (Social Security and Medicare)	√	
FUTA	√	
SUTA*	√	

*depends on state law. AL, CA, and NJ do not allow state HSA deductions.

IRS Notice 2004-2, See Q 20.

563. How do employers switching from traditional insurance to HDHPs explain the change to employees?

Although there is no certain answer to this question, a straight-forward and honest approach to the change will likely work best. Changing from traditional insurance to a high deductible plan with an HSA can be significant because employees likely face a higher deductible (although traditional health plan deductibles have been increasing to the point they are close to HDHPs). Often the largest obstacle to the change is that employees feel something is being taken away from them. An employer that can show that the actual dollars contributed by the employer are level, or increased, versus the previous year helps a lot-- especially if the employer makes a substantial HSA contribution for employees.

If the employer is making the change to reduce its health care expenses then the employer will have to explain and justify that change to employees to get employees' support for the change (e.g., the business is in a tough spot due to a difficult economy, etc.). Depending on the facts, the change will likely be an improvement for some employees and HSA eligibility provides benefits to all employees. Some specific benefits include the following.

- **Saving Money.** The HDHP is generally significantly less expensive. Depending upon the circumstances, this fact often saves not only the employer money but also the employee. Highlighting the savings will help convince employees the change is positive. Although an actual reduction of the employee's portion of the premium expense may be unlikely given increasing health insurance premiums, explaining that without the change the employee's portion of the premium would have increased by more will help reduce tension.

- **Tax Savings.** The HSA enables tax savings. For some employees these tax savings are significant

- **Control.** HSAs give individuals control over their money and accordingly their doctor and treatment choices

- **Flexibility.** An HSA is very flexible and allows for some employees to put aside a large amount and get a large tax benefit. For those that prefer not to do so, the HSA allows that as well. Plus, even better, the HSA allows employees to change their mind mid-year. If an employee believes they are not going to need any medical services, the employee needs to contribute only a minimum deposit to an HSA. If it turns out that the employee does incur some medical treatment, the employee can contribute at that time and still get the tax benefits. Employees are often frustrated by HSA rules because of some confusion, but when explained that the rules are very flexible they appreciate HSAs more.

- **Distribution Reasons.** HSAs allow for more distribution reasons than FSAs: namely to pay for health insurance premiums if unemployed and receiving COBRA, to pay for some health insurance premiums after age sixty-five, to use for any purpose penalty-free after age sixty-five, to carry forward a large balance, and more.

Responsibilities of Employer and Employee

564. What are the employer responsibilities regarding employee HSAs?

If an employer offers pre-tax employer contributions, then the employer has the following responsibilities.

- **Make Comparable Contributions.** If the employer is making a pre-tax employer contribution (non-payroll deferral), it must do so on a comparable basis.

- **Maintain Section 125 Plan for Payroll Deferral.** If the employer allows pre-tax payroll deferral, then the employer must adopt and maintain a Section 125 plan that provides for HSA deferrals. This includes collecting employee deferral elections, sending the deferred amount directly to the HSA custodian, and accounting for the money for tax-reporting purposes.

- **HSA Eligibility and Contribution Limits.** Employers should work with employees to determine eligibility for an HSA and the employee's HSA contribution limit. Although it is legally the employee's responsibility to determine his or her eligibility and contribution limit, a mistake in these areas generally involves work by both the employer and the employee to correct. Mistakes are best avoided by upfront communication. Also, the employer does have some responsibility not to exceed the known federal limits. An employer may not know if a particular employee is ineligible for an HSA due to other health coverage but an employer is expected to know the current HSA limits for the year and not exceed those limits.

- **Tax Reporting.** The employer needs to properly complete employees' W-2 forms and its own tax-filing regarding HSAs (HSA employer contributions are generally deductible as a benefit under IRC Sec. 106).

- **Business Owner Rules.** Business owners generally are not treated as employees and employers need to review HSA contributions for business owners for proper tax reporting.

- **Detailed Rules.** There are various detailed rules that fall within the responsibility of the employer that are too numerous to list here but include items such as: (1) holding employer contributions for an employee that fails to open an HSA, (2) not being able to "recoup" money mistakenly made to an employee's HSA, (3) actually making employer HSA contributions into employees HSAs on a timely basis, and (4) other detailed rules.

IRS Notice 2004-2, See Q 35 (W-2 reporting only), IRC Sec. 106.

565. What are the employee's responsibilities regarding HSAs?

The bulk of the compliance burden for meeting the HSA rules rests with the individual employee including:

- **Substantiation.** The employee must substantiate that the distributions from the HSA were in fact used for qualified medical expenses by saving medical receipts in case of an IRS audit. Placing this burden on the individual relieves the employer of the arduous task of reviewing receipts and issuing reimbursement checks or otherwise facing some potential liability for failure by an employee to use the money appropriately. Employees generally welcome this change as well as it simplifies the process of paying or reimbursing for medical expenses, allows for more privacy, and gives employees the opportunity to be more aggressive in interpreting the definition of qualified medical expense.

- **Eligibility.** Although an employer and a custodian can help educate employees on the requirements to be eligible for an HSA, the ultimate responsibility to determine eligibility rests with the employee. An employee's participation in a spouse's health insurance plan or Flexible Spending Account (FSA) could jeopardize the employee's HSA eligibility as could participation in a government health care system such as the Veterans Administration's plan or Medicare.

- **Maximum Contribution Limit.** The employee is primarily responsible to ensure that the amount contributed to the HSA is within federal guidelines. Employers and custodians share a bit of the responsibility as employers cannot deduct more than the maximum HSA contribution limit for an employee and custodians cannot accept more than the family HSA limit plus one catch-up contribution ($7,650 for 2015).

An employee that exceeds the limit may cause additional administrative work for the employer, the custodian and the individual, so it is in everyone's best interest to educate the employee on the limits.

- **Management of HSA.** Employees manage the balance in the HSA, select investments, choose beneficiaries, update contact information, pay for medical expenses and perform other maintenance issues generally without employer involvement.

- **Tax Reporting/Payments.** Employees are required to file an attachment (IRS Form 8889) to their income tax return each year they make a contribution or take a distribution. This includes employees that receive an employer-made contribution. This form is used by the IRS to ensure that the individual does not take a larger than permitted deduction and also ensures that the individual pays any taxes and penalties owed for non-eligible distributions.

- **Termination of Employment.** Another positive feature of HSAs for both employers and employees is that the HSA remains open and viable after the employee's separation from service. Other than discontinuing any contributions into the HSA, the employer generally does not need to take any action regarding the separating employee's HSA.

IRS Form 8889.

566. How are HSA responsibilities split between the employee, employer, and custodian?

The chart bellows illustrates HSA compliance requirements and which party bears responsibility.

HSA Compliance Requirement	Responsibility		
	Employee	**Employer**	**Custodian**
Eligibility for HSA	√	√*	
Contribution Limit	√	√*	√*
Distributions – Deciding & Validating What Is Eligible	√		
Open HSA	√		
Management of HSA – (Monitor Balance, Maintain Contact Information, Select Investments, Etc.)	√		
Termination of Employment – Close HSA	√		

HSA Compliance Requirement	Responsibility		
	Employee	Employer	Custodian
Employer Contribution – Comparability		√	
Employee Payroll Deferral - §125 Plan Rules		√	
Small Business Owner Rules		√	
Accounting – Custodial Services (Track Activity, Accept Beneficiary Information, Etc.)			√
HSA Legal Documentation – 5305-C	√		√
HSA IRS Reporting – 1099-SA & 5498-SA			√
HSA IRS Reporting – 1040, 8889, & 5329	√		

*Limited responsibility

567. Does the employer need to determine employees' HSA eligibility?

The employer has limited responsibility regarding determining employees' eligibility for an HSA. The employer must determine whether an employee is covered by an HDHP offered by the employer or by a traditional health plan (including FSA and HRA coverage). If the employee is HSA-eligible through a non-employer provided HDHP, the employer can accept the employee's statement to that effect. The employer must not contribute more than the HSA maximum (the legal limit, not necessarily a specific employee's limit) and must determine the employee's age for catch-up purposes, although the employer can rely on a statement by the employee as to the employee's date of birth.

IRS Notice 2004-50, See Q 82.

568. Is the employer responsible for reviewing medical expenses?

No, the employer is not responsible for policing the employee's HSAs. The employee/HSA owner is responsible for determining that their account funds are being properly used and would be required to provide supporting evidence on the use of their funds if requested under IRS audit.

IRS Notice 2004-2, See Q 31.

569. What is the minimum level of HSA involvement for an employer?

There is no requirement that an employer get involved in HSAs. Employers that offer HDHP coverage to employees face the issue of whether and how to implement an HSA program. Employers that offer no assistance for HSAs or only offer after-tax HSA payroll deferrals are often struggling just to pay a portion of the employees' health insurance and lack the ability to add additional funds to employees HSAs. An employer in this position is capitalizing on the unique benefit of HSAs in health benefits law: those individuals can open and contribute to an HSA without employer involvement and still get a tax break.

Without much expense other than the additional compliance and administrative burdens, however, these employers could offer pre-tax payroll deferral into an HSA giving employees a substantial additional benefit. HSAs are tax-driven accounts and not offering pre-tax HSA contributions reduces this main benefit for both employees and employers.

570. Does an employer have to make HSA contributions for its employees or allow payroll deferral?

No. There is no requirement that employers make contributions to their employees' HSAs. Likewise, employers are not required to provide for employee payroll deferrals into an HSA

571. Can an employer restrict HSA distributions to only qualified medical expenses?

No. Only the HSA owner may determine how HSA distributions will be used. Some employers or HSA custodians provide restricted cards that can only be used for qualified medical expenses, but these custodians must provide another means of accessing the HSA money that does not bear this restriction.

IRS Notice 2004-50, See Q 80.

572. When an employee separates from service, is the employer responsible to close the employee's HSA?

No, the HSA belongs to the former employee and the individual can decide whether to keep it open or close it unless the HSA custodial agreement or other agreement provides otherwise. The HSA survives a person separating from service.

Establishment

573. What is the employer's responsibility regarding the establishment of HSAs for employees?

An employer that will make pre-tax employer contributions to its employees' HSAs is generally somewhat involved in the process of opening the HSAs for employees. Employer involvement may include distributing HSA applications and collecting completed applications for forwarding to an HSA custodian or instructing employees how to enroll online. The HSA custodial agreement, however, is a contract between the employee and the HSA custodian and the employer is generally either not part of that agreement or only a very minor player (the agreement may provide for some information sharing with the employer or other terms to facilitate contributions). The legal nature of the HSA as a contract between the employee and the HSA custodian generally limits the employer's involvement for establishing HSAs to educating employees what they need to do to open their HSAs as well as educating HSA owners on general HSA rules.

574. Can employers provide employee information directly to the HSA custodian?

For establishing HSAs, an employer may be able to automate and expedite the HSA establishment process by providing data to the HSA custodian. However, the legal relationship is between the HSA owner and the custodian and the HSA owner will have to review, verify and sign the ultimate HSA custodial agreement (the "signature" may be done through an authentication process rather than a traditional ink signature).

Note: This answer is not addressing any privacy law issues that may arise by an employer sharing confidential employee information with an HSA custodian without the employee's consent.

After the HSA is established, changes to the HSA owner's contact information, beneficiaries, authorized signer, investment choices or otherwise should come directly from the HSA owner. An employer may provide forms on its website or its office to facilitate these changes and may collect and forward the forms for the HSA owner. The HSA custodial agreement or another agreement signed by the employee may grant the employer more authority to directly change the employee's HSA contact information. This is more of a privacy and account authorization question. Nothing in the HSA rules directly address as this issue so it's appropriate to look to contract law or other banking laws (privacy) for the answer.

The employer generally will provide HSA contributions and the information necessary to allocate those contributions directly to the HSA custodian.

575. Can an employer open an HSA on behalf of an employee that neglects or refuses to do so?

No. The employee needs to be involved in opening the HSA for a number of reasons:

- **Signing of the Custodial Agreement**. The employee must sign or otherwise agree to the terms of the HSA custodial account agreement and the employer cannot do that for the employee. This could potentially be done after the opening but the timing creates issues.

- **Determining Eligibility**. The employee may not be eligible for an HSA and it would be difficult for the employer to determine eligibility under a variety of circumstances: (1) eligibility for traditional insurance under a spouse's work or otherwise, (2) a spouse's participation in a Health FSA, (3) participation in Veterans Administration or TRICARE benefits, and (4) potentially other eligibility issues.

- **Correcting Mistakes**. Although most HSA mistakes can be corrected, opening HSAs for employees is likely to increase mistakes causing work for the employer, the employee and the HSA custodian.

- **No Authorization to Open HSAs**. HSA law also does not provide for authorization for anyone to open the HSA other than the HSA owner. There is some support in general benefits law allowing for employers to take action for inactive employees. The Department of Labor must believe it's an acceptable practice as it has stated that an employer that opens an HSA for an employee without that employee's consent does not subject the employer to ERISA rules and does not violate the "completely voluntary" requirement to avoid ERISA for HSAs. Not subjecting a plan to ERISA, however, is different from authorizing the practice of automatically opening HSAs for employees.

The HSA rules do not specifically address this issue but the rules do specifically provide directions for what an employer should do in case an employee does not open an account. The employer is directed to hold the money for the employee outside of the HSA and pay interest during the holding period. The IRS or DOL may come out with clarifying rules allowing for employers to open HSAs on behalf of employees as there are good policy reasons to do so, but as of this writing that clarification is not directly available.

DOL FAB 2006-02.

576. When do employees have to open HSAs?

Employees should open HSAs as soon as possible after becoming eligible. Employees must be eligible for an HSA in order to open an HSA. The HSA paperwork can be completed in advance with the opening occurring when the first funding of the HSA occurs.

See Part IV: Establishment - Establishment Date.

577. Can an employer require all employees to open an HSA at the same HSA custodian?

Yes. An employer that will make pre-tax employer HSA contributions can require that all its employees open an HSA at the same HSA custodian. Having all the HSAs at the same custodian will generally lower the administrative burden on the employer and also facilitate the educational process because the employer will have only one set of custodial rules to explain to employees.

The reason employers ask this question is a concern over becoming an ERISA plan. If an employer exercises too much control over the HSA then the HSA program could be considered to be an employee welfare benefit plan subject to ERISA.

There is a requirement that the employer not make or influence investment decisions. The Department of Labor (DOL) has held that selecting a single custodian is not making or influencing investment decisions so long as employees are afforded a reasonable choice of investment options. The DOL further stated that the selection of a single provider with a single investment option would not afford employees a reasonable choice.

See DOL FAB 2006-2 and FAB 2004-1. See Part XII: Custodial Issues — Investment Offerings.

Fees

578. Can employers pay the HSA fees for employees?

Yes. Employers can pay HSA fees for employees. This can be done either through the HSA or outside the HSA.

- **Paid Through the HSA.** Paying employee HSA fees through the HSA means that the employer will make an employer contribution to the employee's HSA of the amount of the custodian's fee. This HSA contribution will generally be subject to the comparability rules. That means that the employer must do it fairly for all employees (usually give everyone the same amount – *see Comparability* for details). Running the money through the HSA provides some advantages. The tax reporting both at the employer and employee level is handled the same as other employer HSA contributions. The HSA custodian can withdraw the amount of the fee without triggering a taxable distribution to the HSA owner (a distribution for a custodial fee is not reported on the IRS Form 1099-SA). The employee sees the fee and sees that the employer paid the fee. Paying directly avoids possible prohibited transaction issues.

- **Paid Outside the HSA.** The employer can also pay the HSA fee directly. This amount would not be deductible as an employer HSA contribution but employers should be able to deduct the amount as a general business expense although the direct support for this position cannot be found in HSA laws and regulations.

    An employer paying HSA fees for employees can create a potential issue of that payment resulting in the employer's HSA program becoming an ERISA covered program. However, the DOL has issued guidance stating that employer paid HSA fees does not result in an HSA program becoming an ERISA covered plan.

DOL FAB 2006-2, See Q 6, IRS Form 1099-SA.

579. Can employers require the employees to pay HSA custodial fees?

Yes. Any fees imposed by the HSA custodian can be paid directly by the employee/HSA owner rather than the employer. Although employees would prefer employers pay the fees there is no requirement to do so. This is true even if the employer requires the employee to establish an HSA with a custodian it chose. There are rules, however, that prevent an employer from receiving compensation back from the custodian.

See Part IX: Tax Issues - Prohibited Transactions.

ERISA

580. Are HSAs covered by ERISA?

HSAs are generally not subject to the Employee Retirement Income Security Act of 1974 (ERISA). HSA plans avoid much of the complexity that goes with an ERISA covered plan, making it a good choice for employers desiring greater simplicity. An employer that exercises too much discretion over employees' HSAs could cause an employer HSA program to become an ERISA plan, but that is not likely.

581. What happens if the HSA program is covered by ERISA?

If an HSA program is covered by ERISA, the employer must: (1) file the IRS Form 5500 annually, (2) provide employees Summary Plan Descriptions, (3) be a fiduciary for the plan, and (4) meet other ERISA imposed terms. HSAs are not designed as ERISA plans and employers generally should seek to avoid ERISA coverage. If the plan does become an ERISA plan, the employer will face a number of challenging questions in applying ERISA to an HSA program.

IRS Form 5500.

582. What steps should employers take to make sure their HSA program is not covered by ERISA?

To avoid ERISA coverage, the establishment of an HSA must be completely voluntary on the part of the employee and the employer cannot do any of the following.

- Limit the ability of eligible individuals to move their funds to another HSA beyond restrictions imposed by HSA law

- Impose conditions on utilization of HSA funds beyond those imposed by HSA law

- Make or influence the investment decisions with respect to funds contributed to an HSA

- Represent that the HSAs are an employee welfare benefits plan

- Receive any payment or compensation in connection with an HSA

The mere fact that the employer limits the forwarding of contributions to a single HSA provider would not in itself violate any of the above conclusions.

DOL FAB 2004-1.

583. Can an employer limit the choice of HSA providers for employer HSA contributions?

Yes. An employer may limit the choice of HSA providers that receive employer contributions to a single provider, unless the employer or the HSA provider restricts the ability of the employee to move funds to another HSA beyond those restrictions imposed by the law. But see the Question and Answer immediately following this answer.

DOL FAB 2004-1. See also DOL FAB 2006-02, See Q 2.

584. Can an employer contribute to just one HSA custodian if the custodian offers only one investment choice?

Maybe. The Department of Labor (DOL) states "the mere fact that employer selects an HSA provider to which it will forward contributions that offers a limited selection of investment options ... would not, in the view of the Department, constitute the making or influencing of an employee's investment decisions giving rise to an ERISA-covered plan so long as employees are afforded a reasonable choice of investment options and employees are not limited in moving their funds to another HSA."

The DOL, however, also states: "[t]he selection of a single HSA provider that offers a single investment option would not, in the view of the Department, afford employees a reasonable choice of investment options."

DOL FAB 2006-02.

585. Can an employer pay the HSA fees without turning an HSA program into an ERISA plan?

Yes. An employer can pay for fees associated with the HSA. Alternatively, the employer can contribute to the employees' HSA and have the employees pay the fee directly.

DOL FAB 2006-02, See Q 6.

586. Can an employer receive a discount on another product offered by the HSA custodian in exchange for using the custodian for its employees' HSAs?

No. Receiving a discount on another product from an HSA vendor would constitute the employer receiving payment or compensation in connection with an HSA.

DOL FAB 2006-02, See Q 8.

587. May an employer open an HSA for an employee and deposit employer funds into that HSA and still meet the "completely voluntary" requirement to avoid ERISA coverage?

Yes. The intended purpose of the completely voluntary condition is to ensure that any contributions the employees makes to an HSA, including salary reduction amounts, be voluntary. HSA owners have sole control and are exclusively responsible for expending HSA funds and generally may move the funds to another HSA or otherwise withdraw the funds. The fact that an employer unilaterally opens an HSA for an employee and deposits employer funds does not divest the HSA owner of this control and responsibility and, therefore, would not give rise to an ERISA-covered plan.

DOL FAB 2006-02, See Q 1. See Questions & Answers above for more discussion on whether an employer can open an HSA for an employee without employee consent.

Employer Contributions
Overview
588. What are the options for employers to help employees with funding their HSAs?

Employers offering HDHPs face the choice of whether and how to help their employees with the funding of the employees' HSAs. The options include the following.

- **Option 1 - Employee After-Tax Contributions.** Employers are not required to help with the employees' HSAs and may choose not to. In this case, employees may open HSAs on their own and receive the tax deduction on their personal income tax return. This option allows for income tax savings but not payroll taxes. A variation on this option is for employers to allow for post-tax payroll deferral (basically, direct deposit of payroll funds into an HSA without treating the deposit any differently than other payroll which may also be directly deposited into an employee's personal checking account). This does not change the tax or legal situation but it does provide a convenience for employees and will likely increase HSA participation and satisfaction.

- **Option 2 - Employee Pre-Tax Payroll Deferral.** Employers can help employees fund their HSAs by allowing for HSA contributions via payroll deferral. This is inexpensive and can be accomplished by adding a Section 125 Cafeteria plan with HSA deferrals as an option. Employers benefit by not having to pay payroll taxes on the employee's HSA contributions. Employees save payroll taxes as well. Plus, HSA contributions are not counted as income for federal, and in most cases, state income taxes. Setting up automatic payments generally simplifies and improves employee savings.

- **Option 3 - Employer Funded Contributions.** Employers may make direct contributions to their employees' HSAs without a Section 125 plan if the contributions are made directly. The contributions must be "comparable," basically made fairly (with a lot of rules to follow). This type of contribution is tax deductible by the employer and not taxable to the employee (not subject to payroll taxes or federal income taxes and in most cases not subject to state income taxes either).

- **Option 4 - Employer and Employee Pre-Tax Funding.** Employers can combine options 2 and 3 where the employer makes a contribution to the employees'

HSAs and the employer allows employees to participate in a Section 125 plan and enabling them to defer a portion of their pay pre-tax into an HSA. This is a preferred approach for a successful HDHP and HSA program as it ensures that employees get some money into their HSA through the employer contribution and allows for the best tax treatment to allow for employees to contribute more on their own through payroll deferral.

- **Options for More Tax Savings.** Some employers go beyond these options to increase tax savings even more. Although a number of strategies exist to increase tax savings, using a limited-purpose FSA (or HRA) is a common one. Generally, FSAs are not allowed with HSAs, however, an exception exists for limited-purpose FSAs. Limited-purpose FSAs are FSAs that are limited to payments for preventive care, vision and dental care. This provides more tax savings and employees use the FSA to pay for the limited-purpose expenses (dental and vision) and save the HSA for other qualified medical expenses.

    HRAs can also be used creatively in connection with HSA programs. The HRA cannot be a general account for reimbursement of qualified medical expenses but careful planning can allow for a limited-purpose HRA, a post-deductible HRA, or other special types of HRAs.

See Part III: Eligibility — Other Health Plan - Limited-Purpose FSAs and HRAs for more discussion on the requirements of offering these plans in conjunction with HSAs.

589. May employers make matching contributions?

No. Employers cannot match with employer comparable contributions as the matching contributions would almost certainly violate comparability testing (in order not to violate the comparability rules all employees in the same category must get the same dollar amount). However, matching contributions made through a section 125 Cafeteria plan are not subject to comparability testing. This means the matched dollars are contributed into the Section 125 plan and not directly into the HSA. Section 125 plans have their own nondiscrimination rules that must be met for a match to work.

590. Can an employer make HSA contributions into the HSA of an employee's spouse?

No. An employer cannot make HSA contributions into the HSA of an employee's spouse and be entitled to the same tax treatment. Any pre-tax employer contribution must go into the employee's HSA and not the spouse's. Part of the reason for this is income tax reporting. The IRS uses the IRS Form W-2 issued in an individual's Social Security Number to match with the IRS Form 5498 from the HSA custodian also issued in the individual's Social Security Number to ensure compliance with HSA rules. The IRS could provide for this issue for married couples on the income tax return, but does not.

HSA rules allow any person the ability to make an HSA contribution for someone's HSA. Accordingly, an employer can make HSA contributions for non-employees. This type of contribution would not be deductible by the employer as either an employer HSA contribution or an employee payroll deferral.

> *Example.* BBB, Inc. offers a pre-tax HSA payroll deferral option for employees. Samantha, an employee of BBB, is over sixty-five and enrolled in Medicare. Samantha's husband is under sixty-five and eligible for an HSA. Samantha requests that BBB take money out of her pay pre-tax and contribute it to her husband's HSA. BBB cannot accommodate Samantha's request on a pre-tax basis and could only do so by reporting the contribution amount as income to Samantha (negating any benefit to her).

IRS Notice 2008-59, See Q 27, IRS Form 5498, IRS Form W-2.

591. When do employers have to decide how much they are going to contribute to employees' HSAs?

There is no statutory rule on when employers must commit to an HSA contribution amount. As a general rule, employers should decide how much they will contribute before the year begins (calendar or fiscal) and commit to the amount by telling the employees.

> *Example.* Tom's Toys switches to an HDHP plan for its employees. At a company meeting the president announces that the company has not decided what, if anything, they will do regarding HSA contributions. This ambiguity is permissible within HSA laws. If Tom's Toys decides to give each of its employees $500 in June that would be permissible assuming it meets the other rules.

592. Can employers change HSA contribution amounts mid-year?

There is no obligation under HSA law that an employer commit to a certain contribution amount. Accordingly, an employer could tell employees, "I am going to put $100 in each of your HSAs this month and I may or may not do that next month." This approach is permissible under HSA laws and because no promise has been made should also be permissible under contract law. There may be other laws (non-HSA specific) that cover benefits and statements employers make about benefits. In particular, the Affordable Care Act only counts employer HSA contributions in the actuarial value calculation if the amount of the employer contribution is known.

Employers that make oral or written promises to employees have to keep those promises, generally both under contract law and for ethical reasons. Employers that want the flexibility to change the amounts should be very clear about this and put their position in writing.

593. Do employer contributions to an employee's HSA count as earned income for the purposes of the Earned Income Credit (EIC)?

No. An employer's contributions to an employee's HSA are not treated as earned income for EIC purposes.

IRS Notice 2004-50, See Q 86.

Deductibility

594. Are employer HSA contributions deductible health care expenses?

Generally, employer pre-tax HSA contributions (non-payroll deferral) are treated as employer provided coverage for medical expenses under an accident or health plan and are deductible. The tax treatment, however, depends on how the business is incorporated. For sole proprietors, partnerships, and S-corporations, contributions to a partner's HSA will be treated as a distribution to the partner and included in the partner's income and may be deductible by the partner but not by the business (see IRS Notice 2005-8 for treatment of HSA contributions in exchange for guaranteed payments of services rendered for partners and two percent shareholder employees of S-corporations).

IRC Sec. 106(d), IRS Notice 2005-8.

595. How do employers claim a deduction for employee HSA contributions?

Employers can deduct the contributions on the "Employee Benefit Programs" line of the business income tax return for the year in which the employer makes the contribution. If the contribution is allocated to the prior year, the employer can still deduct it in the year in which the contribution is made. If the employer is filing a IRS Form 1040, Schedule C, this contribution is noted in Part II, line 14.

IRS Publication 969, IRS Form 1040 Schedule C.

Reporting

596. Are employer contributions, payroll deferral, and employee direct contributions treated the same for the purposes of IRS reporting?

The HSA custodian treats all of these contributions the same on the IRS Form 5498-SA.

Employers also treat employer contributions and pre-tax payroll deferral HSA contributions the same on the employee's IRS Form W-2. Both types of employer contributions are reported in Box 12 with a Code W.

Employees have to report all types of contributions on the IRS Form 8889 (an attachment to the IRS Form 1040) and employee direct contributions are deductible on line 25 of the IRS Form 1040. The chart below illustrates the reporting for the different types of contributions.

| Type of Contribution | Reporting | | |
	Custodian	Employer	Employee
Pre-Tax Employer Contribution	5498-SA, Normal Contribution	W-2, Box 12, Code W	8889
Pre-Tax Payroll Deferral §125	5498-SA, Normal Contribution	W-2, Box 12, Code W	8889
Employee Contribution Made Personally	5498-SA, Normal Contribution	W-2, Box 1, Ordinary Income	1040 & 8889

IRS Form 8889, IRS Form 1040, IRS Form W-2, IRS 5498-SA.

597. What happens if an employer fails to report HSA contributions on the IRS Form W-2s?

The employer is required to report both pre-tax employer HSA contributions and pre-tax employee payroll deferral contributions in Box 12 of the IRS Form W-2. An employer failing to properly report can file corrected Form W-2s. The W-2 is used to check the employee's IRS Form 8889 to make sure the employee is not taking too large of an HSA deduction or is not attempting to deduct an HSA contribution that was already made pre-tax.

IRS Form W-2.

Prior Year

598. Can employers make prior year HSA contributions?

An employer can choose the year of the contribution for contributions made between January 1 and April 15 (or for non-calendar year taxpayers the date for filing the employees' return without extensions). Of course, an employee must have been eligible in the prior year to receive an employer HSA contribution. Most employer contributions are made for the year they are made in, e.g., contributions made in 2015 are for 2015. The ability to make a prior year contribution can provide additional tax planning opportunities.

An employer desiring to make an employer contribution for the prior year or desiring to allow employees to have payroll deferral HSA contribution taken for the prior year must communicate that the contributions relate to the prior year to both the HSA custodian and the employee. Employers that do not want to allow for prior year HSA contributions should provide a clear default that the tax year of the contribution will be the year the contribution is made unless the employer or the custodian is notified otherwise.

The last pay period of a calendar year is especially prone to this issue where the employer and the employee likely intend the contribution to be for the "prior" year even though the money is not received by the custodian until the "current" year. This situation requires careful planning and communication between the employer, the employee, and the custodian so all parties can coordinate how to report the contributions properly.

IRS Notice 2008-59, See Q 22.

599. How are employer prior year contributions reported by the employer and employee?

Employers report the contribution in the year made on the employees' IRS Form W-2 in Box 12 with a Code W. The employee then needs to adjust the year by modifying the employee's IRS Form 8889 that is attached to the employee's personal income tax return. This modification will need to be done twice -- once to reflect that a contribution was made for the prior year but will not be reported on the Form W-2 until the next year as well as a second time the next year to reflect that the amount shown on the Form W-2 was actually for the prior year.

Example. Big Business, Inc. makes a $500 contribution to each of its employees HSAs on January 31, 2013 for 2012. Big Business, Inc. notifies the HSA custodian and its employees that the contribution is for 2012. Big Business will not report the $500 contribution on the employees' 2012 Forms W-2 but instead will report the $500 on the 2013 Forms W-2 sent out in early 2014.

This reporting will require the employee to complete a special Employer Contribution Worksheet provided in the instructions to the IRS Form 8889 (see below). The employee would have to add the $500 to the amount the employer reported in the employees' 2012 Form W-2 in Box 12 with a Code W. For 2013, when the employer would report the $500 in Box 12 on the W-2, the employee must subtract that amount on the IRS Form 8889. The instructions to the IRS Form 8889 explain how to do this as illustrated below (the instructions below are for the 2013 tax year, the latest available at the time this book was published).

Employer Contribution Worksheet *Keep for Your Records*

1. Enter the employer contributions reported in box 12 of Form W-2, with code W	1. _____
2. Enter employer contributions made in 2013 for tax year 2012	2. _____
3. Subtract line 2 from line 1	3. _____
4. Enter employer contributions made in 2014 for tax year 2013	4. _____
5. **Employer contributions for 2013.** Add lines 3 and 4. Enter here and on Form 8889, line 9	5. _____

IRS Form W-2, IRS Form 8889.

Payroll Deferral
Overview
600. What is payroll deferral into an HSA?

Payroll deferral into an HSA refers to the process where an employee makes an election directing the employer to take a portion of the employee's pay and deposit it directly into an HSA. This can be done on a pre-tax basis or an after-tax basis. Generally, "HSA payroll deferral" means pre-tax as there are substantial benefits to deferring payroll pre-tax and the additional administrative burden to the employer to offer it pre-tax is outweighed by the tax benefits. In order to offer pre-tax HSA payroll deferrals, an employer must establish a Section 125 Cafeteria plan that allows for HSA deferrals.

601. Does an employer that offers HDHP health insurance have to offer payroll deferral into an HSA?

No. Employers are not required to make HSA contributions for employees and are also not required to offer employees pre-tax payroll deferral.

602. If an employer offers an HDHP but does not help with HSA contributions, can the employee open an HSA on her own?

Yes. The HSA belongs to the individual not the employer and any eligible individual may open an HSA.

603. Can an employer allow HSA payroll deferral for an employee not covered by the company health plan?

Yes, provided the employee is otherwise eligible for an HSA.

For employer contributions (non-payroll deferral), the employer can decide whether to include employees that are HSA-eligible but do not have company insurance in the HSA contribution. The employer does not have to give an employee in this situation any HSA contribution (it has to treat all similarly situated employees the same).

> *Example.* Bob and Sally are married and work at separate companies that both offer HDHP coverage. Sally elects to get family HDHP coverage through her company and Bob declines coverage. Both companies also offer HSA payroll deferral. Sally elects to defer a portion of her income into an HSA. Bob would also like to defer a portion of his income into his HSA through his company. He can do so even if he did not obtain the insurance through his company.
>
> In late 2013, the IRS released guidance together with HHS and the DOL that limits some of the ability to offer FSAs and HRAs when the employer does not integrate the FSA or HRA with employer provided health insurance. This limitation does not apply to HSAs as HSAs are not considered a "group health plan" for this purpose (although more direct guidance on this point by the federal authorities would be valued).

IRS Notice 2013-54.

604. How long can an employer hold employee payroll deferral funds prior to depositing the funds into an HSA?

The best guidance is provided by the Department of Labor (DOL). The DOL provides detailed rules on the timing of deposits for certain benefit plans (26 CFR Part 2510) and states that "plan assets" must be deposited "as of the earliest date on which such contribution can reasonable be segregated, but in no event to exceed ninety days from the date the on which such amount are received or withheld by the employer..." Additional DOL regulations for pension plans interpreted the outer limit of the rule as "...the fifteenth business day of the month following the month in which such amounts would otherwise have been payable to the participant in cash (in the case of amounts withheld by an employer from a participant's wages)." The DOL also provides a "safe harbor" for employers with fewer than one hundred participants of seven business days (employers that meet the seven day "safe harbor" and enjoy a guarantee that the contributions are timely).

There are some arguments that the DOL rules above do not apply to HSA deferrals or that the rules may apply differently to HSA payroll deferrals. One argument is that Section 125 plans enjoy a general exception to some of the timing requirements outlined above and that HSA deferrals may come under that exception (this exception applies to assets not held in trust, such as FSAs where expenses are often paid out of general employer funds as they are incurred).

Another argument is that the DOL rules are designed for ERISA covered employee welfare plans and HSA programs are generally not ERISA covered plans. The DOL's comments in its rule appear to be inclusive (the rules cover SEP and SIMPLE IRA programs), but do not specifically mention or include HSA deferrals. HSA deferrals certainly fit within the overall spirit of the regulatory framework for other benefit plans. For these reasons, employers should follow the

DOL guidance outlined above absent a compelling reason or a legal opinion from an advisor that it can deviate from the DOL rules.

Post-Tax

605. Why would an employer offer a post-tax HSA deferral option?

An employer that deposits an employee's pay directly into an HSA on an after-tax basis is generally doing so as an administrative convenience to the employee. Most employers already offer direct deposit of employee paychecks. To expand that to allow for some pay to be directly deposited into an HSA is likely relatively easy for the employer and may provide the employee some structure for making recurring payments (i.e., the HSA savings comes first). An employee can likely accomplish this same goal without employer involvement by setting up a direct deposit from the employee's personal checking account into an HSA.

> *Example.* ABC Inc. does not have a Section 125 plan and does not offer pre-tax payroll deferral into an HSA. Helen, an employee of ABC Inc. asks the Human Resources manager of ABC Inc. to take $100 out of her pay and deposit it directly to her HSA. ABC Inc. can offer this as a service without facing any of the rules involved for offering pre-tax payroll deferral into an HSA. ABC Inc. would issue Helen's Form W-2 as if the HSA deferral amounts were paid directly to her and Helen will deduct the HSA contributions on line 25 of her IRS Form 1040 personal income tax return.

IRS Form W-2, IRS Form 1040.

606. Can an employer allow for HSA contributions through payroll deferral without a Section 125 plan?

No, not if the goal is to save payroll taxes. Employers can offer HSA payroll deferral on an after-tax basis without concern over the comparability rules or the Section 125 plan rules. Amounts contributed under this method are treated as income to the employee and are deductible on the employee's personal income tax return. The lack of any special tax treatment for this approach makes it an unattractive for most employers and with just a small additional investment of money and time a Section 125 plan could be added allowing for pre-tax deferrals.

> *Example.* Waving Flags, Inc. does not offer health insurance or a Section 125 plan to its employees. Waving Flags does provide direct deposit services to its employees that provide it with their personal checking account number and bank routing number. Maggie, an employee of Waving Flags, Inc., approaches the human resources person and asks to have her direct deposit split into two payment streams with $100 per month being directly deposited to her HSA and the balance of her pay being deposited into her personal checking account. She provides Waving Flags the appropriate account and routing numbers and signs the proper election forms.

> Waving Flags is not subject to the Section 125 non-discrimination rules for pre-tax payroll deferral nor is Waving Flags subject to the HSA comparability rules. Waving Flags is simply paying Maggie by making a direct deposit into her HSA. The $1,200 Maggie elects to have directly deposited to her HSA in this manner will be reflected in Box 1 of her IRS Form W-2 from Waving Flags as ordinary income. She will be subject to payroll taxes on the amount. She can claim an HSA deduction on line 25 of her IRS Form 1040 when she files her tax return.

> Maggie benefits from this approach by setting up an automatic contribution to her HSA which often improves the commitment to savings. Most HSA custodians will offer a similar system that HSA owners can

set up on their own by having their HSA custodian automatically draw a certain amount from a personal checking account at periodic intervals. Employer involvement is not necessary. Individuals with online banking tools available to them may be able to set it from their personal checking account as well to push money periodically to an HSA.

IRS Form W-2, IRS Form 1040.

Section 125 Plan

607. What is a Section 125 plan?

A Section 125 plan is an IRS-sanctioned written legal document that the employer signs, maintains and administers. By signing the document, the employer agrees to comply with the rules contained in the document regarding types of benefits allowed, treating employees fairly, and other IRS requirements. The maintenance of the document itself generally means updating the document periodically to comply with law changes or changes to the employer's benefits program. The document generally does not need to be submitted to the IRS but a signed copy should be kept on file in case of an IRS audit.

608. What is involved in administering a Section 125 plan?

For payroll deferral into an HSA through a Section 125 plan, the employer must reduce the employees' pay by the amount of the deferral and contribute that money directly into the employees' HSA. The employer may do this administration itself or it may use a payroll service or another type of third-party administrator. In any case, the cost of the Section 125 plan itself and the ongoing administration are generally small and offset, if not entirely eliminated, by employer savings through reduced payroll taxes.

Another administrative element is the collection of Section 125/HSA payroll deferral election forms from employees. Employers that have offered Section 125 plans prior to introducing an HSA program are familiar with this process. Unlike other Section 125 plan deferral elections which only allow annual changes, the law allows for changes to the HSA deferral election as frequently as monthly. Although frequent changes to the elections create a small administrative burden on the employer, the benefit to employees is significant. Employers are not required to offer changes more frequently than annually.

The full scope of the administrative rules for Section 125 plans is beyond the scope of this book.

609. What are the benefits of using a Section 125 plan combined with an HSA?

There are a number of benefits to this approach:

* Employees can make HSA contributions through payroll deferral on a pre-tax basis

* Employees may pay for their share of insurance premiums on a pre-tax basis

* Employers and employees save payroll taxes (7.65 percent each on FICA and FUTA for contributions)

- Employers avoid the "comparability" rules for HSA contributions although employers are subject to the Section 125 plan rules

610. Is a "Premium-Only Plan (POP) Section 125" set up to work with HSAs?

A Section 125 Premium-Only Plan (POP) contains the legal language to allow employee pre-tax payroll deferral to pay for health insurance premiums. The plan will likely require the addition of legal language to allow for pre-tax deferrals into an HSA. If the Section 125 plan document already contains the language allowing for pre-tax deferrals into an HSA, then the employer should be set to allow HSA payroll deferrals pre-tax. A good practice for employers is to check with the Section 125 plan document provider for verification of compliance.

611. Are Section 125 plans subject to non-discrimination rules?

Yes. A cafeteria plan must meet non-discrimination rules. The rules are designed to ensure that the plan is not discriminatory in favor of highly compensated or key employees. For example, contributions under a cafeteria plan to employee HSAs cannot be greater for higher-paid employees than they are for lower-paid employees. Contributions that favor lower-paid employees are not prohibited.

The cafeteria plan must not: (1) discriminate in favor of Highly Compensated Employees (HCE) as to the ability to participate (eligibility test), (2) discriminate in favor of HCE as to contributions or benefits paid (contributions and benefits test), and (3) discriminate in favor of HCE as measured through a concentration test that looks at the contributions made by key employees (key employee concentration test). Violations generally do not result in plan disqualification, but instead may cause the value of the benefit to become taxable for the highly compensated or key employees.

The non-discrimination rules pre-date the creation of HSAs and how the rules apply to HSA contributions is an area where additional government guidance would be welcome.

IRS Publication 15-B, See Part XI: Comparability - Categories - Highly Compensated versus Non-Highly Compensated (for a full definition of Highly Compensated Employees).

612. Is there an exception to the Section 125 plan non-discrimination rules for small employers?

Yes, if the small employer meets the rules for a "simple" cafeteria plan. The key benefit of a simple cafeteria plan is that it is treated as automatically meeting the non-discrimination rules. An employer must employ an average of 100 or fewer employees during either of the two preceding years. If the employer was not in existence throughout the preceding year, then the employer will meet the rule if the employer reasonably expects to employer 100 or fewer employees in the current year. If an employer establishes a simple cafeteria plan in a year that the employer employed an average of 100 or fewer employees, the employer will be considered eligible for any subsequent year so long as the employer does not employ an average of 200 or more employees in a subsequent year.

The simple cafeteria plan must include all employees that had 1,000 hours of service in the preceding year. An employer can exclude: (1) employees under the age of twenty-one, (2) employees with less than one year of service, (3) union employees (subject to collective bargaining), and (4) nonresident aliens working outside the U.S. whose income did not come from a U.S. source.

The employer must make a contribution on behalf of each qualified employee in the amount equal to: (1) a uniform percentage (not less than 2 percent) of the employee's compensation for the plan year, or (2) an amount which is at least 6 percent of the employees compensation for the plan year or twice the amount of the salary reduction contributions for each qualified employee, whichever is less. If option 2 is used, the rate of contribution to any salary reduction contribution of a highly compensated or key employee cannot be greater than the rate of contribution to any other employee.

IRS Publication 15-B.

613. Can an employer make a matching contribution to employees' HSAs through the Section 125 plan?

Yes, subject to the terms of the Section 125 plan.

Employee Contributions

614. Are employee payroll deferrals into an HSA subject to FICA/FUTA taxes?

No, HSA pre-tax HSA contributions made pursuant to a Section 125 plan are not subject to payroll taxes. This can provide employers and employees with a significant tax benefit.

> *Example.* Quality Cabinets employs twenty-five people and will soon begin offering an HDHP. Quality Cabinets plans to pay the cost of the HDHP for the employees, but does not plan on contributing to the employees' HSAs. Quality Cabinets is questioning whether it should offer a Section 125 plan to allow for its employees to make contributions on a pre-tax payroll deferral basis or just let employees fund their HSA on their own.
>
> For analysis, the employer needs to consider the payroll tax savings (it will have to pay the payroll taxes if it pays the employees the same amount in payroll rather than allow for deferrals pursuant to a Section 125 plan). Assuming each of the twenty-five people would defer $1,000 into the HSA, the employer saves 7.65 percent in payroll taxes (6.2 percent for Social Security and 1.45 percent for Medicare) for a combined annual savings of $1,912.40 ($1,000 x 25 = $25,000 x 7.65 percent = $1,912.40). This likely pays for the cost of a simple Section 125 plan and the savings would also cover or partially offset any administrative cost. When you combine that with the fact the employees collectively also save $1,912.40 in payroll taxes, plus the employer is providing a convenience, it often makes sense to allow for the HSA deferrals.

615. Can an employee change his or her HSA deferral election mid-year?

Yes. Section 125 plans generally require that an employee elect deferral amounts at the beginning of the year and the plans do not allow changes to the election mid-year. An employee may start or stop HSA deferrals through a Section 125 plan on a monthly basis so long as the change is prospective.

The ability to change deferral elections allows employees to adjust mid-year to what the year's expenses actually are versus what they planned. An employee that initially expected a low expense healthy year and elected only a small HSA payroll deferral can adjust when surprised by a large medical expense. Conversely, an employee that elected to defer a large amount into the HSA but later faces lower than anticipated medical expenses (or faces higher than anticipated non-medical expenses) can adjust their deferral downward. Prospective means that the change cannot take effect until the month following the change date.

IRS Notice 2004-50, See Q 59.

616. May an employer accelerate an employee's payroll deferrals to cover a large expense that occurs early in the year?

Yes. An employer may, but is not required to, accelerate payroll deferral contributions into an HSA of the employee. The employer must make this option available equally to all participating employees throughout the plan year and must be offered on the same terms. Employers are also allowed to accelerate non-payroll deferral employer contributions. For non-payroll deferral the employer is required "to establish reasonable uniform methods and requirements for accelerated contributions." Presumably that same logic applies to the acceleration of payroll deferral HSA contributions. The employee of course must repay any accelerated deferral through their normal payroll deferral such that the amount accelerated is repaid by the end of the year.

If the employee separates from service prior to repaying the accelerated amount, the employer is not allowed to recoup that amount. To avoid this result and the extra work involved in administering accelerated payments, employers often do not offer this feature. The choice to not offer accelerated HSA contributions is made easier by the fact that employees can borrow money from any source to pay a medical expense and then reimburse themselves from the HSA once the funds are contributed.

Another approach some employers use is to offer to make an employee a personal loan to cover the amount of the medical expense. The loan would be set up for repayment through deduction from pay. Provided this is kept separate from the HSA, the employee could use the loan proceeds to pay the medical expense. The loan would be repaid through payroll deduction. The employee can then write a check from his or her HSA to pay for the cost of the qualified medical expenses paid through the loan once the HSA has sufficient funds. HSA rules prohibited pledging an HSA as security for a loan, but the employer is not tying the loan to the HSA.

> *Example 1.* XYZ Corporation operates on a calendar year and committed to contributing $100 per month into the HSA of each eligible employee. Jane, an employee, incurred a $1,000 medical bill in January and asked XYZ to accelerate the $100 per month for the next ten months so she can afford to pay the bill with her HSA. XYZ can accelerate the contributions but it will have to establish a policy of doing so and allow similarly situated employees to also take advantage of the policy. Plus, XYZ will run the risk that Jane will separate from service prior to the repayment of the accelerated amount and it will be unable to recoup that money.

> *Example 2.* Assuming the same facts as above, except that XYZ Corporation instead extends Jane a $1,000 personal loan that is repaid through deduction from her pay. Jane can use the $1,000 loan to pay the medical expense in January. Assuming no other medical expenses, Jane's HSA will have $1,000 in it in November

of the year (XYZ is contributing $100 per month). Jane can write herself a check for $1,000 from the HSA to cover her $1,000 medical expense that she had to pay for with after-tax funds because she did not have sufficient dollars in her HSA. She will need the receipt for the medical expense in case she is audited. This allows Jane to pay her medical expense timely but still get the tax benefits of running the expense through the HSA. She does not need to wait until her account has sufficient funds to pay the full $1,000 and she could write herself a check each month for $100 from her HSA as soon as her employer contributes the $100. She also does not need to complete the reimbursement in the same year and could wait until a future year to reimburse herself. If an employer is unwilling to make a personal loan, Jane could accomplish this same result through the use of a credit card or other source of funds.

IRS Notice 2004-50, See Q 61, See Also Treas. Reg. Sec. 54.4980G-4, See Q 15.

617. Can an employer provide a negative election for HSAs (automatic contribution if the employee fails to complete the election form)?

Yes. This assumes that the payroll deferral is offered through a Section 125 Cafeteria plan and that the negative election meets the requirements under that plan.

IRS Notice 2004-50, See Q 62.

618. How long can employers hold HSA payroll deferral amounts before contributing to the HSAs?

The answer depends on the size and sophistication of the employer. The quicker an employer can make the contribution to the employees' HSAs the less of an issue this becomes. HSAs are generally not considered ERISA plans and are not subject the stringent requirements for quick deposits for ERISA plans. Nevertheless, the rules for Section 125 plans do require the deposits to be made on a reasonable basis.

See Part X: Employer Issues – ERISA.

Business Owners

619. What unique HSA rules apply to partnership members, Limited Liability Corporation (LLC) shareholders, S-Corp shareholders and sole proprietors?

Business owners face special HSA rules that limit the owners' ability to get tax benefits through the business. A business can usually deduct HSA contributions for employees as a business expense (IRC Sec. 106) and the HSA contributions do not get reported as income to the employees. The rules are different for owners (other than employees that are also share-holders of C-corporations). The IRS reporting is different and so is how the HSA deduction is claimed. Some business owners are surprised by the different tax treatment of owners versus employees.

These special rules apply to business owners with entity structures other than C-corporations (or just "corporations – the "C" is added to clarify that it's not an "Subchapter S" corporation or other type of corporation). The special rules apply to partners in a partnership, members or partners in Limited Liability Corporations (LLCs), more than 2 percent owners of S-corporations, and sole proprietors. Business entity structure can vary state-by-state but these represent general categories for most businesses.

Beyond just the reporting differences, the key distinction between the treatment of owners versus employees is payroll taxes. Employer pre-tax HSA contributions avoid payroll taxes. Employer contributions to business owners do not automatically avoid payroll taxes as it depends on how the distribution from the business is taxed (e.g., if it is capital gains-payroll taxes do not apply; if income-payroll taxes may apply).

IRS Notice 2004-50, IRC Sec. 106, See Q 85. See the Small Business Owner Worksheet.

620. How are business HSA contributions to non-owner employees treated?

The special rules discussed in this section only apply to owners and do not apply to non-owner employees. The normal rules for business HSA contributions apply to non-owner employee HSA contributions. This means the contributions are generally made comparably and pre-tax and that the employer can allow HSA pre-tax payroll deferral pursuant to a Section 125 plan.

621. Are family members of a business owner also considered owners?

Maybe. An individual may be deemed to constructively own any stock owned by a spouse, a parent, a child and a grandchild.

See IRC Sec. 318 for details.

622. Are HSA contributions to owners subject to the comparability rules?

One positive of the different treatment of business owners is that the owner's contribution is not subject to the comparability rules. This allows a sole proprietor, more than 2 percent owner of an S-Corp or partner in a partnership to give herself a more generous HSA contribution than her employees without violating the comparability rules. This is because the business' contribution to the HSA is not considered an HSA contribution but instead a form of business distribution.

Sole Proprietors

623. Is a sole proprietor allowed to deduct HSA contributions made to herself through the business?

A sole proprietor is not considered an employee for the purposes of business HSA contributions. Accordingly, sole proprietors are not allowed to deduct their own HSA contributions as a business expense. Instead, sole proprietors can deduct HSA contributions on their personal income tax return.

624. Can a sole proprietor open an HSA in the business's name?

Only individuals can open HSAs. A sole proprietorship is generally an individual but the sole proprietor would open the HSA in his or her name and personal Social Security Number. The business owner cannot use a business name or business Taxpayer Identification Number (unless the owner is using his or her Social Security Number for both purposes).

Partners

625. Are partners and members of LLCs allowed to deduct HSA contributions made to themselves through the business?

Generally HSA contributions to partners and LLC members are not deductible by the business but are deductible by the individual business owners on their personal income tax returns.

Partnerships and LLCs are generally treated as flow-through entities for purpose of HSA contributions made on behalf of the owners. HSA contributions to the owners are not deductible by the business but flow through to the owner as a distribution to the partner.

Contributions by a partnership to a bona fide partner's HSA are not contributions by an employer to the HSA of an employee. The HSA contribution would be reported as a distribution of money on the partner's Schedule K-1 and the partner can then take a deduction for the HSA contribution on the partner's personal income tax return. If the HSA contribution is made to the partner as a distribution, the contribution will have no impact on the partner's self-employment tax.

For this reason, partnerships and LLCs often choose to make a larger shareholder distribution for the owners and let the owners make HSA contributions on their own rather than have the business do it directly. The tax treatment is the same. Contributions made pursuant to a Section 125 plan will be added back to the owners as a taxable fringe benefit negating any tax benefit they might have otherwise received from a Section 125 plan.

Example. Johnson & Johnson is a limited partnership with three equal partners: Sally (general partner), Todd (limited partner) and Mike (limited partner). All three partners are eligible for HSAs.

Johnson & Johnson makes a $300 HSA contribution to Sally and Todd. These contributions are treated as distributions (Section 731) and not HSA contributions by the partnership. These contributions do not affect Johnson & Johnson's calculation of its taxable income or loss. Sally and Todd are entitled to an above-the-line taxable deduction (line 25 of the 1040) for the $300 contributed to their HSAs. The $300 is reported as cash distributions to Sally and Todd on their respective K-1s (IRS Form 1065). The distributions are not including in Sally or Todd's net earnings from self-employment (Section 1402(a)) because distributions under Section 731 do not affect a partner's distributive share of the partnership's income or loss under Section 702(a)(8).

IRS Notice 2005-8, See Q 1, IRS Form 1065.

626. Is there an exception for guaranteed payments to partners?

There is an exception for guaranteed payments to partners to the general rule of how business owner HSA contributions are treated. If a partner is entitled to a guaranteed payment from the partnership, the HSA contribution is deductible by the partnership as a business expense. Unlike non-owner employees, the HSA contribution is also reported as income pursuant to a guaranteed payment on the partner's K-1 and the partner can then deduct the HSA contribution on his or her personal income tax return. This amount is generally subject to self-employment taxes.

Example. Johnson & Johnson is a limited partnership with three equal partners: Sally (general partner), Todd (limited partner) and Mike (limited partner). Mike is to be paid $500 annually for a service rendered to the partnership without regard to his the partnership income (a guaranteed payment). The $500 is derived from the partnership's business. All three partners are eligible for HSAs. See the preceding Question & Answer for an explanation of how Sally and Todd's HSA contributions are treated.

Johnson & Johnson makes a $500 HSA contribution to Mike in lieu of paying him his guaranteed payment. Johnson & Johnson cannot include this amount as a deductible HSA contribution (Section 106(d)) because the contribution is considered as a distributive share of partnership income for all purposes (other than Sections 61(a) and 162(a)) and a guaranteed payment to a partner is not treated as compensation to an employee. The payment should be reported on the K-1 as a guaranteed payment. Because the contribution is a guaranteed payment that is derived from the partnership's trade or business and is for services rendered to the partnership, the contribution constitutes net earnings from self-employment to Mike who deducts the $500 on his personal income tax return.

IRS Notice 2005-8, See Q 2.

S-Corporations

627. Are owners of S-Corporations subject to special rules for business HSA contributions?

Yes. Owners of more than 2 percent of an S-corporation are treated as partners in a partnership. *See Employer Issues – Business Owners – Partners.*

Contributions made for services rendered are treated as guaranteed payments following the same process for partnership guaranteed payments. There is a difference in tax treatment depending upon whether an HSA contribution is treated as a distribution of cash or as a guaranteed payment.

Owners also cannot make pre-tax contributions to their HSA via a salary reduction. Any contributions made on their behalf by the corporation are taxable and may be deducted on their personal income tax.

Example. Bob is a more than 2 percent owner of an S-Corp, Bob's Buildings, Inc. Bob's Buildings makes a $5,000 HSA contribution to Bob's HSA. This contribution is treated as a guaranteed payment for services rendered and the S-Corp deducts the amount as compensation paid to Bob (the amount will reflect as income). Bob then claims the $5,000 HSA deduction on his personal income tax return.

IRS Notice 2005-8, See Q 3.

628. Are HSA contributions to the owner of an S-Corp subject to payroll taxes or self-employment taxes?

Generally contributions made to S-Corp owners for services rendered will be deemed guaranteed payments and will be subject to payroll taxes.

However, if the requirements for an exclusion under Section 3121(a)(2)(B) of the Tax Code are satisfied, the S Corporation's contributions to the HSA are not wages subject to FICA tax, though they must be included for income tax withholding purposes on the shareholder-employee's IRS Form W-2.

IRS Notice 2005-8, See Q 3, IRS Form W-2.

C-Corporations

629. How are employees that are also owners of a C-corporation treated concerning HSA contributions?

Shareholders of C-corporations (or a "corporation" that is not a sole proprietor, partnership, LLC, S-Corp, or other special category of corporate entity) that are also employees are treated as employees and are not subject to any special HSA rules.

> *Example*. Jake works at ABC Corp. (a C-Corporation) and also owns 5 percent of its outstanding stock. ABC Corp makes an HSA contribution for its employees. Jake is entitled to receive that HSA contribution and the company can claim it as a deductible expense and report it to Jake in Box 12 of the IRS Form W-2 as pre-tax income rather than taxable income.

IRS Form W-2.

Recoupment

630. What does "recoup" mean?

The IRS uses the word "recoup" to discuss when an employer can work directly with an HSA custodian to fix contribution errors. This means the employer takes the money back from the HSA custodian, or "recoups" it, without necessarily, the consent of the HSA owner. In some situations, an employer can recoup mistaken HSA contributions and in other situations the employer cannot recoup the amounts.

HSA custodial agreements are essentially contracts between the HSA owner and the HSA custodian. An employer may be making a contribution on behalf of the HSA owner but is often either not part of the contractual arrangement or only tangential to the arrangement. The contractual terms together with general HSA law that provides that the interest in the HSA is "nonforfeitable" make correcting employer mistakes troublesome. In general, the rules limit when an employer can fix mistakes involving HSA contributions.

631. Can an employer ever recoup an HSA contribution made on behalf of an employee?

Yes. An employer can recoup employee contributions it made in two circumstances: (1) the employee was never eligible for an HSA, and (2) the amount the employer contributed exceeded the federal HSA limit for the year. At the employer's option, the employer may request that the HSA custodian return the amounts to the employer. However, if the employer does not recover the amounts by the end of the taxable year, then the amounts must be included as gross income and wages on the employee's IRS Form W-2 for the year during which the employer made the contributions.

> *Example 1*. Peak Ski Resort made a $500 HSA contribution to its employee, Melanie, thinking she elected the Resort's HDHP insurance option. Later that same year, Peak Ski Resort learned that Melanie actually elected the traditional health insurance option and was never eligible for an HSA. Peak Ski Resort may request that the HSA custodian return the $500, less administrative fees, directly to Peak Ski Resort. If Peak Ski Resort does not receive the balance of the HSA, it must include the amounts in Melanie's gross income and wages on the IRS Form W-2.

Example 2. Same as above, but Peak Ski Resort first learns of the mistake the next year. Peak Ski Resort will have to issue a corrected IRS Form W-2 for Melanie, and Melanie will have to file an amended income tax return.

IRS Notice 2008-59, See Q 24, See Q 25, See Q 26, IRS Notice 2004-50, See Q 82, IRS Form W-2.

632. How can an employer take an employee's HSA money back if the money is nonforfeitable?

Although the HSA custodial agreement provides that "the account owner's interest in the balance is this custodial account is nonforfeitable," employer recoupment is a very limited exception to that rule allowed by the IRS.

IRS Notice 2008-59, See Q 24, See Q 25, See Q 26.

633. Can the employee agree to a recoupment that would otherwise not be allowed?

No. The recoupment rules are limited to the two specific set of circumstances and cannot be expanded by agreement of the HSA owner, employer and custodian. Whether arrangements can be made outside of the HSA is another question.

Exceeds Annual Limit

634. If an employer contributes amounts to an employee's HSA that exceed the maximum annual contribution, can the employer recoup the excess amounts?

Yes. If the employer contributes amounts to an employee's HSA that exceed the maximum annual contribution due to an error, the employer may correct the error. In that case, at the employer's option, the employer may request that the financial institution return the excess amounts to the employer. Alternatively, if the employer does not recover the amounts, then the amounts must be included as gross income and wages on the employee's IRS Form W-2 for the year during which the employer-made contributions. If, however, amounts contributed are less than or equal to the maximum annual contribution allowed under federal law, the employer may not recoup any amount from the employee's HSA.

IRS Form W-2.

635. Is the HSA limit for employer recoupments the HSA legal maximum limit or the individual's maximum limit?

The IRS guidance is not perfectly clear on this point but logically means the HSA federal limits, not that individual's maximum limit. Otherwise, employers would be able to use the recoupment rules in situations unlikely intended by the rule. For example, an employer that provides HDHP coverage decides to give all its employees their HSA contribution on January 1 so they have the full contribution to use right away. An employee that quits and loses HSA eligibility early in the year would have some of that amount subject to recoupment under a definition where the individual's HSA limit applies although other HSA guidance indicates in that circumstance the contribution is nonforfeitable.

Example 1. Little Company makes a $500 HSA contribution for each of its employees. Barb, a Little Company employee, receives a $5,000 contribution into her HSA due to a clerical error by a Little Company Employee. Assume Barb was eligible for the self-only HSA limit for 2015 of $3,350. Little Company can recoup the difference between $5,000 and $3,350 or $1,650. The rules do not provide for the return of the additional $2,850 ($3,350 in HSA less $500 intended as an employer contribution).

Example 2. In 2014, Big Lake Industries provided self-only HDHP coverage for all its employees and put $100 per month into each employee's HSA. Mike was a Big Lake Industries employee but quit in February of 2014. Mike changed to traditional insurance in February and was only HSA-eligible for one month in 2014. Big Lake Industries forgot to stop the $100 per month HSA contributions for Mike and only discovered its mistake at year end. Big Lake Industries would like to recoup the $1,100 it over-contributed to Mike's HSA (it should have stopped Mike's contributions after the first one in January).

Whether Big Lake Industries can recoup depends on whether or not Mike exceeded the maximum annual contribution allowed in Section 223(b). The code section allows for a $3,300 HSA limit for self-only HDHP insured in 2014, well above the $1,200 contributed. Another method to look at Section 223(b) is that Mike's individual limit is actually 1/12 of $3,300 or $275. The $1,200 did exceed that amount and opens the possibility of Big Lake Industries recouping $925 ($1,200 - $275). The conservative and logical answer is that Big Lake Industries cannot recoup in this situation because Mike is below the Section 223(b) limit of $3,300.

636. If an employer contributes to the HSA of an employee who ceases to be a qualified individual during a year, can the employer recoup amounts that the employer contributed after the employee ceased to be an eligible individual?

Generally, no. Employers generally cannot recoup amounts from an HSA other than in the two specifically allowed cases: (1) the employee was never eligible for an HSA, or (2) the employer contributes more than the maximum contribution limit for the year. The maximum contribution limit for the year is based on the statutory maximum, not the maximum for a particular individual based on that individual losing eligibility mid-year (see Questions and Answers on this issue in this section).

Example. Pita was a qualified individual on January 1, 2014. On April 1, 2014, Pita lost her eligibility because her spouse enrolled in a general purpose health FSA that covers all family members. Pita first realized that she is no longer eligible on July 17, 2014, at which time she notifies her employer to cease HSA contributions. Her employer cannot recoup the HSA contributions made between April 1, 2014 and July 17, 2014 because Pita has a nonforfeitable interest in her HSA. Pita is responsible for determining if the contributions exceeded the maximum annual contribution limit in Section 223(b), and for withdrawing the excess contribution and the income attributable to the excess contribution and including both in gross income.

IRS Notice 2008-59, See Q 26.

637. What if an employee quits mid-year and the employer forgets to stop the HSA payments?

The employer cannot recoup the contributions after the employee separated from service in this situation, assuming the employee was HSA-eligible and the employer contribution was below the HSA maximums for the year.

Example. Garth worked at Sammy's Soda Shop and elected to defer $100 per month from his pay into an HSA. Garth was HSA-eligible and covered by a self-only HDHP. Garth quit Sammy's Soda Shop in June, but Sammy's Soda Shop mistakenly continued to put $100 a month into Garth's HSA until it realized its mistake in November, after putting in $500 too much. Sammy's Soda Shop would like to recoup this money from Garth's HSA but cannot. Garth was eligible for an HSA and the total HSA contributions by Sammy's Soda Shop were less than Garth's HSA limit for the year ($3,350 for 2015).

638. What happens when an employer contribution and an employee payroll deferral combined cause an excess contribution?

The HSA rules do not clearly address this issue, however, the best practice is to stop employee payroll deferrals to avoid additional over-contributions. The employee should remove the personal contributions as an excess and the employer leaves its money in the HSA.

Never HSA Eligible

639. If an employer contributes to an employee who was never eligible for an HSA, can the employer recoup the HSA contributions?

Yes. If the employee was never eligible then no HSA ever existed and the employer may correct the error. This correction can occur at the employer's option. If the employer does not correct the error by the end of the taxable year, then the amounts must be included as gross income and wages on the employee's IRS Form W-2. The employer can also withdraw any earnings on the HSA and will be subject to any fees on the HSA.

IRS Notice 2008-59, See Q 23, IRS Form W-2.

Impact on Comparability

640. Can an employer recoup a mistaken employee contribution if that contribution results in non-comparable contributions?

No. An employer may not recoup from an employee's HSA any portion of the employer's contribution to the HSA (see Questions and Answers covering exceptions in this section). In many cases when an employer makes a mistake in contributing to an employee's HSA it will be because the employer over-contributed. This over-contribution will generally cause a failure in the comparability rules.

Treas. Reg. Sec. 54.4980G-4, See Q 13.

641. Are employers subject to a 35 percent penalty for violation of the comparability rules if the employer mistakenly over contributes to an employee's HSA and cannot recoup?

The rules do not answer this question directly - however, it seems unlikely the IRS would impose the penalty in the case of a legitimate mistake (common mistakes are making an extra contribution after an employee separates from service or making a contribution for an employee after the employee is no longer eligible). The IRS regulations allow employers to pass the comparability rules in the case where an employer gives an upfront HSA contribution and then an employee separates from service such that the employee receives a larger pro-rata HSA contribution than other employees. This same logic should apply to legitimate mistakes. This is especially true given that the IRS rules prohibit the recoupment of the money in most cases. Prohibiting recoupment already punishes the employer.

The IRS rules also provide that an employer can make extra HSA contributions at the end of the year (up until April 15 of the year following the tax year) to allow for a situation where non-comparable contributions were made. This statement does not directly reference mistakes and could be interpreted to only applying to the situation of mid-year hires or employees that fail to open HSAs. This further assumes the employer-made a legitimate mistake.

If an employer "accidently" puts $5,000 into a favored employee's HSA and then claimed it could not recoup it, then a violation of the comparability rules is more likely.

> *Example.* Notebooks, Inc. mistakenly puts $500 too much into Brian's HSA (Notebooks meant to contribute $50). The $500 is below Brian's HSA limit and Brian is eligible for an HSA. Notebooks gave its other employees a contribution of $50. The $500 contribution to Brian technically causes a failed comparability test.

Other Correction Methods

642. Can an employer seek a repayment of the mistaken HSA contribution directly from the employee rather than recouping through the HSA custodian?

The answer to this question is not covered by HSA laws and regulations and is heavily dependent on the facts. HSA law uses the word "nonforfeitable." That's a strong word that implies that the HSA owner gets to keep the money. The rules make it clear the employer cannot get the money back directly from the HSA custodian or that the employee cannot even take the money out of the HSA and give it back to the employer without reporting issues. An employer may be able to seek repayment of legitimate mistakes outside of the HSA under contract, tort or other law. The employer can also simply ask the employee for repayment.

Depending upon the size of the mistake and the reasonableness of the parties there may be situations when the employer and the employee work out an arrangement to correct the mistake (e.g., the employee simply writes a check to the employer for the amount wrongly placed into the employee's HSA).

There is no support for this type of correction in HSA law - however, if all parties agree to an approach to fix a mistake and it otherwise complies with HSA laws it seems unlikely issues would arise. If the approach was questioned, then the answer may lie in a deeper understanding of the word "nonforfeitable" (does that extend beyond the HSA to ancillary agreements made to correct mistakes?) and how HSA law may intersect with other laws (the return of the money may be required pursuant to contract or other law).

643. What if the HSA custodian made the mistake rather than the employer?

The employer is not allowed to recoup that money unless one of the two exceptions exist: (1) the employee receiving the money was never eligible for the HSA (unlikely in case the employee already had an HSA), and (2) if the contribution exceeded the HSA limit for the year. This does not allow for an employers to fix a situation where it puts HSA money into the wrong employee's HSA (if the employee was not eligible it could recoup). Sometimes these mistakes are made by the HSA custodian rather than the employer.

If an HSA custodian makes a mistake, the custodian will generally work to correct the situation. The HSA rules do not provide clear guidance on how custodians are allowed to proceed to fix their own mistakes, so general banking or other applicable laws or industry practice would apply.

Generally, the custodian would withdraw the money from the HSA account of the HSA owner that wrongly received the funds and put the contribution into the HSA of the employee where it should have gone. Most HSA custodial agreements or investment instrument agreements allow for fixes for mistakes. In the case where there are not sufficient funds in the HSA, this is not possible. If the HSA is receiving regular contributions or the HSA owner is willing and able to make an additional contribution, this issue can be resolved.

Reporting

644. How is a recouped HSA contribution reported to the IRS by the custodian and employer?

In the case of an employee never being eligible for an HSA, the reporting is treated as though the HSA never existed. Accordingly, the HSA custodian would not report the contribution on the IRS Form 5498-SA and the employer would not report the contribution on the IRS Form W-2. This same non-reporting occurs for recoupment of contributions exceeding the HSA limit.

> *Example.* Yellow Tree Coffee mistakenly contributes $500 to Sally's HSA. Sally, an employee of Yellow Tree Coffee elected traditional health insurance, but through an honest mistake, Yellow Tree Coffee thought she elected the HDHP plan and made the HSA contribution for her. Yellow Tree Coffee approaches the HSA custodian and requests a return of the $500 as an employer recoupment. Yellow Tree Coffee would not report the $500 on Sally's IRS Form W-2 (or would correct it). The HSA custodian likewise would not report the $500 contribution on a IRS Form 5498-SA.

IRS Form 5498-SA, IRS Form W-2.

HSAs, FSAs and HRAs Compared

645. What are the differences between HSAs, FSAs and HRAs?

Health Savings Accounts (HSAs), Flexible Spending Accounts (FSAs) and Health Care Reimbursement Accounts (HRAs) are all accounts used to pay for health care expenses. The common thread between these accounts is that they all provide employees a means to control a portion of their health care dollars (only HSAs can be opened by individuals outside of an employment arrangement).

Employers are often comparing the differences between these plans in an effort to choose the best one or to offer a combination of the accounts to maximize benefits for employees.

- **What is an HSA?** An HSA requires coverage under a HDHP - FSAs and HRAs do not. Also unlike an FSA or HRA, an HSA is an individual custodial account that is owned by the individual rather than the employer. That legal ownership is significant because it allows employees to use that money as they see fit: spending it on eligible health care expenses, saving it for the future, or even spending it on consumer goods (penalties apply). The fact that the account belongs to the employee also removes many of the compliance and administration requirements from the employer. For example, with HSAs the employer is not required to review receipts. HSAs allow for contributions as large as $3,350 for self-only (2015) and $6,650 for family (2015) plus a $1,000 catch-up for individuals over age fifty-five.

- **What is an FSA?** An FSA is an account established as part of a Section 125 Cafeteria plan that allows employees to defer a portion of their income to pay for medical expenses on a tax-free basis. FSAs are a popular employee benefit in large part because of the tax benefits and FSAs work with a traditional health plan. The employer owns the account and is responsible for its management; including paying claims as they occur (often this is accomplished by hiring an outside administrator). Money left over at the end of the year reverts back to the employer and not the employee. However, a new rule in 2013 allows employers to amend their FSAs to allow for a rollover of up to $500 per year. As part of the Affordable Care Act, FSA contributions are now limited to $2,500 (2014). General health FSAs are considered "other health coverage" and disqualifies a person for an HSA. However, employers may offer limited-purpose FSAs and combine that offering with an HSA offering.

- **What is an HRA?** An HRA is an employer provided account that allows employees to direct a portion of their health care spending. The employer contributes funds to the employees HRA account and the employee can spend the funds on eligible health care expenses. HRAs work very similar to an FSA - however, the rules are more flexible and allow for a variety of different designs. For instance, an HRA may allow employee funds to rollover year-after-year and grow for future use. With an HRA, the employer is also responsible for compliance and administration (often accomplished by hiring an outside administrator).

Criteria	HSA	FSA	HRA
Overview	Opened with HSA custodian. Requires HDHP coverage and other eligibility rules apply.[1]	Set up through employer and generally requires payroll deferral to fund.	HRAs give employers the most control. Employer must fund.
Contribution Limits	$3,350 self-only for 2014 $6,650 family for 2015 $1,000 catch-up for 2015	$2,500 for years after 2012	No limit.

Criteria	HSA	FSA	HRA
Who Can Contribute	Employer – Optional Payroll deferral – Optional Employee direct – Optional	Employer – Optional Payroll deferral – Optional Employee direct – Not allowed	Employer – Required Payroll deferral – Not allowed Employee direct – Not allowed
Tax Savings	Employer – deductible[2] Payroll def – tax free + 7.65%[3] Employee direct – deductible	Employer – deductible Payroll def – tax free + 7.65%[3] Employee direct – Not allowed	Employer – deductible Payroll def – Not allowed Employee direct – Not allowed
Acct Owner	Employee	Employer	Employer
Earnings Investments	Generally interest paid and investments allowed. Earnings grow tax-free.	No earnings paid.	Generally, no earnings paid.
Qualified Expenses & Distributions	213(d) medical expenses, dental, vision, Medicare and LTC premiums, CO-BRA (when unemployed), Health premiums at age 65, and may withdraw at any time for any reason (subject to 20% penalty).[4]	213(d) medical expenses, dental, and vision, (health insurance premiums through Section 125). Cannot access for non-medical reasons. See IRS Publication 502 for details.	213(d) medical expenses, dental, vision, Medicare and vision, LTC premiums, health insurance premiums. Cannot access for non-medical reasons. See IRS Publication 502 for details.
Claims Substantiation	Only employee required to maintain supporting records. Employer need not review.	ERISA plan – Employer or Administrator must substantiate expense	ERISA plan – Employer or Administrator must substantiate expense
Employer Involvement	None Required. Employer may contribute and allow for payroll deferral.	Required. ERISA Plan.	Required. ERISA Plan.
Rollover	Yes, funds roll year-to-year.	Maybe, up to $500 per year.	Maybe.
Ability to Use for Multiple Year's Expenses	Yes, can save and use current year's contributions for future year's expenses. May also use future year's contributions to cover current year's expense.	Limited, generally must elect amount prior to the start of the year and then stick with that amount. Limited ability to roll over for future use.	Employers generally allow some rollover for future year's use; however, money may or may not go with employee if the employee changes jobs.

[1] High Deductible Health Plan, See the Eligibility and Contribution Worksheet for details on eligibility.

[2] See the Comparability Worksheet and Employer Guide for details.

[3] Both the employer and the employee save payroll taxes (approx. 7.65% for each). The 7.65% reflected in the chart assumes employee savings of FICA at 6.2% (only up to $117,000 for 2014) and an additional 1.45% for Medicare. Add .9% for a Medicare surtax for income above $200,000 for single filers and $250,000 for joint filers.

[4] See the Distribution Worksheet for details.

646. Do FSAs allow for rollovers?

The IRS released new guidance in 2013 that allows for employees to rollover year-to-year up to $500 in an FSA. Employers must amend their Section 125 Cafeteria plans in order to allow for this rollover and employers are not required to allow for the rollover and could limit the amount to less than $500. Employers are not allowed to increase the amount of the rollover above $500.

If an employee does rollover some or all of the allowed $500, the amount rolled does not count against the employee's next year FSA contribution limit. Accordingly, an employee rolling over the maximum $500 could still elect to defer $2,500 for the next year (or an amount as adjusted for inflation). The IRS states that "this carryover option provides an alternative to the current grace period rule and administrative relief similar to that rule" so an employer cannot offer both a rollover and a grace period (some transitional relief applies).

> *Example.* Big Lake, Inc. sponsors a Section 125 plan and Health FSA with a calendar year and an annual run-out period from January 1 through March 31 in which participants can submit claims for expenses incurred during the previous plan year. The plan has an annual open enrollment season in November in which participants elect a salary reduction amount (not to exceed $2,500) for the following plan year. Big Lake timely amends the plan to provide for participants to carryover up to $500 of unused health FSA amounts remaining at the end of the run-out period. The plan does not provide a grace period with respect to health FSA.
>
> In November 2014, Jim elects a salary reduction amount of $2,500 for 2015. By December 31, 2014, Jim's unused amount from 2014 is $800. On February 1, 2015, Jim submits claims and is reimbursed with respect to $350 of expenses incurred during the 2014 plan year, leaving a carryover on March 31, 2015 (the end of the run-out period) of $450 of unused health FSA amounts from 2014. The $450 is not forfeited; instead, it is carried over to 2015 and available to pay claims incurred in that year so the $2,950 (that is, $2,500 plus $450) is available to pay claims incurred in 2015.
>
> Jim incurs and submits claims of $2,700 during the month of July 2015, and does not submit any other claims during 2015. Jim is reimbursed with respect to the $2,700 claim, leaving $250 as potential unused amount from 2015 to carryover to 2016 (depending upon whether Jim submits claims during the 2015 run-out period in early 2016).

IRS Notice 2013-71.

647. Which is the best, HSA, FSA or HRA?

Although there is no simple answer to this question, some points to consider are outlined below:

HSAs: An HSA generally works well for employers that want to minimize administration and compliance issues. Employers desiring to offer the most flexible solution for employees are often drawn to the HSA as it allows for portability, the opportunity for investment growth (HRAs may offer this as well), and the distribution of funds for non-medical reasons (including for any purpose at age sixty-five without penalty). Also, employers seeking to minimize their costs and involvement often offer HSAs because the employer does not have to fund any portion of the account. Employees may prefer HSAs to health FSAs because the funds belong to them so they do not need to worry about being as precise in estimating their medical expenses. Further, they benefit personally from lowering their healthcare expenses, unlike FSAs where an employee may end up rushing to spend money on health care at the end of the year in order to avoid losing funds.

FSAs: Employers offering traditional health care plans often prefer FSAs, primarily because HSAs are not an option with traditional insurance (must have an HDHP to be eligible). A traditional health plan limits the deductible so that the rollover feature of HSAs is less important and it's also easier for an employee to estimate expenses. FSAs allow employees to defer extra income into the FSA to pay for co-pays, medical bills not covered by insurance, as well as dental and vision care. One significant benefit of FSAs over HSAs, from the employer's perspective, is that the employer gets to keep unspent money at the end of the year (except up to $500 rollover amount if employer allows for rollovers).

HRAs: HRAs allow the most flexibility in plan design and are favored by more sophisticated employers (generally larger employers that have complex benefit packages). The inability to allow for payroll deferral reduces the attractiveness of HRAs as the only offering, but HRAs can be offered in connection with a health FSA and to a limited extent an HSA. HRAs also work well for employers that self-insure. The HRA provides a method for self-insuring employers to put in consumer-directed efforts to reduce overall health care costs and increase employee satisfaction at the same time. HRAs are more complicated to administer than HSAs. A key limitation of HRAs is that only the employer can fund the HRA.

648. Can an employer offer both an FSA and HSA?

Yes, but either not to the same employee or the FSA must be a limited-purpose FSA. An employee covered under an HDHP and another first-dollar insurance plan is not eligible for an HSA. An FSA that reimburses for qualified medical expenses is considered another insurance plan and would make the covered person ineligible for an HSA. One approach is for an employer to offer an FSA for employees that elect a traditional health plan and an HSA for those that elect an HDHP. Another option is for the employer to offer a limited-purpose FSA that only covers dental and vision expenses and is allowed along with an HSA (a post-deductible FSA or HRA are additional options).

> *Example.* Jane runs a small company and wants to enable her employees to defer as much as possible on a tax-favored basis to pay for medical expenses. Jane can offer an HDHP along with both HSA payroll deferrals and a limited-purpose FSA. Employees could then fully fund the HSA and also the FSA. The FSA funds would only be available for vision, dental and very limited other preventative care.
>
> Bob, an employee of Jane's, wants to maximize his tax benefits and save as much as possible for future medical expenses. Bob knows his daughter will have $2,500 in orthodontics expenses in the next year. Bob elects to defer $2,500 of his pay into the limited-purpose FSA to pay his daughter's orthodontics expenses. He also plans to payroll defer the maximum HSA limit for the year to pay for qualified medical expenses or to save for the future. Bob could use his HSA to pay for the orthodontics expenses but he prefers to save his HSA and get the larger tax break by using the limited-purpose FSA for the expense.

See Part III: Eligibility - Other Health Plan — Limited-Purpose FSA.

649. Can an employer offer both an HRA and an HSA?

Yes, but either not to the same employee or the HRA must be a limited-purpose HRA or a post-deductible HRA. An employee covered under an HDHP and another first-dollar insurance plan is not eligible for an HSA. An HRA that reimburses for qualified medical expenses is considered another insurance plan and would make the covered person ineligible for an HSA.

A limited-purpose HRA that only covers dental, vision and preventive care does not make a person ineligible for an HSA. The HRA can also pay or reimburse premiums for coverage by an accident or health plan.

> *Example.* Fancy Watches, Inc. provides an HRA which reimburses for qualified medical expenses incurred by an employee. Fancy Watches amends its HRA to limit its benefits to expenses for vision, dental, and preventive care and to pay the employee's share of the premiums for the employer-sponsored HDHP. After the amendment, employees of Fancy Watches are otherwise eligible individuals.

IRS Notice 2008-59, See Q 1. See Part III: Eligibility - Other Health Plan — Limited-Purpose HRA.

650. Can an employer offer an HRA, FSA and HSA?

Yes, but the employer will have to be careful if the employer wants its employees to remain HSA-eligible. The employer could offer HDHP coverage, a limited-purpose FSA and a post-deductible HRA and its employees would still be otherwise eligible for HSAs.

651. What FSA rules do not apply to HSAs?

HSAs are not subject to the following FSA rules: (1) the prohibition against rolling more than $500 over year to year, (2) the requirement that the maximum amount of reimbursement must be available at all times during coverage, and (3) the mandatory twelve-month period of coverage.

IRS Notice 2004-50, See Q 58.

652. Are HSAs, FSAs and HRAs taxed in the same fashion?

Basically all three types of plans enjoy tax-free treatment for health care expenses. The rules of deductibility can be different, however.

HSA contributions are deductible by the employer when made by the employer as a "comparable" contribution or when made by employee payroll deferral through a section 125 plan. In both cases the contribution will not show as income on the employee's income tax return. Individuals may also contribute directly to an HSA and deduct the amount on their income tax return.

FSA contributions are deductible by the employer and not income to the employee. The contribution is not subject to FICA/FUTA.

HRA contributions are deductible by the employer and not income to the employee. The contribution is an employee benefit not subject to FICA/FUTA.

653. Do FSAs avoid some of the "group health plan" rules as "excepted benefits"?

A joint release from the IRS, DOL and HHS provides that a health FSA will be classified as excepted benefits if:

- Other (non-excepted benefit) group health plan coverage is made available to employees by the employer, and

- The arrangement is structured so that the maximum benefit payable to any participant cannot exceed two times the participant's salary reduction election for the arrangement for the year (or, if greater cannot exceed $500 plus the amount of the participant's salary reduction election)

IRS Notice 2013-54.

654. Are HSAs subject to the "group health plan" rules under the Affordable Care Act?

A 2013 IRS release on this topic did not address HSAs. Presumably, HSAs are not group health plans for this purpose and an employer can continue to make HSA contributions for employees without integration with a health plan.

IRS Notice 2013-54.

655. How is an HSA similar to a 401(k) or an IRA?

HSAs have some obvious features that are common with retirement accounts including rollovers, portability, choice of investment types and risks, as well as survivor benefits.

In addition to similarities, there are also advantages including

- Exempt for paying FICA tax on contributions made from payroll

- Greater liquidity options – ability to keep funds in insured accounts if one desires as well as being able to move money for investments with greater return

- Can contribute both earned and unearned income

- Funds can be used at any time/any age for qualified medical expenses

- Can continue to contribute to account after end of employment

PART XI: COMPARABILITY

Overview

656. What are the HSA comparability rules?

The comparability rules are designed to ensure that employers that make pre-tax HSA contributions for their employees do so "comparably," or in other words, do so fairly. The rules are patterned after 401(k) or other benefit plan nondiscrimination rules. The rules for all of these plans share a common goal of making sure the plans are fair and do not discriminate in favor of some employees or against others.

For HSAs, employers must give all participating employees that fall into the same category the same HSA contribution or an HSA contribution that is the same percentage of the health insurance deductible. In the words of the IRS, "[i]f an employer makes contributions to any employee's HSA, the employer must make comparable contributions to the HSAs of all comparable participating employees."

This somewhat straight-forward sounding sentence is misleading as the comparability rules are complex. The rules do allow for discrimination between different categories of employees and do allow employers to make decisions that impact employer HSA contributions.

Treas. Reg. §54.4980G-1, See Q 1.

657. When do the comparability rules apply?

The comparability rules only apply to employers that make pre-tax HSA contributions to employees outside of a Section 125 Cafeteria plan.

> *Example.* Pleasure Yachts, Inc. provides self-only HDHP coverage to its employees and puts $100 per month into each employee's HSA. The $100 per month is not a payroll deferral elected by the employees pursuant to a Section 125 plan but is instead an additional benefit offered by the company. The contribution is made pre-tax by Pleasure Yachts and it takes a deduction for the HSA contribution as a business expense (IRC Sec. 106) and reflects the income to the employees in Box 12 of the IRS Form W-2, rather than in Box 1 as taxable income. Pleasure Yachts is subject to the comparability rules because it makes pre-tax employer HSA contributions. Pleasure Yachts meets the comparability rules because it gives all employees the same HSA contribution (it could meet the rules with other contribution arrangements as well).

IRS Form W-2, IRC Sec. 106.

658. Does employer encouragement of employees to fund HSAs on their own result in the comparability rules applying?

No. Only pre-tax employer contributions are subject to the comparability regulations. Employee after-tax contributions made on the employees' own are not subject to comparability.

659. What types of HSA contributions are not subject to the comparability rules?

The comparability rules only apply to employers that make pre-tax HSA contributions to employees. The comparability rules do not apply to the following:

- Individual HSA contributions made directly rather than through the employer

- Employee pre-tax payroll deferral contributions made through the employer's Section 125 plan

- Employee after-tax payroll deferrals

- HSA contributions made by family members, friends, or other non-employer entity or person

- HSA rollover and transfer contributions

- IRA funding of an HSA ("qualified funding distribution")

- Archer MSA transfer or rollover into an HSA

- FSA and HRA funding of an HSA (law allowing this has now expired)

660. Can an employer make comparable contributions to employees if the employer does not offer health insurance?

Yes. Employers can make pre-tax HSA contributions to employees even if the employer does not offer HDHP health insurance coverage. Employers are however, required to follow the comparability rules.

Note: The answer above is accurate for HSAs but not necessarily for HRAs or FSAs. In 2013, the IRS released guidance together with HHS and the DOL that limits some of the ability to offer FSAs and HRAs when the employer does not integrate the FSA or HRA with employer provided health insurance. This means that an employer could not offer an FSA or HRA absent offering group health insurance. This limitation does not apply to HSAs as HSAs are not considered a "group health plan" for this purpose (although more direct guidance on this point by the federal authorities would be valued).

Example. A to Z Inc. does not offer health insurance coverage for its employees. It wants to encourage employees to get health insurance on their own and tells employees that if they buy their own HSA-eligible health insurance and are otherwise eligible for an HSA, they will contribute $100 a month into their HSA on a pre-tax basis." The company can do this but is subject to the comparability rules requiring it to treat similarly situated employees the same. A to Z could not make this offer contingent upon some other requirement such as: "if you buy your own HSA-eligible health insurance AND meet your sales objectives for the month, then we will put $100 in your HSA for that month."

IRS Notice 2013-54.

661. Can an employer allow after-tax payroll deferral into an HSA and avoid the comparability rules?

Yes, if an employee requests that his or her employer deduct after-tax amounts from the employee's compensation and forward these amounts to the employee's HSA the contribution is not subject to the comparability rules. After-tax contributions to an HSA are not subject to the comparability rules because they are not considered employer contributions under the law (IRC Sec. 106(d)).

> *Example.* Safe Boating, Inc. covers its employees under an HDHP. The business does not provide pre-tax payroll deferral into the HSA under a Cafeteria plan nor does it make a direct employer contribution. Safe Boating does allow employees to direct deposit their pay checks. Tina, an employee, directs Safe Boating to send $100 to her HSA custodian from her pay and the balance of her pay to her personal checking account. Safe Boating complies and treats Tina's entire income (including the HSA amount) as taxable wages reported in Box 1 on the IRS Form 1040. This contribution to the HSA is a direct deposit by Tina after tax and is not an employer contribution subject to the comparability rules.

IRS Form 1040, IRC Sec. 106(d).

662. Can an employer make a one-time contribution to employees' HSAs without committing to future HSA contributions?

Yes, employers are allowed to give their employees a one-time contribution to their HSA. The employer would need to be clear in that it is not committing to future contributions to avoid misunderstanding. The employer would need to meet the "comparability" rules for the one-time contribution.

A one-time contribution generally does commit the employer to making HSA contributions for employees that are hired mid-year and become eligible for the HSA contribution. The contribution to mid-year hires is necessary to meet the comparability rules unless the one-time contribution is made at the end of the year when month-to-month coverage is already known (although this approach may require the employer to give an HSA contribution to an employee that separated from service during the year).

Categories

663. What are the acceptable categories for comparability testing?

The chart below illustrates the allowed categories of employees for the purpose of making comparable HSA contributions.

Allowed Categories of Employees
Part Time v. Full Time
Current v. Former
HSA Eligible v. Not Eligible
Non-Union v. Union and Union v. Different Union
Employer Provided HDHP v. Other HDHP
Single HDHP Coverage v. Family Coverage
Within Family: Self +1, Self +2, and Self +3 or More (Cannot decrease amount as family size increases)
Non-Highly Compensated (must not get less, but can get more) v. Highly Compensated (cannot get more)

Treas. Reg. §54.4980G1, See Q 2, Treas. Reg. §54.4980G-3, See Q 6, See Q 7, Treas. Reg. §54.4980G-6, See Q 1.

Single versus Family

664. Can an employer treat employees covered under a family HDHP differently than those covered under a single HDHP?

Yes, the comparability rules require that HSA contributions to employees within a category are comparable. The rules do not require that HSA contributions to employees across categories be comparable. Contributions to self-only HDHP covered employees do not need to bear a relationship to HSA contributions made to family HDHP covered employees (employees might become disgruntled if there is no logic to explain the disparate treatment, but the rules allow it).

Example 1. ABC Corporation elects to give each of its employees that elect self-only coverage under the company's HDHP a $2,000 HSA contribution. ABC Corporation elects not to give any contribution to family HDHP covered employees. Although this treatment may appear unfair, it meet the comparability rules because the employees within the same category of coverage are treated comparably (all self-only covered employees receive $2,000 and all family covered employees receive no HSA contribution).

Employers do not need to have a good reason for treating different categories differently, but employees are likely to question why. Employers may elect to give more to single HDHP covered employees for a number of reasons but most often its due to the fact that single covered employees save the employer money on the insurance premium cost and the employer is using some or all of that savings to make an HSA contribution for the self-only covered employees.

Example 2. Same facts as above, except new management takes over and believes that family HDHP covered employees should receive a larger contribution than self-only HDHP covered employees because families have more individuals and likely more medical expenses. The employer decides to keep its $2,000 for self-only employees but starts giving $3,500 to each family HDHP covered employee in the next plan year. The employer's plan would meet the comparability rules.

Treas. Reg. §54.4980G-1, See Q 2. Treas. Reg. §54.4980G-4, See Q 1.

665. What are the family categories of coverage?

Family HDHP coverage breaks into three subsets:

- Self plus one

- Self plus two

- Self plus three or more

Example 1. ABC Corporation maintains an HDHP plan for its employees and contributes to the HSAs of eligible employees who elect coverage under the HDHP. The HDHP has only self-only coverage and family coverage and ABC Corporation does not distinguish within the family coverage category. ABC Corporation contributes $750 to its self-only HDHP covered employees and $1,000 to its family HDHP covered employees (regardless of whether the size of the family is plus one, plus two or plus three or more). ABC Corporation meets the comparability rules.

Example 2. XYX Corporation maintains an HDHP with the following categories and contributes to its employees HSAs who elect coverage under the HDHP:

- Self-only

- Self plus spouse

- Self plus dependent

- Self plus spouse plus one dependent

- Self plus two dependents

- Self plus spouse and two or more dependents

The self plus spouse category and the self plus dependent category constitute the same category for comparability purposes. Similarly, the self plus spouse plus one dependent constitute the same category as self plus two dependents for comparability purposes.

Treas. Reg. §54.4980G-1, See Q 2.

666. Can an employer treat an employee and spouse covered under a family plan differently than an employee and a child covered under a family plan?

No. The IRS comparability rules only allow the categories of self-only, self plus one, self plus two, or self plus three or more. An employee plus a spouse and an employee plus a child are both considered self-plus one and must receive comparable HSA contributions.

> *Example.* Tina's Tools would like to give $200 a month to the HSAs of its employees that are a family comprised of two spouses and may or may not have children. Tina's Tools would like to give $100 a month to the HSAs of its employees that are a family comprised of one parent and one or more children (the employee is not married). This is not allowed. The family category is defined as employee plus one. The plus one could be a spouse or a children and the employer is not allowed to distinguish between the two.

Treas. Reg. §54.4980G-1, See Q 2.

667. How do the comparability rules apply if an employee switches mid-year from single to family coverage using the pay-as-you-go method?

An employer can adjust the contribution amount to reflect a change in status of an employee in the single versus family category.

> *Example.* Sun Systems, Inc. contributes to its eligible employees' HSAs on a monthly pay-as-you-go method. Sun Systems makes a $50 contribution per month for each eligible employee that elects its self-only HDHP coverage and $100 per month to each eligible employee electing its family HDHP coverage.
>
> From January 1 through March 31, Owen, an employee of Sun Systems, is a qualified employee with self-only coverage. Owen got married in March and switched to family HDHP coverage effective April 1 and he maintained that coverage through December 31. For Owen's HSA, Sun Systems contributed $50 per month for the months of January through March and $100 per month for the months of April through December. Sun Systems meets the comparability rules.

Treas. Reg. §54.4980G-4, See Q 2.

668. Can an employer give a larger contribution to an employee with a larger family?

Yes. An employer is allowed to treat employees electing different categories of family coverage differently provided the HSA contribution amount stays the same or increases as the family size increases. The allowed categories are self plus one, self plus two and self plus three or more.

Example 1. An employer might set up a program where a self plus one employee receives a $500 HSA contribution, a self-plus two receives a $600 contribution and self plus threw or more a $700 contribution. These amounts cannot decrease as more people are added. Self plus two must receive at least as much as self plus one and self plus three or more must receive at least as much as self plus two. So, an employer could not make a $500 to self plus one and a $400 to self plus two, because the amount is less for self plus two.

Example 2. Green Company offers HDHPs with the following coverage options:

- A $2,500 deductible for self-only
- A $3,500 deductible for self plus one dependent (self plus one)
- A $3,500 deductible for self plus spouse (self plus one)
- A $3,500 deductible for self plus spouse and one dependent (self plus two)
- A $3,500 deductible for self plus spouse and two or more dependents (self plus three or more).

Green Company makes the following contributions for the calendar year to the HSA of each full-time employee who is a qualified individual covered under the HDHP:

- $750 for self-only
- $1,000 for self plus one dependent
- $1,000 for self plus spouse
- $1,500 for self plus spouse and one dependent
- $2,000 for self plus spouse and two or more dependents

Green Company satisfies the comparability rules.

Treas. Reg. §54.4890G-4, See Q 1.

Employer Provided HDHP versus Other HDHP

669. Can an employer limit HSA contributions to employees who have health insurance coverage provided by the employer?

Yes. An employer can make HSA contributions only to the HSAs of its eligible employees that receive HDHP coverage through the employer's plan. The employer is not required to make comparable contributions to HSAs of employees who are eligible individuals but are not covered under the employer's HDHP.

Example. WIFI, Inc. offers an HDHP to its full-time employees. Most full-time employees are covered under WIFI's HDHP and WIFI makes comparable contributions only to these employees. Sally, a full-time employee of WIFI, is HSA-eligible but receives her insurance coverage through her husband's employer and not WIFI. WIFI does not make an HSA contribution for Sally. WIFI is not required to make a comparable contribution to Sally because she did not receive her insurance coverage through WIFI's HDHP.

Treas. Reg. §54.4980G-3, See Q 8.

670. Can an employer elect to make HSA contributions to employees who do not receive their health insurance through the business?

Yes. The employer has a choice on whether or not it wants to make HSA contributions to employees who are HSA-eligible but do not receive their HSA-eligible health insurance through the employer. If the employer decides to include these employees in the HSA contribution it must do so for all similarly situated employees.

> *Example 1.* ABC Corporation offers an HDHP for its employees and it makes a $1,000 contribution to the HSAs of comparable participating employees. Bob, an employee of ABC Corporation, is eligible for an HSA but does not receive his HDHP coverage through ABC Corporation. ABC Corporation decides to limit its $1,000 HSA contributions only to employees that receive their health coverage through the employer. This is permissible under the comparability rules.

> *Example 2.* Assume the same example as above, except that Bob convinces ABC Corporation that he should also get the HSA contribution. His logic is that he is actually saving the company money by receiving his health insurance outside the company and he should not be punished by being excluded from the HSA contribution. ABC Corporation agrees and changes it position on the HSA contribution and will now give the HSA contribution to employees that receive their HDHP coverage through the employer and also to employees that receive their HDHP coverage otherwise. ABC Corporation will meet the comparability rules.

671. How does an employer know whether an employee is eligible for an HSA when the employee is not covered by the employer's HDHP?

The employer must make a reasonable good faith effort to identify all comparable participating employees with non-employer provided HDHP coverage.

Treas. Reg. §54.4980G-3, See Q 8.

672. If a husband and wife both work for the same business do the comparability rules require that the business give them each an HSA contribution?

Generally, an employer only needs to make an HSA contribution for the employee that is primarily named on the health insurance policy. If one spouse takes out a family HDHP through the employer that covers both spouses and the employer only makes HSA contributions to employees that receive their HDHP coverage through the employer, then the employer only has to contribute to the HSA of the employee with HDHP coverage through the employer. The employer is not required to give an HSA contribution to the employee that only has HDHP coverage by virtue of his or her spouse's coverage.

However, if an employer contributes to the HSAs of its employees with HDHP coverage that is not an employer provided HDHP, then the employer must make comparable contributions to both employee-spouses if they are both eligible individuals. The employer is not required to contribute an amount in excess of the HSA limits.

> *Example 1.* ABC Corporation makes a $1,000 HSA contribution to its HSA-eligible employees that are covered under its employer provided HDHP. Samantha and Bill, wife and husband, both work for ABC Corporation. Samantha elects family HDHP coverage through the ABC Corporation's insurance offering and Bill receives coverage because he is Samantha's spouse and the policy covers her spouse. ABC Corporation must make a $1,000 contribution to Samantha's HSA but is not required to make the $1,000 contribution to Bill's HSA.

> *Example 2.* Using the same facts as above, except ABC Corporation elects to make HSA contributions to eligible employees that do not receive their HDHP coverage through the employer. In this case, ABC Corporation must make a $1,000 contribution to both Samantha's and Bill's HSAs.

Example 3. Using the same facts as the Example 2, except that ABC Corporation makes an HSA contribution equal to the HSA limit for a family each year ($6,550 for 2014). ABC Corporation would have to make the $6,550 contribution to Samantha's HSA, but not Bill's because the HSA contribution to Bill's HSA would exceed the maximum allowed HSA contribution for the year.

26 CFR §54.4980 G-3, See Q 9.

Current versus Former Employees

673. Do employers have to make HSA contributions for former employees?

No. If an employer elects to make HSA contributions for former employees it must do so on a comparable basis.

Example. ABC Company makes a $1,000 HSA contribution to all its current employees HSAs if they are HSA-eligible with coverage under any HDHP, employer or non-employer provided. ABC Company does not make any HSA contribution to its former employees even if they are still eligible for an HSA. ABC Company meets the comparability rules.

Treas. Reg. §54.4980G-3, See Q 11.

674. Are employers required to make HSA contributions for former employees receiving COBRA continuation coverage?

No, employers are not required to make comparable contributions to the HSAs of former employees with coverage under the employer's HDHP because of an election under a COBRA continuation provision.

Example. Grass Cutters, Inc. provides HSA contributions to its employees. Cindy worked for Grass Cutters and received the HSA contributions. She separated from service but opted to continue the same health plan through COBRA continuation coverage. Grass Cutters, Inc. does not need to fund Cindy's HSA under the HSA comparability rules as she is a former employee, not a current employee.

Treas. Reg. §54.4980G-3, See Q 13.

675. What happens when an employer makes HSA contributions for former employees but cannot find a former employee?

Employers must take "reasonable" action to locate any missing comparable participating employees. In general such actions include the use of certified mail, the Internal Revenue Service Letter Forwarding Program or the Social Security Administration's Letter Forwarding Service.

676. Can an employer make HSA contributions only to former employees that continue to receive their HDHP coverage through the employer?

Yes. An employer can choose to make HSA contributions to former employees that are comparable participating former employees with coverage under an HDHP provided by the employer. An employer that contributes to former employees' HSAs with coverage under an employer provided HDHP are not required to contribute to the HSAs of former employees who are eligible for an HSA but not covered through the employer's HDHP. However, an employer that contributes to the HSA of any former employee who is a qualified individual with coverage under an HDHP that is not an HDHP of the employer, must make comparable contributions to the HSAs of all former employees who are eligible individuals whether or not covered under an HDHP of the employer.

Treas. Reg. §54.4980G-3, See Q 12.

Union versus Non-Union

677. Can an employer treat collectively bargained employees differently for the purpose of HSA contributions?

Yes. An employer can separate union employees as not comparable participating employees, provided that health benefits were the subject of good faith bargaining between the union and the employer (health benefits generally are part of the bargaining agreement). Basically, an employer can make HSA contributions for non-union workers and not have to make them for union workers, or vice versa.

> *Example 1.* ABC Company has collectively bargained and non-collectively bargained employees. The collectively bargained employees are covered by a collective bargaining agreement under which health benefits were bargained in good faith. ABC Company contributes $500 to the HSAs of all eligible non-collectively bargained employees with self-only coverage under the Company's HDHP. ABC Company does not contribute to the collectively bargained employees. ABC Company's HSA contributions satisfy the comparability rules. The comparability rules do not apply to collectively bargained employees.

> *Example 2.* Assume the same facts as above, except that ABC Company contributes $500 into the HSA of each collectively bargained employee and makes no contribution to its non-collectively bargained employees. ABC Company's HSA contributions to the collectively bargained employees are not subject to the comparability rules. ABC Company's failure to contribute to the HSAs of non-collectively bargained employees does not violate the comparability rules.

> *Example 3.* Assume the same facts as above, except that ABC Company pursuant to the terms of its collective bargaining agreement contributes an amount equal to the specific number of cents per hour for each hour worked to the HSAs of all eligible collectively bargained employees. Although this contribution method would fail the comparability rules, the comparability rules do not apply because the rules do not apply to collectively bargained employees.

Treas. Reg. §54.4980G-3, See Q 7.

678. What if an employer has two different collective bargaining units, can the employer treat those two unions differently for HSA contributions?

Yes. HSA contributions made to employees in collective bargaining units where health care benefits were negotiated in good faith are not subject to the comparability rules.

> *Example.* ABC Company has two collectively bargained employer units, unit A and unit B, each covered by a collective bargaining agreement under which health benefits were bargained in good faith. According to the respective collective bargaining agreements, ABC Company makes a $500 HSA contribution to each eligible employee in unit A and no contribution to the employees in unit B. ABC Company's contributions, or lack thereof, to the HSAs of collectively bargained employees are not subject to the comparability rules.

Highly Compensated versus Non-Highly Compensated

679. Can an employer give non-highly compensated employees a larger HSA contribution than highly compensated employees?

Yes, the law allows employers to give larger HSA contributions to non-highly compensated employees than highly compensated employees. The rule does not work in reverse. An employer may not give a larger HSA contribution to its highly compensated employees versus its non-highly compensated employees.

The definition for highly compensated employee includes any employee: (1) who was a 5 percent owner at any time during the year or the preceding year, or (2) for the preceding year (A) had compensation from the employer in excess of $115,000 (for 2014) or (B) if elected by the employer, was in the group consisting of the top 20 percent of employees ranked based on compensation.

> *Example 1.* An employer may make a $1,000 HSA contribution to each eligible non-highly compensated employee without making a contribution for its highly compensated employees.

> *Example 2.* An employer makes a $1,000 HSA contribution to each eligible non-highly compensated employee. The employer makes a $500 HSA contribution to each eligible highly compensated employee. The employer meets the comparability rules because the highly compensated are getting the same or less than the non-highly compensated employees.

Treas. Reg. §54.4980G-5, See Q 2.

680. Can an employer give highly compensated employees a larger HSA contribution than non-highly compensated employees?

No. The category of highly compensated employees versus non-highly compensated employees has a special rule. The non-highly compensated employees must get the same HSA contribution or more as compared to highly compensated employees.

> *Example.* Johnson Law Office wants to contribute $1,200 to the HSAs of each full-time self-only HDHP insured non-highly compensated employee and $2,400 to the HSAs of each full-time self-only HDHP insured highly compensated employee. Johnson Law Office cannot proceed with this program and will fail the comparability rules if it does.

> In order to meet the comparability rules, Johnson Law Office changes its HSA contribution plan to giving $2,400 to the HSAs of each full-time self-only HDHP insured employee (and otherwise HSA-eligible). Johnson Law Office meets the comparability rules as all comparable employees are receiving the same HSA contribution.

Treas. Reg. §54.4980G-5, See Q 2.

681. What is a highly compensated employee?

The definition for highly compensated employee includes any employee: (1) who was a 5 percent owner at any time during the year or the preceding year, or (2) for the preceding year (A) had compensation from the employer in excess of $115,000 (for 2014) or (B) if elected by the employer, was in the group consisting of the top 20 percent of employees ranked based on compensation.

IRC Sec. 414(q).

682. What if by coincidence all of an employer's highly compensated employees fall into an allowed HSA category, can the employer give a larger contribution for that category?

Yes. Employers are allowed to categorize employees pursuant to the approved categories. Level of compensation is not an approved category for general purposes although there is an exception allowing employers to give larger contributions to non-highly compensated employees versus highly compensated. That exception does not allow for larger contributions to highly compensated employees. However, if all the highly compensated employees fall within the same category and no non-highly compensated employees fall within that category it is possible that an employer will be making larger contributions for highly compensated versus non-highly compensated employees. This result would have to be based on an approved category.

> *Example.* Seaside Restaurant contributes $1,000 for the calendar year to the HSA of each full-time employee who is a qualified individual with self plus one HDHP coverage. Seaside Restaurant contributes $1,500 for the calendar year to the HSA of each employee who is a qualified individual with self plus two coverage. Sam, a non-highly compensated employee, is a qualified individual with self plus one coverage and receives a $1,000 HSA contribution. Paula, a highly compensated employee, is an individual with self plus two coverage and receives a $1,500 contribution. Seaside's HSA contributions meet the comparability rules even though a highly compensated employee received a larger contribution than a non-highly compensated employee. The difference is acceptable because the employees fall into different approved categories.

Treas. Reg. §54.4980G-5, See Q 3.

683. Can an employer base HSA contributions on management versus non-management as a category?

No. Although giving more to non-management employees appears to comply with the spirit of the exception allowing employers to give more to non-highly compensated employees, the two are not the same. The law and regulations allow for different treatment of highly versus non-highly compensated employees. The law and regulations do not allow for different treatment of management versus non-management employees, even if non-management gets a larger contribution.

If all management employees are also highly compensated employees, then the employer could use the highly compensated versus non-highly compensated exception to meet its objectives of giving more to non-highly compensated employees.

> *Example.* Best Computers, Inc. maintains an HDHP covering all management and non-management employees. Best Computer contributes to the HSAs of non-management employees who are eligible individuals covered under its HDHP. Best Computers does not contribute to the HSAs of its management employees who are eligible individuals under its HDHP. The comparability rules are not satisfied (unless all the management happen to also be highly compensated employees).

Treas. Reg. §54.4980G-5, See Q 2.

Part-Time versus Full-Time

684. Can an employer exclude part-time employees from an HSA contribution?

Yes. Part-time employees are their own category for comparability purposes. Employers must treat all part-time employees comparably, but that could mean all part-time employees receive no HSA contribution.

Treas. Reg. §54.4980G-3, See Q 6.

685. What is the definition of "part-time" for comparability purposes?

Part-time employees are those that customarily are employed for fewer than thirty hours per week and full-time employees are customarily employed for thirty hours or more per week.

686. What if an employee is full-time for some months and part-time for other months?

Employers must determine eligibility for employer comparable HSA contributions on a monthly basis. Accordingly, an employee that is a full-time comparable employee in a certain month will count as full-time for that month's HSA contribution.

> *Example.* Sun Systems, Inc. contributes $240 to the HSA of each eligible employee that works full-time for the full calendar year. Jake, works full time for June, July and August and part-time for the rest of the year. Jake must receive a $60 HSA contribution from Sun Systems as a pro-rata amount of the annual contribution ($240 annually divided by twelve months = $20 per month).

Treas. Reg. §54.4980G-4, See Q 4.

HSA-Eligible versus Non-Eligible

687. How are ineligible employees treated for comparability purposes?

Employees that are not eligible for an HSA are not considered comparable participating employees and do not have to receive an HSA contribution.

> *Example.* Purple Company offers an HDHP and makes HSA contributions for comparable eligible participating employees. Jane, an employee of Purple Company, is married and her spouse is enrolled in a health FSA at his work. He can use his FSA to pay for Jane's medical expenses. Purpose Company does not need to make a contribution to Jane's HSA because Jane is not eligible for an HSA due to her husband's FSA coverage.

Treas. Reg. §54.4980G4 See Q 1.

688. Do employers need to make HSA contributions for employees enrolled in Medicare?

No, employers only need to make comparable contributions to eligible individuals.

Not Allowed Categories

689. What categories are not allowed for comparability purposes?

The IRS lists the specifically allowed categories and all other categories are not allowed. The chart below illustrates examples of commonly desired, but not allowed, categories for the purpose of HSA contributions.

Categories Not Allowed
Management Employees v. Non-Management
Age Based
Wellness Plan Participation Based
Length of Service Based
Any Other Category Not Specifically Allowed

Treas. Reg. §54.4980G-3, See Q 10.

690. Can employers treat employees differently based on where the employee works?

Generally, no. Discriminating based on the location of the employee is not permitted for the comparability test as it is not one of the allowed categories. However, if the employees working in the different location are treated differently for other allowed categories for comparability testing then giving different HSA contribution amounts might be allowed (for example, the employees in one location are unionized).

> *Example 1.* Kitchens, Inc. operates out of two cities: Big City and Little City. Kitchens, Inc. offers HDHP coverage to its employees in both locations. Kitchens, Inc. makes a $500 HSA contribution to its eligible participating employees in Big City but no HSA contribution to the employees in Little City. Kitchens, Inc. fails the comparability rules for failing to treat Little City employees comparably.

> *Example 2.* Assume the same facts as above, except that Kitchens, Inc. does not provide HDHP coverage for the employees in Little City. Kitchens, Inc. now meets the comparability rules because the employees in Little City are not covered by the employer provided HDHP.

Treas. Reg. §54.4980G-3, See Q 10.

691. Can two divisions of a business receive different HSA contributions?

An employer cannot categorize employees by the division they work in for the purposes of the comparability rules.

> *Example 1.* Kitchens, Inc. operates two divisions: new development and remodeling. Kitchens, Inc. maintains an HDHP for employees working in both divisions. Kitchens, Inc. contributes to the HSAs of employees working in the new development division but not in the remodeling division. Kitchens, Inc. fails the comparability rules.

Example 2. Assuming the same facts as above, expect that the employees in the remodeling division are subject to a collective bargaining agreement under which health benefits were negotiated in good faith. Kitchens, Inc. meets the comparability rules because employees subject to collective bargaining agreements are not subject to the comparability rules.

Treas. Reg. §54.4980G-3, See Q 10.

692. Can an employer give the extra catch-up contribution amount to employees over age fifty-five?

No. Age is not a permissible category for discrimination under the comparability rules. Accordingly, an employer cannot give additional funds to employees based on the employee's eligibility for a catch-up contribution. If all the employees do not meet the age requirement, all comparable participating employees would not receive the same amount and would not satisfy the comparability rules.

Treas. Reg. §54.4980G-4, See Q 11.

693. Can an employer require some length of service before being eligible for HSA contributions?

No. If all the employees do not meet the length of service requirements, all comparable participating employees would not receive the same amount and would not satisfy the comparability rules.

Note: This rule does not include new hires that may be in a probationary period or waiting period for up to ninety days before benefit coverage begins. An employer can limit HSA contributions to only those covered under its employer provided health insurance and employees that are in the probationary period would not yet be covered under the employer's health insurance.

Example. Longevity, Inc. wants to wait until an employee completes three years of service prior to allowing that employee to participate in its $200 a month employer HSA contribution. This policy is not permitted under the comparability rules as it is not an approved category for discriminating. Longevity, cannot adopt this policy.

Treas. Reg. §54.4980G-4, See Q 11.

694. Can an employer "match" employees' HSA contributions?

No. Matching contributions fail comparability testing because comparability testing requires the same dollar amount or the same percentage of the deductible (unless all employees elect to defer exactly the same dollar amount). Simply making matching available to everyone on an equal basis does not satisfy the rules.

However, employers may be able to match employee HSA contributions through a Section 125 plan rather than directly. HSA contributions made through a Section 125 plan, both employer and employee payroll deferral, are not subject to the comparability rules.

Treas. Reg. §54.4980G-4, See Q 9.

695. Can an employer give a bonus amount into the HSAs of employees that participate in a health assessment exam process?

No. If all comparable participating employees do not participate in the program, all comparable participating employees will not receive the same dollar contribution and that violates the comparability rules. This same logic prevents extra HSA payments to employees that contribute in disease management or wellness programs.

Treas. Reg. §54.4980G-4, See Q 10.

696. Can an employer give a bonus amount to an employee that participates in a health assessment process into a Section 125 plan that the employee then elects to put in an HSA?

The Section 125 plan non-discrimination rules apply, not the comparability rules. If the Section 125 plan rules allow for the contribution then it is permissible.

Employee Fails to Open an HSA
Overview
697. What if an employee fails to open an HSA?

If an employee has not established an HSA at the time the employer funds it employees' HSAs, the employer complies with the comparability rules by contributing comparable amounts plus reasonable interest to the employee's HSA when the employee establishes the HSA, taking into account each month the employee was a comparable participating employee.

> *Example.* An employer contributes $50 per month to each comparable participating employee beginning on January 1. Pete is a comparable participating employee for the entire calendar year, but he failed to open his HSA in January when other employees did so and waited instead until July 1. The employer must make up for the missed HSA contributions, plus reasonable interest for January through June, by April 15 of the next calendar year.

Treas. Reg. §54.4980G-4, See Q 7.

698. How are the comparability rules satisfied if a qualified employee fails to open an HSA?

The comparability rules provide an exception when an employee fails to open an HSA. The employer will not fail the comparability rules if the employer does the following:

- **Provides Notice.** The employer needs to provide a timely notice (the IRS provides a model notice) that the employer will make an HSA contribution for eligible employees that both establish an HSA and notify the employer they established an HSA

- **Make Contribution.** The employer needs to make an HSA contribution, plus interest, for any employee that initially failed to open the HSA but then does so by the timeline provided in the notice

Example. In a calendar year, Special Ties Company, contributes to the HSAs of current full-time employees with family coverage under any HDHP. For the 2014 calendar year, Special Ties Company provides all its employees timely and accurate written notice regarding failing to open an HSA. Special Ties Company makes identical monthly HSA contributions to all eligible employees (meaning full-time employees with family HDHP coverage) that establish HSAs. Special Ties Company contributes comparable amounts plus reasonable interest to the HSAs of eligible employees that establish HSAs and provide the necessary information by the end of February 2015. Special Ties Company does not make any HSA contribution to otherwise eligible employees that fail to open an HSA by the end of February 2015 (or fail to notify and provide the employer the information). Special Ties satisfies the comparability rules.

Treas. Reg. §54.4980G-4, See Q 15.

Model Notice

699. What is the IRS model language for notice to employees regarding employer HSA contributions and the consequences of failing to open an HSA?

The IRS model notice language is included below.

Notice to Employees Regarding Employer Contributions to HSAs:

This notice explains how you may be eligible to receive contributions from [employer] if you are covered by a High Deductible Health Plan (HDHP). [Employer] provides contributions to the Health Savings Account (HSA) of each employee who is [insert employer's eligibility requirements for HSA contributions] ("eligible employee"). If you are an eligible employee, you must do the following in order to receive an employer contribution:

(1) Establish an HSA on or before the last day in February of [insert year after the year for which the contribution is being made] and;

(2) Notify [insert name and contact information for appropriate person to be contacted] of your HSA account information on or before the last day in February of [insert year after year for which the contribution is being made]. [Specify the HSA account information that the employee must provide (e.g., account number, name and address of trustee or custodian, etc.) and the method by which the employee must provide this account information (e.g., in writing, by e-mail, on a certain form, etc.)].

If you establish your HSA on or before the last day of February in [insert year after year for which the contribution is being made] and notify [employer] of your HSA account information, you will receive your HSA contributions, plus reasonable interest, for [insert year for which contribution is being made] by April 15 of [insert year after year for which contribution is being made]. If, however, you do not establish your HSA or you do not notify us of your HSA account information by the deadline, then we are not required to make any contributions to your HSA for [insert applicable year]. You may notify us that you have established an HSA by sending an [e-mail or] a written notice to [insert name, title and, if applicable, e-mail address]. If you have any questions about this notice, you can contact [insert name and title] at [insert telephone number or other contact information].

---

700. Can an employer modify the model notice?

Yes. The notice requires some modification by inserting relevant dates and employer information. More modification is also allowed but straying too far from an IRS-provided model carries some risk.

See Appendix - HSA Notice to Employees Regarding Employer Contributions to HSAs.

701. Can the notice be sent to employee electronically?

Yes, employers can provide the notices electronically but need to comply with the IRS rules for electronic communications.

Treas. Reg. §54.4980G-4, See Q 15. Treas. Reg. §1.401(a)-21.

702. When does the notice need to be sent to employees?

The notice must be provided to each eligible employee that has not established an HSA, or if the employer is not aware an HSA was established, no earlier than 90 days before the first HSA employer contribution for that calendar year and no later than January 15 of the following calendar year.

> *Example.* Boating Inc. offers an HDHP to its employees and contributes $100 per month to eligible employees HSAs. On October 30, Boating Inc. gives all its employees the Notice to Employees Regarding Employer Contributions to HSAs. The October 30 date is less than 90 days before Boating Inc.'s first planned HSA contribution for the new year as is required for employer's desiring to make the required notice early.

Treas. Reg. §54.4980G-4, See Q 15.

703. What if an employer hires a new employee after it sent the model notice?

New employees must also receive the notice. The notice must be provided to each eligible employee that has not established an HSA, or if the employer is not aware an HSA was established, no earlier than 90 days before the first HSA employer contribution for that calendar year and no later than January 15 of the following calendar year. If a new employee missed the earlier employer notice, the employer must provide the new employee with the notice.

> *Example.* Boating Inc. offers an HDHP to its employees and contributes $100 per month to eligible employees HSAs. On October 30 of the year before the plan year, Boating Inc. gives all its employees the Notice to Employees Regarding Employer Contributions to HSAs.
>
> Boating Inc. makes its first HSA contribution in mid-January and several of its eligible employees who received the notice in October failed to open an HSA and accordingly do not receive this $100. Boating Inc. has satisfied its notice requirements for these employees. Boating Inc. also hires a number of new employees who become HSA-eligible prior the end of the calendar year. Boating Inc. must give any of these new employees that fail to open an HSA, or that Boating Inc. is not aware of the open HSA, the notice prior to January 15 of the next year.

Treas. Reg. §54.4980G-4, See Q 15.

704. Does the model notice go to all employees or only those that did not open an HSA?

Only employees that fail to open an HSA need to receive the notice. The employer, however, could just give the notice to all employees if it prefers to provide notice in that manner.

705. Do employers have to give the notice for payroll deferral or employer matching contributions made through a Cafeteria plan?

No. The notice only applies to employer pre-tax contributions subject to the comparability rules. Employee pre-tax payroll deferral contributions and employer matching contributions made through a Section 125 Cafeteria plan are not subject to the comparability rules.

Treas. Reg. §54.4980G-4, See Q 15.

706. Is the notice required if all eligible employees establish HSAs?

No. The notice is required only for employees that fail to establish HSAs. If all qualified employees have established HSAs, then the employer is not required to give any employees the notice.

For many employers, especially small employers, this will be the case. The employer HSA contribution is "free" money for the employees so the logical answer for employees is to open the HSA and receive the money. As the number of employees increases, an employer is more likely to confront a situation where an employee fails to open an HSA due to a lack of understanding of the benefits of the HSA, has some other life event that is pre-occupying the employee's time, or otherwise simply fails to take the logical action of opening an HSA.

> *Example.* Boating Inc. offers an HDHP and makes $100 per month comparable HSA contribution to its eligible participating employees. All ten of Boating Inc.'s employees opt to be covered by the HDHP, are otherwise eligible for HSAs, open HSAs, and receive all of Boating Inc.'s HSA contributions. Boating Inc. is not required to give the notice because all eligible employees have opened HSAs.

Treas. Reg. §54.4980G-4, See Q 15.

Making Missed Contributions

707. How long do employers have to hold the money for employees that fail to open HSAs?

Employees must open HSAs by the end of February of the year after the calendar year of the contributions in order to be eligible for the contribution. If an otherwise eligible employee fails to open an HSA by the end of February or fails to provide the employer proper notification that it did open an HSA, then the employer is relieved of the obligation of making that HSA contribution for the employee.

708. Are employers required to account separately for missed contributions?

Employers must "hold" the missed HSA contributions for an employee that fails to open an HSA. An employer does not need to open a separate account for the HSA money its holding but can instead just hold the funds as part of general employer funds until contributed to the HSA.

709. After notified that an employee did open an HSA, how long does the employer have to make any missed HSA contributions?

The employer must make comparable HSA contributions into employees' HSAs for employees who failed to timely open an HSA by April 15 of the year following the tax year of the contributions.

> *Example.* For 2013, Sailing Lessons LLC contributes to the HSAs of current full-time employees with family coverage under any HDHP. Sailing Lessons LLC has 500 current full-time employees eligible for the HSA contribution. As of the date of Sailing Lessons' first HSA contribution, 450 eligible employees have established HSAs. Sailing Lessons provides timely written notice satisfying the content requirements of the IRS rules only to those 50 employees that have not established HSAs. Sailing Lessons makes identical quarterly contributions to the 450 eligible employees who have established HSAs. By April 15, 2014, Sailing Lessons contributes comparable amounts to the other eligible employees who establish and provide the necessary information on or before the last day of February, 2014. Sailing Lessons makes no contribution to the HSAs of eligible employees that do not establish an HSA or that do not provide the necessary information on or before the last day of February, 2014. Sailing Lessons satisfies the comparability rules.

Treas. Reg. §54.4980G-4, See Q 15.

710. Do employers have to pay interest on HSA money held for employees that fail to open an HSA?

Yes. The determination of whether a rate of interest used by an employer is reasonable will be based on all of the facts and circumstances. If an employer calculates interest using the Federal short-term rate as determined by the Secretary in accordance with section 1274(d), the employer is deemed to use a reasonable interest rate (.33 percent as of May 2014). The IRS updates the rates monthly in Revenue Rulings.

Treas. Reg. §54.4980, See Q 14. Rev. Rul. 2013-21.

711. Does an employer have to set aside HSA contributions for ineligible employees?

No. Employers are not required to make HSA contributions to employees who are not eligible for an HSA.

> *Example.* Sally's employer makes a $100 HSA contribution for each employee that elects self-only HDHP coverage through the employer. Sally elected self-only HDHP coverage. Sally's husband works at another company that provides traditional family health insurance (non-HSA-eligible insurance) to both Sally's husband and Sally. Sally is double covered and not eligible for an HSA. Sally's employer is not required to make an HSA contribution for her and does not fail the comparability testing rules.

712. What if the failure to open the HSA is caused by a refusal of the HSA custodian to accept the employee's HSA Application?

Most HSA custodians are banks, credit unions or other federally regulated entities that must meet a host of federal and state laws regarding security and "know your customer" rules. To comply with these rules or for other reasons, HSA custodians will refuse to open HSA for some people.

The IRS rules do not directly address whether an employee who fails to open an HSA because the employee was rejected by the HSA custodian falls within the same rule for employees that have not established an HSA prior to the end of the year. The logical answer is that the same rule applies and that the employer must make the HSA contribution plus interest if the employee opens the HSA prior to April 15 of the year following the calendar year of the contribution.

Custodians and employers should make every effort to open an HSA for a willing employee. An employee with credit, banking or fraud problems may meet more lenient rules for stored value cards, savings accounts with limited access, or other methods to allow an employee to open an HSA while still complying with safe banking practices.

Business Owner Issues

713. Can a sole proprietor contribute to his or her own HSA without contributing to employees' HSAs?

Yes, but only because the law does not consider the owner of a sole proprietorship to be an employee. Sole proprietors' contributions to their own HSAs made through their business do not receive the same tax treatment as contributions for employees. Any HSA contributions a sole proprietor makes to employees will have to meet the comparability rules.

> *Example.* Jay's Bar is a sole proprietorship owned 100 percent by Jay. Jay has ten employees. Jay decides to have Jay's Bar make a $3,000 contribution to his HSA and a $500 contribution to each of his eligible participating employee's HSAs. Jay's Bar contributions meet the comparability rules.
>
> The larger contribution to Jay does not violate the comparability rules because the contribution is considered a distribution to Jay and not an employer HSA contribution (the business will not take a IRC Sec. 106 deduction and Jay will claim the HSA deduction on his personal income tax return). Jay is not an employee of Jay's Bar.

Treas. Reg. §54.4980G-3, IRC Sec. 106, See Q 2.

714. Are HSA contributions to partners in a partnership subject to the comparability rules?

No. Contributions by a partnership to a bona fide partner's HSA are not subject to the comparability rules because the contributions are not contributions by an employer to the HSA of an employee. Any HSA contributions made to employees (non-partners will have to meet the comparability rules.

Example. Partnership X is a limited partnership with three partners: Jim, Steve and Sally. Sally is entitled to a guaranteed payment of $300 without regard to partnership income. Jim, Steve and Sally otherwise share partnership income equally. Partnership X also has ten employees. Partnership X contributes $300 to Jim and Steve's HSA. Partnership X also contributes $300 to Sally's HSA in lieu of her guaranteed payment. Partnership X contributes $200 to each of its comparable participating employees.

The tax treatment for these various contributions are as follows:

- **Jim and Steve.** The HSA contributions by the partnership into Jim and Steve's HSA are treated as cash distributions to Jim and Steve (Section 731)

- **Sally.** The HSA contribution to Sally is treated as a guaranteed payment (under Section 707(c))

- **Ten Employees.** The HSA contributions to the ten employees are treated as HSA contributions deductible by the partnership (Section 106(d))

The comparability rules do not apply to the HSA contributions to Jim, Steve or Sally. The HSA contributions are subject to the comparability rules for the ten employees and the partnership meets the comparability rules by giving the same amount to all comparable participating employees.

CFR §54.4980G-3, See Q 4.

Controlled Groups

715. How do the comparability rules apply when our company is part of a controlled group of corporations?

In some situations, multiple business entities are treated as a single employer for comparability testing. The law and IRS regulations require this to prevent businesses from circumventing the non-discrimination rules by forming multiple business entities. The HSA comparability rules refer to the controlled group of corporation regulations. The controlled group of corporations' regulations apply to other tax issues as well so businesses that face this issue for HSA contributions may already be familiar with the regulations.

See IRC Secs. 4980G(b), 4980E(e), and 414(b), (c), (m) or (o). Treas. Reg. §54.4980G-3, See Q 5. Treas. Reg. §1.414(b)

716. Can an employer create two separate companies to avoid the comparability rules?

The rules regarding controlled groups of corporations will likely require employers to treat the separate companies as one controlled group of corporations.

717. What is a controlled group?

The HSA laws require that controlled groups of corporations must be treated as a single employer for the purposes of comparability testing. The detail rules are complex and beyond the scope of this book. Employers should seek professional guidance in this area.

The rules are designed to prevent a business owner from simply creating multiple businesses in order to give more generous benefits to some employees versus others.

A controlled group is two or more corporations connected through stock ownership. This includes:

- **Parent-Subsidy Group.** This controlled group happens when one organization (the parent) owns 80 percent of the stock of each corporation (the subsidiary). More complicated examples also exist, for instance, if the subsidiary owns 80 percent of another organization then that organization gets pulled into the controlled group.

- **Brother-Sister Group.** This type of controlled group happens when the same five or fewer individuals own at least 80 percent of the stock of the organizations corporations and more than 50 percent of the ownership is identical.

- **Combined Group.** This happens when a combination of the above occur. A group of three or more organizations if each is a member of a parent-subsidiary or brother-sister and at least one organization is the common parent in the parent-subsidiary controlled group and a member of the brother-sister controlled group.

To understand these rules requires a review of the full regulations. To decide whether the rules apply to a particular fact situation requires professional assistance. A few key points: (1) the rules encompass all types of business entitles, not just corporations, (2) family attribution rules apply (you cannot just give your spouse shares to avoid the rules), and (3) rules for trusts and estates also exist.

> *Example.* Health Medical Clinic has five doctors and fifteen staff members. It decides to create a new company, Medical Services Corporation, and puts the fifteen staff members into the Medical Services Corporation. Medical Services Corporation will then enter into a contract with Health Medical Clinic to provide services. If Health Medical Clinic owns 100 percent of Medical Services Corporation this would be a parent–subsidiary controlled group and must be combined for comparability testing. This means that the employees of Health Medical Clinic and Medical Services Corporation must be treated comparability.

Treas. Reg. §1.414(b).

Section 125 Plans and Comparability

718. Do the comparability regulations apply to payroll deferral done through a Section 125?

No. Section 125 plans are subject to their own testing requirements.

> *Example.* Lake Association offers a written Cafeteria plan that permits employees to elect to make pre-tax salary reduction contributions to their HSAs. Employees making this election have the right to receive cash or other taxable benefits in lieu of their HSA pre-tax contributions. The Section 125 plan discrimination rules and not the comparability rules apply.

26 CFR §54.4980 G-5, See Q 1.

719. Do the comparability regulations apply to employer matching contributions made through a Section 125?

No. Section 125 plans are subject to their own testing requirements.

Example. Lake Association offers a written Cafeteria plan that permits employees to elect to make pre-tax salary reduction contributions to their HSAs. Employees making this election have the right to receive cash or other taxable benefits in lieu of their HSA pre-tax contributions. Lake Association automatically contributes a non-elective matching contribution or seed money to the HSA of each employee who makes a pre-tax HSA contribution. The Section 125 plan non-discrimination rules and not the comparability rules apply.

26 CFR §54.4980G-5, See Q 2.

720. Do the comparability regulations apply to employer contributions made through a Section 125 for health assessments?

No. The comparability rules do not apply to HSA contributions made through a Section 125 plan.

Example. Lake Association offers a written Cafeteria plan that permits employees to elect to make pre-tax salary reduction contributions to their HSAs. Employees making this election have the right to receive cash or other taxable benefits in lieu of their HSA pre-tax contributions. Lake Association makes a non-elective contribution through the Section 125 plan to the HSAs of all employees who complete a health risk assessment and participate in Lake Association's wellness program. The Section 125 plan discrimination rules and not the comparability rules apply.

26 CFR §54.4980 G5, See Q 4.

721. Do the comparability regulations apply to employer contributions made through a Section 125 not associated with a match or health assessments?

No. The comparability rules do not apply to HSA contributions made through a Section 125 plan. Whether this type of contribution is allowed must be determined by reference to the Section 125 plan and the Section 125 plan rules.

Example. Lake Association offers a written Cafeteria plan that permits employees to elect to make pre-tax salary reduction contributions to their HSAs. Employees making this election have the right to receive cash or other taxable benefits in lieu of their HSA pre-tax contributions. Lake Association makes an automatic HSA contribution to employees participating in the plan. Employees make no election with respect to Lake Association's contribution and do not have the right to receive cash or other taxable benefits in lieu of Lake Association's contribution but are permitted to make their own pre-tax salary deferral contributions to fund their HSAs. The Section 125 plan discrimination rules and not the comparability rules apply.

26 CFR §54.4980 G5, See Q 4.

Calculating Comparable Contributions.

722. How are comparable contributions calculated?

HSA contributions are comparable if, for each month in a calendar year, the contributions are either the same amount or the same percentage of the deductible under the HDHP for employees who are eligible individuals with the same category of coverage on the first day of the month.

Example 1. Global Exports offers its full-time employees three health plans, including a self-only HDHP coverage and a family HDHP. Global Exports contributes $1,000 for the calendar year into the HSA of each employee who is eligible and selects the self-only HDHP. Global Exports makes no HSA contribution to employees that select non-HDHP coverage or family HDHP coverage. Global Exports meets the comparability rules.

Example 2. Global Exports offers two HDHPs. Plan A has a $2,000 deductible for self-only coverage and a $4,000 deductible for family coverage. Plan B has a $2,500 deductible for self-only coverage and a $4,500 deductible for family coverage. Global Exports makes contributions to the HSAs of each full-time employee who is an eligible individual covered under Plan A of $600 for self-only coverage and $1,000 for family coverage. Global Exports satisfies the comparability rules if it makes either of the following contributions for each full-time employee who is a qualified individual under Plan B.

- **$600/$1000.** It can make the same HSA contribution for Plan B participants as it does for Plan A. In this case $600 to self-only HDHP coverage employees and $1,000 to family covered employees.

- **$750/$1,125.** Global Exports can make a contribution that is the same percentage of the deductible and still satisfy the comparability rules. A $600 contribution under Plan A for a self-only HDHP employee is made at 30 percent of the deductible ($600/$2,000). Multiplying 30 percent times the $2,500 deductible for Plan B results in a $750 HSA contribution. A $1,000 HSA contribution under Plan A for family HDHP coverage is made at 25 percent of the deductible ($1,000/$4,000). Multiplying 25 percent time the $4,500 family deductible for Plan B results in a $1,125 HSA contribution for Plan B family participants.

Example 3. Assume the same facts as above, except that Global Exports also offers both plans to part-time employees. Global Exports makes a $300 HSA contribution to part-time employees covered under Plan A with self-only HDHP coverage and a $500 contribution for part-time family HDHP coverage individuals under Plan A. Global Exports satisfies the comparability rules with either of the following contributions for each part-time employee who is a qualified individual covered under Plan B.

- **$300/$500.** Global Exports can elect to make the same HSA contributions for Plan B eligible participants as it does for Plan A. In this situation, $300 to self-only HDHP covered participants and $500 for family HDHP coverage.

- **$375/$563.** Global Exports can make a contribution that is the same percentage of the deductible and still satisfy the comparability rules. A $300 contribution under Plan A for part-time self-only HDHP employee is made at 15 percent of the deductible ($300/$2,000). Multiplying 15 percent times the $2,500 deductible for Plan B results in a $375 HSA contribution. A $500 HSA contribution under Plan A for family HDHP coverage is made at 12.5 percent of the deductible ($500/$4,000). Multiplying 12.5 percent time the $4,500 family deductible for Plan B results in a $562.50 (rounded to $563) HSA contribution for Plan B part-time family participants.

Treas. Reg. §54.4980G-4, See Q 1.

723. Is rounding allowed in calculating comparable contributions?

Yes, the IRS regulations allow rounding to the nearest 1/100th of a percentage point and the dollar amount can be rounded to the nearest whole dollar.

Example. Carpet Magic, Inc. maintains two HDHPs: Plan A has a $3,000 self-only deductible limit and Plan B has a $3,500 self-only deductible limit. Carpet Magic contributes $1,000 to the HSA of each eligible employee selecting Plan A coverage. Carpet Magic satisfies the comparability rules if it contributes either:

(1) $1,000 to eligible individuals selecting plan B (the same dollar amount), or (2) $1,167 (the same percentage of the deductible). The $1,167 amount is calculating by first determining the percentage for the participants in Plan A: $1,000/$3,000 = 33.33 percent. Then that percentage is multiplied by the deductible for Plan B: 33.33 percent X $3,500 = $1,166.55. Finally, that amount can be rounded to the nearest whole dollar: $1,167.

Treas. Reg. §54.4980G-4, See Q 8.

Penalty

724. What is the penalty for failing the comparability rules?

An employer faces a 35 percent excise tax if it fails to meet the comparability rules. The 35 percent applies to the aggregate amount contributed by the employer to the HSAs of all employees, not just the amount that caused the failure of the comparability rules.

> *Example.* Tip Top, Inc. contributes $2,000 into the HSAs of its two managers, both of whom have self-only coverage. Tip Top, Inc. contributes $1,000 into the HSAs of each of its six non-managers that also all have self-only HDHP coverage. Tip Top's total HSA contribution is $10,000. Tip Top failed the comparability rules and owes a penalty of 35 percent of its $10,000 contribution.

Treas. Reg. §54.4980G-1, See Q 5.

725. How does an employer pay the penalty for failing the comparability rules?

Employers should file the IRS Form 8928 to pay the penalty for failing to make comparable contributions.

Treas. Reg. §54.4980G-1, See Q 6, IRS Form 8928.

726. Can the government waive the 35 percent penalty for failure to follow the comparability rules?

Yes, in the case of a failure which is due to a reasonable cause and not due to willful neglect, all or a portion of the tax can be waived to the extent that payment of the tax would be excessive relative to the failure involved.

Treas. Reg. §54.4980G-5, See Q 5. IRS Instructions to IRS Form 8928.

Miscellaneous

727. Do the comparability rules apply to amounts rolled over from employees' HSAs or Medical Savings Accounts?

No.

728. How do the comparability rules apply if some employees have HSAs and other employees have Archer MSAs?

The comparability rules apply separately to employees who have HSAs and employees who have Archer MSAs. However, if an employee has both an HSA and an Archer MSA, the employer may contribute to either the HSA or the Archer MSA, but not to both.

Example. Convenience Mart, Inc. contributes $600 to the Archer MSA of each employee who is a qualified individual and who has an Archer MSA. Convenience Mart contributes $500 for the calendar year to the HSA of each employee who is a qualified individual and who has an HSA. If the employee has both an Archer MSA and an HSA, Convenience Mart contributes to the Archer MSA and not the HSA. John, an employee, has both an Archer MSA and an HSA. Convenience Mart contributes $600 to John's MSA but does not contribute to his HSA. Convenience Mart satisfies the comparability rules.

Treas. Reg. §54.4980G-3, See Q 14.

729. Do employers have to make comparable HSA contributions to independent contractors?

No. The comparability rules only require that employers treat employees' comparability and does not require that employers give HSA contributions to independent contractors who are not employees.

Treas. Reg. §54.4980G-3, See Q 1.

730. Can an employer stop contributing to an HSA of an employee that exceeds the HSA limit and still meet the comparability rules?

Yes, an employer can stop contributing to an employee that exceeds the HSA eligibility limits.

Example. Assume ABC Inc. contributes the maximum HSA limit to each employee's HSA under the comparability rules. In July 2011, Jim, a family HDHP covered employee turns sixty-five. Jim will only be eligible for 6/12 of the $6,150 HSA limit plus 6/12 of the $1,000 catch-up for a total contribution of $3,575. The employer can and should stop contributing to Jim's HSA when the employer has contributed that amount and the employer will not violate the comparability rules even though other employees get a larger HSA contribution.

Timing of Contributions

731. How often do employers have to calculate whether employer contributions are comparable?

One positive aspect of the comparability rules as compared to other types of discrimination testing is that an employer can know upfront whether the HSA contributions will meet the comparability rules. This ability to get it correct from the beginning reduces an employer's need to do periodic and post-testing. However, even if an employer properly sets up comparable HSA contributions, there is a need for ongoing maintenance and review in order to ensure comparability throughout the entire year.

The comparability rules are determined based on month-to-month eligibility and then viewed annually to ascertain if the rules are met. An employee is considered within the category if the employee is a qualified individual in that same category as of the first day of the month. Employees' eligibility for an HSA could change, an employee could change health care plans, new employees are hired, employees separate from service and other events cause ongoing review of the comparability rules to ensure compliance.

Employers that set up comparable HSA contributions to be made monthly and adjust each month to changes in employee status, including adding new employees, should meet the comparability rules automatically. An employer that makes monthly or more frequent contributions will likely not have to make any adjustments based on the year-end review because the employer could contribute the correct amounts monthly.

Employers who make HSA contributions less frequently will encounter situations where adjustments are necessary.

732. Is the comparability test run on a fiscal or calendar year?

The calendar year is used for comparability testing.

Treas. Reg. §54.4980G1, See Q 4.

733. What are the timing methods for employer comparable HSA contributions?

The IRS refers to three types of funding methods for employer HSA contributions:

- **Pre-Funding.** Employers may choose to make the entire year's HSA contribution up-front at the beginning of the calendar year

- **Pay-As-You-Go/Periodic Funding.** An employer may establish a reasonable and consistent basis for making contributions periodically

- **Look-Back.** An employer can meet the comparability rules by waiting until the end of the calendar year and making an employer contribution into eligible employees' HSAs based on their monthly eligibility for any employer HSA contribution

Please note these payment methods refer to non-payroll deferral employer pre-tax HSA contributions and do not apply to employee pre-tax payroll deferral contributions made through a Section 125 plan (also referred to as employer contributions).

734. Which payment method works best, pre-funding, pay-as-you-go, or look back?

The answer depends on the facts and circumstances of each employer group. Important factors include: employee retention rate, cash flow, employee need for upfront contributions, employer ability/desire to manage frequent contributions, and more. From an HSA rules perspective, following a pay-as-you-go method using a monthly or more frequent contribution offers significant advantages. The advantages are as follows:

- **No Lost Money for Employees that Separate from Service.** The HSA comparability rules and contribution amounts are determined monthly. Employers that make monthly or more frequent HSA contributions can adjust their HSA contributions for employees that separate from service. This prevents the pre-funding issue where an employee receives a full year of HSA funding and then separates from service without obligation to return the money.

- **New Employees Enter System Timely.** The pay-as-you-go method allows for new employees to begin receiving their HSA contribution the month after they become eligible and there is no need to do an end-of-the year calculation to make contributions for new employees.

- **Employees Receive Regular Funding.** With pay-as-you-go funding, employees receive a regular contribution to their HSA and are able to plan accordingly. This method is not as advantageous to the employee as the pre-funding method but is better than the look-back method.

- **Coordinates with Payroll Deferral.** HSA payroll deferral contributions made through a Section 125 plan have different and likely more frequent contribution deadlines (the deadline depends upon factors relating to the size and sophistication of the employer and the size of the payroll). Employers that make comparable contributions and allow employee pre-tax payroll deferral can likely coordinate the contributions if done on a periodic basis (monthly or more frequent).

Pre-Funding

735. Does an employer have to use the same funding method for all employees?

Yes. If an employer makes comparable HSA contributions on a pay-as-you-go basis, it must do so for each employee who is a comparable participating employee as of the first day of the month. If an employer makes comparable contributions on a look-back basis, it must do so for each employee who was a comparable participating employee for any month during the calendar year. If an employer makes HSA contributions on a pre-funded basis, it must do so for all employees who are comparable participating employees at the beginning of the calendar year and must make comparable HSA contributions for all employees who are comparable participating employees for any month during the calendar year, including employees who are eligible individuals hired after the date of the initial funding.

Treas. Reg. §54.4980G-4, See Q 6, See Part XI: Comparability – Timing of Contributions – Pay-as-you-go.

736. May an employer fully fund the employee's HSA at the beginning of the year?

Yes. An employer may fully fund the employee's HSA at the beginning of the year-however, HSAs belong to the individual and not the employer. The employer may not recoup HSA contributions if the employee separates from service.

Treas. Reg. §54.4980G-4, See Q 5.

737. What's wrong with the pre-funding option for employer HSA contributions?

Employees logically prefer to get their full HSA contribution at the beginning of the year as it gives employees more flexibility to pay for medical expenses incurred early in the year.

The negative for the employer is that if the employee separates from service, the employer cannot recoup any of the HSA contribution. This can be frustrating for employers especially if the employee leaves under adverse circumstances (e.g., goes to work for a competitor or is fired for cause). Also, the positive cash flow feature for employees of the pre-funding option is the converse for the employer and paying the full contribution up front may not work well with the employer's cash flow.

738. Does an employer violate the comparability rules if it pre-funds and then an employee quits?

No. Although the comparability rules look at monthly eligibility for the employer HSA contribution, an exception exists for an employer that pre-funds and then the employee quits. Even though that employee will receive a larger HSA contribution than other employees when calculated on a monthly basis, the employer is not in violation of the comparability rules.

> *Example.* Rajesh's Cars, Inc. pre-funds its employer HSA contributions by making a $1,200 HSA contribution to each of its comparable participating employees on January 15 of the calendar year. Tim, an employee of Rajesh's Cars, receives the $1,200 contribution in January but quits his job on March 18 of the same year. Rajesh's Cars cannot recoup the extra money in Tim's HSA. Rajesh's Cars meets the comparability test because of the exception for pre-funding of HSA contributions and an employee separating from service prior to working the full year.

Treas. Reg. §54.4980G-4, See Q 2.

739. If an employer makes the full year's HSA contribution on January 1, is it done for the year?

Pre-funding does complete the employers' involvement in the HSA contribution for employees who received the HSA contribution. New employees are still entitled to a pro-rata share of the employer HSA contribution based on their months of eligibility. The employer will have to make that pro-rata contribution to new employees using either the look-back or pay-as-you-go method or be in violation of the comparability rules.

> *Example.* Rajesh's Cars, Inc. prefunds HSA contributions by making a $1,200 HSA contribution to each of its comparable participating employees on January 15. In July of the same year, Rajesh's Cars hires Boyd and Boyd become eligible for an employer HSA contribution on August 1. Rajesh's Cars can begin funding Boyd's HSA in August at the rate of $100 per month or it must make a $500 contribution after the end of the calendar year using the look-back method (Boyd was eligible for the HSA contribution in five of the twelve months of the year and is entitled to 5/12 of the HSA contribution).

740. If an employer pre-funds for its existing employees, can it choose to fund new employees' HSAs either on a pay-as-you-go method or a look back method?

Yes. An employer that prefunds and subsequently hires a new employee can: (1) make the full pre-funded HSA contribution for the new employee, (2) start a pay-as-you-go method for the new employee making monthly or more frequent contributions of a pro-rata amount of the pre-funded contribution, or (3) wait until the end of the year and make a pro-rata contribution of the pre-funded HSA contribution.

741. Can an employer contribute the maximum HSA contribution to an employee that starts mid-year?

Yes, employers are allowed to make an HSA contribution (up to the HSA limits for the year) to all eligible employees regardless of their start date. In order to be eligible for a maximum HSA contribution, the employee must be a qualified participating employee (eligible for an HSA) no later than December 1 of the tax year to qualify for the full contribution rule. An employer is not required to pro-rate the HSA contribution for employees that are not employed when the initial pre-funded HSA contribution is made.

However, employers that contribute more than a pro-rata pre-funded HSA contribution to employees hired after January 1 are required to do so on an equal and uniform basis to the HSAs of all comparable participating employees who are hired after January 1.

> *Example.* In January Rajesh's Cars makes a $1,000 HSA contribution for the calendar year to employees who were eligible individuals with family HDHP coverage. In mid-March of the same year, Rajesh's Cars hires Peter, a qualified individual with family coverage. On April 1, Rajesh's Cars contributes $1,000 to Peter's HSA.
>
> In September, Mary becomes a qualified individual with family HDHP coverage. On October 1, Rajesh's Cars contributes $1,000 to Mary's HSA. Rajesh's Cars satisfies the comparability requirements even though Peter and Mary are getting the same HSA contribution as employees with more months of eligibility.

Treas. Reg. §54.4980G-4, See Q 2.

742. Can an employer accelerate employer HSA contributions into earlier months to help an employee with large medical bills?

Yes. An employer may, but is not required to, accelerate comparable HSA contributions into an HSA of the employee in cases where the an employee has incurred, during the calendar year, qualified medical expenses exceeding the employer's cumulative HSA contributions at that time. The employer must make this option available equally to all participating employees throughout the plan year and must be offered on the same terms (on an equal and uniform basis). The employer must establish reasonable uniform methods and requirements for accelerated contributions and determination of medical expenses.

An employer that does this will not fail the comparability rules because some employees receive accelerated HSA contributions and others do not. The employer will also not fail the comparability rules if an employee that received an accelerated HSA contribution separated from service prior to accruing the full accelerated amount received (i.e., the terminating employee got a larger HSA contribution on a monthly basis than employees that worked the entire year). The employer cannot recoup amounts of accelerated payments in the case of separation from service. An employer that offers accelerated payments is not required to pay interest on either the accelerated or non-accelerated HSA contributions.

The IRS rules do not provide examples of acceptable systems for determining whether the employee's medical expenses have exceeded the employer's contributions. A likely solution is that an employer asks to see receipts to verify the amount spent. Another potential system is to have employees sign an affidavit (a form) that testifies to the fact that they have spent more on qualified medical expenses during the calendar year than the employer has contributed to the

HSA. The affidavit would include additional information and possibly insert the amount spent. This method provides a couple of benefits over asking for receipts: (1) it's easier, and (2) it keeps employee medical issues more private. The disadvantage is that it is more prone to fraud (probably not too likely given the limited benefits of accelerated HSA contributions).

> *Example.* XYZ Corporation contributes $100 per month into the HSA of each eligible employee. Jane, a qualified employee, incurred a $2,000 medical bill in January and asked XYZ to accelerate the $100 per month for the next twelve months so she can better afford to pay the bill with her HSA. Jane wants the full $1,200 HSA contribution to be made in January rather than $100 per month over a twelve month period. XYZ can accelerate the contributions but it will have to establish a policy of doing so and allow similarly situated employees to also take advantage of the policy. Part of the policy will be a system to determine whether the employee's qualified medical expenses have exceeded the amount contributed by the employer. Plus, XYZ will run the risk that Jane will separate from service prior to the repayment of the accelerated amount and will be unable to recoup that money.

Treas. Reg. §54.4980G-4, See Q 16.

Pay-as-you-go Method
743. How does the pay-as-you-go method work?

The pay-as-you-go basis allows for an employer to comply with the comparability rules by contributing amounts at one or more dates during the calendar year to the HSAs of employees who are eligible individuals as of the first day of the month.

> *Example.* Spot Cleaners, Inc. contributes $50 per month on the first day of each month to the HSA of each employee who is a qualified individual on that date. Spot Cleaners does not contribute to former employees. Spot Cleaners made contributions from January through June but stopped and did not make any HSA contributions from July through December. Spot Cleaners experiences the following scenarios with its eligible employees during the calendar year.
>
> - John terminates employment in mid-March and Spot Cleaners stops HSA contributions. Spot Cleaners contributed $150 to John's HSA
>
> - Sally is hired mid-April and Spot Cleaners begins HSA contributions on May 1. Spot Cleaners contributed $100 to Sally's HSA (May and June)
>
> - Petra is hired in mid-August. Spot Cleaners makes no HSA contributions to Petra
>
> - Spot Cleaners contributed $300 to all its eligible employees employed from January 1 through June 30
>
> Spot Cleaners meets the comparability rules.

Treas. Reg. §54.4980G-4, See Q 2.

744. Can employers adjust the timing of HSA contributions to match payroll when salaried employees are paid monthly and hourly employees are paid bi-weekly?

Yes. HSA contributions made at the employer's usual payroll interval for different groups of employees are considered made at the same time.

> *Example.* Yellow Trucks pays salaried employees monthly and hourly employees bi-weekly. Yellow Trucks makes a $100 a month HSA contribution to its eligible participating employees with family HDHP coverage. Yellow Trucks makes the salaried employees' HSA contribution with the monthly payroll and the hourly

employees' HSA contribution are pro-rated and made bi-weekly. At the end of the calendar year, both groups of employees that were eligible all twelve months will have received $1,200.

Treas. Reg. §54.4980G-4, See Q 2.

745. What if an employer uses a different pay period for exempt versus non-exempt employee?

Contributions made at an employer's usual payroll interval for different groups of employees are considered made at the same time. For example, if salaried employees are paid monthly and hourly employees are paid bi-weekly, an employer may contribute to the HSAs of salaried employees on a monthly basis and to the HSAs of hourly employees bi-weekly without violating the comparability rules.

Treas. Reg. §54.5980G-4, See Q 2.

746. How does it work if an employee switches mid-year from single to family coverage using the pay-as-you-go method?

An employer can adjust the contribution amount to reflect a change in status of an employee in the single versus family category.

> *Example.* Sun Systems, Inc. contributes to its eligible employees' HSAs on a monthly pay-as-you-go method. Sun Systems makes a $50 contribution per month for each eligible employee that elects its self-only HDHP coverage and $100 per month to each eligible employee electing its family HDHP coverage. From January 1 through March 31, Owen, an employee of Sun Systems, is a qualified employee with self-only coverage. From April 1 through December 31, Owen is a qualified employee with family coverage. For Owen's HSA, Sun Systems contributed $50 per month for the months of January – March and $100 per month for the months of April through December. Sun Systems meets the comparability rules.

Treas. Reg. §54.4980G-4, See Q 2.

747. Does pay-as-you-go work if HSA contributions are made quarterly?

An employer can elect to make quarterly HSA contributions under the pay-as-you-go method but quarterly contributions may result in employees separating from service receiving a larger contribution than they would be entitled to under a monthly contribution and employers will have to account for new hires.

> *Example.* Sun Systems, Inc. contributes $150 per quarter to its eligible employees' HSAs. Sun Systems makes the payments on January 1, April 1, July 1 and October 1. Sun Systems experiences the following:
>
> - Brittany, a qualified employee, quits on January 15 after Sun Systems had already contributed $150 to her HSA for the first quarter
>
> - Rachel is hired immediately on January 15 to replace Brittany and Rachel becomes eligible for the HSA on February 1. On April 1, Sun Systems makes an extra $100 contribution to Rachel for her missed HSA contributions for February and March.
>
> Sun Systems meets the comparability rules. Brittany received a larger than pro-rata share based on her months but this situation is allowed under the comparability rules (although most employers prefer to avoid larger funding for employees separating from service). Sun Systems has to make up for Rachel's

missed contribution for February and March because of Sun Systems use of quarterly funding rather than monthly funding.

Treas. Reg. §54.4980G-4, See Q 2.

Look-back Method
748. What is the look-back method for making comparable contributions?

The look-back method is when an employer waits until the end of the calendar year and looks-back at its employees' eligibility by month and makes a comparable contribution with the benefit of knowing each employee's eligibility throughout the year.

> *Example.* On December 31, Spot Cleaners contributes $50 per month on a look-back basis to each employee's HSA for each month in the calendar year that the employee was a qualified individual. Spot Cleaners experienced the following employee scenarios:
>
> - In mid-March, Sonja, a qualified employee, terminated employment. Spot Cleaners makes a $150 HSA contribution for Sonja.
>
> - Bree, a qualified employee, is hired in mid-April and begins HSA eligibility on May 1. Spot Cleaners makes a $400 HSA contribution for Bree.
>
> - All eligible employees that worked January 1 through December 31 received a $600 HSA contribution.
>
> Spot Cleaners satisfies the comparability rules.

Treas. Reg. §54.4980G-4, See Q 2.

749. How does it work if an employee switches mid-year from single to family coverage using the look-back method?

An employer can adjust the contribution amount to reflect a change in status of an employee in the single versus family category.

> *Example.* Sun Systems, Inc. contributes to its eligible employees' HSAs on a look-back basis. Sun Systems makes a $50 contribution per month for each eligible employee that elects its self-only HDHP coverage and $100 per month to each eligible employee electing its family HDHP coverage. From January 1 through March 31, Owen, an employee of Sun Systems, was a qualified employee with self-only coverage. From April 1 through December 31, Owen was a qualified employee with family coverage. For Owen's HSA, Sun Systems contributed $50 per month for the months of January through March and $100 per month for the months of April through December. Owen's total contribution received is $1,050. Sun Systems meets the comparability rules.

Treas. Reg. §54.4980G-4, See Q 2.

750. Can employers change the amount of an HSA contribution mid-year?

The HSA rules are very flexible and do not require an employer to commit to an HSA funding level. Employers may be bound to any promise of HSA funding made to employees. The employer also needs to meet the comparability rules which require looking back at the end of the year to ensure that new hires are treated comparably.

> *Example.* Used Cars, Inc. announced to its employees that it would begin making a $50 monthly HSA contribution to comparable participating employees in the new calendar year. Used Cars makes the

$50 contribution from January through August but due to difficult economic times had to announce to its employees that it was ceasing payments after the August HSA contribution. Stopping the HSA contribution is permissible under the HSA comparability rules. If an employee begins after August, the employer is not required to make an HSA contribution for the employee.

751. Must an employer use the same method for all comparable employees?

Yes, although if the employer chooses the pre-funding or look-back methods that could result in different employees receiving their HSA contribution at different times.

Employers that pre-fund must make the pre-funding contribution to all employees that were comparable participating employees at the beginning of the calendar year. Employers can use the look-back method or the pay-as-you-go method for new hires throughout the year so the new hires will not get the pre-funding treatment but are still considered to have had a comparable contribution made. Note: See exception to this rule for "accelerated" HSA contributions.

An employer that uses the look-back method must make comparable contributions. It must do so for each employee who was a comparable participation employee for any month during the calendar year.

Employers that select the pay-as-you-go method must make a contribution for all comparable participating employees as of the first day of the month.

PART XII: CUSTODIAL ISSUES

Overview

752. What is an HSA custodian or trustee?

Congress created the role of HSA custodian or trustee as an intermediary between the taxpayer and the tax-favored money in an HSA. This intermediary role is important to the tax reporting integrity of HSAs. Only approved entities can serve as HSA custodians or trustees. This requirement gives the IRS the ability to obtain tax reporting on HSA activity from the HSA custodian or trustee. This third-party information reporting allows the IRS to triangulate its HSA reporting among the HSA owner, the HSA custodian and trustee, and in some cases employer HSA reporting on the IRS Form W-2s. The information reporting role is the key function of an HSA custodian or trustee. To satisfy that key role, the custodian must establish rules and procedures to properly account for all HSA contributions, distributions and gains in investments.

The custodian or trustee must also "administer the trust ... consistent with the requirements of..." HSA law. This includes using an HSA custodial agreement provided by the IRS or approved for use by the IRS. Custodians must also follow numerous other rules imposed by HSA law including: (1) not investing the assets in life insurance contracts, (2) not commingling the assets with other property except in a common trust or common investment fund, (3) and contracting that the balance in the HSA is nonforfeitable.

IRC Sec. 223(d)(1)(B), IRS Form W-2.

753. Who is qualified to serve as an HSA custodian or trustee?

A qualified HSA custodian can be a bank, insured credit union, a life insurance company or anyone already approved by the IRS to be a custodian for Individual Retirement Arrangements (IRAs) or Archer Medical Savings Accounts (MSAs). Other entities can apply to the IRS to be approved as HSA custodians or trustees.

See Part III: Establishment – Overview for a list of non-bank HSA custodians, IRC Sec. 223(d)(1)(B), IRS Notice 2004-2, See Q 10.

754. Are banks and credit unions automatically approved to be HSA custodians?

Yes. Banks and some other regulated financial institutions, including credit unions, and certain insurance companies are automatically approved.

755. Are all insurance companies qualified to serve as HSA custodians?

No. Generally, only a life insurance company (defined in IRC Sec. 816) can be an HSA trustee or custodian. However, any entity can apply to be an approved custodian or trustee of HSAs.

IRS Notice 2005-50, IRC Sec. 816, See Q 73.

Fiduciary

756. Is an HSA custodian a fiduciary?

No. In most cases, an HSA custodian or trustee is not be a fiduciary to the HSA owner. The legal duties imposed on the HSA custodian or trustee by the HSA laws are of a recordkeeping nature, not of a fiduciary nature. The actual language in the custodial or trust agreement and the actual relationship between the parties can impact this answer.

For most financial institutions, it makes sense to use the "custodial" agreement rather than the "trust" agreement to avoid the use of the word "trust" and its implied higher standard of duty. HSAs run through trust departments or in cases where the financial institution intends to be a fiduciary are exceptions. To avoid misunderstanding, financial institutions should add clear language to their custodial agreements outlining the duties of the custodian and specifically stating the custodian is not a fiduciary.

757. What is the difference between a custodian and a trustee?

HSAs law treat the two the same with no appreciable difference. The common and legal understanding of the term "custodial" better describes the relationship between the financial institution holding the HSA funds and the HSA owner. The financial institution is providing reporting to the IRS on contributions and distributions and serves as an intermediary between the HSA owner and the HSA owner's HSA money. This role of the financial institution is primarily administrative or "custodial" in nature.

The term "trust," however, could imply a fiduciary relationship between the HSA owner and the financial institution. Generally, the relationship between an HSA owner and the financial institution serving as either a custodian or a trustee is not a fiduciary relationship. If the HSA is offered through a trust department or an actual fiduciary then the use of the trust agreement may be more appropriate.

To simplify and shorten questions and answers, this book uses the word "custodian" in place of "custodian and trustee" in most instances.

Contribution Responsibilities

758. Is an HSA custodian required to determine if an individual is eligible for an HSA?

No. The HSA owner bears the responsibility to determine whether or not he or she is eligible for an HSA. Many custodians will provide assistance in educating individuals on the eligibility rules, but it is ultimately the HSA owner's responsibility.

759. What is the maximum HSA contribution an HSA custodian can accept?

HSA custodians are not allowed to accept more than the family contribution limit plus one catch-up amount ($7,650 for 2015). Some HSA custodians have systems in place to stop contributions exceeding the limit before they are made. Other custodians will have to run periodic system queries and notify HSA owners if they go over this limit.

IRS Notice 2004-50, See Q 74.

760. Is the custodian responsible for determining whether a particular HSA owner exceeded his or her HSA limit?

No. The HSA owner is responsible for making contributions below the HSA owner's personal HSA limit.

> *Example.* Every year on January 1, Tom contributes the maximum family limit to his HSA. In July 2014, Tom enrolled in Medicare and lost HSA eligibility. Tom's 2014 HSA limit is accordingly reduced to a pro-rata amount. Tom has an excess in his HSA as he already contributed the full 2014 family maximum and not his reduced limit. Tom has to notify his HSA custodian of this excess contribution. The custodian has no duty to notify Tom of the excess.

IRS Notice 2004-50, See Q 75.

761. Is the custodian required to determine an HSA owner's limit based on whether the person has family or self-only HDHP coverage?

No., The HSA owner is responsible for staying within the applicable HSA limit for self-only or family HDHP coverage. The HSA custodian has no duty to ask the type of insurance coverage when first opening an HSA or to track the coverage on an ongoing basis.

762. Is the HSA custodian responsible to track the age of the HSA owner?

Yes. The HSA custodian is required to track the age of the HSA owner, although the custodian can rely on the HSA owner's representation as to their age.

IRS Notice 2004-50, See Q 75.

763. Do custodians have to accept the return of mistaken distributions?

No. Whether or not an HSA custodian accepts the return of mistaken distributions is optional for the custodian.

IRS Notice 2004-50, See Q 77, See Part VIII: Distributions – Mistaken Distributions.

764. If the custodian does accept the return of a mistaken distribution may it rely on the HSA owner's representation that it was a mistake?

Yes. The HSA custodian can rely on the owner's representation that the return fits within the rules for returning mistaken distributions.

IRS Notice 2004-50, See Q 40, See Part VIII: Distributions – Mistaken Distributions.

Employer Contributions

765. Are HSA custodians required to differentiate between employer and employee contributions?

No. HSA custodians must treat all of the following types of contributions the same for the purposes of IRS contribution reporting: (1) employer contributions, (2) employee payroll deferral contributions, and (3) contributions made directly by the employee or others on behalf of the employee.

Some custodians' internal reporting systems might differentiate between these types of contributions as the information could be useful for a number of purposes. For example, the HSA owner will generally have to treat these contribution types differently for tax purposes and an HSA owner may ask the custodian for detail that separate reporting could provide. There is no requirement for custodians to track the contribution types separately for IRS reporting purposes.

IRS Notice 2004-50, See Q 76.

766. Are custodians responsible for recording whether employer contributions are pre-tax or post-tax?

No. Custodians report all contributions the same regardless of whether an employer makes the contribution pre-tax or post-tax. All HSA contributions are tax deductible so the pre-tax or post-tax refers to how the deduction is taken and not whether or not it is deductible. The HSA owner needs to sort out the deductibility with the help of IRS Forms W-2, 1040 and 8889.

Distribution Responsibilities

767. Can a custodian restrict distributions to only qualified medical expenses?

No. HSA custodians must allow for distributions for any purpose. HSA custodians cannot add a contractual term that restricts distributions to just qualified medical expenses. Custodians can add restriction on access to HSA funds by limiting access (i.e., not offering checking, debit card, or ATM access and requiring a distribution form or other access method instead).

IRS Notice 2004-50, See Q 80.

768. Does a custodian have to ensure that HSA owners' distributions were for qualified medical expenses?

No. The HSA owner must maintain adequate records to prove expenses were eligible if audited by the IRS. HSA custodians report distributions for qualified medical expenses the same as distributions that are not qualified.

IRS Notice 2004-2, See Q 30.

769. Are custodian's required to "spot-check" documentation to prove distributions were for qualified medical expenses?

No. Custodians are not responsible for validating distribution reasons and have no reason to review distributions for the purpose of determining whether the distribution was for a qualified medical expense or not.

770. Can an HSA custodian use a health only debit card that prevents use for non-medical items?

Debit cards that only allow for eligible medical expense purchases are a popular idea. However, These cards are difficult to manage and not necessary for HSAs. Restricted health-only debit cards are more important for health FSAs and HRAs where the employer must substantiate that the money in the accounts is only used for eligible health expenses. HSA owners bear the substantiation requirement for HSAs, not the employers or the custodian. Some employers and HSA custodians, nonetheless, value the restricted cards as the cards serve as an additional check to assist employees with compliance and may also reduce employee intentional use for non-qualified medical expenses (simply because it makes it harder to access the HSA funds).

IRS rules prevent HSA custodians from limiting HSA use to only qualified medical expenses. This rule limits the appeal of a restricted card for HSAs as the HSA custodian must also offer another unrestricted method to access the HSA funds. The other access could be via online transfers, ATM access, or check writing. An employee intent on using the funds for non-eligible expenses could still do so.

The Affordable Care Act's change regarding over-the-counter drugs also complicates the use of restricted cards. The cards can only be used for over-the-counter drugs if special conditions are met. The ACA states that an HSA owner cannot use HSA funds for over-the-counter drugs unless a prescription is obtained. For an HSA, a person could get a written prescription from a doctor and then file the prescription in their tax file. With an unrestricted card, the HSA owner can simply buy the over-the-counter drug with the debit card and be confident that in the case of an audit the prescription would defend the purchase.

Individuals using a restricted debit card must do the substantiation in advance. Substantiation is accomplished by submitting the subscription for the over-the-counter medicine or drug and any other necessary information prior to reimbursement. This is generally accomplished only at pharmacies that are Inventory Information Approval System (IIAS) certified. This system can identify whether an item is a qualified medical expense or not. If a pharmacy does not have IIAS certification but 90 percent of the store's gross receipts during the prior taxable year consists of items which qualify as qualified medical expenses then a health debit card can be used. The prescription for the over-the-counter drug still requires substantiation. This could be done at the point-of-sale if the pharmacy is set up to accomplish that review.

Rev. Rul. 2010-23, IRS Notice 2010-59, IRS Notice 2011-5, IRS Notice 2004-50, See Q 80, IRS Notice 2008-59, See Q 28.

771. Will the law change requiring HSA custodians to substantiate that distributions were used for qualified medical expenses?

Congress has considered bills that would require HSA custodians to verify qualified medical expenses. None of these bills has passed and as of this writing none are in a position to pass in the near future. If a substantiation bill did pass, the bill would likely treat HSAs similar to Flexible Spending Accounts (FSAs) and require the HSA custodian to substantiate each eligible medical expense distribution. A substantiation law would represent a major change for custodians and increase the cost of administering HSAs.

772. How long does a Custodian have to retain contribution and distribution forms?

The HSA laws and regulations do not contain any special document retention rules. Accordingly, HSA custodians should follow their document retention rules already in place for similar accounts.

Establishment

773. Can an HSA custodian require that an employer open all its employees' HSAs with the custodian?

HSA custodians cannot force an employer to open all its employees' HSAs with it. An HSA custodian can certainly encourage this choice and HSA laws allow an employer to elect to make all HSA contributions to a single HSA custodian. Employers generally do restrict the choice to one HSA custodian as that limits the employer's administrative burden and simplifies the educational process because the HSA account terms would be the same for all employees.

DOL Field Assistance Bulletins 2004-1 & 2006-2.

774. Can HSA custodians set up an individual's HSA before the individual is eligible?

An HSA owner cannot establish an HSA until after the HSA owner is eligible and HSA custodians should assist individuals in complying with that rule. The first step to compliance is to determine what "established" means in the applicable state. Although HSAs are based on federal law, when an HSA is established is determined by state law. Generally established means the HSA is both opened (application completed) and funded (money is placed into the HSA).

For individuals who want to get their HSA established as soon as possible after becoming eligible, one practice is to get the HSAs ready on the custodian's system before eligibility begins. This means having the individual complete an application and for the custodian to begin any identity verification or other necessary steps. The custodian will be careful not to put any money into the HSA until the individual is eligible. In this manner the paperwork is done and all that is left to do on the first day of eligibility is to add the money to the HSA.

With group plans, advance preparation is even more important to ensure employees can use their HSAs close to beginning HDHP coverage and becoming eligible. Providing employees with the ability to use their HSA the first day of eligibility may be difficult to accomplish so it's important for both HSA custodians and employers to set proper expectations for employees. The custodian can help by providing clear timelines and clear information to the employer and employees that they cannot use their HSA for medical expenses until after established and that it cannot be established until the person is eligible. If the first funding (first payroll) is not until two weeks or so after the employee completed the HSA application process, that delay can be problematic for some employees. Employers can solve this issue by making an initial contribution, even a very small one, for all employees to get their HSAs opened timely. Ultimately, it's not the custodian's responsibility to determine when to establish an HSA as the individual is responsible for determining his or her eligibility and for the timing of that eligibility.

Note: The IRS Form 5498-SA does not collect the date the HSA was established, just the year, so although the establishment date is very important for tax benefits it's difficult for the IRS to enforce the rule against individuals who use their HSA for medical expenses incurred prior to the establishment of the HSA but in the same year.

IRS Form 5498-SA.

775. Is the custodian responsible to disclose new HSA law changes?

HSA custodians generally do not have an ongoing legal responsibility to provide HSA owners with updates to law changes on HSAs. Periodically, the IRS will require that all HSA custodians amend their custodial account agreements (IRS Form 5305-C) to reflect significant changes in the law and to provide a copy of that amendment to its HSA customers.

IRS Form 5305-C.

Investment Offerings

776. What types of investments can a custodian offer?

HSA custodians are allowed to offer a wide range of investments including checking accounts, savings accounts, Certificates of Deposit, money market accounts, stocks, bonds, mutual funds as well as even more exotic choices.

777. Can an HSA custodian provide a cash incentive to open an HSA?

Yes, provided the cash is deposited into the HSA. If the cash incentive is paid directly to the HSA owner, outside of the HSA, it is likely a prohibited transaction as the "sale or exchange" of property between the custodian and the HSA owner.

DOL Advisory Opinion 2004-09A.

778. Can stored value cards be used for HSAs?

Yes. Stored value cards may be used in connection with HSAs.

IRS Notice 2004-2, See Q 38.

779. Does a custodian have to offer more than one investment choice?

No. However, an HSA custodian that works with employer groups should be aware of an issue if they offer only one investment option (usually a checking account). Most employers want to avoid their HSA program being covered by ERISA. To avoid ERISA coverage, the employer is not allowed to exercise too much control over the investment choices for the HSA.

The Department of Labor (DOL) provides guidance in this area by stating: "the mere fact that employer selects an HSA provider to which it will forward contributions that offers a limited selection of investment options ... would not, in the view of the Department, constitute the making or influencing of an employee's investment decisions giving rise to an ERISA-covered plan so long as employees are afforded a reasonable choice of investment options and employees are not limited in moving their funds to another HSA."

Although the DOL makes it clear that an employer can limit employees to one HSA custodian, the requirement to "afford reasonable choice of investments" must be met. The DOL further states that "[t]he selection of a single HSA provider that offers a single investment option would not, in the view of the Department, afford employees a reasonable choice of investment options." This does not mean that the custodian must offer more than one investment. An employer should exercise caution, because using a single custodian with only one investment offering may be subject to ERISA. An argument exists that ERISA would still not apply because HSA owners are free to transfer their HSA funds to a new custodian.

DOL FAB 2006-02.

780. May an HSA custodian serve as the HSA custodian for its own employees?

Yes. An HSA custodian can serve as the HSA custodian for its own employees provided the custodian offers the same product to the general public in the regular course of business.

DOL FAB 2006-2, See Q 7.

781. Can an HSA custodian offer an employer a discount on other services it offers if the employer agrees to open its employees' HSA with the custodian?

No. This is likely a prohibited transaction. For the employer, this would also likely constitute the employer receiving a payment or compensation in connection with an HSA. That means the employer could be subject to ERISA if it accepts a discounted service in exchange for opening its employees HSAs with the HSA custodian.

DOL FAB 2006-2, See Q 8, See Part Nine: Tax Issues — Prohibited Transactions.

Fees

782. What types of fees are typically charged on an HSA?

HSA fees vary and the list below is only representative of some of the more common fees:

- Set-up fee

- Annual/monthly administration fee

- Check printing fee

- Online-banking fee

- Account closing fee

- Investment fees

- Debit card/other transaction fee

- Fees for failing to meet minimum balance requirements

- Excess contribution correction fee

- Return of mistaken distribution correction fee

- Fees for administrative work to correct or replace IRS reporting documents

HSA fees are more prevalent than fees for other types of accounts because HSAs require additional IRS reporting and can be complex leading to additional support needs. Support in answering questions is especially needed. Unlike IRAs, HSAs generally do not enjoy as large balances. HSA balances, however, have grown dramatically over the years and are beginning to reach the levels where fee waiver is making sense.

783. Can fees be directly withdrawn from the HSA account?

Yes. HSA administrative fees may be deducted directly from the HSA and the HSA owner does not have to pay taxes or penalties on the amount of the fee. Paying fees by directly debiting the HSA allows HSA owners to pay the fees with tax-free dollars, a welcome approach for most HSA owners.

IRS Notice 2004-50, See Q 70.

784. If HSAs fees are paid from the HSA, does that increase the annual contribution limit by the amount of the fee?

No. For example, if the maximum annual contribution is $3,350 (2015) and the HSA custodian charges a $25 annual fee that is deducted from the HSA balance. The annual contribution limit remains $3,350 (not $3,350 plus $25).

IRS Notice 2004-50, See Q 69.

785. Can HSA administrative fees be paid outside of the HSA?

Yes. Some HSA owners prefer to maximize their HSA contribution by paying HSA fees separately. This is also allowed and in this case the payment does not count as an HSA contribution or distribution. Since the amount is never contributed to the HSA it is not considered an HSA contribution.

Caution: Some fees are integral to the underlying investment and must be paid from the HSA to avoid prohibited transaction rules. For example, real estate taxes owed on real estate held within an HSA must be paid from the HSA.

> *Example.* Mark wants to maximize his HSA contribution. He is eligible with self-only HDHP coverage and can contribute up to $3,350 for 2015. His HSA charges a $25 annual fee. He would like to make an HSA contribution of $3,350 plus pay the $25 fee separately, outside of the HSA. This is permissible under HSA rules and the $25 will not be counted as an HSA contribution. Many HSA owners prefer to pay any fees using HSA funds as the funds get favorable tax treatment.

IRS Notice 2004-50, See Q 71, See Q 72.

786. Must HSA custodians report ATM and other administrative fees as distributions?

No. HSA fees are not reportable on the 1099-SA. HSA administrative fees, including ATM fees, may be deducted directly from the HSA and not reported as a distribution. The money is removed from the HSA but is not reported as a distribution (the money just disappears from the HSA as far as the IRS reporting is concerned). This provides advantageous tax treatment as the HSA owner is essentially paying the fees with tax-free money. Any deduction of a fee would reduce the Fair Market Value of the account and accordingly the fee reduction is indirectly reflected in the FMV box of the IRS Form 5498-SA.

IRS Form 5498-SA.

787. If HSA fees are paid by an employer does that count against the annual HSA limit?

Depends. Whether or not an employee paid HSA fee counts against the HSA owner's annual contribution limit depends upon how the fee is paid. Often employers contribute some set amount of money and state that a portion of that should be used to offset fees. In that case, the annual fee contribution would count against the HSA annual limit.

If an employer separately pays the fee and consciously asks that it be made outside of the HSA, then the fee payment does not count against the annual limit for the year.

IRS Notice 2004-50, See Q 72.

Overdrafts

788. Can HSA custodians allow overdrafts on HSA accounts?

No. Loans and extensions of credits to HSAs are prohibited. Accordingly, overdrafts should not occur and should not be allowed in any HSA custodial agreement or investment agreement. Processes should be put in place to stop transactions before causing the HSA to be overdrawn.

Basically, the prohibited transaction rules do not allow for a custodian to extend credit to an HSA. The consequence of that is that the HSA has engaged in a prohibited transaction and is destroyed as of the first day of the calendar year. This requires custodians to report a special code on the 1099-SA and will likely result in taxes and penalties to the HSA owner.

> *Example 1.* National Sky Bank serves as the custodian for Bill's HSA. National Sky extends a line of credit to Bill's HSA. The line of credit causes Bill's HSA to cease to be an HSA because of the prohibited transaction rules.

> *Example 2.* National Sky Bank serves as the custodian for Bill's HSA. National Sky offers Bill a separate line of credit that is not related to his HSA, is not connected to his HSA, and the HSA cannot be directly used to repay the line of credit. This line of credit is permissible.

IRS Notice 2008-59, See Q 35, See Part Nine: Tax Issues - Prohibited Transactions.

789. Must a custodian report an overdraft as a prohibited transaction if it does occur?

Depends. A proper HSA agreement will specifically disallow overdrafts. However, overdrafts can still occur outside of the account agreement rules (although good procedures should be in place to stop the HSA from becoming overdrawn). The issue is whether the custodian must report this as a prohibited transaction on the IRS Form 1099-SA.

One interpretation of the rules is that custodians must report overdrafts as prohibited transactions. The prohibited transaction rules do not allow a custodian to extend credit to an HSA owner's HSA. An overdraft is likely construed as an extension of credit especially because the rules state that "indirect" extensions of credit also result in prohibited transactions

The author called the IRS and asked. "What happens if an HSA owner writes a check or uses an HSA debit card in a fashion that causes the HSA to overdraft against the rules of the account agreement, does this result in a prohibited transaction?"

The IRS stated that because this overdraft is not part of an overdraft protection program and no interest is being charged on the overdraft, it is not the type of transaction the IRS was referring to as a prohibited transaction in the IRS Notice. This statement cannot be relied upon as an oral answer but it does provide some comfort to HSA custodians. The Department of Labor issued an Advisory Opinion (DOL Advisory Option 2003-02A) on overdrafts in connection with the ERISA prohibited transaction rules that also supports this interpretation. That advisory option provides that an overdraft that results from the payment process but is not intended to be a loan and is otherwise discouraged is not a prohibited transaction, but an overdraft that is part of a specific loan or extension of credit is prohibited. That Advisory Opinion pre-dates HSAs but the logic still applies.

An alternative to reporting the overdraft as a prohibited transaction would be to contact the HSA owner and get the problem corrected immediately. The HSA owner may be able to make an additional HSA contribution to resolve the issue. If that's not possible because the HSA owner has already contributed the limit for the year or is no longer HSA-eligible, the HSA owner could re-contribute money using the return of a mistaken distribution rule (the HSA owner mistakenly took money out of the HSA that he or she did not have and now needs to return it).

Failing these measures, the HSA needs to be closed timely. These approaches are not directly supported by any IRS rulings, but make common sense. Please seek your own legal advice for more specific direction on how to proceed in this area. Reporting routine overdrafts (relatively small amounts) as prohibited transactions will place unwarranted scrutiny on the HSA owner and the custodian for a situation where the rules arguably are not meant to apply (the account agreement does not allow for overdrafts and every effort was made to prevent the overdraft from occurring).

IRS Form 1099-SA, DOL Advisory Option 2003-02A.

Account Terms

790. Do HSA custodians have to send monthly statements?

No. HSA laws do not require monthly or specific periodic statements. How often statements are required is a function of the law governing the investment instrument (generally a checking account) or possibly some other general state or federal banking law.

791. Can custodians limit the number of transactions in an HSA and require minimum distribution amounts?

Yes. Custodians may place reasonable restrictions on both the frequency and the minimum amount of distributions. For example, the custodian may prohibit distributions for amounts less than $50 or only allow a certain number of distributions per month. Generally, terms of frequency or minimum amounts are matters of contract between the HSA custodian and the HSA owner.

IRS Notice 2004-50, See Q 81.

APPENDIX A

Forms

(these worksheets are available online at http://pro.nuco.com/booksupplements/hsa)

The following forms have been created by the authors to assist you in various actions involving Health Savings Accounts. They are provided for your use but do not constitute advice. If you have any questions, please contact the appropriate legal counsel or financial or tax advisors.

- HSA Application Form
- HSA Custodial Agreement
- HSA Transfer Form
- HSA Designation of Beneficiary Form
- HSA Contribution Form
- HSA Distribution Form
- HSA Authorized Signer Form
- HSA Payroll Deferral Form
- HSA Notice to Employees Regarding Employer Contributions to HSAs

HSA Application (Example)

Initial Application to create a Health Savings Account

HSA Application

Complete electronically (optional).

Send applications here →

1 Personal Information.

Name _____ Soc. Sec. _____ Date of Birth _____

Street Address _____ City _____ State ____ Zip _____

Mailing Address _____ City _____ State ____ Zip _____

Home Phone _____ Work Phone _____ Employer _____ Occupation _____

E-mail _____ Driver's License _____ (attach copy- **required**) State Issued _____

Mother's Maiden Name_____ Birthplace _____ Agent/Broker _____

2 Contribution Information.

(**Employer Plans:** Do **not** complete this section if your HSA contributions are coming directly from your employer.)

Make check payable to Financial Institution above.	
Initial Contribution:	$_____
Fees (if applicable):	$_____
Other:	$_____
Total:	$_____

A. **Type** ☐ Regular   ☐ Rollover   ☐ Transfer (complete Transfer Form)

B. **Tax Year:** ☐ Current Year or ☐ Prior Year

C. **Automated Contributions:** If you want to set up monthly constributions to your HSA from your checking account, complete the following. You must attach a voided check from the account you would like to withdraw from.

Amount $_____   Day of Month ☐ 15th **or** ☐ 30th

3 Signatures.
I have received, read and agree to the terms in the Custodial Agreement and Disclosure Statement and I agree that those terms and conditions apply to this HSA and that I am bound to those terms and conditions. If applicable, I hereby designate the beneficiaries of this HSA as those named on the second page of this Application in the HSA Designation of Beneficiary section. If applicable, I hereby authorize the person named on the second page in the Authorized Signer section as an authorized signer for this HSA. I understand that I am solely responsible to determine my eligibility to make this HSA contribution and to determine the tax deductibility of the contribution; including an understanding that I must be covered under a "High Deductible Health Plan" for annual contribution eligibility. I agree that I will consult with my tax or legal advisor if I need advice. I acknowledge that the Custodian named above cannot and does not provide me with tax or legal advice. I am solely responsible for determining the tax consequences of all distributions. I acknowledge and agree that the Custodian may share limited information with my employer or insurance agents. I certify that the information provided by me on this application is accurate.

T.I.N./Backup Withholding. (Cross out item (3) if you are subject to backup withholding) Under penalties of perjury, I certify (1) that the number shown is my correct taxpayer ID number or social security number, (2) that I am a U.S. person (including U.S. resident alien), (3) and that I am not subject to backup withholding because (a) I am exempt from backup withholding or (b) because I have not been notified by the IRS that I am subject to backup withholding as a result of failure to report all interest or dividends or (c) because the IRS has notified me that I am no longer subject to backup withholding. The Internal Revenue Service does not require your consent to any provision of this document other than the certifications required to avoid backup withholding.

_____ _____
HSA Owner Signature   Date

☐ Check here if you completed the second page of this application.

Page 1 (this page) – Required information to open an HSA.
Page 2 (next page) – Optional beneficiary and authorized signer information can be completed at any time.

HSA Designation of Beneficiary Form

Send applications here →

(optional)

HSA Owner Name: _____

4 *Designation of Beneficiary.*

A. Primary Beneficiaries. In the event of my death, pay my HSA balance to the following primary beneficiaries according to the percentages indicated. If more than one primary beneficiary is designated and no percentages are indicated, the beneficiaries will be deemed to own equal share percentages in the HSA. If a primary beneficiary dies before me, his or her share shall be reallocated on a pro-rata basis to any remaining primary beneficiaries.

Name and Address	SSN	Relationship	Date of Birth	Percentage

B. Contingent Beneficiaries. If all of my primary beneficiaries die before me, pay my HSA balance to the following contingent beneficiaries according the percentages indicated. If a contingent beneficiary dies before me, his or her share shall be reallocated on a pro-rata basis to any remaining contingent beneficiaries.

Name and Address	SSN	Relationship	Date of Birth	Percentage

C. Spousal Consent. *Complete only if you name someone other than your spouse as a primary beneficiary.* Consult your tax or legal advisor with questions regarding naming beneficiaries in community or marital property states.

_____ _____ _____ _____
Spouse's Signature   Date   Witness' Signature   Date

HSA Authorized Signer (Optional)

5 *Authorized Signer.* If you want your spouse or other party to have access to the HSA, please complete the following section with the authorized signer's information. The authorized signer must sign below.

Authorized Name _____ Soc. Sec. # _____ Date of Birth _____

Mailing Address _____ City _____ State ___ Zip _____

Driver's License _____ (attach copy) State Issued _____ Phone _____

Mother's Maiden Name _____ Employer _____ Employer Phone _____

_____ _____
Signature of Additional Signer (Authorized Signer)   Date

> Page 1 (previous page) - Required information to open an HSA
> Page 2 (this page) - Optional beneficiary and authorized signer information can be completed at any time.

© 2010 HSA Authority, LLC - HSA Application 8/17/2010

HSA Custodial Agreement (Example)

Health Savings Custodial Account and Disclosure terms and agreement including: contributions, contribution limits, responsibilities, distributions, reporting requirements, custodians, investments, distributions, eligibility, expenses

Form **5305-C** (Rev. December 2011) Department of the Treasury Internal Revenue Service	**Health Savings Custodial Account** (Under section 223(a) of the Internal Revenue Code)	**Do not** file with the Internal Revenue Service
Name of account owner	Date of birth of account owner	**Identifying number** (see instructions)
Address of account owner (Street address, city, state, ZIP code)		
Name of custodian	Address or principal place of business of custodian	

The account owner named above is establishing this health savings account (HSA) exclusively for the purpose of paying or reimbursing qualified medical expenses of the account owner, his or her spouse, and dependents. The account owner represents that, unless this account is used solely to make rollover contributions, he or she is eligible to contribute to this HSA; specifically, that he or she: (1) is covered under a high deductible health plan (HDHP); (2) is not also covered by any other health plan that is not an HDHP (with certain exceptions for plans providing preventive care and limited types of permitted insurance and permitted coverage); (3) is not enrolled in Medicare; and (4) cannot be claimed as a dependent on another person's tax return.

$ _____ dollars in cash is assigned to this custodial account.
The account owner and the custodian make the following agreement:

Article I

1. The custodian will accept additional cash contributions for the tax year made by the account owner or on behalf of the account owner (by an employer, family member, or any other person). No contributions will be accepted by the custodian for any account owner that exceeds the maximum amount for family coverage plus the catch-up contribution.

2. Contributions for any tax year may be made at any time before the deadline for filing the account owner's federal income tax return for that year (without extensions).

3. Rollover contributions from an HSA or an Archer Medical Savings Account (Archer MSA) (unless prohibited under this agreement) need not be in cash and are not subject to the maximum annual contribution limit set forth in Article II.

4. Qualified HSA distributions from a health flexible spending arrangement or health reimbursement arrangement must be completed in a trustee-to-trustee transfer and are not subject to the maximum annual contribution limit set forth in Article II.

5. Qualified HSA funding distributions from an individual retirement account must be completed in a trustee-to-trustee transfer and are subject to the maximum annual contribution limit set forth in Article II.

Article II

1. For calendar year 2011, the maximum annual contribution limit for an account owner with single coverage is $3,050. This amount increases to $3,100 in 2012. For calendar year 2011, the maximum annual contribution limit for an account owner with family coverage is $6,150. This amount increases to $6,250 in 2012. These limits are subject to cost-of-living adjustments after 2012.

2. Contributions to Archer MSAs or other HSAs count toward the maximum annual contribution limit to this HSA.

3. For calendar year 2009 and later years, an additional $1,000 catch-up contribution may be made for an account owner who is at least age 55 or older and not enrolled in Medicare.

4. Contributions in excess of the maximum annual contribution limit are subject to an excise tax. However, the catch-up contributions are not subject to an excise tax.

Article III

It is the responsibility of the account owner to determine whether contributions to this HSA have exceeded the maximum annual contribution limit described in Article II. If contributions to this HSA exceed the maximum annual contribution limit, the account owner shall notify the custodian that there exist excess contributions to the HSA. It is the responsibility of the account owner to request the withdrawal of the excess contribution and any net income attributable to such excess contribution.

Article IV

The account owner's interest in the balance in this custodial account is nonforfeitable.

Article V

1. No part of the custodial funds in this account may be invested in life insurance contracts or in collectibles as defined in section 408(m).

2. The assets of this account may not be commingled with other property except in a common trust fund or common investment fund.

3. Neither the account owner nor the custodian will engage in any prohibited transaction with respect to this account (such as borrowing or pledging the account or engaging in any other prohibited transaction as defined in section 4975).

Article VI

1. Distributions of funds from this HSA may be made upon the direction of the account owner.

2. Distributions from this HSA that are used exclusively to pay or reimburse qualified medical expenses of the account owner, his or her spouse, or dependents are tax-free. However, distributions that are not used for qualified medical expenses are included in the account owner's gross income and are subject to an additional 20 percent tax on that amount. The additional 20 percent tax does not apply if the distribution is made after the account owner's death, disability, or reaching age 65.

3. The custodian is not required to determine whether the distribution is for the payment or reimbursement of qualified medical expenses. Only the account owner is responsible for substantiating that the distribution is for qualified medical expenses and must maintain records sufficient to show, if required, that the distribution is tax-free.

Cat. No. 38257X   Form **5305-C** (Rev. 12-2011)

Article VII

If the account owner dies before the entire interest in the account is distributed, the entire account will be disposed of as follows:

1. If the beneficiary is the account owner's spouse, the HSA will become the spouse's HSA as of the date of death.

2. If the beneficiary is not the account owner's spouse, the HSA will cease to be an HSA as of the date of death. If the beneficiary is the account owner's estate, the fair market value of the account as of the date of death is taxable on the account owner's final return. For other beneficiaries, the fair market value of the account is taxable to that person in the tax year that includes such date.

Article VIII

1. The account owner agrees to provide the custodian with information necessary for the custodian to prepare any report or return required by the IRS.

2. The custodian agrees to prepare and submit any report or return as prescribed by the IRS.

Article IX

Notwithstanding any other article that may be added or incorporated in this agreement, the provisions of Articles I through VIII and this sentence are controlling. Any additional article in this agreement that is inconsistent with section 223 or IRS published guidance will be void.

Article X

This agreement will be amended from time to time to comply with the provisions of the Code or IRS published guidance. Other amendments may be made with the consent of the persons whose signatures appear below.

Article XI

Article XI may be used for any additional provisions. If no other provisions will be added, draw a line through this space. If provisions are added, they must comply with the requirements of Article IX.

Account owner's signature _____ Date _____

Custodian's signature _____ Date _____

Witness' signature _____

(Use only if signature of account owner or custodian is required to be witnessed.)

What's New

Additional Tax Increased. For tax years beginning after December 31, 2010, the additional tax on distributions not used for qualified medical expenses increases from 10% to 20%.

General Instructions

Section references are to the Internal Revenue Code.

Purpose of Form

Form 5305-C is a model custodial account agreement that has been approved by the IRS. An HSA is established after the form is fully executed by both the account owner and the custodian. The form can be completed at any time during the tax year. This account must be created in the United States for the exclusive benefit of the account owner.

Do not file Form 5305-C with the IRS. Instead, keep it with your records. For more information on HSAs, see Notice 2004-2, 2004-2 I.R.B. 269, Notice 2004-50, 2004-33 I.R.B. 196, Pub. 969, Health Savings Accounts and Other Tax-Favored Health Plans, and other IRS published guidance.

Definitions

Identifying Number. The account owner's social security number will serve as the identification number of this HSA. For married persons, each spouse who is eligible to open an HSA and wants to contribute to an HSA must establish his or her own account. An employer identification number (EIN) is required for an HSA for which a return is filed to report unrelated business taxable income. An EIN is also required for a common fund created for HSAs.

High Deductible Health Plan (HDHP). For calendar year 2011, an HDHP for self-only coverage has a minimum annual deductible of $1,200 and an annual out-of-pocket maximum (deductibles, co-payments and other amounts, but not premiums) of $5,950. In 2012, the $1,200 minimum annual deductible remains the same and the annual out-of-pocket maximum increases to $6,050. For calendar year 2011, an HDHP for family coverage has a minimum annual deductible of $2,400 and an annual out-of-pocket maximum of $11,900. In 2012, the $2,400 minimum annual deductible remains the same and the annual out-of-pocket maximum increases to $12,100. These limits are subject to cost-of-living adjustments after 2012.

Self-only coverage and family coverage under an HDHP. Family coverage means coverage that is not self-only coverage.

Qualified medical expenses. Qualified medical expenses are amounts paid for medical care as defined in section 213(d) for the account owner, his or her spouse, or dependents (as defined in section 152) but only to the extent that such amounts are not compensated for by insurance or otherwise. With certain exceptions, health insurance premiums are not qualified medical expenses.

Custodian. A custodian of an HSA must be a bank, an insurance company, a person previously approved by the IRS to be a custodian of an individual retirement account (IRA) or Archer MSA, or any other person approved by the IRS.

Specific Instructions

Article XI. Article XI and any that follow it may incorporate additional provisions that are agreed to by the account owner and custodian. The additional provisions may include, for example, definitions, restrictions on rollover contributions from HSAs or Archer MSAs (requiring a rollover not later than 60 days after receipt of a distribution and limited to one rollover during a one-year period), investment powers, voting rights, exculpatory provisions, amendment and termination, removal of custodian, custodian's fees, state law requirements, treatment of excess contributions, distribution procedures (including frequency or minimum dollar amount), use of debit, credit, or stored-value cards, return of mistaken distributions, and descriptions of prohibited transactions. Attach additional pages if necessary.

Form **5305-C** (Rev. 12-2011)

HSA Rollover and Transfer Form (Example)

Form used to transfer or rollover assets from another HSA, MSA, IRA, FSA, or an HRS

HSA Transfer Form

HSA Custodian/Trustee Named Above

Purpose and Instructions: Use this form to transfer funds into your Health Savings Account at the custodian/trustee named above. Complete and return it to the custodian/trustee named above along with an HSA Application if you are a new client. You can use this form to transfer assets from another Health Savings Account, a Medical Savings Account (MSA), an Individual Retirement Account (IRA), a Flexible Savings Account (FSA) or a Healthcare Reimbursement Account (HRA) into this HSA.

1. Personal Information (information about you)

Name _____ Soc. Sec # _____

Street _____ Address

City _____ State _____ Zip

Phone _____ Date of Birth _____

2. Transfer Request (information about the current holder of the funds)

A. Transfer Type (select one)

☐ Transfer from another HSA or MSA (most common)

☐ Transfer from an IRA (only allowed once per lifetime – check rules)

☐ Transfer from FSA or HRA (only allowed in limited circumstances)

B. Current Holder of Assets (provide information on the current holder of your HSA, MSA, IRA, HRA or FSA assets)

Current Custodian/Trustee/FSA Administrator Name

Current Custodian Address

Current Account # _____

C. Instructions on Transfer (select one)

☐ Immediately liquidate all assets and send the cash proceeds (most common)

☐ Other (for special circumstances – please write instructions below)

_____

_____

_____

3. Signatures. I have an HSA, MSA, FSA, HRA or IRA at the above listed custodian, trustee or administrator and I certify that all the above information is correct. I understand the rules regarding transferring the funds and I agree to seek my own tax or legal advice, if I deem it necessary. I authorize and request that you, the present holder of my funds, transfer the assets to my HSA custodian/trustee named on the top right of this form.

HSA Owner's Signature _____ Date _____

The HSA custodian or trustee listed on the top right of this form agrees to accept the transfer described above and serve as the custodian or trustee for the HSA.

Receiving Custodian/Trustee's Signature _____ Date _____

HSA Designation of Beneficiary (Example)

Form used to name or change beneficiaries for an HSA

HSA Designation of Beneficiary Form

HSA Custodian/Trustee Named Above

Purpose: Use this form to name or change beneficiaries for your HSA.

1. Personal Information

Name (HSA Owner) _____ Soc. Sec # _____

Date of Birth _____ Account # _____

2. Designation of Beneficiary

A. Primary Beneficiaries. In the event of my death, pay my HSA balance to the following primary beneficiaries according to the percentages indicated. If more than one primary beneficiary is designated and no percentages are indicated, the beneficiaries will be deemed to own equal share percentages in the HSA. If a primary beneficiary dies before me, his or her share shall be reallocated on a pro-rata basis to any remaining primary beneficiaries.

Name and Address	SSN	Relationship	Date of Birth	Percentage

B. Contingent Beneficiaries. If all of my primary beneficiaries die before me, pay my HSA balance to the following contingent beneficiaries according the percentages indicated. If a contingent beneficiary dies before me, his or her share be reallocated on a pro-rata basis to any remaining contingent beneficiaries.

Name and Address	SSN	Relationship	Date of Birth	Percentage

3. Spousal Consent.

If you are married and name someone other than your spouse as the primary beneficiary, complete this section. Consult your tax or legal advisor with questions regarding naming beneficiaries in community or marital property states.

Spouse's Signature _____ Date _____

Witness's Signature _____ Date _____

4. Signatures.

I hereby designate the beneficiaries above. If I marry in the future I will complete a new Designation of Beneficiary form which includes the spousal consent.

HSA Owner's Signature _____ Date _____

Witness's Signature _____ Date _____

HSA Contributions (Example)

Form used to make contribution to an HSA.

Can be used for one-time contribution or automatic monthly contributions or to change amounts.

HSA Contribution Form

> Purpose: Use this form to make contributions to your HSA. This may be a one-time contribution or to set up automatic monthly contributions. You can also use this form to change your monthly contribution amounts.

1 Personal Information

Name:_____

Social   Security   #:

HSA Account Number (if available): _____

2 Contribution Type (check only one – unless you are making multiple types of contributions)

a) ☐ **Regular Contribution.** ☐ for current tax year or ☐ prior tax year

b) ☐ **Rollover Contribution.** Rollover from another HSA (this form is not needed if you are also completing an Application along with this rollover).

c) ☐ **Transfer Contribution.** Transfer from another HSA – Please Use a Transfer Form for this purpose.

d) ☐ **Return of Mistaken Distribution.** If you mistakenly take a distribution for an expense that you thought was "eligible," but which you later learn is not, you can repay the amount into your HSA so long as the mistake of fact was due to a "reasonable cause," and the mistake is corrected no later than April 15 following the year you knew or should have known of the mistake. Check this box to make sure we report your contribution appropriately.

3 Contribution Amount

a) **Amount (if paid by check).** _____

b) **Amount (if paid electronically via ACH)** (complete this section for automated monthly contributions or to make a one-time contribution using the ACH system from your personal checking account)

    (1) ☐ **Automated Monthly Contributions.** If you want to set up automatic monthly withdrawals from another checking account, complete the following. You must attach a voided check from the account you wish to withdraw.

    (a) Monthly Amount $_____ Date ☐ 15th ☐ 30th

    (2) ☐ **One Time ACH Contribution.** If you want to make a one time contribution to your HSA using the ACH system (transfer from another financial institution).

    (a) **Account to Be Debited** (or attach check).

    Name on Account:_____

    Account:_____

    Bank Name:_____ Routing #:_____

    (b) **Amount.** _____

4 Signatures. I hereby agree to make the HSA contribution described above.

_____   _____
HSA Owner Signature   Date

HSA Distributions (Example)

Form is used to obtain distributions.

This can include normal distributions, death distributions, prohibited transaction distributions, and transfers to a spouse due to death or divorce

HSA Distribution Form

> **Purpose:** Use this form for distributions from your HSA in cases when you want a check from us (or a transfer to a spouse) rather than using your debit card, checking or ACH access. This may include: normal distributions, death distributions, disability distributions, prohibited transaction distributions and transfers to a spouse due to death or divorce.

1. Personal Information

Name _____ Soc. Sec # _____
Date of Birth _____ HSA Account # _____ Phone # _____

2. Distribution Information

A. **Amount:** $_____ A check will be mailed to your address on record or, in the case of a death distribution or transfer to a spouse, the address listed by a beneficiary or spouse on this form. Please include special instructions here:

_____

B. **Distribution Reason** (*select one*)

☐ **Normal Distribution** Are you closing your HSA? ☐ No ☐ Yes (taxes, penalties, and fees may apply)
☐ **Excess:** Return of Excess Contribution For Tax Year _____ Amount of Excess $_____
    ☐ corrected by my tax-filing due date, including extensions
        Earning attributable to the excess amount $_____
    ☐ corrected after my tax-filing due date, including extensions
☐ **Death Distribution** (for distributions to beneficiaries – death certificate required)
    Distribution in ☐ year of death ☐ after year of death
    ☐ spouse beneficiary (use transfer below) ☐ non-spouse beneficiary
    Beneficiary Name:_____ Address _____
    SSN/TIN_____ Phone _____
☐ **Transfer to Spouse** ☐ Due to Death ☐ Due to Divorce
    Spouse's Name_____ Address_____
    SSN _____ Phone _____
    Spouse's HSA Account # _____ Financial Institution_____
    Address_____ Phone_____
☐ **Disability** (avoids the additional 10% (20% penalty starting 1/1/11) if you do not meet another exception – must meet IRS definition of "disabled" to qualify)
☐ **Prohibited Transaction**
☐ **Return HSA Contribution to Employer.** An employer may complete this form and request funds be returned directly to the employer in two situations: (1) the employee was never eligible for the HSA and (2) the employer contributed more than the maximum HSA limit for the year. An authorized party for the employer signs below. Write address for check and company name in the "special instructions" line in Part A.

3. Signatures. I certify that I am solely responsible for this HSA distribution and understand the tax consequences. I certify that I am the HSA owner, the beneficiary, or the individual authorized to complete this transaction. I have not received tax advice from the Custodian of this account and agree to seek my own tax or legal advice, if I deem it necessary. I indemnify and hold the HSA Custodian harmless for any resulting liabilities for this transaction.

HSA Owner's/Responsible Party's Signature _____ Date _____

HSA Authorized Signer Form (Example)

Form is used to name or change an authorized signer for an existing HSA.

HSA Authorized Signer Form

Purpose: Use this form to name or change an authorized signer for your existing HSA.

1. Personal Information of HSA Owner

Name (HSA Owner) _____ Soc. Sec # _____

Date of Birth _____ Account # _____

2. Authorized Signer Information

Complete this section to add or delete an authorized singer. The authorized signer must sign below if you are adding the authorized signer.

CHECK ONE ☐ Add Authorized Signer
(or both, if applicable)   Complete part A below

☐ Remove Existing Authorized Signer
     Complete part B below

A. Add New Authorized Signer (Complete this section to add a new authorized signer).

Authorized Signer Name _____

Authorized Signer Social Security Number _____

Authorized Signer Date of Birth _____

Mailing Address_____City _____State_____ Zip_____

Authorized Signer Driver's License (or state ID)[1] _____State Issued _____

           [1]INCLUDE A COPY OF DRIVER'S LICENSE OR STATE ID

Birth Place _____

Second debit card for authorized signer?   Yes ☐ No ☐

B. Remove Existing Authorized Signer (complete to remove an existing authorized signer)

Please note the authorized signer does not need to sign below.

Authorized Signer Name _____

Authorized Signer Social Security Number _____

3. Signatures

Authorized Signer Signature Statement. You (the Authorized Signer) understand that we have a current need to verify your identity and creditworthiness, therefore, by signing below, you authorize us to verify your credit record and employment history by any means necessary, including preparation of a credit report by a credit agency.

HSA Owner Signature Statement. I hereby authorize the person named above in Section 2: Add New Authorized Signer Information as an authorized signer for my HSA. If a debit card was selected, I am a current HSA owner and understand that I remain subject to that Agreement. I hereby request that you remove any authorized signer designated in Section B, above, Remove Existing Authorized Signer.

HSA Owner's Signature _____ Date _____

Authorized Signer's Signature_____ Date _____

Please remember to review and name beneficiaries for your HSA. Use our HSA Beneficiary form to name and change beneficiaries.

HSA Payroll Deferral Form (Example)

Form is used to allow defer money from a paycheck into an HSA.

HSA Payroll Deferral Form

1 *General Information.*

Your Name: _____

Company Name: _____ ("Employer")

2 *Payroll Deferral Request.*

Payroll Deferral. I request that my Employer defer the following amount from my pay and direct the money into an HSA with the custodian named above. (Please make sure you know how much you are eligible to contribute.) Check **only one** box.

☐ Per Pay Period. $_____   Multiply by number of pay periods to get annual contribution amount.

☐ Annual Amount. $_____   This amount will be divided by the # of pay periods per year (or the remaining number of pay periods).

☐ Other. $_____   Use for unique situations- please explain: _____ _____

3 *Signature and Submission Information.*

I agree to the above deferral request and will submit this form to my Employer for processing. I also authorize my Employer to make withdrawls from my HSA in the event that a credit entry is made in error. I understand that the custodian may provide my HSA account number to my Employer to facilitate the money transfer. I further understand that the date of my payroll may differ from the date the funds are actually deposited and are available for use.

_____   _____
HSA Owner Signature   Date

Employer Instructions: Use this form when you allow payroll deferral into an HSA. Please collect this data from each employee (print or copy this form for more copies of it) and consolidate employee deferrals onto one spreadsheet, use "The Employee Contribution Worksheet", or one of your own. Then forward that spreadsheet to the HSA Custodian along with a check or ACH instructions for payment. Keep this Employee Payroll Deferral Form for your records, the HSA Custodian does not need a copy.

HSA Notice to Employees Regarding Employer Contributions to HSAs (Example)

This notice is required to be provided by employers that make HSA contributions to each eligible employees who has not established an HSA by December 31 (or if the employer does not know if the employee established an HSA.)

HSA Notice to Employees Regarding Employer Contributions to HSAs

For Employer - Instructions: Employers that make employer HSA contributions are required to provide this notice to each eligible employee who has not established an HSA by December 31 or if the employer does not know if the employee established an HSA. The employer may provide this notice to other employees as well. However, if an employee earlier notified the employer that he or she has established an HSA, the employer may not condition making the HSA contribution on receipt of any additional notice from that employee. For each calendar year, a notice is deemed to be timely if the employer provides the notice no earlier than 90 days before the first HSA employer contribution for that calendar year and no later than January 15 of the following calendar year.

For Employees - Purpose: This notice explains that you may be eligible to receive Health Savings Account (HSA) contributions from your employer if you are covered by a High Deductible Health Plan (HDHP).

1. Employer Information (completed by employer)

Employer/Business Name: _____
Year of HSA Contribution: _____ (insert year HSA contribution is being made for)
Contact: Name: _____ (Contact person for HSA questions and to notify of HSA establishment)
Address: _____

E-Mail: _____ Phone: _____
HSA Eligibility Requirements: _____
_____
_____ (Include a short description of your HSA program and include the requirements the employee must meet to receive the HSA contribution.)

2. Notice of HSA Contributions (Legal notice for employee to read)

The employer named above provides contributions to the Health Savings Account (HSA) of each employee who meets the employer's eligibility requirements stated above ("eligible employee"). If you are an eligible employee, you must do the following in order to receive an employer contribution:

(1) **Establish an HSA** on or before the last day in February of the year after the year of the HSA contribution (the year of the HSA contribution is listed in Section 1 above), and;

(2) **Notify the contact person** named above of your HSA account information on or before the last day in February of the year after year for which the contribution is being made. Please provide the information required in Section 3 of this form regarding the details of your HSA.

If you establish your HSA on or before the last day of February in the year after the year for which the contribution is being made and notify the contract person above of your HSA account information, you will receive your HSA contributions, plus reasonable interest (if established late), for the HSA contribution by April 15 of the year after the year for which the contribution is being made. If, however, you do not establish your HSA or you do not notify us of your HSA account information by the deadline, then we are not required to make any contributions to your HSA for the year of the HSA contribution. You may notify us that you have established an HSA by sending a written notice to the contact person named (complete and return this form). If you have any questions about this notice, please connect with the contact person named above.

3. Personal HSA Account Information (Completed by employee and returned to contact person)

Name _____ Soc. Sec # _____
HSA Custodian/Trustee Name: _____ HSA Account # _____
Address of Custodian/Trustee: _____

_____
Signature   Date

APPENDIX B
Worksheets

(these worksheets are available online at http://pro.nuco.com/booksupplements/hsa)

The following worksheets have been created by the authors to assist you in various actions involving Health Savings Accounts. These worksheets are provided for your use but do not constitute advice. If you have any questions, please contact the appropriate legal counsel or financial or tax advisors.

- Age 65 Worksheet

- Distribution Worksheet

- Eligibility and Contribution Worksheet

- Employer Comparability Worksheet

- Employer Funding Worksheet

- HSA/FSA/HRA Comparison Worksheet

- IRA to HSA Worksheet

- Qualified Medical Expenses Worksheet

- Small Business Owner Worksheet

- Tax Savings Worksheet

- Testing Period Worksheet

Age Sixty-Five Worksheet (Example)

This worksheet is designed to educate HSA owners that are aged sixty-five or older on three changes to the HSA law including: penalty-free withdrawals, paying for health insurance premiums, and loss of HSA eligibility

Changes to your HSA When You Reach 65

Purpose: This worksheet is designed to educate HSA owners reaching age 65 on three key HSA changes.
(1) **Penalty Free Withdrawals.** At age 65, you are eligible to take money out of your HSA for any reason.
(2) **Pay for Health Insurance Premiums.** At age 65 you can use your HSA to pay for some insurance premiums.
(3) **Loss of HSA Eligibility.** At age 65, most Americans lose HSA eligibility because they begin Medicare.

1 Age 65 General Distributions

At age 65, you can take penalty-free distributions from the HSA for any reason. However, in order to be both tax-free and penalty-free the distribution must be for a qualified medical expense. Withdrawals made for other purposes will be subject to ordinary income taxes. Given that Medicare does not cover all of your medical expenses, most HSA owners over 65 continue to use their HSA funds for qualified medical expenses. This will ensure they get the maximum benefits from their HSA.

Example. Bill, age 66, wants to take money out of his HSA to pay for general retirement expenses (not qualified medical expenses). Bill will __not__ have to pay the 20% penalty for non-eligible HSA withdrawals because he is over the age 65, but he will be subject to income taxes on the distribution. If instead Bill uses his HSA for a qualified medical expense he can use the funds tax-free __and__ penalty-free.

2 Health Insurance Premiums

At age 65, you can use your HSA to pay for Medicare parts A, B, D and Medicare HMO premiums tax-free and penalty-free. You cannot use your HSA to pay for Medigap insurance premiums. You can also use your HSA to pay the employee share of premiums for employer-sponsored health care (employee paid portions of employer sponsored health care may already be pre-tax). Using HSA money is an especially good method to pay for Medicare as it is challenging to pay for Medicare with pre-tax dollars. If your Medicare premium is automatically deducted from your Social Security check, you simplify reimburse yourself directly from your HSA for the Medicare premiums paid from your Social Security payment.

3 Continued Eligibility for an HSA

Most Americans become eligible for Medicare at age 65. Americans that begin receiving Social Security benefits prior to age 65 are automatically enrolled in Medicare at age 65. Participation in any type of Medicare (Part A, Part B, Part C - Medicare Advantage Plans, Part D, and Medicare Supplement Insurance - Medigap), makes you ineligible to contribute to an HSA. However, you can continue to use your HSA for qualified medical expenses and for other expenses for as long as you have funds in your HSA.

Loss of Eligibility in Month You Turn 65. You lose eligibility as of the first day of the month you turn 65 and enroll in Medicare.

Example. Sally turns 65 on July 21 and enrolls in Medicare. She is no longer eligible to contribute to her HSA as of July 1. Her maximum contribution for that year would be 6/12 (she was eligible the first 6 months of the year) times the applicable federal limit (remember to include the catch-up amount). See our Eligibility and Contribution Worksheet and the next page for details.

See Page 2 for More Details

Changes to your HSA When You Reach 65

Calculating Your HSA Contribution for the Year You Turn 65

Final Year's Contribution is Pro-Rata. You can make an HSA contribution after you turn 65 and enroll in Medicare, if you have not maximized your contribution for your last year of HSA eligibility. You have until April 15 of the year following the tax year you lose HSA eligibility to make your HSA contribution. You can do so even if you are no longer eligible for an HSA so long as you are making a contribution for a period when you were eligible.

Example. Jim was covered by a self-only HDHP and eligible for an HSA in 2014 but turned 65 on July 2, 2014, and enrolled in Medicare. Jim lost eligibility for an HSA as of July 1, 2014. For 2014, Jim was eligible for 6 months of the year. The federal HSA limit for Jim is $4,300 ($3,300 individual HSA limit plus a $1,000 catch-up). Accordingly, Jim's calculation is 6/12 X $4,300 = $2,150. Jim's maximum contribution for 2014 is $2,150. Jim has until April 15, 2015 to make this contribution. See our Eligibility and Contribution Worksheet for details.

Remaining HSA Eligible Past Age 65

To be able to contribute to an HSA after age 65, you must not enroll in Medicare. HSA rules make a distinction between being merely "eligible" for Medicare (keep HSA eligibility) and being "entitled" to or "enrolled" in Medicare (lose HSA eligibility). You become enrolled in Medicare under Part A by filing an application or being approved automatically. The Social Security Administration automatically "enrolls" you in Medicare Part A when you begin collecting Social Security benefits. Accordingly, if you are receiving Social Security payments and are over 65, you are almost certainly enrolled in Medicare Part A and ineligible to contribute to an HSA. Some people; however, avoid enrolling in Medicare and being automatically enrolled by waiting to receive Social Security. If you are not enrolled in Medicare and are otherwise HSA eligible, you can continue to contribute to an HSA after age 65. You are also allowed to contribute the $1,000 catch-up.

Stopping Medicare to Reclaim HSA Eligibility

If you signed up for Medicare Part A and now want to decline it, you can do so by contacting the Social Security Administration. Assuming you have not begun receiving Social Security checks this will reestablish your eligibility for an HSA. If you have applied for or have begun receiving Social Security, you cannot opt out of Medicare Part A without paying the government back all the money you received from Social Security payments plus paying the government back for any money Medicare spent on your medical claims. This action will also stop future Social Security payments (until you reapply and start this cycle over again).

Spouse Under Age 65

If your spouse is under age 65 that may provide an avenue for continued HSA contributions. An employer; however, cannot make HSA contributions into the HSA of an employee's spouse.

Example. Dick and Adelle are covered under a family HDHP provided through Dick's employer. Dick reaches age 65 in July and enrolls in Medicare. Dick's employer makes HSA contributions and allows Dick to make pre-tax payroll deferrals as well. Dick's employer continues to provide family HDHP coverage for both Dick and Adelle. Adelle, age 58, can now open an HSA and contribute the family maximum (plus the catch-up as she is over age 55) because she remains covered by a family HDHP and is otherwise eligible. Adelle can use her HSA for Dick's medical expenses. Adelle cannot put her HSA contribution into Dick's HSA and will have to open her own HSA. Dick's employer will stop HSA employer contributions and cannot allow Dick to defer pay pre-tax into Adelle's HSA.

Distribution Worksheet (Example)

This worksheet helps illuminate the federal income tax consequences of a distribution.

HSA Distribution Worksheet

Purpose: Use this worksheet to guide you in the federal income tax consequences of HSA distributions. Please consult with your tax or legal counsel. We do not provide tax or legal advice. See p.2 for details.

1 Is your distribution for a "qualified" medical expense?
The primary purpose of an HSA is to use the funds to pay for the health care expenses of yourself and dependents. Distributions for qualified medical expenses are tax-free and penalty-free.

a. **Was the expense incurred by yourself or a family member?** HSA funds may only be used for yourself, your spouse and your dependents. Note: there is no requirement that you or your family member be currently eligible for an HSA (covered by an HDHP). Eligibility is only important when contributing to an HSA, not in being allowed to use the funds. See the Eligibility and Contribution Worksheet for detail on contributing to an HSA.

b. **Was the expense incurred after you established the HSA?** You must open your HSA before you incur the medical expense. This is a good reason to open your HSA as soon as you become eligible. Once your HSA is open you can use your HSA funds to pay for qualified medical expenses incurred now or in the future. You can even pay for current expenses out of future contributions or reimburse yourself for eligible medical expenses that you paid for with other funds.

> *Example: you incur a $2,000 eligible medical expense this year but only have $500 in your HSA. You can pay $500 out of the HSA and the other $1,500 out of other funds. You can then pay yourself back with future year HSA contributions (provided you remain eligible to make HSA contributions).*

c. **Is your expense "qualified"?** Most traditional medical expenses such as doctor visits and prescriptions are covered, see page 2 for a list of qualified expenses.

> Note: The HSA custodian does not review your medical expenses for eligibility. You should save receipts and keep a tax record in case of an IRS audit.

2 Does your distribution qualify for another tax-free and penalty-free exception?

Long-term Care	Long-term care insurance is an eligible expense subject to dollar limitations – see page 2.
COBRA Benefits	Paying for COBRA continuation health benefits is eligible – see also "Insurance Premiums" below.
Insurance premiums	Health coverage for an HSA owner aged 65 is eligible (see back for detail). Also, COBRA health care coverage, and health care coverage while receiving unemployment compensation is eligible.
Medicare Premiums	You can use your HSA to pay for Medicare premiums (other than Medi-Gap). If your premiums are deducted from Social Security, you can reimburse yourself for the cost.
Rollover/Transfer	A rollover or transfer to another HSA is not taxed or penalized so long as the rollover is completed within 60 days and you have not completed another rollover within the previous 12 months.

3 Does your distribution qualify for a taxable, but penalty-free exception?

Age 65 or over	Non-qualified distributions after age 65 are not penalized but are taxable (similar to IRAs and 401(k)s).
Death/Inheritance	Distributions to named beneficiaries of HSAs are not penalized but are taxed. Spouse beneficiaries can treat the HSA as their own and are not subject to tax or penalty – see page 2.
Disability	Distributions taken by disabled persons are not penalized.

4 Fail to meet any of the above? You are subject to taxes plus a 20% penalty.
See back (p.2) for additional exceptions and distribution reasons.

> *Example: a 25 year old takes a $1,000 distribution from his HSA to pay for a new motorcycle for recreation. The motorcycle is not an eligible medical expense so the $1,000 distribution is taxable and subject to a 20% penalty ($1,000 x 20% = $200). Non-eligible distributions are reported on IRS Form 8889 along with your income tax return.*

HSA Distribution Guide – Additional Detail

This Worksheet is based on IRS guidance regarding HSAs including IRS Notice 2004-2, IRS Notice 2004-50, IRS Publication 969, and IRS Publication 502. The following list of qualified and non-qualified medical expenses is intended to provide a quick guide and is not exhaustive. For more information review the IRS materials or talk to a tax or financial advisor. This Worksheet does not cover state taxes issues. Many, but not all, states provide similar tax treatment for HSAs.

Qualified Medical Expenses

Abortion	Guide Dogs	Orthopedist
Acupuncture	Gynecologist	Osteopath
Alcoholism*	Hearing Aids	Oxygen
Ambulance Services	Hospital Services	Pediatrician
Anesthetists	Insulin	Physician
Artificial Limbs	Laboratory Tests	Postnatal Treatments
Artificial Teeth	Prepaid Insurance Premiums*	Prenatal Care
Bandages	Lab Fees	Prescription Drugs
Breast Recon. Surgery*	Lead Based Paint Removal*	Prosthesis
Birth Control Pills	Legal Fees*	Psychiatric Care
Blood Tests	Lodging*	Psychoanalysis
Braces	Long Term Care*	Psychologist
Braille Books and Magazines*	Long Term Care Services*	Registered Nurse
Car - modifications*	Meals*	Spinal Fluid Test
Cardiographs	Medical Information Plan	Splints
Chiropractor	Medical Services	Sterilization
Christian Science Practitioner	Medicines - prescriptions	Stop Smoking Programs*
Contact Lenses	Mentally Retarded, Homes*	Surgeon
Contraceptives	Nonprescription medicine*	Telephone*
Crutches	Neurologist	Therapy
Dental Treatment*	Nursing Home*	Transplants
Dermatologist	Nursing Services	Transportation
Diagnostic Devices and Fees	Obstetrician	Vaccines
Disabled Dependent Care	Operating Room expenses	Vasectomy
Drug Addiction Therapy*	Operations	Vision Correction Surgery
Eyeglasses	Ophthalmologist	Weight Loss Programs*
Eye Surgery	Optician	Wheelchair
Fertility Treatments	Oral Surgery	Wigs*
Future Medical Care*	Orthopedic Shoes	X-rays

Non-Qualified

Over-the-counter drugs (see below)
Child Care
Cosmetic Surgery
Hair Transplants*
Health Club Dues
Household Help
Insurance Premiums*
Maternity Clothes
Nutritional Supplements*
Teeth Whitening
Vitamins

Over-the-Counter Drugs

Over-the-counter drugs and medicines are no longer eligible medical expenses starting January 1, 2011. If you get a prescription for an over-the-counter drug then you can still use your HSA. Insulin is an exception. This rule does not apply to non-drug over-the-counter items; such as, bandages or blood pressure monitors.

* Additional rules apply. For more information see IRS Publication 502, or a tax professional.

Additional Distribution Events and Other Details on Distributions:

1. **Divorce.** In the case of a divorce with a "divorce or separation agreement," an HSA owner may transfer HSA assets to the spouse without taxes or penalties. A private separation agreement is not sufficient for this tax treatment.
2. **Spouse as Beneficiary.** A spouse named as a beneficiary is automatically deemed to be the HSA owner upon death of the original HSA owner. The surviving spouse may rollover, transfer and use the HSA as his or her own.
3. **Long-Term Care Premiums.** Long-term care distributions are limited in amount based on age (for 2013 it ranges from $360 for individuals under age 40 to $4,550 for individuals age 71 or over). The amount adjusts annually for cost-of-living increases. See Revenue Code 213(d)(10).
4. **Prohibited Transactions.** HSA owners engaging in "prohibited transactions" face potentially severe consequences and should seek professional help. The rules surrounding prohibited transactions are too complex for this Worksheet. Basically, a prohibited transaction occurs when a disqualified person (the HSA owner and others) engages in dealings with the HSA that permit opportunities for tax fraud. For example, an HSA owner cannot sell his or her HSA an asset the HSA owner owns (e.g., real estate).
5. **Pledging the HSA as Security for a Loan.** An HSA owner is not allowed to pledge the HSA as security for a loan and the amount so pledged is treated as a distribution and is subject to taxes and a penalty.
6. **Mistaken Distributions.** If there is clear and convincing evidence that amounts were distributed from an HSA because of a mistake of fact due to reasonable cause, the account owner can repay the mistaken distribution no later than April 15 following the first year the account owner knew or should have known the distribution was mistaken (subject to the custodian's allowance of this).
7. **Return of Excess Contributions.** If you contribute more to your HSA than you are eligible to contribute, you must remove the excess amount by your tax filing due date plus extensions. If you fail to remove the excess amount, plus any earning (e.g. interest) attributable to the excess by your tax filing due date, plus extensions, you will be subject to a 6% excise tax for years that you allow the excess to remain.
8. **Reimburse Yourself.** You can reimburse yourself for medical expenses that you pay for with personal funds (not tax favored).
9. **Use Contributions for Future Expenses.** You can use a current year contribution to pay for future medical expenses.
10. **Use Future Contributions to Pay Current Expenses.** Assuming you established an HSA, you can pay for current medical expenses (expenses incurred after HSA established) with future year HSA contributions.
11. **Insurance Premiums at Age 65.** Individuals over the age 65 can use the HSA to pay for premiums for Medicare Part A or B, Medicare HMO, and the employee share of premiums for employer-sponsored health insurance, including premiums for employer sponsored retiree health insurance. Premiums for Medigap policies are not qualified medical expenses. This applies to both insured and self-insured plans.

© 2013 HSA Authority, LLC HSA Distribution Worksheet 11/18/13

Eligibility and Contribution Worksheet (Example)

This worksheet is used to determine a person's eligibility for an HSA and the amount they can contribute

HSA Eligibility and Contribution Worksheet

Purpose: Use this form to verify your eligibility for an HSA and determine the amount you may contribute. You are responsible for properly determining your eligibility and contribution amount. This worksheet is simply a tool to aid you in that effort. If you have any questions, please consult with your tax or legal counsel.

1 **HSA Eligibility.** You must answer "True" to each of the following in order to be eligible for an HSA. See definitions on back for help.

a.	I am covered under an HDHP	True	False	Not Eligible
b.	I am not covered by another non-HDHP health plan other than "permitted insurance"	True	False	
c.	I am not enrolled in Medicare (age 65)	True	False	
d.	I am not a dependent on another person's tax return	True	False	

2 **Contribution Amount.** Use the table below to determine your amount.

	Contribution Worksheet	Individual	Family
A	Federal Limit[1]	$3,300 (2014) $3,350 (2015)	$6,550 (2014) $6,650 (2015)
B	Catch Up[2] if Age 55 - 65 + $1,000 (2014 or 2015)		
C	Total (add Federal Limit plus Catch-Up)		

[1]**Issues that Impact Contribution Amounts.** A number of issues potentially affect the amount of your HSA contribution.

A. Less Than Full Year Eligibility – Eligible on December 1. If you become eligible for an HSA sometime during the year, rather than on January 1, you can still contribute and deduct the full amount of the Federal Limit above if you remained eligible on December 1 of that year (this assumes you are a calendar year taxpayer and this rule applies even if your first day of eligibility was December 1). However, if you fail to maintain your eligibly for a *testing period* then the amount you contributed under this rule is subject to taxation and a 10% penalty (except in the case of disability or death). The *testing period* is the period beginning in the last month of the taxable year (generally December 1) and ending on the last day of the 12th month following such month (generally December 31 of the next year). Please see the HSA Testing Period Worksheet for details.

B. Less Than Full Year Eligibility – Not Eligible on December 1. If you are not eligible for the HSA in all months of the year and are not eligible on December 1, a different rule applies. You must apply the *Sum of the Months* rule to determine the maximum amount of your HSA contribution. The Sum of the Months calculation requires you to determine your eligibility month-by-month and only contribute a pro-rata amount of the maximum federal HSA limit. Please use the chart on page 2.

C. Multiple HSAs. The total contribution amount may be split among multiple HSAs. For family coverage, the amount may be split between eligible spouses' HSAs.

D. IRA to HSA Transfers. You are allowed a one time transfer of funds from your Individual Retirement Account into your HSA. This is limited to the amount you are eligible to contribute for the year and counts against that contribution (i.e. you cannot put in more than the Federal Limit counting any IRA transfer). You cannot deduct the amount transferred from an IRA to an HSA; however, the amount taken from the IRA is not taxable as a distribution from the IRA. Please see the IRA to HSA Transfer Worksheet for details.

E. Employer Contributions. Caution: Employer contributions made to your HSA on a pre-tax basis count towards your total contribution amount but may not be deductible from your personal income.

[2]**Catch-Up Contributions.** For individuals (and their spouses covered under the HDHP) age 55 and over, the HSA contribution limit is increased by $1,000. If both you and your spouse are age 55 or over and not enrolled in Medicare, you each get a catch-up. You cannot contribute more than $7,650 ($6,650+$1,000) into one HSA for 2015. Catch-up contributions should be made into each spouses' respective HSA.

Catch-Up Amount	Tax Year	2012	2013	2014	2015
	Amount	$1,000	$1,000	$1,000	$1,000

3 **Need More Help?** You are encouraged to talk to a tax professional, your insurance representative or another professional to help determine your eligibility and contribution amount. IRS Notice 2008-59 and IRS Notice 2004-50 both provide examples and more detail on eligibility (caution some points in the 2004 IRS Notice are outdated).

HSA Eligibility and Contribution Worksheet - Definitions and Instructions

1. **HDHP Defined**. The quickest and easiest method to determine if you are covered by a HDHP is to ask your insurance provider. Generally, an HDHP is a health plan that satisfies certain requirements with respect to deductibles and out-of-pocket expenses.

   a) **Self-only coverage**. Specifically, for self-only coverage, an HDHP has an annual deductible of at least $1,300 (2015) and annual out-of-pocket expenses required to be paid (deductibles, co-payments and other amounts, but not premiums) not exceeding $6,450 (2015 limit).

   b) **Family coverage**. For family coverage, an HDHP has an annual deductible of at least $2,600 (2015) and annual out-of-pocket expenses required to be paid not exceeding $12,900 (2015 limit). In the case of family coverage, a plan is an HDHP only if, under the terms of the plan and without regard to which family member or members incur expenses, no amounts are payable from the HDHP until the family has incurred annual covered medical expenses in excess of the minimum annual deductible. Amounts are indexed for inflation.

   c) **Preventative care**. A plan does not fail to qualify as an HDHP merely because it does not have a deductible (or has a small deductible) for preventive care (*e.g.*, first dollar coverage for preventive care).

   d) **Permitted insurance defined**. If you are covered under a HDHP, you are not allowed to also be covered under another health plan, other than certain "Permitted" types of insurance. Permitted insurance is insurance under which substantially all of the coverage provided relates to liabilities incurred under workers' compensation laws, tort liabilities, liabilities relating to ownership or use of property (*e.g.*, automobile insurance), insurance for a specified disease or illness, and insurance that pays a fixed amount per day (or other period) of hospitalization. In addition to permitted insurance, an individual does not fail to be eligible for an HSA merely because, in addition to an HDHP, the individual has coverage (whether provided through insurance or otherwise) for accidents, disability, dental care, vision care, or long-term care. If a plan that is intended to be an HDHP is one in which substantially all of the coverage of the plan is through permitted insurance or other coverage as described in this answer, it is not an HDHP. You are covered by another health plan if you are covered under a health Flexible Spending Account (FSA) or Health Reimbursement Account (HRA) unless it's a *Limited Purpose FSA or HRA* (other exceptions apply). You are also considered covered under another health plan if your spouse is covered under a FSA or HRA and can use the funds for your expenses.

2. **Sum of The Months Calculation**. Use this chart if you were not eligible for an HSA for the entire year and were not eligible on December 1 of the year.

   Example. Jim is covered by a self-only HDHP and eligible for an HSA in 2015 but turns 65 on July 2, 2015, and enrolls in Medicare. Jim is no longer eligible for an HSA as of July 1, 2015. For 2015, Jim was eligible for 6 months of the year. The federal HSA limit for Jim is $4,350 ($3,350 single limit plus a $1,000 catch-up). Accordingly, Jim's calculation is 6/12 X $4,350 = $2,175. Jim's maximum contribution for 2014 is $2,175. The chart below assists in the calculation.

	Sum of the Months Contribution Worksheet	Individual	Family
A	Federal Limit (Choose individual or family column based on whether you have self-only or family HDHP coverage.)	$3,300 (2014) $3,350 (2015)	$6,550 (2014) $6,650 (2015)
B	Catch-Up Contribution – Add $1,000 if over 55[1]	$1,000	
C	Add A +B = Total Federal Limit	$4,350	
D	Divide C by 12 = Monthly Contribution Eligibility	$362.50	
E	Insert # of Months you were eligible for an HSA in the Year[2]	6	
F	Multiply D x E = Total Eligible Amount Based on Sum of the Months	$2,175	

[1] If both you and your spouse are age 55 or over, HSA eligible and not enrolled in Medicare, you each get a catch-up contribution. You cannot contribute two catch-up contributions into the same HSA, you must make the contributions into each spouse's respective HSA.

[2] HSA contribution amounts are determined on a monthly basis and then aggregated. To determine how much you may contribute, you must determine the number of months you were covered by a HDHP and otherwise eligible. Count months that you were eligible as of the first day of that month and every day of the month.

Need More Help? You are encouraged to talk to a tax professional, your insurance representative or another professional to help determine your eligibility and contribution amount. IRS Notice 2004-50 and IRS Notice 2004-2 both provide examples and more detail on eligibility; however, some of the contribution questions are outdated.

Employer Comparability Worksheet (Example)

This worksheet is used to illuminate the "comparability" rules for employer contributions = used by employers that are required to treat like employees in a similar fashion

HSA Employer Comparability Worksheet

Purpose: Use this worksheet to gain an understanding of the "comparability" rules for employer contributions. Employers subject to comparability testing (section 1) are required to treat like employees (section 2) similarly (section 3). Employers are responsible for properly determining whether the HSA contributions meet the rules. This worksheet is a tool to aid you in that effort, but it is not advice. If you have any questions, please consult with your tax or legal counsel. See the back of this form for details (p.2).

1 Are You Subject to Comparability Testing?
You are only subject to the comparability rules if you make pre-tax contributions for your employees outside of a Section 125 Cafeteria plan, i.e. If you answer "Yes" to the following questions.

a. Do you offer or plan to offer pre-tax HSA contributions? Yes   No ⟶ Not Subject to HSA

b. Will you make the HSA contributions outside of a Section 125 plan? Yes   No ⟶ Comparability Testing

2 Have You Properly Categorized Employees?
Employers are allowed to treat different "categories" of employees differently for HSAs contributions. See the table below for categories and p. 2 for details on categories. Employers must treat employees within the same category "comparably" – see section 3 below.

Allowed Categories of Employees		Not Allowed Categories - Samples
1. Part time v. Full time	5. Single HDHP coverage v. Family HDHP coverage. Plus categories of Self +1, Self +2, and Self +3 or more Cannot decrease contribution - see back for details	Management employees v. Non-management, but see non-highly compensated employee exception
2. Current v. Former		
3. HSA eligible v. Not eligible	6. Employer provided HDHP v. Other HDHP	Age based
4. Union v. Non-union	7. Non-highly compensated employees – see back!	Wellness plan participation based

3 Are You Making Comparable Contributions?
You must make "comparable" contributions to employees falling within the same categories from Step 2. Special rules for Self+ categories – on back

a. **Amount.** Contributions are "comparable" if they are the same dollar amount (Example 1) or same percentage of the deductible for the HDHP (Example 2). Employers offering multiple plans with multiple deductibles may result in multiple HSA contribution amounts.

b. **Timing.** Employers can pre-fund HSA contributions, fund periodically, or fund at the end of the year. Pre-funding does not result in comparability violations if an employee separates from service. Periodic funding results in employees receiving different contribution amounts based on number of eligible periods (Example 3). Employers may also use a "look back" method (Example 4).

c. **Testing Period.** The testing period is the calendar year.

Example 1 Employer contributes $1,000 on behalf of all employees with individual HDHP coverage. This meets the comparability test.

Example 2 Employer offers two different HDHP plans with different deductibles. Plan A with a $2,000 deductible and Plan B with a $2,500 deductible. The employer can contribute either the same amount to those covered under Plan A and B, say $1,000, or the same percentage of the deductible, for example, $1,000 (50%) for Plan A enrollees and $1,250 (50%) for those in Plan B.

Example 3 Employer contributes $100 per month to each employee who is eligible. In March, Jane quits after receiving $300 to her HSA. Employer stops additional contributions for Jane. In June, Sara begins employment. In July, employer begins contributing $100 per month for Sara and contributes a total of $600. Ted worked for employer the entire year and received $1,200 in HSA contributions. Employer made comparable contributions.

Example 4 Same facts as Example 3, except that the employer waits until the end of the year to contribute rather than on a month-to-month basis. This meets the test. Note: the employer may have to pay employees that left.

35% Penalty for Failure To Comply.
The penalty for failure to comply with the comparability rules is 35% of the *aggregate* HSA contributions by the employer.

Example Consider an employer that wrongly contributed $1,000 to 10 employees and only $500 to another 10 employees. That's a total HSA contribution of $15,000 x 35% = a potential fine of $5,250.

HSA Employer Comparability Worksheet – Additional Detail

This worksheet is based on Final Regulations issued by the Internal Revenue Service (IRS 26 CFR Part 54).

1. **Are You Subject to Comparability Testing?** Employers that do not make employer contributions are not subject to comparability testing.
   a) Section 125 Cafeteria Plan. Employers making contributions through a Section 125 Cafeteria plan are not subject to HSA comparability testing. Section 125 plans; however, have their own non-discrimination testing procedures to ensure you treat employees fairly. Employee pre-tax payroll deferral contributions are considered "employer contributions."
   b) After-Tax Contributions. Employers allowing employees to request that the employer deduct after-tax amounts from the employee's compensation (payroll) and forward these amounts as employee contributions to an HSA are not subject to the comparability rules because the employer is not making employer contributions.
2. **Have You Properly Categorized Employees?** Employers are only allowed to categorize employees in a limited number of methods for the purpose of making different HSA contributions to different categories. Listed below are more details on common categories and whether or not they are permissible categories. Seek professional help for categories not listed or for more detailed questions.
   a) Part-Time Versus Full-Time. Part time employees are customarily employed for fewer than 30 hours per week and full-time employees are customarily employed for 30 or more hours. It is permissible to make different HSA contributions to part-time employees.
   b) Former Employees. An employer is allowed to treat current employees differently than former employees. "Former employees" does not include former employees with coverage under the employer's HDHP because of an election under a COBRA continuation provision. An employer is not required to make comparable contributions to a employee that separated from service with coverage under COBRA. **c) Employer Provided HDHP.** It is permissible for an employer to contribute only to employees that are covered through the employer provided HDHP. Accordingly, the employer would not have to make an HSA contribution to an employee that is an eligible employee but not covered through the employer provided HDHP. However, an employer that contributes to the HSA of any employee who is an eligible individual, regardless of the HDHP coverage, must make comparable contributions to the HSAs of all comparable participating employees, even those with coverage under a non-employer provided HDHP.
   d) Family HDHP and Single HDHP. Employers may treat employees covered under family coverage different than single coverage.
   e) Family HDHP and Self +1, +2 and +3 or More. If the "family" HDHP choice has sub-options, additional rules apply. The sub-options allowed are Self +1, Self +2 and Self +3 or more. If more than one category exists that cover the same number of individuals, all such categories are treated as one for the purpose of comparability testing. An employer may make different HSA contribution amounts to these sub-categories; PROVIDED THAT, the contribution with respect to the self +2 category may not be less than the contribution with respect to the self +1 category and the contribution with respect to the self +3 or more category may not be less than the contribution with respect to the self +2 category. See the regulation for examples.
   f) Collectively Bargained Employees. Collectively bargained employees covered by a bona fide collective bargaining agreement are not subject to the comparability rules provided that health care benefits were the subject of good faith negotiation. This includes the ability to treat separate collective bargaining units differently. See the regulations for more details and examples.
   g) Both Spouses Employees. If the employer makes contributions only to the HSAs of employees who are eligible individuals covered under its HDHP, the employer is not required to contribute to the HSAs of both employee-spouses when both spouses are covered under one spouse's family insurance coverage provided through the employer.
   h) Management Versus Non-Management. This is not a permissible category. If management employees and non-management employees are comparable participating employees, the employer must make comparable contributions to the management and non-management employees. Some employers provide different medical coverage to management and non-management employees. Differentiating based on coverage is permissible. For example, an employer maintains a HDHP for management employees only and not for non-management employees. The employer makes a $1,000 contribution to the HSA of its management employees and no contribution to its non-management employees not covered under its HDHP. The employer meets the comparability rules.
   i) Non-Highly Compensated Employees. An employer is allowed to make larger HSA contributions for non-highly compensated employees than *highly compensated employees*. The definition for highly compensated employee includes any employee (1) who was a 5% owner at any time during the year or the preceding year, or (2) for the preceding year (A) had compensation from the employer in excess of $115,000 (for 2014) or (B) if elected by the employer, was in the group consisting of the top-20 percent of employees ranked based on compensation. For example, an employer may make a $1,000 HSA contribution to each non-highly compensated employee without making a contribution for its highly compensated employees.
   j) Age. An employer is not allowed to discriminate in making HSA contributions based on age. For example, an employer could not add $1,000 to all employees over the age 55 for the catch-up amount.
   k) Independent Contractors. The employer does not need to make contributions on behalf of independent contractors for comparability.
   l) Participation in Wellness Program. An employer is not allowed to categorize employees by employees' participation in health assessments, disease management programs, or wellness programs.
   m) Seasonal Employees. Employers must make comparable contributions to employees that work full-time for less than the entire calendar year. The rules are satisfied if the contribution amount is comparable when determined on a month-to-month basis.
3. **Other Considerations**
   a) Control Group. In some situations, multiple companies are treated as a single employer for comparability testing. The law and IRS regulations require this to prevent companies from circumventing non-discrimination rules by forming multiple corporations. Seek professional help for determining how the control group rules apply. See IRC Section 4980G(b) and 4980E(e), 414(b), (c), (m), and (o).
   b) Sole Proprietor. A sole proprietor may contribute to his or her own HSA without contributing to the HSAs of employees. A sole proprietor is not considered an employee. If a sole proprietor does contribute on behalf of employees, he or she must make comparable contributions; however, contributions that a sole proprietor makes to his or her own HSA are not taken into account.
   c) Partnership. Partners follow the same rule as sole proprietors in that they are not considered employees.
   d) Employee Fails to Open HSA. If an employee fails to establish an HSA at the time the employer funds its employees' HSA, the employer complies with the comparability rules by contributing comparable amounts to the employee's HSA when the employee establishes the HSA (the employee must establish an HSA no later than the end of February in the year after the year of the contribution), taking into account each month that the employee was a participating employee, plus interest.
   e) Medical Savings Accounts. The comparability rules apply separately to employees who have HSAs and employees who have Archer MSAs. If an employee has both an HSA and an MSA, the employer may contribute to either the HSA or the Archer MSA, but not both.

Employer Funding Worksheet (Example)

This worksheet reviews a variety of alternatives for funding high deductible insurance plans (HDHPs) and Health Savings Accounts (HSAs)

Employer HDHP and HSA Funding Guide

Purpose: This form reviews a variety of alternatives for funding high deductible health insurance plans (HDHPs) and Health Savings Accounts (HSAs). Please consult with your tax counsel for assistance in implementing your plan.

Funding of Insurance Premiums

Many employers have elected to share the cost burden of health insurance with their employees. The employer paid portion of insurance premiums is generally deductible by the employer as an employee benefit but, without a cafeteria plan, the employee portion of the insurance cost will have to be paid with after-tax income.

Adding a Section 125 Premium Only Plan (POP). A Premium Only Plan (POP) is a simple, low cost method that allows employees to make insurance payments via pre-tax payroll deferrals.
    Employer Benefit: Employers save payroll taxes on the amounts paid by the employees, typically 7.65% of the amounts paid plus state unemployment taxes (where applicable).
    Employee Benefit: Employee insurance payments through a POP are tax-free, resulting in a savings of roughly 15% to 32% in income taxes (depending on the employee's tax rate) plus 7.65% for payroll taxes (FICA/FUTA).

Funding of Health Savings Accounts

Employers offering High Deductible Health Insurance Plans (HDHPs) also face the choice of whether and how to help their employees with the funding of the employees' Health Savings Account (HSA). The options include:

Option 1 - Employee Funded, After-Tax on Employee's Own

Employers are not required to help with the employees HSAs and may choose not to. In this case, employees may open HSAs on their own and receive the tax deduction on their personal income tax return resulting in savings of about 15-32% depending upon the tax bracket (there is no savings of FICA/FUTA). See the Tax Savings Worksheet to calculate tax savings. This option could include after-tax payroll deferral into an HSA (basically direct deposit to an HSA)

Option 2 - Employee Funded, Pre-Tax Through Payroll Deferral

Employers can help employees fund their HSAs by allowing for HSA contributions via payroll deferral. This is inexpensive and can be accomplished by adding Section 125 plan with an HSA module. The administration is limited because the HSA custodian generally does much of the work.
    Employer Benefit: Employers benefit by not having to pay payroll taxes on the employee's HSA contributions, typically 7.65% of the amounts paid plus state unemployment taxes (where applicable).
    Employee Benefit: Employees save 7.65% on payroll taxes on HSA contributions made through this method (FICA and FUTA are not withheld). Plus, the HSA contribution is also never counted as income, saving approximately 15-32% on income taxes (depending upon state and federal tax brackets and personal income). Note: HSA contributions made outside of payroll are deductible on personal tax returns.

Option 3 - Employer Contributions to an HSA

Employers may make direct contributions to their employees' HSAs without a Section 125 plan however, the contributions must be "comparable" in order to be tax deductible (see our Comparability Worksheet for details).
    Employer Benefit: Employer HSA contributions are tax deductible by the employer as an employee benefit.
    Employee Benefit: Employees receive HSA funds tax-free.

Option 4 - Employer and Employee Pre-tax HSA Contributions through Payroll Deferral

Employers can combine options 2 and 3 (adding a Section 125 POP with an HSA module) allowing themselves and their employees to make tax-free HSA contributions. Employers may contribute some money to the HSAs and the employee can add more through payroll deferral (see our Contribution Worksheet for contribution limits).

Achieving further tax savings -- add a Limited Purpose FSA or HRA to an HSA

To maximize tax benefits for health care expenses, employers can add a limited purpose Flexible Spending Account (FSA) or Healthcare Reimbursement Account (HRA) to an HSA. Generally, FSAs and HRAs are not allowed with HSAs, however, an exception exists for "limited purpose" plans (plans that are limited to payments for preventive care, vision and dental care). This provides more tax savings for employees that need money for dental or vision.

Note: Special rules apply for sole proprietors, partners and most LLC members and shareholders owning more than 2% of an S-corporation. See our Small Business Owners Guide for more detail. We do not provide tax or legal advice.

Examples

Corporation

ABC Corp employs 10 people at an annual payroll cost of $500,000. ABC offers an HDHP with an annual premium of $4,800 per person and offers to pay 50% of the cost of the insurance with employees paying the other 50% of the cost. Subsequent columns assume that the employer has modified the Section 125 plan to allow for employee HSA contributions of $1,500 and limited purpose FSA contributions of $1,000.

	Without POP	With POP	With POP & HSA	With POP, HSA & FSA
Payroll	500,000	$500,000	$500,000	$500,000
Pre-Tax Payroll Deductions				
Insurance Premiums	-	(24,000)	(24,000.00)	(24,000.00)
HSA Contributions	-	-	(15,000.00)	(15,000.00)
FSA Contributions	-	-	-	(10,000.00)
Total	-	(24,000)	(39,000.00)	(49,000.00)
Taxable Payroll	500,000	$476,000	$461,000	$451,000
Payroll Taxes	38,250	36,414	35,267	34,502
Payroll Tax Savings		$1,836	$2,984	$3,749

Employee

Bob, an employee of ABC corp, has an annual salary of $50,000. He is single individual with no exemptions. This example is illustrating his payment for half the insurance premium ($4,800/2 = $2,400) and estimating that he would spend $1,500 on medical related expenses and $1,000 on preventative care, vision and dental expenses.

	Without POP	With POP	With POP & HSA	With POP, HSA & FSA
Annual Salary	50,000	50,000	50,000	50,000
Pre-tax payroll contributions				
Insurance premiums		2,400	2,400	2,400
HSA Contributions			1,500	1,500
FSA Contributions				1,000
Total pre-tax contributions	0	2,400	3,900	4,900
Taxable Income	50,000	47,600	46,100	45,100
After Tax Costs				
Insurance	(2,400)			
Medical Expenses	(1,500)	(1,500)		
Prevent, Vision, Dental	(1,000)	(1,000)	(1,000)	
Estimated Taxes (30.65%[1])	(15,325)	(14,589)	(14,130)	(13,823)
Net Pay - After Expenses	29,775	30,511	30,970	31,277
Savings		736	1,195	1,502

[1] Estimated average tax rates of: 20% Federal, 7.65% FICA and 3% State

HSA/FSA/HRA Comparison Worksheet (Example)

This attachment includes a comparison of Health Savings Accounts, Flexible Spending Accounts, and Healthcare Reimbursement Accounts.

HSA/FSA/HRA Comparison Chart

Purpose: This chart provides a comparison of Health Savings Accounts (HSAs), health Flexible Spending Accounts (FSAs) and Healthcare Reimbursement Accounts (HRAs). All three accounts are used to pay for qualified medical expenses not covered by insurance including: expenses before the deductible is met, co-pays and non-covered medical services (e.g. dental and vision).

Criteria	HSA	FSA	HRA
Overview	Opened with HSA custodian. Requires HDHP coverage and other eligibility rules apply.[1]	Set up through employer and generally requires payroll deferral to fund.	HRAs give employers the most control. Employer must fund.
Contribution Limits	$3,350 self-only for 2015 $6,650 family for 2015 $1,000 catch-up for 2015	$2,500 for years after 2012	No limit.
Who Can Contribute	Employer – Optional Payroll deferral - Optional Employee direct – Optional	Employer – Optional Payroll deferral - Optional Employee direct - Not allowed	Employer – Required Payroll deferral – Not allowed Employee direct – Not allowed
Tax Savings	Employer – deductible[2] Payroll def – tax free +7.65%[3] Employee direct –deductible	Employer – deductible Payroll def – tax free + 7.65%[3] Employee direct – Not allowed	Employer – deductible Payroll def – Not allowed Employee direct – Not allowed
Acct Owner	Employee	Employer	Employer
Earnings Investments	Generally interest paid and investments allowed. Earnings grow tax-free.	No earnings paid.	Generally, no earnings paid.
Qualified Expenses & Distributions	213(d) medical expenses, dental, vision, Medicare and LTC premiums, COBRA (when unemployed), Health premiums at age 65, and may withdraw at any time for any reason (subject to 20% penalty).[4]	213 (d) medical expenses, dental, and vision (health insurance premiums through Section 125). Cannot access for non-medical reasons. See IRS Publication 502 for details.	213(d) medical expenses, dental, vision, Medicare and vision, LTC premiums, health insurance premiums. Cannot access for non-medical reasons. See IRS Publication 502 for details.
Claims Substantiation	Only employee required to maintain supporting records. Employer need not review.	ERISA plan - Employer or Administrator must substantiate expenses.	ERISA plan - Employer or Administrator must substantiate expenses.
Employer Involvement	None Required. Employer may contribute and allow for payroll deferral.	Required. ERISA Plan.	Required. ERISA plan.
Rollover	Yes, funds roll year-to-year.	Maybe, up to $500 per year.	Maybe.
Ability to Use for Multiple Year's Expenses	Yes, can save and use current year's contributions for future year's expenses. May also use future year's contributions to cover current year's expense.	Limited, generally must elect amount prior to the start of the year and then stick with that amount. Limited ability to roll over for future use.	Employers generally allow some rollover for future year's use; however, money may or may not go with employee if the employee changes jobs.

[1] High Deductible Health Plan, See the Eligibility and Contribution Worksheet for details on eligibility
[2] See the Comparability Worksheet and Employer Guide for details.
[3] Both the employer and the employee save payroll taxes (approx. 7.65% for each). The 7.65% reflected in the chart assumes employee savings of FICA at 6.2% (only up to $117,000 for 2014) and an additional 1.45% for Medicare. Add .9% for a Medicare surtax for income above $200,000 for single filers and $250,000 for joint filers.
[4] See the Distribution Worksheet for details.

HSA/FSA/HRA Comparison Chart – Additional Detail

The Comparison Chart and detail below are for illustrative purposes only and should not substitute for legal or tax advice. This worksheet does not provide tax or legal advice.

What are HSAs, FSAs and HRAs? Health Savings Accounts (HSAs), Flexible Spending Accounts (FSAs) and Health Care Reimbursement (HRAs) are accounts some employers choose to offer to employees usually in conjunction with health insurance coverage. The common thread between these accounts is that they all provide tax advantages to pay for medical expenses and all three give employees some control over a portion of their health care dollars.

- **What is an HSA?** A unique aspect of HSAs versus FSAs and HRAs is that a person must be eligible for an HSA. One key eligibility rule is that an employee must be covered by a High Deductible Health Plan ("HDHP") in order to fund an HSA. Also unlike an FSA or HRA, an HSA is an individual custodial account that is owned by the individual rather than the employer. That legal ownership is significant because it allows employees to use that money as they see fit: spending it on eligible health care expenses, saving it for the future, or even spending it on consumer goods (penalties apply). The fact that the account belongs to the employee also removes many of the compliance and administration requirements from the employer. HSA programs are generally not ERISA plans. For example, with HSAs the employer is not required to review medical receipts.
- **What is an FSA?** An FSA is an account established as part of a Section 125 Cafeteria plan that allows employees to defer a portion of their income to pay for medical expenses on a tax-free basis. FSAs are a popular employee benefit in large part because of the tax benefits and because FSAs work well with a traditional health plan. The employer owns the account and is responsible for its management, including paying claims as they occur (often this is accomplished by hiring an outside administrator). Money left over at the end of the year (or period) reverts back to the employer and not the employee. A 2013 IRS ruling provides that employers can choose to allow employees to rollover up to $500 a year. One benefit of FSAs for employees is that the full amount of the employee's deferral is available for use at the beginning of the year. Limited purpose FSAs may be offered in conjunction with HSAs.
- **What is an HRA?** An HRA is an employer provided account that allows employees to direct a portion of their health care spending. The employer contributes funds to the employees HRA account and the employee can spend the funds on eligible health care expenses. HRAs work very similar to an FSA and HSA with one key difference being they do not allow for payroll deferral. An advantage of HRAs is their flexibility as they allow for a variety of different designs. For instance, an HRA may allow employee funds to rollover year after year and grow for future use; however, the HRA belongs to the employer. Any remaining funds generally belong to the employer when the employee separates from service (although even this feature is flexible). With an HRA, the employer is also responsible for compliance and administration (often accomplished by hiring an outside administrator). HRAs give employers the most flexibility in plan design and that flexibility may aid in developing an overall benefits package that best suits that group.

Which plan is best? Although there is no simple answer to this question, some points to consider are covered below.
- **HSA.** An HSA generally works well for employers that want to minimize administration and compliance issues. Also, employers seeking to minimize their costs and involvement often offer HSAs because the employer does not have to fund any portion of the account (FSAs offer this too). Employers desiring to offer the most flexible solution for employees are often drawn to the HSA as it is the only one that allows for portability, the opportunity for significant investment growth, and the distribution of funds for non-medical reasons (including for any purpose at age 65 without penalty). Employees may prefer HSAs to FSAs because the funds belong to them so they do not need to worry about being as precise in estimating their medical expenses. This is especially important given that employees with HSAs are covered under High Deductible Health Plans where it is more difficult to accurately estimate expenses. The HSA contribution limits are higher than FSAs and HSAs offer more distribution reasons.
- **FSA.** Employers offering traditional health care plans often prefer FSAs partly because HSAs are not an option. A traditional health plan limits out-of-pocket expenses so that the limited ability to rollover funds is less important. FSAs allow employees to defer extra income into the FSA to pay for co-pays, medical bills not covered by insurance, as well as dental and vision care. One significant employer benefit of FSAs over HSAs from the employer's perspective is that the employer gets to keep unspent money at the end of the year.
- **HRA.** HRAs are generally offered by employers that self-insure all or a portion of their health care or otherwise desire a lot of flexibility in plan design. The HRA provides a method for self-insuring employers to put in consumer-directed efforts to reduce overall health care costs and increase employee satisfaction at the same time. HRAs are more complicated to administer than HSAs. A key limitation of HRAs is that only the employer can fund the HRA.

Are HSAs, FSAs, and HRAs taxed the same? Basically all three types of plans enjoy tax-free treatment for health care expenses. How each of them arrive at this is a bit more complex. HSAs are deductible by the employer when made by the employer as a "comparable" contribution or when made by the employees through a section 125 plan. In both cases the contribution will not show as income on the employee's income tax return. Individuals may also contribute directly to an HSA and deduct the amount on their income tax return. FSA and HRA expenses are deductible by the employer and not reported as income to the employee.

IRA to HSA Worksheet (Example)

This worksheet explains the special rules for moving funds from an IRA to an HSA

IRA to HSA Worksheet

Purpose: Use this Worksheet to gain a better understanding of the special rules for moving funds from an Individual Retirement Account (IRA) into a Health Savings Account (HSA). Please see IRS Notice 2008-51 for additional information. We do not provide tax or legal advice. Please seek tax or legal advice from your own tax or legal advisors.

IRA to HSA Overview. The law allows you to move money from your IRA into your HSA and avoid the taxation and penalties generally associated with early withdrawals from an IRA. HSA owners face a potentially troubling issue of large medical expenses without the funds to pay for it. Allowing HSA owners to access their IRA funds provides another option to fund the HSA. This option; however, is limited by the rules discussed below and on page 2.

1 Are You Eligible for an IRA to HSA Contribution?

A. Are you eligible for an HSA?[1] Yes No
B. You have <u>not</u> already moved an IRA to an HSA?[2] Yes No
C. You have an IRA?[3] Yes No

Eligible*

*You must answer all questions "Yes" to be eligible.

Not Eligible

Footnotes

[1] You must be eligible for an HSA to move money from an IRA to an HSA. Please see the HSA Eligibility and Contribution Worksheet to determine your HSA eligibility.

[2] You are only allowed to do an IRA to HSA qualified funding distribution once-in-a-lifetime. See "change in HDHP status" in the next step for an exception and see p.2 for additional details.

[3] You can only move money from a traditional or Roth IRA and in some cases a SEP or SIMPLE IRA into an HSA. You <u>cannot</u> move funds directly from a 401(k) to an HSA. See p.2 for details.

2 How Much of the IRA Can You Move to the HSA? See definitions and examples on page 2 for help.

A. **Federal HSA Limits Apply.** You cannot contribute more than the applicable HSA federal limit: $3,350 for individuals in 2015 and $6,650 for family HDHP coverage in 2015 plus a catch up of $1,000 if you are over age 55. You can contribute any amount up to the applicable federal HSA limit for the year taking into account the paragraphs immediately below. See HSA Eligibility and Contribution Worksheet for details on your eligible amount.

B. **IRA to HSA Contribution Counts Against Federal Limit.** Your IRA to HSA contribution counts against the applicable federal limit. All of the following types of contributions count against the HSA federal limit: IRA to HSA funding, employer HSA contributions, payroll deferral HSA contributions and regular HSA contributions.

C. **Change in HDHP Status.** If your status changes from self-only HDHP coverage to family HDHP coverage during the year of the contribution, you may be able to move additional funds from your IRA to your HSA. See page 2 for details.

3 What Are the Tax Ramifications? See additional tax issues on p.2 – plus consult with your tax advisor.

A. **HSA Treatment - Not Deductible.** IRA to HSA contributions are not tax deductible as an HSA contribution.

B. **IRA Treatment - Not Taxable.** A qualified HSA funding distribution from an IRA enjoys an exception to the normal rule that IRA distributions are subject to tax and possibly a 10% penalty. The law allows for the basis (after-tax dollars) to remain in the IRA to the extent that such amount does not exceed the aggregate amount which would have been so included if there were a total distribution from the IRA or Roth IRA owner's accounts. Basis is an important, but confusing, tax concept - See p. 2 for details.

C. **Testing Period.** You will be subject to a testing period if you complete an IRA to HSA qualified funding distribution. If you fail to maintain your HSA eligibility for the testing period, taxes and penalties apply. See p.2 for details.

4 How Do I Move My IRA to My HSA?

The IRA to HSA funding must be done as a "direct transfer." That means the IRA assets must move directly to the HSA and cannot be paid to the IRA owner. A common approach is for you to request and complete a "transfer form" from your HSA provider. The HSA provider forwards the form to the IRA provider. The IRA provider then writes a check directly to the HSA provider for the benefit of the HSA owner and sends the check directly to the HSA provider. The rules permit the IRA/HSA owner to hand carry a check made payable to the HSA custodian or trustee.

IRA to HSA – Definitions and Additional Detail

1. **Additional Background.** The IRA to HSA direct transfer (qualified HSA funding distribution) allows you to fund your HSA with your IRA. Generally, distributions from an IRA are subject to taxation plus a 10% penalty if you fail to meet a qualified distribution reason (age 59 ½, death, disability, etc.). The taxes and penalties do not apply to HSA to IRA qualified funding distributions that meet the requirements. The IRS refers to the process of moving funds from an IRA to an HSA as a trustee-to-trustee "direct transfer" and it refers to the distribution from an IRA for use in funding an HSA as a "qualified HSA funding distribution" from the IRA.

2. **Types of IRAs Permitted for HSA Funding.** A qualified HSA funding distribution may be made from a traditional IRA or a Roth IRA, but not from an ongoing SIMPLE IRA or a SEP IRA. A SEP or a SIMPLE is considered ongoing if an employer contribution is made for the plan year ending with or within the IRA owner's taxable year in which the qualified HSA funding distribution would be made. You cannot move money directly from a 401(k) into an HSA; however, you may be able to move the money from a 401k to an IRA and then to an HSA. You also cannot use your spouse's or someone else's IRA. But see "inherited IRAs."

3. **Inherited IRAs.** After the death of an IRA or Roth IRA owner, a qualified HSA funding distribution may be made from an IRA or Roth IRA maintained for the benefit of an IRA or Roth IRA beneficiary. This distribution will be taken into account in determining whether the required minimum distribution has been satisfied from the IRA.

4. **Once Per Lifetime Rule.** Generally only one qualified HSA funding distribution is allowed during your lifetime. An exception exists if you changed your HDHP status from single to family during the same taxable year – see paragraph 6 below.

5. **Multiple IRAs.** If you own two or more IRAs, and want to use amounts in multiple IRAs to fund your HSA, you must first consolidate the IRAs into a single IRA, and then make the one-time qualified HSA funding distribution from that IRA.

6. **Change from Single HDHP Coverage to Family HDHP Coverage.** You are allowed a second qualified HSA funding distribution if you change your HDHP status from single coverage to family coverage in the same taxable year. Both distributions count against your maximum HSA contribution for that taxable year. For example, Jim enrolls in self-only HDHP coverage on July 1, 2015. Jim completes a qualified funding distribution from his IRA to his HSA in the amount of $3,350 to fund the HSA. On September 1, 2015, Jim switches insurance to a family HDHP. Jim may do a second IRA to HSA funding distribution prior to the end of the year in an amount up to $3,350 ($6,650 family federal maximum - $3,300 already contributed in the first IRA to HSA transaction). Jim would have two different testing periods for the two separate IRA to HSA transactions. See paragraph 9 below.

7. **Change from Family HDHP Coverage to Single HDHP Coverage.** You are not eligible to do a second IRA to HSA funding transaction if you change from family HDHP coverage to single HDHP coverage. However, you also do not need to adjust your contribution, taxes or penalties provided you meet your testing period. For example, assume you enroll in a family HDHP on January 1, 2015 and remain eligible for an HSA through March 31, 2015. On March 18, 2015 you complete an IRA to HSA direct transfer of $6,650. On June 1, 2015, you change your family HDHP to a single HDHP policy. The $6,650 IRA to HSA direct transfer met the maximum limit at the time of the transfer and is permissible because you met (or will meet) the testing period.

8. **Two IRA to HSA Direct Transfers In Violation of Once-in-Lifetime Rule.** If you complete two IRA to HSA transactions and do not meet the exception for change in status discussed above, your second IRA to HSA transfer is not a qualified HSA funding distribution and will be included in gross income and subject to the additional tax for early withdrawals from an IRA. The treatment from an HSA perspective depends upon whether the federal HSA limit was exceeded. If not, the amount is deductible as an HSA contribution. If exceeded, the amount is treated as an excess contribution to the HSA.

9. **Testing Period.** If you complete an IRA to HSA direct transfer you are subject to a testing period. You must maintain your HSA eligibility for the testing period. The testing period begins with the month in which the qualified HSA funding distribution is contributed to the HSA and ends on the last day of the 12th month following that month. Each qualified funding distribution allowed has a separate testing period. If at any time during the testing period, you cease to be eligible for the HSA, the amount of the IRA to HSA distribution is included in income for the taxable year in which you first failed to be an eligible individual. Plus, you will face an additional penalty tax, unless the failure to meet the testing period is due to death or disability. Please see the HSA Testing Period Worksheet for additional details.

10. **IRA to HSA Attributable to Year Actually Made.** A qualified HSA funding distribution relates to the taxable year in which the distribution is actually made. You cannot complete an IRA to HSA direct transfer for the previous year.

11. **Basis Recovery Rules for Roth and Nondeductible IRAs.** This rule allows for an IRA owner to protect her non-deductible basis in a traditional IRA or Roth IRA to the extent possible by allowing for basis to remain with the IRA and to transfer the taxable portion to the HSA. For example, suppose an individual who has $200 of basis in an IRA with a fair market value of $2,000 makes a qualified HSA funding distribution of $1,500, the individual retains $200 of basis in an IRA that has a fair market value of $500. If a qualified funding distribution from an individual's IRA or Roth IRA exceeds the aggregate amount which would have been included in gross income if there were a total distribution from that individual's IRA or Roth IRA account, the basis does not carry over to the HSA. Assume the same facts as the previous example, except that the individual directly transferred all $2,000 from the IRA to the HSA. The $200 of basis is lost in the IRA because the IRA is empty and the basis does not transfer to the HSA. You cannot maintain basis in an HSA. Get tax advice if you plan to move Roth or nondeductible IRA assets to an HSA.

12. **IRA to HSA Contribution More than Federal HSA Limits.** Special rules apply if you move more than the federal HSA limits from your IRA to your HSA. For example, assume you have a family HDHP and are eligible for an HSA contribution of $6,650 (2015). You transfer $10,000 from your IRA to your HSA. The $3,350 ($10,000-$6,650) does not enjoy the benefit of the tax-free penalty-free withdrawal rules from the IRA and will be subject to taxes and penalties on the IRA distribution. Additionally, the $3,350 is also subject to the taxes and penalties from the HSA for exceeding the federal HSA limits unless corrected. Seek professional guidance if you are in this situation.

13. **IRA Substantially Equal Period Payments.** If the qualified IRA to HSA funding distribution results in a modification of a series of substantially equal periodic payments that, prior to the modification, qualified as an exception to the early distribution penalty for IRAs, then the recapture tax applies to the payments made before the date of the qualified HSA funding distribution if you complete the IRA to HSA transfer. If you are currently taking substantially equal period payments from your IRA seek professional guidance before taking a qualified HSA funding distribution from your IRA because of the potentially serious adverse tax impact.

14. **FSA/HRA Direct Transfers to HSA.** This Worksheet is not intended for individuals moving money from a Flexible Spending Account (FSA) or Healthcare Reimbursement Account (HRA). The rules for FSA or HRA direct transfers are complex and very different than the rules for IRA to HSA. FSA/HRA direct transfers are no longer allowed.

Qualified Medical Expenses Listing (Example)

This attachment serves has a guide to help determine if a medical expense is a qualified expense for an HSA distribution

Qualified Medical Expenses List

Use these three lists as a guide to help you determine whether a medical expense is qualified or not for an HSA distribution. Your particular factual situation may impact the answer. You ultimately decide whether an expense is qualified or not. Please consult with your tax or legal counsel. We do not provide tax or legal advice.

The following items are qualified medical expenses and may be paid for using your HSA:

- Ambulance
- Annual Physical
- Artificial Limb
- Artificial Teeth
- Nursing Home (for medical care)
- Thermometers
- Abortion
- Acupuncture
- Bandages
- Birth Control Pills
- Blood Pressure Monitor
- Blood Sugar Test Kit
- Blood Tests
- Body Scan
- Body Scan
- Braille Books
- Breast Pump/Supplies
- Breast Reconstruction
- Christian Science (fees to
- practitioners for care)
- Cold/Hot Pack for medical care
- Condoms
- Contact Lenses and supplies
- Contraceptives
- Crutches
- Dental Treatment
- Dentures and cleaners
- Dermatologist
- Diabetic Supplies
- Diagnostic Devices
- Doctor's Fees not covered by insurance
- Drug Addiction (inpatient treatment)
- Drugs (with prescription)
- Eye Exam
- Eye Surgery
- (including laser eye surgery)
- Eyeglasses
- Fertility Enhancement
- First Aid Supplies
- Flu Shot
- Guide Dog (incl. maintenance costs - food, vets, etc....)
- Gynecologist
- Hearing Aids (incl. batteries and repair)
- Homeopathic Care
- Immunizations
- Laboratory Fees
- Lactation Expenses (see breast pump)
- Medical Alert Bracelet
- Operations (non cosmetic)
- Optometrist
- Orthopedist
- Orthotic Inserts
- Osteopath
- Out-of-Network
- Oxygen for medical condition
- Physical Examination
- Pregnancy Test Kit
- Prosthesis
- Psychiatric Care
- Psychoanalysis
- Psychologist
- Splints
- Sterilization
- Surgery (non-cosmetic)
- Therapy.
- Vasectomy
- Vision Surgery
- Wheelchair
- X-Ray

The following items are NOT qualified medical expenses

- Baby Sitting
- Bottled Water
- Controlled Substances
- Cosmetic Surgery
- Cosmetics
- CPR Class
- Dancing Lessons
- Dental Floss
- Diaper Service
- Diet Foods
- Electrolysis Hair Rem.
- Exercise Equip.
- Facial Tissues
- Finance Charge
- Funeral Expenses
- Funeral Expenses
- Health Club Dues
- Household Help
- Illegal Treatments
- Marijuana
- Maternity Clothes
- Medigap Premiums
- Personal Use Items
- Swimming Lessons
- Teeth Whitening
- Veterinary Fees

Qualified Medical Expenses List

Items that may be considered qualified medical expenses or may be subject further limitations

• Acne Treatment	Prescription required if medicine. Doctor visit covered.
• Airfare	See Transpiration in IRS Pub 502.
• Alcoholism	Inpatient treatment for addiction. Transportation to AA meetings.
• Allergy Medicines	Prescription required.
• Allergy Products	Medical need. Excess cost over normal product only.
• Alternative Medicine	Must be treating a specific medical condition.
• Antacids	Must get prescription.
• Aspirin	Must get prescription.
• Asthma Medicines	Must get prescription.
• Blood Storage	Temporary storage for known procedure likely applies.
• Car - Modifications	The extra cost to make car accessible if medically necessary.
• Carpal Tunnel Brace	Wrist brace.
• COBRA Premiums	See IRS Pub 969 for limiting rules.
• Cold Medicines	Must get prescription.
• Counseling	Covered for medical purposes: psychological, etc.
• Ergonomic Chair	Must be doctor recommended. Only increased cost allowed.
• Health Institute	If prescribed by a doctor with statement of necessity.
• Homeopathic Medicine	If used to treat specific illness.
• Humidifier	If used to treat specific illness. Doctor Rec.
• Imported Medicines	Must be legally imported.
• Insurance Premiums	See IRS Pub 969.
• Legal Fees	If necessary to authorize treatment for mental illness. Limited.
• Lodging	Many rules and limitations apply - see IRS Pub 502.
• Long-term Care Ins.	Dollar limits apply (see IRS Pub 969 for details)
• Mattress	Not likely. If medically necessary and only cost difference - see capital.
• Meals	In hospital. Very limited.
• Medical Conference	If conference concerns chronic illness. Limited.
• Medical Information Plan	Plan to keep medical information available.
• Medicare Premiums	If over 65 - see IRS Pub 969 for details.
• Medicines	If prescribed.
• Nonprescription Drugs	Must get prescription.
• Nursing Services	Medical services only - see IRS Pub 502 for details.
• Nutritional Supp.	No, unless practitioner recommended for specific condition.
• Orthopedic Shoes	Medically necessary and only extra cost can be paid from HSA.
• Sleep Aids	Prescription required.
• Smoking Cessation Program	Classes. Nicotine gum or patches require prescription.
• Special Home	Intellectually and developmentally disabled if necessary.
• Sunglasses	Prescription glasses only.
• Telephone	If necessary for hearing disability.
• Television	If necessary, pay for the part that displays the audio (subtitles)
• Transplants	See IRS Pub 502 for details.
• Transportation	See IRS Pub 502 for details.
• Trips	See IRS Pub 502 for details.
• Weight-Loss Program	See IRS Pub 502 for details.
• Wig	If physician advised after disease caused hair loss.

Small Business Owners Worksheet (Example)

This attachment helps identify some of the tax issues for health insurance and HSAs for small business owners, including sole proprietors, partners, LLCs and greater than two percent shareholders of S-Corporations

Small Business Owner
HSA Contribution Guide

Purpose: This Guide identifies some of the tax issues of health insurance and Health Savings Accounts (HSAs) for Small Business *Owners*: sole proprietors, partners, LLC members and >2% shareholders of S-Corporations. A separate Employer Funding Guide covers HSA contribution issues for employees and a separate Small Business Guide covers issues for small business owners. Please consult with your tax or legal counsel. This is not tax or legal advice.

Overview
HSA contributions and health insurance payments for employees are usually deductible expenses for most businesses however, HSA contributions and Health Insurance payments made on behalf of Small Business Owners are subject to different rules. Further, the specific treatment varies depending on the particular form of organization; sole proprietorship, LLC, partnership or S-corporation. A high level overview of the treatment for each organization is discussed further below.

Sole Proprietors
Sole proprietors are treated similarly to individuals making HSA contributions on their own, the sole proprietor may deduct the amount of their HSA contributions and health insurance payments on their personal income tax. Sole proprietors are not allowed to deduct their own HSA contributions as a business expense; however, amounts contributed on behalf of employees may be deductible on their Schedule C. The owners HSA contribution is not a deduction attributable to the self-employed individual's trade or business so it is not taken as a deduction on Schedule C, nor is it taken into account in determining net earnings from self-employment on Schedule SE.

Partnerships, LLC's and S-Corporations
Partnerships, LLC's and S-corporations are generally treated as flow through entities for purpose of HSA contributions made on behalf of the owners. That is, HSA contributions and health insurance payments benefiting the owners are not deductible by the business but flow through to the owner.

Partnerships and multiple member LLCs[2,3] Contributions on behalf of partners by the partnership are treated as distributions to the partners (under §731), they are not deductible by the partnership and do not affect the distributive shares of partnership income and deductions. The contributions are reported as distributions of money on Schedule K-1 and the partner can then take a deduction for the HSA contribution on their personal income tax return. Contributions made pursuant to a Section 125 plan will be added back to the owners as a taxable fringe benefit negating any tax benefit they might have otherwise received from a Section 125 plans.

Note – an exception exists for Guaranteed Payments[4] to partners, if the partner is entitled to a Guaranteed Payment from the partnership, then a special rule applies. The HSA contributions are still not treated the same as contributions to other employees. These contributions are deductible by the partnership (under IRC §162) and are includable in the partner's gross income. The contribution is also reported as a Guaranteed Payment on the K-1. The partner can then deduct the HSA contribution on his or her personal income tax return.

>2% shareholders of S-corporations – anyone that owns more than 2% of an S-corporation is regarded as an owner of the corporation with regards to HSA contributions. This means the rules above under partnership apply to employer HSA contributions to anyone owning 2% or more of an S-corporation. Plus, they can not make pre-tax contributions to their HSA via a salary reduction. Any contributions made on their behalf by the corporation are taxable and they may be deducted on their personal income tax.

Notes:
1. LLC tax treatment varies state by state, check with your tax counsel for determination of the treatment that applies in your state.
2. Single member LLCs are treated the same as sole proprietors.
3. Does not include multiple member LLCs that have elected to be treated as a corporation.
4. Guaranteed Payments as defined in section 707(c) include contributions by a partnership to a partner's HSA for services rendered to the partnership (See IRS Notice 2005-8 Q&A 2 for further details). Guaranteed payments to partners are reported on the partner's K-1, are not excludible from the partner's gross income and HSA contributions of eligible individuals may be deducted from the partner's personal income tax return.

Sole Proprietor - Example

J's Pizzeria is a sole proprietorship with 5 employees. This year Jay, the owner, decided to pay $2,500 towards the insurance costs of himself and each of employees as well as up $2,000 towards everyone's HSA (for eligible individuals).

The contributions that Jay makes for his own expenses are included on his Form 1040 in the Adjusted Gross Income Section (see Form 1040 example). Note: self-employed health insurance deductions may be limited based on net income, see the IRS' Self-Employed Health Insurance Deduction Worksheet for further details.

The contributions that Jay makes on behalf of his employees are included in Jay's Schedule C Line 14, Employee benefit programs (see Schedule C example). In this case Jay would have $12,500 in employee related insurance expenses and $10,000 in HSA contributions for a total $22,500.

Form 1040

Adjusted Gross Income	23	Educator expenses (see page 29)	23	
	24	Certain business expenses of reservists, performing artists, and fee-basis government officials. Attach Form 2106 or 2106-EZ	24	2,000
	26	Moving expenses. Attach Form 3903	26	
	27	One-half of self-employment tax. Attach Schedule SE	27	
	28	Self-employed SEP, SIMPLE, and qualified plans	28	2,500
	30	Penalty on early withdrawal of savings	30	
	31a	Alimony paid b Recipient's SSN ▶	31a	
	32	IRA deduction (see page 31)	32	
	33	Student loan interest deduction (see page 33)	33	
	34	Tuition and fees deduction (see page 34)	34	
	35	Domestic production activities deduction. Attach Form 8903	35	
	36	Add lines 23 through 31a and 32 through 35		

Schedule C
(Form 1040)

	37	Subtract line		Part II	Expenses. Enter expenses for business use of y...		
		8	Advertising			8	
		9	Car and truck expenses (see page C-3)			9	
		10	Commissions and fees			10	
		11	Contract labor (see page C-4)			11	
		12	Depletion			12	
		13	Depreciation and section 179 expense deduction (not included in Part III) (see page C-6			13	
		15	Insurance (other than health)			15	22,500
		16	Interest				
		a	Mortgage (paid to banks, etc)			16a	
		b	Other			16b	
		17	Legal and professional services			17	

Partnership - Example

Bob's Copy Shop is a partnership with 2 employees. A and B, are equal partners in the business. This year Bob's decided to contribute $1,500 towards everyone's insurance plus $500 towards everyone's HSA.

The implications of offering the benefits to the employees are covered our Employer Funding Guide.

The contributions by the partnership to the partner's HSA are not treated as contributions by the partnership to an employee so they are not deductible by the partnership. Instead the contributions are treated as distributions to the partner (shown on Line 19 to the right), not affecting distributive shares of the partnership income which may then be carried forward as a deduction on the partner's individual income tax. The payments for health insurance would be shown on as a deduction for health insurance (shown on Line 13 to the right).

Schedule K-1 (For Partner A)

Part III	Partner's Share of Current Year Income, Deductions, Credits, and Other Items		
1	Ordinary business income (loss)	15	Credits & credit recapture
2	Net rental real estate income (loss)		
3	Other net rental income (loss)		
4	Guaranteed payments		
5	Interest income	16	Foreign transactions
6a	Ordinary dividends		
6b	Qualified dividends		
7	Royalties		
8	Net short-term capital gain (loss)		
9a	Net long-term capital gain (loss)		
9b	Collectibles (28%) gain (loss)		
9c	Unrecaptured section 1250 gain	17	Alternative minimum tax (AMT) items
10	Net section 1231 gain (loss)		
11	Other income (loss)		
		18	Tax-exempt income and nondeductible expenses
12	Section 179 deduction		
13	Other deductions M 1,500	19	Distributions A 500
14	Self-employment earnings (loss)	20	Other information

13. Other deductions
A Cash contributions (50%)   See Partner's Instr. (Form 1065)
B Cash contributions (30%)   See Partner's Instr. (Form 1065)
C Noncash contributions (50%)   See Partner's Instr. (Form 1065)
D Noncash contributions (30%)   See Partner's Instr. (Form 1065)
E Capital gain property to a 50% organization (30%)   See Partner's Instr. (Form 1065)
F Capital gain property (20%)   See Partner's Instr. (Form 1065)
G Cash Contributions (100%)   See Partner's Instr. (Form 1065)
H Investment interest expense   Form 4952, line 1
I Deductions—royalty income   Schedule E, line 18
J Section 59(e)(2) expenditures   See Partner's Instr. (Form 1065)
K Deductions—portfolio (2% floor)   Schedule A, line 22
L Deductions—portfolio (other)   Schedule A, line 27
M Amounts paid for medical insurance   Schedule A, line 1 or Form 1040, line 29
N Educational assistance benefits   See Partner's Instr. (Form 1065)
O Dependent care benefits   Form 2441, line 12
P Preproductive period expenses   See Partner's Instr. (Form 1065)
Q Commercial revitalization deduction from rental real estate activities   See Form 8582 Instructions
R Pensions and IRAs   See Partner's Instr. (Form 1065)
S Reforestation expense deduction   See Partner's Instr. (Form 1065)
T Domestic production activities information   See Form 8903 instructions
U Qualified production activities income   Form 8903, line 7
V Employer's W-2 wages   Form 8903, line 18
W Other deductions   See Partner's Instr. (Form 1065)

19. Distributions
A Cash and marketable securities
B Other property

©HSA Authority, LLC 2008 Small Business Owners Guide 2/10/08

Tax Savings Worksheet (Example)

This worksheet provides an estimate of your tax savings if you contribute to an HSA

HSA Tax Savings Worksheet

Purpose: This worksheet provides you an estimate of your tax savings if you contribute to an HSA. You are responsible for understanding your tax situation and you should consult with your tax or legal counsel for specific questions.

1 Income and Payroll Tax Savings. Your HSA contribution may be eligible for federal and state tax savings.
Complete the chart to estimate your tax savings.

A. HSA Contribution Amount – Enter the amount you intend to contribute to your HSA on line A. Use our Eligibility and Contribution Worksheet to determine your maximum amount.

B. Federal Tax Rate – Use the Federal Tax Table below to determine your marginal Federal tax rate based on your "taxable" income and enter it on line B (see p. 2 of this form for additional details).

2014 Federal Tax Table

Single	Married Filing Jointly	Marginal Tax Rate
$0 – $9,075	$0 - $18,150	10%
$9,075 - $36,900	$18,150 - $73,800	15%
$36,900 - $89,350	$73,800 - $148,850	25%
$89,350 - $186,350	$148,850 - $226,850	28%
$186,350 - $405,100	$226,850 - $405,100	33%
$405,100 - $406,750	$405,100 - $457,600	35%
$406,750+	$457,600+	39.6%

HSA Tax Savings Calculator

	A	HSA Contribution Amount	
Federal Income Savings	B	Federal Income Tax Rate	
	C	Estimated Federal Income Tax Savings (Multiply A x B)	
State Income Savings	D	State Income Tax Rate	
	E	Estimated State Income Tax Savings (Multiply A x D)	
Payroll Taxes Savings	F	Payroll Tax Savings, if applicable (7.65%)	
	G	Estimated Payroll Tax Savings (Multiply all or part of A x F)	
	H	Estimated Income Tax Savings (Add C + E + G)	

C. Federal Tax Savings – Multiply your HSA contribution, line A, by your federal tax rate, line B, and enter the result on line C.

D. State Tax Bracket – You may also be eligible for an HSA state income tax deduction. If your state has an income tax and allows you to deduct your HSA contribution, then enter your personal state tax bracket on line D. Most states with income taxes provide the same tax break for HSA contributions that the federal government allows. However, some states (e.g., AL, CA, & NJ) do not provide an income tax deduction for HSAs, please check with your tax advisor to obtain the most current information.

E. State Tax Savings – Multiply your HSA contribution, line A, by your state tax rate, line D, and enter the result on line E.

F. Payroll Tax (FICA and FUTA) – Most people will enter 7.65% (.0765) on this line. The 7.65% assumes employee savings of 6.2% for Social Security (only up to $117,000 for 2014) and an additional 1.45% for Medicare. Add .9% for a Medicare surtax for income above $200,000 for single filers and $250,000 for joint filers. Employers also save payroll taxes for these HSA contributions. You may also save unemployment taxes (SUTA and FUTA).

G. Payroll Tax Savings – If your employer makes pre-tax HSA contributions (comparable contributions) on your behalf or if your employer allows pre-tax payroll deferral to an HSA through a Section 125 plan, these HSA contributions are not subject to payroll taxes. Multiple the amount of your HSA Contribution from line A that meets this description by the percentage in Line F.

H. Total Income Tax Savings – Add the federal savings, line C; the state savings, line E; and the payroll tax savings, line G; to get an estimate of your total tax savings for your HSA contribution.

Additional Tax Savings - Earnings on HSA assets grow tax-free while held in the HSA. This works similar to investments in other tax-deferred plans, such as 401k or IRA plans with the added bonus of tax-free withdrawals for qualified medical expenses.

2 How To Take Your HSA Federal Tax Deduction. Either your HSA contribution is never counted
as income to you or you may deduct your eligible HSA contribution directly on your tax return.

A. Employer HSA Contributions (Pre-Tax).
Pre-tax employer contributions (including pre-tax payroll deferral) are never considered as income to you so you automatically get the tax benefits. See box 12 of your W-2 and look for Code W for HSA contributions. You must still file Form 8889.

B. Personal HSA Contributions.
HSA contributions you make outside of your tax return. See line 25 of the IRS Form 1040. You do not have to itemize your taxes to receive this benefit and no income limits apply.

Form 1040 Department of the Treasury—Internal Revenue Service (99)
U.S. Individual Income Tax Return

| Adjusted Gross Income | 24 | Certain business expenses of reservists, performing artists, and fee-basis government officials. Attach Form 2106 or 2106-EZ | 24 | |
| | 25 | Health savings account deduction. Attach Form 8889. 25 | | |

HSA Tax Savings
Federal Tables & Chart

Below are two charts: (1) a 2014 Federal Tax Table and (2) a HSA Tax Savings table published by the U.S. Treasury to guide you in determining your HSA tax savings from a federal income tax perspective. The U.S. Treasury table gives you another method to estimate your Federal income tax savings from an HSA contribution (the U.S. Treasury has not updated the table).

1 Tax Table - Notes

This tax table includes married filing separate and head of household in addition to single and joint on the previous page.
Please note: your "taxable" income is reduced by the amount of your HSA contribution. Accordingly, if your HSA contribution amount reduces your tax rate, your tax savings are also reduced. If your taxable income is near one of the tax rate thresholds then your tax savings may require the use of two tax rates to determine your actual savings. This Worksheet

		2014 Federal Tax Table			
	Single	Married Filing Jointly	Married Filing Separately	Head of Household	Marginal Tax Rate
	$0 – $9,075	$0 - $18,150	$0 – $9,075	$0 - $12,950	10%
	$9,075 - $36,900	$18,150 - $73,800	$9,075 - $36,900	$12,950 - $49,400	15%
	$36,900 - $89,350	$73,800 - $148,850	$36,900 - $74,425	$49,400 - $127,550	25%
	$89,350 - $186,350	$148,850 - $226,850	$74,425 - $113,425	$127,550 - $206,600	28%
	$186,350 - $405,100	$226,850 - $405,100	$113,425 - $202,550	$206,600 - $405,100	33%
	$405,100 - $406,750	$405,100 - $457,600	$202,550 - $228,800	$405,100 - $432,200	35%
	$406,750+	$457,600+	$228,800+	$432,200+	39.6%

does not provide for that instance. Use this Worksheet only to estimate your tax savings. Your actual tax savings may vary. Table 2 below gives you another method to estimate your Federal Tax savings. If you use both estimating tools, you should achieve a representative estimate of your tax savings.

2 US Treasury Table

US Government Prepared Table Reflects Tax Rates Government Has Not Updated for Recent Years

Reduction in Federal Income Tax from HSA Contributions in 2007
Illustrative Examples

HSA Contribution	Income					
	$20,000	$40,000	$60,000	$80,000	$100,000	$120,000
Single Taxpayer						
$500	75	75	125	125	140	140
$1,000	150	150	250	250	280	280
$1,500	225	225	375	375	420	420
$2,000	300	300	500	500	545	560
$2,500	375	375	625	625	670	700
$2,850 1/	428	428	713	713	758	798
Head of Household with 1 Dependent Child						
$1,000	100	150	150	300	260	260
$2,000	200	300	300	600	520	520
$3,000	300	450	450	900	780	780
$4,000	400	600	600	1,200	1,040	1,040
$5,000	500	750	750	1,500	1,300	1,300
$5,650 1/	535	848	848	1,663	1,469	1,469
Married Couple with No Dependents						
$1,000	100	150	150	150	250	260
$2,000	200	300	300	300	500	520
$3,000	250	450	450	450	750	780
$4,000	250	600	600	600	1,000	1,040
$5,000	250	750	750	750	1,250	1,300
$5,650 1/	250	848	848	848	1,413	1,469
Married Couple with 2 Dependent Children						
$1,000	0	103	150	150	260	310
$2,000	0	203	300	300	520	620
$3,000	0	303	450	450	780	930
$4,000	0	403	600	600	1,040	1,240
$5,000	0	503	750	750	1,300	1,550
$5,650 1/	0	568	848	848	1,469	1,719

April 10, 2007

1/   Maximum contribution allowable.

Note: Assumes: all income is from wages and salaries; taxpayers use the larger of the standard deduction or itemized deductions of 18 percent of income before HSA contributions; heads of household and married couples with children have dependents eligible for the child tax credit and the earned income tax credit; and the Alternative Minimum Tax (AMT) exemptions will be $45,000 for married taxpayers filing jointly and $33,750 for single and head of household taxpayers.

Testing Period Worksheet

This worksheet is used to explain the HSA testing period and helps determine if a person is: covered by the testing period, passes or fails the test, and the consequences of failing the test.

Purpose: Use this Worksheet to learn more about the HSA testing period and to determine if: (1) you are covered by the HSA testing period, (2) if you pass or fail the test, and (3) the consequences of failure. This Worksheet is designed to work in conjunction with the HSA Eligibility and Contribution Worksheet that determines HSA eligibility and HSA contribution limits as well as the IRA to HSA Worksheet that gives an overview of the IRA to HSA contribution rules. You are responsible for properly determining whether or not you are subject to and meet the test – not the HSA custodian or trustee. This Worksheet does not provide tax or legal advice – please consult with your own tax or legal advisor.

Testing Period **Overview.** The testing period is a concept created by Congress to prevent you from receiving greater tax benefits than the government intended in two limited circumstances: (1) you become eligible for an HSA mid-year and remain eligible on December 1 (assuming a calendar year tax year), and (2) you move money from an IRA to an HSA. In these cases, the rule requires that you maintain your HSA eligibility for a testing period. Individuals that fail to maintain their HSA eligibility during the testing period face taxes and a 10% penalty on the amount over contributed. The rules are different for regular contributions and IRA funding direct transfers. See page 2 for additional detail.

1 Are You Subject to the Testing Period? Answer the applicable question(s). Regular HSA contributions follow different testing period rules than IRA contributions. If you have both types of contributions, run the tests separately. See page 2 for help. ASSUMPTIONS: This worksheet assumes you were eligible for the HSA on the day of the contribution and that you are a calendar year taxpayer (most people).

For Regular HSA Contributions
Did you contribute this year and remain eligible on December 1?*

*If you ended eligibility mid-year see page 2.

For Contributions From an IRA
Did you move money into your HSA from an IRA?

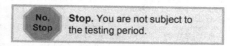

| Yes, Go to Step 2 | **Testing Period Applies.** Go to Step 2 | No, Stop | **Stop.** You are not subject to the testing period. |

2 Do You Pass the Testing Period? See page 2 for detail. Note: run tests separately if multiple contribution types.

For Regular HSA Contributions
Were you eligible for the HSA on December 1 of the year of the HSA contribution and did you remain eligible through December 31 of the year following the year of the contribution?

For Contributions from an IRA
Did you remain eligible for the HSA from the month of the distribution from the IRA until the last day of the 12th month following such month? For example, if you complete the funding on Dec 31, 2015, the test runs from Dec 1, 2015 – Dec 31, 2016.

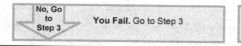
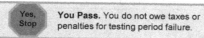

| No, Go to Step 3 | **You Fail.** Go to Step 3. | Yes, Stop | **You Pass.** You do not owe taxes or penalties for testing period failure. |

3 Failed the Test? If you failed the test, you may owe taxes plus a 10% penalty. See below. Note: this worksheet assumes you did not contribute more than the maximum applicable federal HSA limit. Different rules apply if you did (for example, you moved $20,000 from your IRA to your HSA). Special rules also apply if you do both types of contributions. See page 2.

  a. **Failure Due to Death or Disability.** You do not owe taxes or penalties if the failure to meet the testing period is because of the HSA owner's death or disability.
  b. **Regular HSA Contribution Failed Test.** To determine the amount of your tax and penalty you first determine the proper contribution amount using the "sum of the months" calculation. Use the table in paragraph 6 on page 2. See paragraph 7 on page 2 for tax and penalty detail. Important: do <u>not</u> remove the amount as an excess.
  c. **IRA Contribution Failed Test.** You need to pay taxes plus a 10% penalty on the amount you moved from your IRA. Important: do <u>not</u> remove the amount as an excess.

HSA Testing Period Worksheet - Definitions and Instructions

1. **Additional Background for Regular Contributions.** The HSA rules allow you to contribute the full federal HSA contribution limit even if you are only eligible for an HSA starting as late as December 1 of the year (this is for calendar year taxpayers – use the first day of the last month of the tax year if not a calendar year taxpayer). This is beneficial for individuals starting HSA eligibility mid-year. The pre-2007, "sum of the months," rule stated that individuals could only contribute 1/12 times the number of months eligible for the HSA times the applicable federal HSA limit (a pro-rata amount). The current law; however, has a catch. In order to get the benefit of the full federal HSA limit, you need to meet the testing period. If you fail to meet the testing period, the pre-2007 sum of the months rule becomes a factor. If you fail the test, you will owe taxes plus a 10% penalty on the amount over contributed – see paragraphs 5 - 7 below. For additional guidance and examples, please refer to IRS Notice 2008-52. See also the HSA Eligibility and Contribution Worksheet.

2. **Additional Background for IRA Contributions.** The law allows people to move money from an Individual Retirement Account (IRA) into an HSA. See also the IRA to HSA Worksheet for more information on IRA funding of HSAs. This worksheet covers only the testing period for IRA direct transfers. IRA transfers are subject to different testing period rules than regular contributions.

3. **Change in HDHP Coverage Type.** You are not required to maintain the same type of High Deductible Health Plan (HDHP) coverage to remain eligible. For example, if you change from family HDHP coverage to single HDHP coverage during the testing period that does not result in test failure. The HDHP coverage as of December 1 is used to determine contribution limits.

4. **Not Eligible on December 1.** Whether or not the testing period applies is determined by whether or not you were eligible as of December 1. If you are not eligible on December 1, you are not subject to the testing period. Instead, you are simply not allowed to contribute more than the sum of the months method allows. For example, assume Ted starts his HSA in 2015 but knows that he will turn turns 65 in July, 2016. Ted knows in advance that he will fail his testing period for any 2015 contributions (because he will not remain eligible through December 31, 2016) and must plan accordingly (not contribute more than the sum of the months amount). For 2016, Ted is not allowed to make a full contribution because he will not be eligible on December 1, 2016. He must use the sum of the months method to calculate his eligible contribution amount. If he contributes too much for 2016, he must remove it as an excess contribution or face a penalty of 6% per year it remains in the HSA. This is very different treatment than the testing period. See the HSA Eligibility and Contribution Worksheet for that situation.

5. **Eligible on December 1 with Example of Failed Testing Period.** If you were eligible on December 1, the testing period applies.
   Example – Part A: Jim, age 53, enrolls in a family HDHP on December 1, 2014. Jim is not an eligible individual for any months prior to December 1. Jim can contribute the greater of the 2014 HSA federal limit for families, $6,550, or the sum of the months limit, $545.83 (1/12 x $6,550 – only one month's eligibility). Jim contributes $6,550 and is subject to the testing period.
   Example – Part B: Now assume that Jim ceases to be an eligible individual in June 2015. Jim's testing period for 2014 ends on December 31, 2015, so Jim failed the testing period. In 2015, Jim must include in gross income $5,912.50, the amount contributed to the HSA for 2014 minus his sum of the monthly contributions limit for 2014 ($6,550-$545.83 = $6,004.17). Jim must also pay a 10% penalty of $600.42 ($6,004.17 x .10). The $6,004.17 remains in the HSA.

6. **Calculating The Sum of the Months Amount to Determine Tax and Penalty Amounts.** CAUTION: This chart is for regular contributions only. If you funded your HSA from your IRA do not use this chart, you owe taxes and penalties on the full amount.

	Sum of the Months Contribution Worksheet	Individual	Family *(Jim Example from above)*
A	Enter Total Amount Actually Contributed to HSA for Tax Year[1]		$6,550
B	Federal Limit (this limit changes every year for inflation).	$3,300 (2014) $3,350 (2015)	$6,550 (2014) $6,650 (2015)
C	Catch-Up Contribution (if between ages 55-65 add $1,000)		$0
D	Add B + C = Total Federal Limit		$6,550
E	Divide D by 12 = Monthly Contribution Eligibility		$545.83
F	Insert # of Months Eligible in the Year[2]		1
G	Multiply E x F = Total Eligible Amount Based on Sum of Months		$545.83
H	Subtract G from A = Base for Taxes & Penalty[3]		$6,004.17

[1]This includes all employer and individual contributions – not HSA to HSA rollover or transfer amounts.
[2]HSA contribution amounts are determined on a monthly basis and then aggregated. To determine how much you may contribute, you must determine the number of months you were covered by a HDHP and otherwise eligible as of the first day of that month.
[3]If zero or negative, no taxes or penalty owed. If a positive number, you owe taxes and a 10% penalty on this amount. File IRS Form 8889. You should leave this amount in the HSA and use it for eligible medical expenses. Do not take out as the return of an excess contribution or you may owe additional taxes and penalties on that distribution as well.

7. **Taxes and Penalties Detail.** For regular contributions, you owe federal income taxes plus a 10% penalty on the amount as calculated above. For IRA funding transfers, you owe federal income taxes plus a 10% penalty for the amount moved if you fail the testing period test. Any interest or earnings on the amount is not subject to tax or penalty. The 10% penalty applies even if you are over age 65. The amount should remain in the HSA or you will be subject to additional taxes and penalties for using your HSA for non-qualified distributions. Do <u>not</u> take the amount out as the return of an excess contribution. If you use these funds for non-eligible medical expenses you will be subject to taxes plus the 20% penalty applicable to non-qualified HSA distributions.

8. **Both Regular and IRA to HSA Contributions.** If you make both regular HSA contributions and an IRA to HSA contribution, then you run the tests separately. The tests do not interact and you can pass one and fail the other. If you fail the regular contribution test but not the IRA to HSA test (it's a shorter test), then the amount included in gross income depends upon how you split the contributions. See IRS Notice 2008-51, Q&A 6-8 for details.

APPENDIX C

References to Laws, Regulations and Other Government Guidance

Internal Revenue Code

- IRC Sec. 223 (HSA law)

Treasury Regulations

- Treas. Reg. section 1.408-11 (Calculating earnings)
- Treas. Reg. section 54.4980 (Comparability)

IRS Revenue Rulings

- Rev. Rul. 2005-25 (Spousal with non-qualifying coverage)
- Rev. Rul. 2004-45 (Other health coverage)

IRS Notices and Memorandum

- IRS Notice 2004-2 (General guidance)
- IRS Notice 2004-23 (Preventive care)
- IRS Notice 2004-25 (Establishment date)
- IRS Notice 2004-50 (General guidance)
- IRS Notice 2005-8 (2 percent owner of S-Corp)
- IRS Notice 2005-86 (FSA grace period and HSA)
- IRS Notice 2007-22 (FSA/HRA and HSA)
- IRS Notice 2008-51 (IRA to HSA)
- IRS Notice 2008-52 (Testing period)
- IRS Notice 2008-59 (General guidance)
- IRS Notice 2010-59 (Over-the-counter drugs)
- IRS Notice 2010-38 (Age twenty-six for FSA/HRA)
- IRS Notice 2011-5 (Medical debit cards)
- IRS Notice 2012-14 (Indian Health Services)
- IRS Notice 2013-57 (Preventive care)

- IRS Notice 2013-71 (FSA $500 rollover)

- IRS Notice 2013-54 (ACA and FSAs and HRAs)

- IRS Memorandum 201413005 (FSA $500 rollover)

DOL Materials

- Field Assistance Bulletin No. 2004-01 (ERISA and HSAs)

- Field Assistance Bulletin No. 2006-02 (ERISA and HSAs)

IRS Publications

- IRS Publication 502 – Medical and Dental Expenses (including the Health Coverage Tax Credit) http://www.irs.gov/pub/irs-pdf/p502.pdf

- IRS Publication 969 – Health Savings Accounts and Other Tax-Favored Health Plans http://www.irs.gov/pub/irs-pdf/p969.pdf

IRS Forms

- **IRS Form 1040**

  - **IRS Form 1040 (Individual Income Tax Return)** http://www.irs.gov/pub/irs-pdf/f1040.pdf

- **IRS Forms 1099-SA and IRS Form 5498-SA**

  - **IRS Form 1099-SA (Distributions from an HSA, Archer MSA, or Medicare Advantage MSA)** http://www.irs.gov/pub/irs-pdf/f1099sa.pdf

    o This form is used to report distributions made from a Health Savings Account (HSA), Archer Medical Savings Account (Archer MSA), or Medicare Advantage Medical Savings Account (MA MSA). The distribution may have been paid directly to a medical service provider or to the account holder. A separate return must be filed for each plan type.

  - **IRS Form 5498-SA (HSA contributions to an HSA, Archer MSA, or Medicare Advantage MSA)** http://www.irs.gov/pub/irs-pdf/f5498sa.pdf

    o Trustees and custodians of a Health Savings Account (HSA), Archer Medical Savings Account (Archer MSA), and Medicare Advantage Medical Savings Account (MA MSA) file this form for each person for whom they maintained an HSA, Archer MSA, or Medicare Advantage MSA (MA MSA). A separate form is required for each type of plan.

  - **Instructions for IRA Form 5498-SA and IRS Form 1099-SA** http://www.irs.gov/pub/irs-pdf/i1099sa.pdf

    o Detailed instructions for Forms 5498-SA and 1099-SA

- **IRS Form 5305-C**

  - **IRS Form 5305-C (Health Savings Account Custodial Account)** http://www.irs.gov/pub/irs-pdf/f5305c.pdf

    o Establishes the HSA Custodial Account Agreement

- **IRS Form 5329**

  - **IRS Form 5329 (Additional Taxes on Qualified Plans including IRAs and Other Tax-Qualified Accounts)** http://www.irs.gov/pub/irs-pdf/f5329.pdf

  - **Instructions to IRS Form 5329** http://www.irs.gov/pub/irs-pdf/i5329.pdf

    o Used to report additional taxes on IRAs, other qualified retirement plans, modified endowment contracts, Coverdell ESAs, QTPs, Archer MSAs, or HSAs.

- **IRS Form 8889**

  - **IRS Form 8889** http://www.irs.gov/pub/irs-pdf/f8889.pdf

  - **Instructions for IRS Form 8889** http://www.irs.gov/pub/irs-pdf/i8889.pdf

    o Used to report health savings account (HSA) contributions (including those made on your behalf and employer contributions), calculate your HSA deduction, report distributions from HSAs, and figure amounts you must include in income and additional tax you may owe if you fail to be an eligible individual.

  - **IRS Form W-2**

  - **IRS Form W-2 (Employee pay reporting)** http://www.irs.gov/pub/irs-pdf/fw2.pdf

  - **Instructions to IRS Form W-2** http://www.irs.gov/pub/irs-pdf/iw2w3.pdf

    o Employers engaged in a trade/business who pay remuneration for services performed by an employee must file a Form W-2 for each employee

INDEX

References are to question numbers.

References are to question numbers.

References are to question numbers.

References are to question numbers.

References are to question numbers.